THE PROBLEM OF UNIVERSALS

*Edited and
with Introductions by*

Andrew B. Schoedinger

HUMANITIES PRESS
NEW JERSEY

First published 1992 by Humanities Press International, Inc.
Atlantic Highlands, New Jersey 07716

This collection © 1992 by Humanities Press International, Inc.
Reprinted 1995

Library of Congress Cataloging-in-Publication Data

The Problem of universals / edited and with introductions by Andrew B.
  Schoedinger.
        p.   cm.
    Includes bibliographical references and index.
    ISBN 0–391–03725–0. — ISBN 0–391–03726–9 (pbk.)
    1. Universals (Philosophy)   I. Schoedinger, Andrew B.
B105.U5P76   1992
111'.2—dc20   91–10228
                                               CIP

British Library Cataloguing in Publication Data

A catalog record for this book is available
from the British Library.

#23214727

Printed in the United States of America

THE PROBLEM OF UNIVERSALS

CONTENTS

INTRODUCTION

The problem of universals has a rich tradition that dates back, at least, to Plato. It is a distinctively philosophical problem demonstrated by the fact that people other than philosophers are generally unaware that the problem even exists. Nevertheless, it is a real problem because particulars are, and can only be, described by their characteristics. Such characteristics are qualities and qualities are what are generally understood to be universals. Not withstanding that qualities determine particulars to be the (types of) things that they are, it is indubitable that relations exist, e.g., that San Francisco is north of Los Angeles. Once it is understood that qualities and relations are ontologically inescapable, it remains to determine the nature of such beasts.

The readings herein attest to the fact that the views concerning the nature of universals have differed widely. One runs the gamut from the position that universals constitute a world unto themselves (e.g., Plato) to the position that there are no universals at all (e.g., Bambrough à la Wittgenstein). There are straightforward views about the matter (e.g., Baylis) versus more complex views (e.g., Aaron). One thing seems clear: one cannot escape the existence of universals. This, in turn, entails not being able to escape an analysis as to their nature. Just exactly what are they? Upon reflection, it appears that several analyses are viable. On the one hand, it seems reasonable to maintain that there are virtues that no one has, indicating that such unpossessed virtues subsist in some sort of way. Plato and his cohorts would undoubtedly think that virtues so described are real. Other theorists would analyze the nature of a virtue, be it possessed or otherwise, to be a product of the mind, namely a concept. However, if the nature of a concept cannot be determined and if concepts have no independent existence, then it would appear that what characterizes a virtue is a general word. But unless the word 'justice', for example, denotes something other than the word itself, it would have no meaning. Therefore, from whence do words derive their meaning? They get their meaning by linguistically representing the qualities that characterize the concept or thing which is the object of description. At this point, we come full circle, because of the inescapable reliance upon qualities to describe any and every sort of reality at hand.

There is another way of viewing the primacy of universals. Without them there could be no language as we understand it. That is to say, without predicates we would have only subject-words within our command. Ultimately, this reduces to proper nouns and the two pronouns 'this' and 'that'. These two pronouns are useful only in conjunction with pointing. Ostension, by itself, does not constitute language. This observation has everything to say about human thinking. Thinking and language go hand in hand. It is apparent that the recognition of characteristics and the formulation of nouns is symbiotic. Consequently, the nature of universals is ultimately associated with human thinking (e.g., Price). Organizing—classifying—is an integral part of thinking. Such a process is made possible via the identification, at the very least, of resemblances that exist in the world around us. One ultimate question that demands a satisfactory answer is, "On the basis of objective resemblances, are there universals?" To a great extent the readings in this book seek an answer to that question.

As a methodological note: in this volume the spelling and punctuation of the originals—whether British or American—has been retained. Thus, because the material was drawn from a wide variety of sources, the reader will notice variations in spelling, grammatical usage, style, and punctuation. For the convenience of the reader, however, original notes referring to portions of the original not reprinted have been removed, and full bibliographical information has been added (in brackets) to notes when not supplied in the original.

1 PLATO

Due primarily to his analysis of numbers, Plato concluded that essences are unchanging and are, in that sense, absolute. Consider the number five, disregarding any exemplification of it. It never changes. Its essence is independent of any spatio-temporal coordinate. If this is true of the essence of number, then it must be a characteristic of all essences. Since essences constitute reality, it must be the case that reality transcends spatio-temporal existence.

Our bodies are defined by spatio-temporal coordinates. We know we have a soul *qua* mind that provides an imperfect understanding of essences. Consequently, (1) it must be the case that our bodies inhibit a perfect understanding of reality and (2) our souls must be capable of existence independent of the body. This independence makes possible a perfect understanding of reality. Therefore, the soul must have existed in a non-physical realm prior to its association with any body whereby it gained a perfect understanding of reality. Then the soul temporarily inhabits and is inhibited by the body, and upon death it departs the body, whereupon it regains its pure state—manifested by its perfect understanding of essences and universals. The world of Forms (i.e., essences and universals) is absolute and unchanging. The physical world is ever changing, according to the Heraclitean Doctrine of Flux. The body is of the latter world. It is our soul (mind) that through recollection makes an understanding of the World of Forms (reality) possible. Consequently, Plato is understood to be a dualistic realist.

Phaedo

And now, O my judges, I desire to prove to you that the real philosopher has reason to be of good cheer when he is about to die, and that after death he may hope to obtain the greatest good in the other world. And how this may be, Simmias and Cebes, I will endeavour to explain. For I deem that the true votary of philosophy is likely to be misunderstood by other men; they do not perceive that he is always pursuing death and dying; and if this be so, and he has had the desire of death all his life long, why when his time comes should he repine at that which he has been always pursuing and desiring?

Simmias said laughingly: Though not in a laughing humor, you have made me laugh, Socrates; for I cannot help thinking that the many when they hear your words will say how truly you have described philosophers,

1

and our people at home will likewise say that the life which philosophers desire is in reality death, and that they have found them out to be deserving of the death which they desire.

And they are right, Simmias, in thinking so, with the exception of the words 'they have found them out'; for they have not found out either what is the nature of that death which the true philosopher deserves, or how he deserves or desires death. But enough of them:—let us discuss the matter among ourselves. Do we believe that there is such a thing as death?

To be sure, replied Simmias.

Is it not the separation of soul and body? And to be dead is the completion of this; when the soul exists in herself, and is released from the body and the body is released from the soul, what is this but death?

Just so, he replied.

There is another question, which will probably throw light on our present enquiry if you and I can agree about it:—Ought the philosopher to care about the pleasures—if they are to be called pleasures—of eating and drinking?

Certainly not, answered Simmias.

And what about the pleasures of love—should he care for them?

By no means.

And will he think much of the other ways of indulging the body, for example, the acquisition of costly raiment, or sandals, or other adornments of the body? Instead of caring about them, does he not rather despise anything more than nature needs? What do you say?

I should say that the true philosopher would despise them.

Would you not say that he is entirely concerned with the soul and not with the body? He would like, as far as he can, to get away from the body and to turn to the soul.

Quite true.

In matters of this sort philosophers, above all other men, may be observed in every sort of way to dissever the soul from the communion of the body.

Very true.

Whereas, Simmias, the rest of the world are of opinion that to him who has no sense of pleasure and no part in bodily pleasure, life is not worth having; and that he who is indifferent about them is as good as dead.

That is also true.

What again shall we say of the actual acquirement of knowledge?—is the body, if invited to share in the enquiry, a hinderer or a helper? I mean to say, have sight and hearing any truth in them? Are they not, as the poets are always telling us, inaccurate witnesses? and yet, if even they are inaccurate and indistinct, what is to be said of the other senses?—for you will allow that they are the best of them?

Certainly, he replied.

Then when does the soul attain truth?—for in attempting to consider anything in company with the body she is obviously deceived.

True.

Then must not true existence be revealed to her in thought, if at all?

Yes.

And thought is best when the mind is gathered into herself and none of these things trouble her—neither sounds nor sights nor pain nor any pleasure,—when she takes leave of the body, and has as little as possible to do with it, when she has no bodily sense or desire, but is aspiring after true being?

Certainly.

And in this the philosopher dishonors the body; his soul runs away from his body and desires to be alone and by herself?

That is true.

Well, but there is another thing, Simmias: Is there or is there not an absolute justice?

Assuredly there is.

And an absolute beauty and absolute good?

Of course.

But did you ever behold any of them with your eyes?

Certainly not.

Or did you ever reach them with any other bodily sense?—and I speak not of these alone, but of absolute greatness, and health, and strength, and of the essence or true nature of everything. Has the reality of them ever been perceived by you through the bodily organs? or rather, is not the nearest approach to the knowledge of their several natures made by him who so orders his intellectual vision as to have the most exact conception of the essence of each thing which he considers?

Certainly.

And he attains to the purest knowledge of them who goes to each with the mind alone, not introducing or intruding in the act of thought sight or any other sense together with reason, but with the very light of the mind in her own clearness searches into the very truth of each; he who has got rid, as far as he can, of eyes and ears and, so to speak, of the whole body, these being in his opinion distracting elements which when they infect the soul hinder her from acquiring truth and knowledge—who, if not he, is likely to attain to the knowledge of true being?

What you say has a wonderful truth in it, Socrates, replied Simmias.

And when real philosophers consider all these things, will they not be led to make a reflection which they will express in words something like the following? 'Have we not found,' they will say, 'a path of thought which seems to bring us and our argument to the conclusion, that while we are in the body, and while the soul is infected with the evils of the body, our desire will not be satisfied? and our desire is of the truth. For the body is a source of endless trouble to us by reason of the mere requirement of food; and is liable also to diseases which overtake and impede us in the search after true being: it fills us full of loves, and lusts, and fears, and fancies of all kinds, and endless foolery, and in fact, as men say, takes away from us the power of thinking at all. Whence come wars, and fightings, and factions? whence but from the body and the lusts of the body? Wars are occasioned by the love of money, and money has to be acquired for the sake and in the service of the body; and by reason of all these impediments we have no time to give to philosophy; and, last and worst of all, even if we are at leisure and betake ourselves to some speculation, the body is always breaking in upon us, causing turmoil and confusion in our enquiries, and so amazing us that we are prevented from seeing the truth. It has been proved to us by experience that if we would have pure knowledge of anything we must be quit of the body—the soul in herself must behold things in themselves: and then we shall attain the wisdom which we desire, and of which we say that we are lovers; not while we live, but after death; for if while in company with the body, the soul cannot have pure knowledge, one of two things follows— either knowledge is not to be attained at all, or, if at all, after death. For then, and not till then, the soul will be parted from the body and exist in herself alone. In this present life, I reckon that we make the nearest approach to knowledge when we have the least possible intercourse or communion with the body, and are not surfeited with the bodily nature, but keep ourselves pure until the hour when God himself is pleased to release us. And thus having got rid of the foolishness of the body we shall be pure and hold converse with the pure, and know of ourselves the clear light everywhere, which is no other than the light of truth.' For the impure are not permitted to approach the pure. These are the sort of words, Simmias, which the true lovers of knowledge cannot help saying to one another, and thinking. You would agree; would you not?

Undoubtedly, Socrates.

But, O my friend, if this be true, there is great reason to hope that, going whither I go, when I have come to the end of my journey, I shall attain that which has been the pursuit of my life. And therefore I go on my way rejoicing, and not I only, but every other man who believes that his mind has been made ready and that he is in a manner purified.

Certainly, replied Simmias.

And what is purification but the separation of the soul from the body, as I was saying before; the habit of the soul gathering and collecting herself into herself from all sides out of the body; the dwelling in her own place alone, as in another life, so also in this, as far as she can;—the release of the soul from the chains of the body?

Very true, he said.

And this separation and release of the soul from the body is termed death?

To be sure, he said.

And the true philosophers, and they only, are ever seeking to release the soul. Is not the separation and release of the soul from the body their especial study?

That is true.

And, as I was saying at first, there would be a ridiculous contradiction in men studying to live as nearly as they can in a state of death, and yet repining when it comes upon them.

Clearly.

And the true philosophers, Simmias, are always occupied in the practice of dying, wherefore also to them least of all men is death terrible. Look at the matter thus:—if they have been in every way the enemies of the body, and are wanting to be alone with the soul, when this desire of theirs is granted, how inconsistent would they be if they trembled and repined, instead of rejoicing at their departure to that place where, when they arrive, they hope to gain that which in life they desired—and this was wisdom—and at the same time to be rid of the company of their enemy. Many a man has been willing to go to the world below animated by the hope of seeing there an earthly love, or wife, or son, and conversing with them. And will he who is a true lover of wisdom, and is strongly persuaded in like manner that only in the world below he can worthily enjoy her, still repine at death? Will he not depart with joy? Surely he will, O my friend, if he be a true philosopher. For he will have a firm conviction that there, and there only, he can find wisdom in her purity. And if this be true, he would be very absurd, as I was saying, if he were afraid of death.

He would indeed, replied Simmias.

And when you see a man who is repining at the approach of death, is not his reluctance a sufficient proof that he is not a lover of wisdom, but a lover of the body, and probably at the same time a lover of either money or power, or both?

Quite so, he replied.

And is not courage, Simmias, a quality which is specially characteristic of the philosopher?

Certainly.

There is temperance again, which even by the vulgar is supposed to consist in the control and regulation of the passions, and in the sense of superiority to them—is not temperance a virtue belonging to those only who despise the body, and who pass their lives in philosophy?

Most assuredly.

For the courage and temperance of other men, if you will consider them, are really a contradiction.

How so?

Well, he said, you are aware that death is regarded by men in general as a great evil.

Very true, he said.

And do not courageous men face death because they are afraid of yet greater evils?

That is quite true.

Then all but the philosophers are courageous only from fear and because they are afraid; and yet that a man should be courageous from fear, and because he is a coward, is surely a strange thing.

Very true.

And are not the temperate exactly in the same case? They are temperate because they are intemperate—which might seem to be a contradiction, but is nevertheless the sort of thing which happens with this foolish temperance. For there are pleasures which they are afraid of losing; and in their desire to keep them, they abstain from some pleasures, because they are overcome by others; and although to be conquered by pleasure is called by men intemperance, to them the conquest of pleasure consists in being conquered by pleasure. And that is what I mean by saying that, in a sense, they are made temperate through intemperance.

Such appears to be the case.

Yet the exchange of one fear or pleasure or pain for another fear or pleasure or pain, and of the greater for the less, as if they were coins, is not the exchange of virtue. O my blessed Simmias, is there not one true coin for which all things ought to be exchanged?—and that is wisdom; and only in exchange for this, and in company with this, is anything truly bought or sold, whether courage or temperance or justice. And is not all true virtue the companion of wisdom, no matter what fears or pleasures or other similar goods or evils may or may not attend her? But the virtue which is made up of these goods, when they are severed from wisdom and exchanged with one another, is a shadow of virtue only, nor is there any freedom or health or truth in her; but in the true exchange there is a purging away of all these things, and temperance, and justice, and courage, and wisdom herself are the purgation of them. The founders of the mysteries would appear to have had a real meaning, and were not talking nonsense when they intimated in a figure long ago that he who passes unsanctified and uninitiated into the world below will lie in a slough, but that he who arrives there after initiation and purification will dwell with the gods. For 'many,' as they say in the mysteries, 'are the thyrsus-bearers, but few are the mystics,'—meaning, as I interpret the words, 'the true philosophers.' In the number of whom, during my whole life, I have been seeking, according to my ability, to find a place;—whether I have sought in a right way or not, and whether I have succeeded or not, I shall truly know in a little while, if God will, when I myself arrive in the other world—such is my belief. And therefore I maintain that I am right, Simmias and Cebes, in not grieving or repining at parting from you and my masters in this world, for I believe that I shall equally find good masters and friends in another world. But most men do not believe this saying; if then I succeed in convincing you by my defence better than I did the Athenian judges, it will be well.

Cebes answered: I agree, Socrates, in the greater part of what you say. But in what concerns the soul, men are apt to be incredulous; they fear that when she has left the body her place may be nowhere, and that on the very day of death she may perish and come to an end—immediately on her release from the body, issuing forth dispersed like smoke or air and in her flight vanishing away into nothingness. If she could only be collected into herself after she has obtained release from the evils of which you were speaking there would be good reason to hope, Socrates, that what you say is true. But surely it requires a great deal of argument and many proofs to show that when the man is dead his soul yet exists, and has any force or intelligence. . . .

So much is clear—that when we perceive something, either by the help of sight, or hearing, or some other sense, from that perception we are able to obtain a notion of some other thing like or unlike which is associated with it but has been forgotten. Whence, as I was saying, one of two alternatives follows:—either we had this knowledge at birth, and continued to know through life; or, after birth, those who are said to learn only remember, and learning is simply recollection.

Yes, that is quite true, Socrates.

And which alternative, Simmias, do you prefer? Had we the knowledge at our birth, or did we recollect the things which we knew previously to our birth?

I cannot decide at the moment.

At any rate you can decide whether he who has knowledge will or will not be able to render an account of his knowledge? What do you say?

Certainly, he will.

But do you think that every man is able to give an account of these very matters about which we are speaking?

Would that they could, Socrates, but I rather fear that tomorrow, at this time, there will no longer be any one alive who is able to give an account of them such as ought to be given.

Then you are not of opinion, Simmias, that all men know these things?

Certainly not.

They are in process of recollecting that which they learned before?

Certainly.

But when did our souls acquire this knowledge?—not since we were born as men?

Certainly not.

And therefore, previously?

Yes.

Then, Simmias, our souls must also have existed without bodies before they were in the form of man, and must have had intelligence.

Unless indeed you suppose, Socrates, that these notions are given us at the very moment of birth; for this is the only time which remains.

Yes, my friend, but if so, when do we lose them? for they are not in us when we are born—that is admitted. Do we lose them at the moment of receiving them, or if not at what other time?

No, Socrates, I perceive that I was unconsciously talking nonsense.

Then may we not say, Simmias, that if, as we are always repeating, there is an absolute beauty, and goodness, and an absolute essence of all things; and if to this, which is now discovered to have existed in our former state, we refer all our sensations, and with this compare them, finding these ideas to be pre-existent and our inborn possession—then our souls must have had a prior existence, but if not, there would be no force in the argument? There is the same proof that these ideas must have existed before we were born, as that our souls existed before we were born; and if not the ideas, then not the souls.

Yes, Socrates; I am convinced that there is precisely the same necessity for the one as for the other; and the argument retreats successfully to the position that the existence of the soul before birth cannot be separated from the existence of the essence of which you speak. For there is nothing which to my mind is so patent as that beauty, goodness, and the other notions of which you were just now speaking, have a most real and absolute existence; and I am satisfied with the proof.

Well, but is Cebes equally satisfied? for I must convince him too.

I think said Simmias, that Cebes is satisfied: although he is the most incredulous of mortals, yet I believe that he is sufficiently convinced of the existence of the soul before birth. But that after death the soul will continue to exist is not yet proven even to my own satisfaction. I cannot get rid of the feeling of the many to which Cebes was referring—the feeling that when the man dies the soul will be dispersed, and that this may be the extinction of her. For admitting that she may have been born elsewhere, and framed out of other elements, and was in existence before entering the human body, why after having entered in and gone out again may she not herself be destroyed and come to an end?

Very true, Simmias, said Cebes; about half of what was required has been proven; to wit, that our souls existed before we were born:—that the soul will exist after death as well as before birth is the other half of which the proof is still wanting, and has to be supplied; when that is given the demonstration will be complete.

But that proof, Simmias and Cebes, has been already given, said Socrates, if you put the two arguments together—I mean this and the former one, in which we admitted that everything living is born of the dead. For if the soul exists before birth, and in coming to life and being born can be born only from death and dying, must she not after death continue to exist, since she has to be born again?—Surely the proof which you desire has been already furnished. Still I suspect that you and Simmias would be glad to probe the argument further. Like children, you are haunted with a fear that when the soul leaves the body, the wind may really blow her away and scatter her; especially if a man should happen to die in a great storm and not when the sky is calm.

Cebes answered with a smile: Then, Socrates, you must argue us out of our fears—and yet, strictly speaking, they are not our fears, but there is a child within us to whom death is a sort of hobgoblin: him too we must persuade not to be afraid when he is alone in the dark.

Socrates said: Let the voice of the charmer be applied daily until you have charmed away the fear.

And where shall we find a good charmer of our fears, Socrates, when you are gone?

Hellas, he replied, is a large place, Cebes, and has many good men, and there are barbarous races not a few: seek for him among them all, far and wide, sparing neither pains nor money; for there is no better way of spending your money. And you must seek among yourselves too; for you will not find others better able to make the search.

The search, replied Cebes, shall certainly be made. And now, if you please, let us return to the point of the argument at which we digressed.

By all means, replied Socrates; what else should I please?

Very good.

Must we not, said Socrates, ask ourselves what that is which, as we imagine, is liable to be scattered, and about which we fear? and what again is that about which we have no fear? And then we may proceed further to enquire whether that which suffers dispersion is or is not of the nature of soul—our hopes and fears as to our own souls will turn upon the answers to these questions.

Very true, he said.

Now the compound or composite may be supposed to be naturally capable, as of being compounded, so also of being dissolved; but that which is uncompounded, and that only, must be, if anything is, indissoluble.

Yes; I should imagine so, said Cebes.

And the uncompounded may be assumed to be the same and unchanging, whereas the compound is always changing and never the same.

I agree, he said.

Then now let us return to the previous discussion. Is that idea or essence, which in the dialectical process we define as essence or true existence—whether essence of equality, beauty, or anything else—are these essences, I say liable at times to some degree of change? or are they each of them always what they are, having the same simple self-existent and unchanging forms, not admitting of variation at all, or in any way, or at any time?

They must be always the same, Socrates, replied Cebes.

And what would you say of the many beautiful—whether men or horses or garments or any other things which are named by the same names and may be called equal or beautiful,—are they all unchanging and the same always, or quite the reverse? May they not rather be described as almost always changing and hardly ever the same, either with themselves or with one another?

The latter, replied Cebes; they are always in a state of change.

And these you can touch and see and perceive with the senses but the unchanging things you can only perceive with the mind—they are invisible and are not seen?

That is very true, he said.

Well then, added Socrates, let us suppose that there are two sorts of existences—one seen, the other unseen.

Let us suppose them.

The seen is the changing, and the unseen is the unchanging?

That may be also supposed.

And, further, is not one part of us body, another part soul?

To be sure.

And to which class is the body more alike and akin?

Clearly to the seen—no one can doubt that.

And is the soul seen or not seen?

Not by man, Socrates.

And what we mean by 'seen' and 'not seen' is that which is or is not visible to the eye of man?

Yes, to the eye of man.

And is the soul seen or not seen?

Not seen.

Unseen then?

Yes.

Then the soul is more like to the unseen, and the body to the seen?

That follows necessarily, Socrates.

And were we not saying long ago that the soul when using the body as an instrument of perception, that is to say, when using the sense of sight or hearing or some other sense (for the meaning of perceiving through the body is perceiving through the senses)—were we not saying that the soul too is then dragged by the body into the region of the changeable, and wanders and is confused: the world spins round her, and she is like a drunkard, when she touches change?

Very true.

But when returning into herself she reflects, then she passes into the other world, the region of purity, and eternity, and immortality, and unchangeableness, which are her kindred, and with them she ever lives, when she is by herself and is not let or hindered; then she ceases from her erring ways, and being in communion with the unchanging is unchanging. And this state of the soul is called wisdom?

That is well and truly said, Socrates, he replied.

And to which class is the soul more nearly alike and akin, as far as may be inferred from this argument, as well as from the preceding one?

I think, Socrates, that, in the opinion of every one who follows the argument, the soul will be infinitely more like the unchangeable—even the most stupid person will not deny that.

And the body is more like the changing?

Yes.

Yet once more consider the matter in another light: When the soul and the body are united, then nature orders the soul to rule and govern, and the body to obey and serve. Now which of these two functions is akin to the divine? and which to the mortal? Does not the divine appear to you to be that which naturally orders and rules, and the mortal to be that which is subject and servant?

True.

And which does the soul resemble?

The soul resembles the divine, and the body the mortal—there can be no doubt of that, Socrates.

Then reflect, Cebes: of all which has been said is not this the conclusion?—that the soul is in the very likeness of the divine, and immortal, and intellectual, and uniform, and indissoluble, and unchangeable; and that the body is in the very likeness of the human, and mortal, and unintellectual, and multiform, and dissoluble, and changeable. Can this, my dear Cebes, be denied?

It cannot.

But if it be true, then is not the body liable to speedy dissolution? and is not the soul almost or altogether indissoluble?

Certainly.

And do you further observe, that after a man is dead, the body, or visible part of him, which is lying in the visible world, and is called a corpse, and would naturally be dissolved and decomposed and dissipated, is not dissolved or decomposed at once, but may remain for some time, nay even for a long time, if the constitution be sound at the time of death, and the season of the year favorable? For the body when shrunk and embalmed, as the manner is in Egypt, may remain almost entire through infinite ages; and even in decay, there are still some portions, such as the bones and ligaments, which are practically indestructible:—Do you agree?

Yes.

And is it likely that the soul, which is invisible, in passing to the place of the true Hades, which like her is invisible, and pure, and noble, and on her way to the good and wise God, whither, if God will, my soul is also soon to go,—that the soul, I repeat, if this be her nature and origin, will be blown away and destroyed immediately on quitting the body, as the many say? That can never be, my dear Simmias and Cebes. The truth rather is, that the soul which is pure at departing and draws after her no bodily taint, having never voluntarily during life had connection with the body, which she is ever avoiding, herself gathered into herself;—and making such abstraction her perpetual study—which means that she has been a true disciple of philosophy; and therefore has in fact been always engaged in the practice of dying? For is not philosophy the study of death?—

Certainly—

That soul, I say, herself invisible, departs to the invisible world—to the divine and immortal and rational; thither arriving, she is secure of bliss and is released from the error and folly of men, their fears and wild passions and all other human ills, and for ever dwells, as they say of the initiated, in company with the gods. Is not this true, Cebes?

Yes, said Cebes, beyond a doubt.

But the soul which has been polluted, and is impure at the time of her departure, and is the companion and servant of the body always, and is in love with and fascinated by the body and by the desires and pleasures of the body, until she is led to believe that the truth only exists in a bodily form, which a man may touch and see and taste, and use for the purposes of his lusts,—the soul, I mean, accustomed to hate and fear and avoid the intellectual principle, which to the bodily eye is dark and invisible, and can be attained only by philosophy;—do you suppose that such a soul will depart pure and unalloyed?

Impossible, he replied.

She is held fast by the corporeal, which the continual association and constant care of the body have wrought into her nature.

Very true.

And this corporeal element, my friend, is heavy and weighty and earthy, and is that element of sight by which a soul is depressed and dragged down again into the visible world, because she is afraid of the invisible and of the world below—prowling about tombs and sepulchers, near which, as they tell us, are seen certain ghostly apparitions of souls which have not departed pure, but are cloyed with sight and therefore visible.

That is very likely, Socrates.

Yes, that is very likely, Cebes; and these must be the souls, not of the good, but of the evil, which are compelled to wander about such places in payment of the penalty of their former evil way of life; and they continue to wander until through the craving after the corporeal which never leaves them, they are imprisoned finally in another body. And they may be supposed to find their prisons in the same natures which they have had in their former lives.

What natures do you mean, Socrates?

What I mean is that men who have followed after gluttony, and wantonness, and drunkenness, and have had no thought of avoiding them, would pass into asses and animals of that sort. What do you think?

I think such an opinion to be exceedingly probable.

And those who have chosen the portion of injustice, and tyranny, and violence, will pass into wolves, or into hawks and kites;—whither else can we suppose them to go?

Yes, said Cebes; with such natures, beyond question.

And there is no difficulty, he said, in assigning to all of them places answering to their several natures and propensities?

There is not, he said.

Some are happier than others; and the happiest both in themselves and in the place to which they go are those who have practised the civil and social virtues which are called temperance and justice, and are acquired by habit and attention without philosophy and mind.

Why are they the happiest?

Because they may be expected to pass into some gentle and social kind which is like their own, such as bees or wasps or ants, or back again into the form of man, and just and moderate men may be supposed to spring from them.

Very likely.

No one who has not studied philosophy and who is not entirely pure at the time of his departure is allowed to enter the company of the Gods, but the lover of knowledge only. And this is the reason, Simmias and Cebes, why the true votaries of philosophy abstain from all fleshly lusts, and hold out against them and refuse to give themselves up to them,—not because they fear poverty or the ruin of their families, like the lovers of money, and the world in general; nor like the lovers of power and honor, because they dread the dishonor or disgrace of evil deeds.

No, Socrates, that would not become them, said Cebes.

No indeed, he replied; and therefore they who have any care of their own souls, and do not merely live molding and fashioning the body, say farewell to all this; they will not walk in the ways of the blind; and when philosophy offers them purification and release from evil, they feel that they ought not to resist her influence, and whither she leads they turn and follow.

What do you mean, Socrates?

I will tell you, he said. The lovers of knowledge are conscious that the soul was simply fastened and glued to the body—until philosophy received her, she could only view real existence through the bars of a prison, not in and through herself; she was wallowing in the mire of every sort of ignorance, and by reason of lust had become the principal accomplice in her own captivity. This was her original state; and then, as I was saying, and as the lovers of knowledge are well aware, philosophy, seeing how terrible was her confinement, of which she was to herself the cause, received and gently comforted her and sought to release her, pointing out that the eye and the ear and the other senses are full of deception, and persuading her to retire from them and abstain from all but the necessary use of them, and be gathered up and collected into herself, bidding her trust in herself and her own pure apprehension of pure existence, and to mistrust whatever comes to her through other channels and is subject to variation; for such things are visible and tangible, but what she sees in her own nature is intelligible and invisible. And the soul of the true philosopher thinks that she ought not to resist this deliverance, and therefore abstains from pleasures and desires and pains and fears, as far as she is able; reflecting that when a man has great joys or sorrows or fears or desires, he suffers from them, not merely the sort of evil which might be anticipated—as for example, the loss of his health or property which he has sacrificed to his lusts—but an evil greater far, which is the greatest and worst of all evils, and one of which he never thinks.

What is it, Socrates? said Cebes.

The evil is that when the feeling of pleasure or pain is most intense, every soul of man imagines the objects of this intense feeling to be then plainest and truest: but this is not so, they are really the things of sight.

Very true.

And is not this the state in which the soul is most enthralled by the body?

How so?

Why, because each pleasure and pain is a sort of nail which nails and rivets the soul to the body, until she becomes like the body, and believes that to be true which the body affirms to be true; and from agreeing with the body and having the same delights she is obliged to have the same habits and haunts, and is not likely ever to be pure at her departure to the world below, but is always infected by the body; and so she sinks into another body and there germinates and grows, and has therefore no part in the communion of the divine and pure and simple.

Most true, Socrates, answered Cebes.

And this, Cebes, is the reason why the true lovers of knowledge are temperate and brave; and not for the reason which the world gives.

Certainly not.

Certainly not! The soul of a philosopher will reason in quite another way; she will not ask philosophy to release her in order that when released she may deliver herself up again to the thraldom of pleasures and pains, doing a work only to be undone again, weaving instead of unweaving her Penelope's web. But she will calm passion, and follow reason, and dwell in the contemplation of her, beholding the true and divine (which is not matter of opinion), and thence deriving nourishment. Thus she seeks to live while she lives, and after death she hopes to go to her own kindred and to that which is like her, and to be freed from human ills. Never fear, Simmias and Cebes, that a soul which has been thus nurtured and has had these pursuits, will at her departure from the body be scattered and blown away by the winds and be nowhere and nothing.

When Socrates had done speaking, for a considerable time there was silence; he himself appeared to be meditating, as most of us were, on what had been said; only Cebes and Simmias spoke a few words to one another.

And Socrates observing them asked what they thought of the argument, and whether there was anything wanting? For, said he, there are many points still open to suspicion and attack, if any one were disposed to sift the matter thoroughly. Should you be considering some other matter I say no more, but if you are still in doubt do not hesitate to say exactly what you think, and let us have anything better which you can suggest; and if you think that I can be of any use, allow me to help you.

Simmias said: I must confess, Socrates, that doubts did arise in our minds, and each of us was urging and inciting the other to put the question which we wanted to have answered but which neither of us liked to ask, fearing that our importunity might be troublesome at such a time.

Socrates replied with a smile: O Simmias, what are you saying? I am not very likely to persuade other men that I do not regard my present situation as a misfortune, if I cannot even persuade you that I am no worse off now than at any other time in my life. Will you not allow that I have as much of the spirit of prophecy in me as the swans? For they, when they perceive that they must die, having sung all their life long, do then sing more lustily than ever, rejoicing in the thought that they are about to go away to the god whose ministers they are. But men, because they are themselves afraid of death, slanderously affirm of the swans that they sing a lament at the last, not considering that no bird sings when cold, or hungry, or in pain, not even the nightingale, nor the swallow, nor yet the hoopoe; which are said indeed to tune a lay of sorrow, although I do not believe this to be true of them any more than of the swans. But because they are sacred to Apollo, they have the gift of prophecy, and anticipate the good things of another world; wherefore they sing and rejoice in that day more than ever they did before. And I too, believing myself to be the consecrated servant of the same god, and the fellow-servant of the swans, and thinking that I have received from my master gifts of prophecy which are not inferior to theirs, would not go out of life less merrily than the swans. Never mind then, if this be your only objection, but speak and ask anything which you like, while the eleven magistrates of Athens allow.

NOTE

From *The Dialogues of Plato*, trans. B. Jowett. Originally published by Random House, New York, 1937. Reprinted by permission of Oxford University Press.

2 ARISTOTLE

In *De Interpretatione* Aristotle states that "Some things are universal, others individual. By the term 'universal' I mean that which is of such a nature as to be predicated of many subjects, by 'individual' that which is not thus predicated. Thus 'man' is a universal, 'Callias' an individual." It should be noted that 'man' can function as either a predicate or a subject, i.e.,

(1) Callias is a man.
(2) Man is an animal.

In other words, the subject of a sentence can be a universal; from this Aristotle concludes (a) that universals are real but different from the primary substance that constitutes individuals, and (b) that to which universal terms refer are classes. Although classes are not tangible, as are the individuals of which they are comprised, classes are nevertheless real because there is nothing arbitrary about the manner in which we classify individuals. For example, alligators are in fact essentially different from hummingbirds. Consequently, Aristotle is understood to be a moderate realist.

The Categories

1   Things are said to be named 'equivocally' when, though they have a common name, the definition corresponding with the name differs for each. Thus, a real man and a figure in a picture can both lay claim to the name 'animal'; yet these are equivocally so named, for, though they have a common name, the definition corresponding with the name differs for each. For should any one define in what sense each is an animal, his definition in the one case will be appropriate to that case only.

On the other hand, things are said to be named 'univocally' which have both the name and the definition answering to the name in common. A man and an ox are both 'animal', and these are univocally so named, inasmuch as not only the name, but also the definition, is the same in both cases: for if a man should state in what sense each is an animal, the statement in the one case would be identical with that in the other.

Things are said to be named 'derivatively', which derive their name from some other name, but differ from it in termination. Thus the grammarian derives his name from the word 'grammar' and the courageous man from the word 'courage'.

2   Forms of speech are either simple or composite. Examples of the

latter are such expressions as 'the man runs', 'the man wins'; of the former 'man', 'ox', 'runs', 'wins'.

Of things themselves some are predicable of a subject, and are never present in a subject. Thus 'man' is predicable of the individual man, and is never present in a subject.

By being 'present in a subject' I do not mean present as parts are present in a whole, but being incapable of existence apart from the said subject.

Some things, again, are present in a subject, but are never predicable of a subject. For instance, a certain point of grammatical knowledge is present in the mind, but is not predicable of any subject; or again, a certain whiteness may be present in the body (for color requires a material basis), yet it is never predicable of anything.

Other things, again, are both predicable of a subject and present in a subject. Thus while knowledge is present in the human mind, it is predicable of grammar.

There is, lastly, a class of things which are neither present in a subject nor predicable of a subject, such as the individual man or the individual horse. But, to speak more generally, that which is individual and has the character of a unit is never predicable of a subject. Yet in some cases there is nothing to prevent such being present in a subject. Thus a certain point of grammatical knowledge is present in a subject.

3   When one thing is predicated of another, all that which is predicable of the predicate will be predicable also of the subject. Thus, 'man' is predicated of the individual man; but 'animal' is predicated of 'man'; it will, therefore, be predicable of the individual man also: for the individual man is both 'man' and 'animal'.

If genera are different and co-ordinate, their differentiae are themselves different in kind. Take as an instance the genus 'animal' and the genus 'knowledge'. 'With feet', 'two-footed', 'winged', 'aquatic', are differentiae of 'animal'; the species of knowledge are not distinguished by the same differentiae. One species of knowledge does not differ from another in being 'two-footed'.

But where one genus is subordinate to another, there is nothing to prevent their having the same differentiae: for the greater class is predicated of the lesser, so that all the differentiae of the predicate will be differentiae also of the subject.

4   Expressions which are in no way composite signify substance, quantity, quality, relation, place, time, position, state, action, or affection. To sketch my meaning roughly, examples of substance are 'man' or 'the horse', of quantity, such terms as 'two cubits long' or 'three cubits long', of quality, such attributes as 'white', 'grammatical'. 'Double', 'half', 'greater', fall under the category of relation; 'in the market place', 'in the Lyceum', under that of place: 'yesterday', 'last year', under that of time. 'Lying', 'sitting', are terms indicating position; 'shod', 'armed', state; 'to lance', 'to

cauterize', action; 'to be lanced', 'to be cauterized', affection.

No one of these terms, in and by itself, involves an affirmation; it is by the combination of such terms that positive or negative statements arise. For every assertion must, as is admitted, be either true or false, whereas expressions which are not in any way composite, such as 'man', 'white', 'runs', 'wins', cannot be either true or false.

5   Substance, in the truest and primary and most definite sense of the word, is that which is neither predicable of a subject nor present in a subject; for instance, the individual man or horse. But in a secondary sense those things are called substances within which, as species, the primary substances are included; also those which, as genera, include the species. For instance, the individual man is included in the species 'man', and the genus to which the species belongs is 'animal'; these, therefore—that is to say, the species 'man' and the genus 'animal'—are termed secondary substances.

It is plain from what has been said that both the name and the definition of the predicate must be predicable of the subject. For instance, 'man' is predicated of the individual man. Now in this case the name of the species 'man' is applied to the individual, for we use the term 'man' in describing the individual; and the definition of 'man' will also be predicated of the individual man, for the individual man is both man and animal. Thus, both the name and the definition of the species are predicable of the individual.

With regard, on the other hand, to those things which are present in a subject, it is generally the case that neither their name nor their definition is predicable of that in which they are present. Though, however, the definition is never predicable, there is nothing in certain cases to prevent the name being used. For instance, 'white' being present in a body is predicated of that in which it is present, for a body is called white: the definition, however, of the color 'white' is never predicable of the body.

Everything except primary substances is either predicable of a primary substance or present in a primary substance. This becomes evident by reference to particular instances which occur. 'Animal' is predicated of the species 'man', therefore of the individual man, for if there were no individual man of whom it could be predicated; it could not be predicated of the species 'man' at all. Again, color is present in body, therefore in individual bodies, for if there were no individual body in which it was present, it could not be present in body at all. Thus everything except primary substances is either predicated of primary substances, or is present in them, and if these last did not exist, it would be impossible for anything else to exist.

Of secondary substances, the species is more truly substance than the genus, being more nearly related to primary substance. For if any one should render an account of what a primary substance is, he would render a more instructive account, and one more proper to the subject, by stating the species than by stating the genus. Thus, he would give a more instructive account of an individual man by stating that he was man than by stating that he was animal, for the former description is peculiar to the individual in a greater degree, while the latter is too general. Again, the man who gives an account of the nature of an individual tree will give a more instructive account by mentioning the species 'tree' than by mentioning the genus 'plant'.

Moreover, primary substances are most properly called substances in virtue of the fact that they are the entities which underlie everything else, and that everything else is either predicated of them or present in them. Now the same relation which subsists between primary substance and everything else subsists also between the species and the genus: for the species is to the genus as subject is to predicate, since the genus is predicated of the species, whereas the species cannot be predicated of the genus. Thus we have a second ground for asserting that the species is more truly substance than the genus.

Of species themselves, except in the case of such as are genera, no one is more truly substance than another. We should not give a more appropriate account of the individual man by stating the species to which he belonged, than we should of an individual horse by adopting the same method of definition. In the same way, of primary substances, no one is more truly substance than another; an individual man is not more truly substance than an individual ox.

It is, then, with good reason that of all that remains, when we exclude primary substances, we concede to species and genera alone the name 'secondary substance', for these alone of all the predicates convey a knowledge of primary substance. For it is by stating the species or the genus that we appropriately define any individual man; and we shall make our definition more exact by stating the former than by stating the latter. All other things that we state, such as that he is white, that he runs, and so on, are irrelevant to the definition. Thus it is just that these alone, apart from primary substances, should be called substances.

Further, primary substances are most properly so called, because they underlie and are the subjects of everything else. Now the same relation that subsists between primary substance and everything else subsists also between the species and the genus to which the primary substance belongs, on the one hand, and every attribute which is not included within these, on the other. For these are the subjects of all such. If we call an individual man 'skilled in grammar', the predicate is applicable also to the species and to the genus to which he belongs. This law holds good in all cases.

It is a common characteristic of all substance that it is never present in a subject. For primary substance is neither present in a subject nor predicated of a subject; while, with regard to secondary substances, it is clear from the following arguments (apart from others) that they are not present in a subject. For 'man' is predicated of the individual man, but is not present in any subject: for manhood is not present in the individual man. In the same way, 'animal' is also predicated of the individual man, but is not present in him. Again, when a thing is present in a subject, though the name may quite well be applied to that in which it is present, the definition cannot be applied. Yet of secondary substances, not only the name, but also the definition, applies to the subject: we should use both the definition of the species and that of the genus with reference to the individual man. Thus substance cannot be present in a subject.

Yet this is not peculiar to substance, for it is also the case that differentiae cannot be present in subjects. The characteristics, 'terrestrial' and 'two-footed' are predicated of the species 'man', but not present in it. For they are not *in* man. Moreover, the definition of the differentia may be predicated of that of which the differentia itself is predicated. For instance, if the characteristic 'terrestrial' is predicated of the species 'man', the definition also of that characteristic may be used to form the predicate of the species 'man': for 'man' is terrestrial.

The fact that the parts of substances appear to be present in the whole, as in a subject, should not make us apprehensive lest we should have to admit that such parts are not substances: for in explaining the phrase 'being present in a subject ', we stated that we meant 'otherwise than as parts in a whole'.

It is the mark of substances and of differentiae that, in all propositions of which they form the predicate, they are predicated univocally. For all such propositions have for their subject either the individual or the species. It is true that, inasmuch as primary substance is not predicable of anything, it can never form the predicate of any proposition. But of secondary substances, the species is predicated of the individual, the genus both of the species and of the individual. Similarly the differentiae are predicated of the species and of the individuals. Moreover, the definition of the species and that of the genus are applicable to the primary substance, and that of the genus to the species. For all that is predicated of the predicate will be predicated also of the subject. Similarly, the definition of the differentiae will be applicable to the species and to the individuals. But it was stated above that the word 'univocal' was applied to those things which had both name and definition in common. It is, therefore, established that in every proposition, of which either substance or a differentia forms the predicate, these are predicated univocally.

All substance appears to signify that which is individual. In the case of primary substance this is indisputably true, for the thing is a unit. In the case of secondary substances, when we speak, for instance, of 'man' or 'animal', our form of speech gives the impression that we are here also indicating that which is individual, but the impression is not strictly true; for a secondary substance is not an individual, but a class with a certain qualification; for it is not one and single as a primary substance is; the words 'man', 'animal', are predicable of more than one subject.

Yet species and genus do not merely indicate quality, like the term 'white'; 'white' indicates quality and nothing further, but species and genus determine the quality with reference to a substance: they signify substance qualitatively differentiated. The determinate qualification covers a larger field in the case of the genus than in that of the species: he who uses the word 'animal' is herein using a word of wider extension than he who uses the word 'man'.

Another mark of substance is that it has no contrary. What could be the contrary of any primary substance, such as the individual man or animal? It has none. Nor can the species or the genus have a contrary. Yet this characteristic is not peculiar to substance, but is true of many other things, such as quantity. There is nothing that forms the contrary of 'two cubits long' or of 'three cubits long', or of 'ten', or of any such term. A man may contend that 'much' is the contrary of 'little', or 'great' of 'small', but of definite quantitative terms no contrary exists.

Substance, again, does not appear to admit of variation of degree. I do not mean by this that one substance cannot be more or less truly substance than another, for it has already been stated that this is the case; but that no single substance admits of varying degrees within itself. For instance, one particular substance, 'man', cannot be more or less man either than himself at some other time or than some other man. One man cannot be more man than another, as that which is white may be more or less white than some other white object, or as that which is beautiful may be more or less beautiful than some other beautiful object. The same quality, moreover, is said to subsist in a thing in varying degrees at different times. A body, being white, is said to be whiter at one time than it was before, or, being warm, is said to be warmer or less warm than at some other time. But substance is not said to be more or less that which it is: a man is not more truly a man at one time than he was before, nor is anything, if it is substance, more or less what it is. Substance, then, does not admit of variation of degree.

The most distinctive mark of substance appears to be that, while remaining numerically one and the same, it is capable of admitting contrary qualities. From among things other than substance, we should find ourselves unable to bring forward any which possessed this mark. Thus, one and the same color cannot be white and black. Nor can the same one action be good and bad: this law holds good with everything that is not substance. But one and the self-same substance, while retaining its identity, is yet capable of admitting contrary qualities. The same individual person is at one time white, at another black, at one time warm, at another cold, at one time good, at another bad. This capacity is found nowhere else, though it might be maintained that a statement or opinion was an exception to the rule. The same statement, it is agreed, can be both true and false. For if the statement 'he is sitting' is true, yet, when the person in question has risen, the same statement will be false. The same applies to opinions. For if any one thinks truly that a person is sitting, yet, when that person has risen, this same opinion, if still held, will be false. Yet although this exception may be allowed, there is, nevertheless, a difference in the manner in which the thing takes place. It is by themselves changing that substances admit contrary qualities. It is thus that that which was hot becomes cold, for it has entered into a different state. Similarly that which was white becomes black, and that which was bad good, by a process of change; and in the same way in all other cases it is by changing that substances are capable of admitting contrary qualities. But statements and opinions themselves remain unaltered in all respects: it is by the alteration in the facts of the case that the contrary quality comes to be theirs. The statement 'he is sitting' remains unaltered, but it is at one time true, at another false, according to circumstances. What has been said of statements applies also to opinions. Thus, in respect of the manner in which the thing takes place, it is the peculiar mark of substance that it should be capable of admitting contrary qualities; for it is by itself changing that it does so.

If, then, a man should make this exception and contend that statements and opinions are capable of admitting contrary qualities, his contention is unsound. For statements and opinions are said to have this capacity, not because they themselves undergo modification, but because this modification occurs in the case of something else. The truth or falsity of a statement depends on facts, and not on any power on the part of the statement itself of admitting contrary qualities. In short, there is nothing which can alter the nature of statements and opinions. As, then, no change takes place in themselves, these cannot be said to be capable of admitting contrary qualities.

But it is by reason of the modification which takes place within the substance itself that a substance is said to be capable of admitting contrary qualities; for a substance admits within itself either disease or health, whiteness or blackness. It is in this sense that it is said to be capable of admitting contrary qualities.

To sum up, it is a distinctive mark of substance, that, while remaining numerically one and the same, it is capable of admitting contrary qualities, the modification taking place through a change in the substance itself.

Let these remarks suffice on the subject of substance.

NOTE

From *The Categories*, trans. E. M. Edghill. *The Basic Works of Aristotle*, ed. Richard McKeon. Originally published by Random House, New York, 1941. Reprinted by permission of Oxford University Press.

3 ABELARD

To avoid the problems of both extreme realism (namely, that universals possess independent existence or subsistence and are therefore inevitably particulars) or nominalism (i.e., that the only basis for predication of qualities to particulars is ultimately arbitrary) Abelard develops a theory of abstraction. The mind is capable of distinguishing between matter and form although the two never, in fact, exist in isolation. Such is the power of abstraction. The process of abstraction is such that it allows one to concentrate on one or another aspects of a particular. This mental power to focus has a parallel to sense perception. If one perceives an object composed partly of gold and partly of silver, he can concentrate his attention at one moment on the gold and at another instant on the silver. This attention to different aspects of the composite object in no way leads one to conclude with respect to that specific perception that the two aspects, gold and silver, are separate from the object being perceived. So too with abstractions one does not conclude that the quality that is the subject of concentration is something separate from the substance it qualifies. Universals, then, are the products of abstraction. Universals are *sermones,* concepts. On this basis, Abelard has very often been judged a conceptualist. Such a conclusion, however, would be hasty. He also refers to universal terms as *sermones.* They are that which are predicable of many and imply a judgement about particulars — the judgement that many different particulars possess common qualities. Consequently, there is a real basis for predication. This reality, consisting of both matter and form, also provides the subject matter for abstraction. Therefore, one can safely argue that Abelard is a moderate realist.

On Universals

Porphyry, as Boethius points out [in his Commentary on the *Isagoge*], raises three profitable questions whose answers are shrouded in mystery and though not a few philosophers have attempted to solve them, few have succeeded in doing so. The first is: Do genera and species really exist or are they simply something in the mind? It is as if [Porphyry] were asking whether their existence is a fact or merely a matter of opinion. The second is: Granting they do exist, are they corporeal or incorporeal? The third is: Do they exist apart from sensible things or only in them? For there are two types of incorporeal things. Some, like God or the soul, can subsist in their incorporeality apart from anything sensible. Others are unable to exist apart from the sensible objects in which they are found. A line, for example, is unable to exist apart from some bodily subject.

Porphyry sidesteps answering them with the remark: "For the present I refuse to be drawn into a discussion as to whether genus and species exist in reality or solely and simply in thought; or if they do exist whether they are corporeal or incorporeal, or whether, on the admission they are incorporeal, they are separated from sensibles or exist only in and dependent upon sensible things, and other things of this sort."

"Other things of this sort" can be interpreted in various ways. We could take him to mean: "I refuse to discuss these three questions and other related matters." For other relevant questions could be raised that pose similar problems. For instance, what is the common basis or reason for applying universal names to things, which boils down to explaining to what extent different things agree; or how should one understand those universal names wherein one seems to conceive of nothing, where the universal term in a word seems to have no referent? And there are many other difficult points. By understanding "other things of this sort" in this way, we can add a fourth question: Do genera and species, as long as they remain such, require that the subject they name have some reality or, if all the things they designate were destroyed, could the universal consist simply in its significance for the mind, as would be the case with the name "rose" when no roses are in bloom which it could designate in general? . . .[1]

Since genera and species are obviously instances of universals and in mentioning them Porphyry touches on the nature of universals in general, we may distinguish the properties common to universals by studying them in these samples. Let us inquire then whether they apply only to *words* or to *things* as well.

Aristotle[2] defines the universal as "that which is of such a nature as to be predicated of many." Porphyry, on the other hand, goes on to define the singular or individual as "that which is predicated of a single individual."[3]

Authorities then seem to apply "universal" to things as much as they do to words. Aristotle himself does this, declaring by way of preface to his definition of the universal, that "some things are universal, others individual. Now by 'universal' I mean that which is of such a nature as to be predicated of many, whereas 'individual' is not something of this kind."[4] Porphyry too, having stated that the species is composed of a genus and difference, proceeds to locate it in the nature of things. From this it is clear that things themselves fall under a universal noun.

Nouns too are called universals. That is why Aristotle says: "The genus specifies the quality with reference to substance, for it signifies what sort of thing it is."[5]

"It seems then that things as well as words are called universals. . . ."[6]

However, things taken either singly or collectively cannot be called universals, because they are not predicable of many. Consequently it remains to ascribe this form of universality to words alone. Just as grammarians call certain nouns proper and others appellative, so dialecticians call certain simple words particulars, that is, individuals, and others universals. A universal word is one which is able to be predicated of many by reason of its intention, such as the noun "man," which can be joined with the names of particular men by reason of the nature of the subject on which they are imposed. A particular word, however, is one which is predicable only of a single subject, as *Socrates* when it is taken as the name of but one individual. For if you take it equivocally, you give it the signification not of one word but of many. For according to Priscian, many nouns can obviously be brought together in a single word.[7] When a universal then is described as "that which is predicable of many," *that which* indicates not only the simplicity of the word as a discrete expression, but also the unity of signification lacking in an equivocal term. . . .[8]

Now that we have defined "universal" and "particular" in regard to words, let us investigate in particular the properties of those which are universal. For questions have been raised about universals, since serious doubts existed as to their meaning because there seemed to be no subject to which they referred. Neither did they express the sense of any one thing. These universal terms then appeared to be imposed on nothing, since it is clear that all things subsisting in themselves are individuals and, as has been shown, they do not share in some one thing by virtue of which a universal name could be given to them. Since it is certain then that (a) universals are not imposed on things by reason of their individual differences, for then they would not be common but singular, (b) nor can they designate things which share in some identical entity, for it is not a thing in which they agree, there seems to be nothing from which universals might derive their meaning, particularly since their sense is not restricted to any one thing. . . . Since "man" is imposed on individuals for an identical reason, viz. because each is a rational, mortal animal, the very generality of the designation prevents one from understanding the term of just one man in the way, for example, that one understands by Socrates just one unique person, which is why it is called a particular. But the common term "man" does not mean just Socrates, or any other man. Neither does it designate a collection, nor does it, as some think, mean just Socrates insofar as he is man. For even if Socrates alone were sitting in this house and because of that the proposition "A man sits in this house" is true, still by the name "man," there is no way of getting to Socrates except insofar as he too is a man. Otherwise, from the proposition itself, "sitting" would be understood to inhere in Socrates, so that from "A man sits in this house," one could infer "Socrates sits in this house." And the same applies to any other individual man. Neither can "A man sits in this house" be understood of a collection, since the proposition can be true if only one man is there. Consequently, there is not a single thing that "man" or any other universal term seems to signify, since there is not a single thing whose sense the term seems to express. Neither does it seem there could be any sense if no subject is thought of. Universals then appear to be totally devoid of meaning.

And yet this is not the case. For universals do signify distinct individuals to the extent of giving names to them, but this significative function does not require that one grasps a sense which arises out of them and which belongs to each of them. "Man," for example, does name individual things, but for the common reason that they are all men. That is why it is called a universal. Also there is a certain sense—common, not proper—that is applicable to those individuals which one conceives to be alike.

But let us look carefully now into some matters we have touched on only briefly, viz. (a) what is the common reason for imposing a universal name on things, (b) what is this intellectual conception of a common likeness, and (c) is a word said to be common because of some common cause by virtue of which all the things it designates are alike, or is it merely because we have a common concept for all of them, or is it for both of these reasons?

Let us consider first the question of the common cause. As we noted earlier, each individual man is a discrete subject since he has as proper to himself not only an essence but also whatever forms [or qualifications] that essence may have. Nevertheless, they agree in this that they are all men. Since there is no man who is not a discrete or distinct individual thing, I do not say they agree "in man," but "in being a man." Now if you consider the matter carefully, man or any other thing is not the same as "to be a man," even as "not to be in a subject" is not a thing, nor is there anything which is "not to undergo contrariety" or "not to be subject to greater or lesser degrees," and still Aristotle says these are points in which all substances agree. Since there is no *thing* in which things could possibly agree, if there is any agreement among certain things, this must not be taken to be some *thing*. Just as Socrates and Plato are alike in being men, so a horse and donkey are alike in not being men. It is for this reason that they are called "nonmen." Different individuals then agree either in being the same or in not being the same, e.g. in being men or white, or in not being men or being white.

Still this agreement among things (which itself is not a thing) must not be regarded as a case of bringing together things which are real on the basis of nothing. In point of fact we do speak of this agreeing with that to the extent of their having the same status, that of man, i.e. the two agree in that they are men, and there is not the slightest difference between them, I say, in their being men, even though we may not call this an essence. But "being a man" (which is not a thing) we do call "the status of man" and we have also called it "the common cause for imposing on individuals a universal name." For we frequently give the name "cause" to some characteristic that is not itself a thing as when one says "He was beaten because he did not wish to appear in court." His not wishing to appear in court, cited here as a cause is not a [constitutive] essence [of his being beaten].

We can also designate as "the status of man" those things themselves in a man's nature which the one who imposed the word conceives according to a common likeness.

Having shown how universals signify, namely by functioning as names of things, and having presented what the reason for imposing such general names is, let us indicate just what these universal meanings consist of.

To begin with, let us point out the distinguishing features of all intellectual conception or understanding. Though sense perception as well as intellectual conception are both functions of the soul, there is a difference between the two. Bodies and what inhere in them are objects of sensory knowledge, e.g. a tower or its sensory qualities. In the exercise of this function, however, the soul makes use of corporeal instruments. In understanding or conceiving something intellectually, the soul needs no corporeal organ and consequently no bodily subject in which the thought object inheres is required. It is enough that the mind constructs for itself a likeness of these things and the action called intellection is concerned with this [cognitive content]. Hence, if the tower is removed or destroyed, the sense perception that dealt with it perishes, but the intellectual conception of the tower remains in the likeness preserved in the mind. As the act of sense perception is not the sensed thing itself, so the act of the intellect is not itself the form understood or conceived intellectually. Understanding is an activity of the soul by virtue of which it is said to understand, but the form toward which understanding is directed is a kind of image or construct (*res ficta*) which the mind fashions for itself at will, like those imaginary cities seen in dreams or the form of a projected building which the architect conceives after the manner of a blueprint. This construct is not something one can call either substance or accident.

Nevertheless, there are those who simply identify it with the act itself through which it is understood or conceived. Thus they speak of the tower building itself, which I think of when the tower is not there and which I conceive to be lofty, square, and situated in a spacious plain, as being the same as thinking of a tower. But we prefer to call the [conceptual] image as such the likeness of the thing.

There is of course nothing to prevent the act of understanding itself from being called in some sense a "likeness" because it obviously conceives what is, properly speaking, a likeness of the thing. Still, as we have said—and rightly so—the two are not the same. For, I ask: "Does the squareness or loftiness represent the actual form or quality possessed by the act of understanding itself when one thinks of the height and the way the tower is put together?" Surely the actual squareness and height are present only in bodies and from an imagined quality no act of understanding or any other real essence can be constructed. What remains then but that the substance, like the quality of which it is the subject, is also fictive? Perhaps one could also say that a mirror or reflected image is not itself a true "thing," since there often appears on the whitish surface of the mirror a color of contrary quality. . . .⁹

Having treated in general the nature of understanding, let us consider how a universal and a particular conception differ. The conception associated with a universal name is an image that is general and indiscriminate [*imago communis et confusa*], whereas the image associated with a singular word represents the proper and characteristic form, as it were, of a single thing, i.e. it applies to one and only one person. When I hear the word "man," for instance, a certain likeness arises in my mind which is so related to individual men that it is proper but common to all. But when I hear "Socrates," a certain form arises in my mind which is the likeness of a particular person. . . . Hence it is correct to say "man" does not rightly signify Socrates or any other man, since by virtue of this name no one in particular is identified; yet it is a name of particular things. "Socrates," on the other hand, must not only name a particular thing, but it must also determine just what thing is its subject. . . . To show what pertains to the nature of all lions, a picture can be constructed which represents nothing that is the peculiar property of only one of them. On the other hand, a picture suited to distinguish any one of them can be drawn by depicting something proper to the one in question, for example, by painting it as limping, maimed, or wounded by the spear of Hercules. Just as one can paint one figure that is general and another that is particular, so too can one form one conception of things that is common and another conception that is proper.

There is some question, however, and not without reason, whether or not this [universal] name also signifies this conceptual form to which the understanding is directed. Both authority and reason, however, seem to be unanimous in affirming that it does.

For Priscian, after first showing how universals were applied commonly to individuals, seemed to introduce another meaning they had, namely the common form. He states that "the general and special forms of things which were given intelligibility in the divine mind before being produced in bodies could be used to reveal what the natural genera and species of things are."¹⁰ In this passage he views God after the fashion of an artist who first conceives in his mind a [model or] exemplar form of what he is to fashion and who works according to the likeness of this form, which form is said to be embodied when a real thing is constructed in its likeness.

It may be all right to ascribe such a common conception to God, but not to man. For those works of God like a man, a soul, or a stone represent general or special states of nature, whereas those of a human artisan like a house or a sword do not. For "house" and "sword" do not pertain to nature as the other terms do. They are the names not of a substance but of something accidental and therefore they are neither genera nor ultimate species. Conceptions by abstraction [of the true nature of things] may well be ascribed to the divine mind but may not be ascribed to that of man, because men, who know things only through the medium of their senses, scarcely ever arrive at such an ideal understanding and never conceive the [underlying] natures of things in their purity. But God knew all things he created for what they were and this even before they actually existed. He can discriminate between these individual states as they are in themselves; senses are no hindrance to him who alone has true understanding of things. Of those things which men have not experienced through the senses, they happen to have opinions rather than understanding, as we learn from experience. For having thought of some city before seeing it, we find on arriving there that it is quite different than we had thought.

And so I believe we have only an opinion about those forms like rationality, mortality, paternity, or what is within. Names for what we experience, however, produce understanding to the extent they can do so, for the one who coined the terms intended that they be imposed in accord with the [true] nature or properties of things, even though he himself was unable to do justice in thought to the nature or property of the thing. It is these common concepts, however, which Priscian calls general and special [i.e. generic and specific], that these general names or the names of species bring to the mind. He says that the universals function as proper names with regard to such conceptions, and although these names refer to the essences named only in an indiscriminate fashion, they direct the mind of the hearer immediately to that common conception in the same way that proper names direct attention to the one thing that they signify.

Porphyry too, in distinguishing between things constituted only in the likeness of matter and form and those actually composed of matter and form, seems to understand this common conception by the former. Boethius also, when he calls the conception gathered from a likeness of many things a genus or a species, seems to have in mind this same common conception. Some think that Plato subscribed to this view, i.e. to these common ideas—which he located in the *nous*—he gave the names of genus and species. On this point, perhaps, Boethius indicates some disagreement between Plato and Aristotle, where he speaks of Plato claiming not only that genera, species, and the rest should be understood to be universals, but also that they also have true existence and subsistence apart from bodies, as if to say that Plato understood these common concepts, which he assumed to exist in a bodiless form in the *nous*, to be universals. He means here by universal "a common likeness of many things" perhaps, rather than "predicable of many" as Aristotle understood the term. For this conception [itself] does not seem to be predicated of many in the way that a name is able to be applied to each of many things.

But his [i.e. Boethius'] statement that Plato thinks universals subsist apart from sensibles can be interpreted in another way, so that there is no disagreement between the philosophers. For Aristotle's statements about universals always subsisting in sensibles is to be understood of the way they actually do exist, because the animal nature (which the universal name "animal" designates and which is called a kind of universal in a transferred sense of the term) is never found to exist in anything which is not sensible. Plato, however, thinks this nature has such a natural subsistence in itself that it would retain its existence if it were not subject to sense [i.e. if it were not clothed with sensible accidents]. Hence what Aristotle denies to be actually the case, Plato, the investigator of the nature, ascribes to a natural capacity. Consequently there is no real disagreement between them.

Reason too seems to agree with these authorities in their apparent claim that the universal names designate these common concepts or forms. For what else does to conceive of them by name mean but that names signify them? But since we hold that these forms conceived are not simply the same as the acts of knowing them, there is in addition to the real thing and the act of understanding a third factor, viz. the signification or meaning of the name. Now while there is no authority for holding this, still it is not contrary to reason.

At this point, let us give an answer to the question we promised earlier to settle, namely whether the ability of universal words to refer to things in general is due to the fact that there is in them a common cause for imposing the words on them, or whether it is due to the fact that a common concept of them exists, or whether it is for both of these reasons. Now there seems to be no ground why it should not be for both of these reasons, but if we understand "common cause" as involving something of the nature of the things, then this seems to be the stronger of the two reasons.

Another point we must clarify is the one noted earlier, namely that these universal conceptions are formed by abstraction, and we must show how one can speak of them as isolated, naked, and pure without their being empty. But first about abstraction. Here we must remember that while matter and form are always fused together, the rational power of the mind is such that it can consider matter alone or form alone or both together. The first two are considerations by way of abstraction, since in order to study its precise nature, they abstract one thing from what does not exist alone. The third type of consideration is by way of synthesis. The substance of man, for instance, is a body, an animal, a man; it is invested with no end of forms. But when I turn my attention exclusively to the material essence of a substance, disregarding all its additional forms or qualifications, my understanding takes the form of a concept by abstraction. If I direct my attention, however, to nothing more than the corporeity of this substance, the resulting concept, though it represents a synthesis when compared with the previous concept (that of substance alone), is still formed by abstraction from the forms other than corporeity, such as animation, sensitivity, rationality, or whiteness, none of which I consider.

Such conceptions by abstraction might appear to be false or empty, perhaps, since they look to the thing in a way other than that in which it exists. For since they consider matter or form exclusively, and neither of these subsists separately, they clearly represent a conception of the thing otherwise than the way it is. Consequently, they seem to be vacuous, yet this is not really the case. For it is only when a thing is considered to have some property or nature which it does not actually possess that the conception which represents the thing otherwise than it is, is indeed empty. But this is not what happens in abstraction. For when I consider this man only in his nature as a substance or a body, but not as an animal, a man, or a grammarian, certainly I do not think of anything that is not in that nature, and still I do not attend to all that it has. And when I say that I attend only to what is in it, "only" refers to my attention and not to the way this characteristic exists, for otherwise my conception would be empty. For the thing does not only have this, but I only consider it as having this. And while I do consider it in some sense to be otherwise than it actually is, I do not consider it to be in a state or condition other than that in which it is, as was pointed out earlier. "Otherwise" means merely that the mode of thought is other than the mode of existing. For the thing in question is thought of not as separated, but separately from the other, even though it does not exist separately. Matter is perceived purely, form simply, even though the former does not exist purely nor the latter simply. Purity and simplicity, in a word, are features of our understanding, not of existence; they are characteristic of the way we think, not of the way things exist. Even the senses often function discriminatively where composite objects are concerned. If a statue is half gold, half silver, I can look separately at the gold and silver combined there, studying first the gold, then the silver exclusively, thus viewing piecemeal what is actually joined together, and yet I do not perceive to be divided what is not divided. In much the same way "understanding by way of abstraction" means "considering separately" but not "considering [it] as separated." Otherwise such understanding would be vacuous. . . .[11]

But let us return to our *universal* conceptions, which must always be produced by way of abstraction. For when I hear "man" or "whiteness" or "white," I do not recall in virtue of the name all the natures or properties in those subjects to which the name refers. "Man" gives rise to the conception, indiscriminate, not discrete, of animal, rational and mortal only, but not of the additional accidents as well. Conceptions of individuals also can be formed by abstraction, as happens for example when one speaks of "this substance," "this body," "this animal," "this white," or "this whiteness." For by "this man," though I consider just man's nature, I do so as related to a certain subject, whereas by "man" I regard this nature simply in itself and not in relation to some one man. That is why a universal concept is correctly described as being *isolated, bare,* and *pure*: i.e. "isolated from sense," because it is not a perception of the thing as sensory; "bare," because it is abstracted from some or from all forms; "pure," because it is unadulterated by any reference to any single individual, since there is not just one thing, be it the matter or the form, to which it points, as we explained earlier when we described such a conception as indiscriminate.

Now that we have considered these matters, let us proceed to answer the questions posed by Porphyry about genera and species. This we can easily do now that we have clarified the nature of universals in general. The point of the first question was whether genera and species exist. More precisely, are they signs of something which really exists or of something that merely exists in thought, i.e. are they simply vacuous, devoid of any real reference, as is the case with words like "chimera," or "goat-stag," which fail to produce any coherent meaning? To this one has to reply that as a matter of fact they do serve to name things that actually exist and therefore are not the subjects of purely empty thoughts. But what they name are the selfsame things named by singular names. And still, there is a sense in which they exist as isolated, bare, and pure only in the mind, as we have just explained. . . .

The second question, viz. "Are they corporeal or incorporeal?" can be taken in the same way, that is, "Granting that they are signs of existing things, are these things corporeal or incorporeal?" For surely everything that exists, as Boethius puts it, is either corporeal or incorporeal, regardless of whether these words mean respectively: (1) a bodily or a bodiless substance, (2) something perceptible to the senses like man, wood, and whiteness, or something imperceptible in this way like justice or the soul. (3) "Corporeal" can also have the meaning of something discrete or individual, so that the question boils down to asking whether genera and species signify discrete individuals or not. A thoroughgoing investigator of truth considers not only what can be factually stated but also such possible opinions as might be proposed. Consequently, even though one is quite certain that only individuals are real, in view of the fact that someone might be of the opinion that there are other things that exist, it is justifiable to inquire about them. Now this third meaning of "corporeal" makes better sense of our question, reducing it to an inquiry as to whether it is discrete individuals or not that are signified. On the other hand, since nothing existing is incorporeal, i.e. nonindividual, "incorporeal" would seem to be superfluous in Boethius' statement that everything existing is either corporeal or incorporeal. Here the order of the questions, it seems, suggests nothing that would be of help except perhaps that corporeal and incorporeal, taken in another sense, do represent divisions of whatever exists and that this might also be the case here. The inquirer in this case would seem to be asking, in effect: "Since I see that some existing things are called corporeal and others incorporeal, I would like to know which of these names we should use for what universals signify?" The answer to this would be: "To some extent, 'corporeal' would be appropriate, since the *significata* are in essence discrete individuals. 'Incorporeal' would be a better description, however, of the way a universal term names things, for it does not point to them in an individual and specific fashion but points only in an indiscriminate way, as we have adequately explained above." Hence universal names are described both as corporeal (because of the nature of the things they point to) and as incorporeal (because of the way these things are signified, for although they name discrete individuals, universals do not name them individually or properly).

The third question ("Do they exist apart from or only in sensible things?") arises from the admission that they are incorporeal, since, as we noted [in the opening paragraph], there is a certain sense in which "existing in the sensible" and "not existing in the sensible" represent a division of the incorporeal. Now universals are said to exist in sensible things to the extent that they signify the inner substance of something which is sensible by reason of its external forms. While they signify this same substance actually existing in sensible garb, they point to what is by its nature something distinct from the sensible thing [i.e. as substance it is other than its accidental garb], as we said above in our reinterpretation of Plato. That is why Boethius does not claim that genera and species exist apart from sensible things, but only that they are understood apart from them, to the extent namely that the things conceived generically or specifically are viewed with reference to their nature in a rational fashion rather than in a sensory way, and they could indeed subsist in themselves [i.e. as individual substances] even if stripped of the exterior or [accidental] forms by which they come to the attention of the senses. For we admit that all genera and species exist in things perceptible to the senses. Since our understanding of them has always been described as something apart from the senses, however, they appeared not to be in sensible things in any way. There was every reason, then, to ask whether they could be in sensibles. And to this question, the answer is that some of them are, but only to the extent, as was explained, that they represent the enduring substrate that lies beneath the sensible.

We can take corporeal and incorporeal in this second question as equivalent to sensible and insensible, so that the sequence of questions becomes more orderly. And since our understanding of universals is derived solely from sense perceptions, as has been said, one could appropriately ask whether universals were sensible or insensible. Now the answer is that some of them are sensible (we refer here to the nature of those things classed as sensible) and the same time not sensible (we refer here to the way they are signified). For while it is sensible things that these universals name, they do not designate these things in the way they are perceived by the senses, i.e. as distinct individuals, and when things are designated only in universal terms the senses cannot pick them out. Hence the question arose: "Do universals designate only sensible things or is there something else they signify?" And the answer to that is that they signify both the sensible things themselves and also that common concept which Priscian ascribes above all to the divine mind.

As for the fourth question we added to the others, our solution is this. We do not want to speak of there being universal *names*[12] when the things they name have perished and they can no longer be predicated of many and are not common names of anything, as would be the case when all the roses were gone. Nevertheless, "rose" would still have meaning for the mind even though it names nothing. Otherwise, "There is no rose" would not be a proposition.[13]

NOTES

Reprinted by permission of the Free Press from *Medieval Philosophy: From St. Augustine to Nicholas of Cusa*, ed. J. F. Wippel and A. B. Wolter, O.F.M. Copyright © 1969 by the Free Press, a division of Macmillan, Inc. The notes are those of the translator, A. B. Wolter.

1. *Peter Abaelards philosophische Schriften*, ed. B. Geyer, in *Beiträge zur Geschichte der Philosophie des Mittelalters* XXI (Münster: Aschendorff, 1933), 7–8.
2. Aristotle, *De interpretatione*, chap. 7 (17a 38).
3. Cf. Boethius, *In Isagogen Porphyrii commenta*, ed. G. Schepss and S. Brandt, *Corpus Scriptorum Ecclesiasticorum Latinorum*, Vol. 48 (Vienna: Tempsky, 1906), 148.
4. Aristotle, *loc. cit.*
5. Aristotle, *Categoriae*, chap. 5 (3b 20).
6. Abelard, *op. cit.*, 9–10.
7. Priscian, *Institutiones grammaticae*, XVII, in H. Keil, *Grammatici latini*, Vol. 3 (Lipsiae: in aedibus B. G. Teubneri, 1858), 145.
8. Abelard, *op. cit.*, 16.
9. *Ibid.*, 18–21.
10. Priscian, *op. cit.*, 135.
11. Abelard, *op. cit.*, 21–26.
12. When Abelard speaks of "there being universal names," he has in mind terms that have actual reference; he distinguishes in a word between signification in the sense of having meaning or sense and denominating, i.e., actually naming or referring to existing things.
13. Abelard, *op. cit.*, 27–30.

4 AQUINAS

Aquinas flatly rejected the extreme realist theory which supposes that because one can correctly use the same word to refer to any number of particulars that there must be only one thing corresponding to that word. For example, one can say that Peter is a man and that John is a man. From this it does not follow that there is one universal "thing" present in both Peter and John.

For Thomas essences are universals. Essences are what determine a particular to be the type of thing that it is. Here it is crucial not to confuse essence with form. Form and matter are inextricably tied to one another for one cannot exist without the other although humans can make an intellectual distinction between them by way of abstraction. However, the essence of say, man, is not simply identical to the form man because essential to man (or any sensible object) is matter. Part of what it is to be a man is to possess the substance characteristic of a man as opposed to, say, a rock which has as its essence a different sort of matter. Consequently, essence entails both matter and form. Essences are real and grounded in the sensible world. We identify essences via sense experience. It is our power of abstraction that makes it possible for essences to become the subject of ideas resulting, for example, in the universal idea of man. We have, however, the power by way of abstraction to conjure ideas of things whose essences are not exemplified. For example, one can conceive of a mermaid without that conception entailing exemplification. In other words, exemplified existence is not a necessary element of the essence of a thing.

On Being and Essence

INTRODUCTION

A slight error in the beginning is large in the end, according to the Philosopher in *De Caelo et Mundo,* and being and essence are what is first conceived in the intellect, as Avicenna says in the *Metaphysics.* So, lest from ignorance of these error should occur, one should first set out the difficulty regarding them by telling what is signified by the terms 'essence' and 'being', how being and essence are found in various cases, and how they stand with respect to the logical intentions, i.e. genera, species and differentia.

Moreover, as we ought to take knowledge of what is simple from what is complex, and come to what is prior from what is posterior, so learning is helped by beginning with what is easier. Hence we should proceed from the signification of being to the signification of essence.

CHAPTER I

One should be aware that, as the Philosopher remarks in the *Metaphysics*, being just as being has two senses. One is that which is divided through the ten categories; the other is that which signifies the truth of propositions. The difference between these is that in the second sense everything can be called being about which an affirmative proposition can be formed, even if it calls for nothing real; this is the sense in which privations and negations are called beings. For we say that affirmation is opposed to negation, and that blindness is in the eye. But in the first sense it cannot be said that anything is being unless it calls for something real; so that in the first sense, blindness and such as that are not beings. Thus the term 'essence' is not taken from being in the second sense, for some are called beings in that sense which do not have an essence, as is obvious in the case of privations. But essence is taken from being in the first sense. Whence the Commentator, in the same place, says, "Being in the first sense is what signifies real substance."

And since, as was remarked, being in this sense is divided through the ten categories, it is required that essence signify something common to all natures through which various beings are organized into various species in various genera, as humanity is the essence of man, and so for other cases. And since that through which a thing is constituted into its own genus or species is what we signify through the definition indicating what a thing is, the term 'essence' has been changed by philosophers into the term 'quiddity' (whatness). And this is what the Philosopher often calls "what it was to be," that is, that through which something is *what* it is. It is also called form, in the sense in which the certitude of any thing is signified through form, as Avicenna says in Book II of his *Metaphysics*. By another name it is also called nature, taking nature in the first of the four senses which Boethius gives in his *De Duabis Naturis*. According to this, nature is said to be all that the intellect can grasp in any way, for a thing is only intelligible through its definition and essence. And the Philosopher also says in Book V of the *Metaphysics* that every substance is nature. But the term 'nature' taken in this sense seems to signify the essence of a thing ordered to the proper operation of the thing, since no thing lacks its own operation. But the term 'quiddity' is taken from what is signified through the definition, and it is called essence since through it and in it a thing has being.

CHAPTER II

But since being is primarily and unqualifiedly said of substances, and secondarily in a qualified sense of accidents, essence is truly and properly found in substances, but only in a qualified way in accidents.

Of substances, some are simple and some composite, and there is essence in both; but in a truer and nobler way in simples. . . .

In composite substances, form and matter are characteristic, such as are soul and body in man. But it cannot be said that either of these alone is called essence. It is clear that matter alone is not essence, since a thing is knowable and ordered in species or genus through its essence. But matter is not the basis of knowledge, nor is anything determined to species or genus in accordance with it, but rather only in accordance with that by which it is in act. Nor can form alone be called the essence of composite substance, howevermuch some try to maintain this. From what has been said, it is obvious that essence is what is signified through the definition of a thing, but the definition of natural substances does not contain form alone, but also matter. Otherwise, natural and mathematical definitions would not differ. Nor can it be said that matter is to be taken as a mere addition to essence in the definition of natural substance, as a being outside of its essence. For this manner of definition is more proper to accidents, which do not have perfect essence, and hence take substance or a subject outside of their genus in their definition. Thus it is obvious that essence includes matter and form. But it cannot be said that essence signifies a relation between matter and form or anything over and above them, since this would necessarily be an accident or extraneous to the thing, and the thing would not be known through it, all of which pertains to essence. For matter is brought into a being in act and a definite thing through form, which is the act of matter. So that which is added over and above does not give unqualified being in act to matter, but being in act in a certain way, as accidents do, as whiteness makes something white in act. When a form such as that is taken on, it is not said to be absolutely generated, but qualifiedly.

What remains, therefore, is that the term 'essence' signifies in the case of composite substances that which is compounded from matter and form. . . . however much it is form alone that in its way is the cause of being of this type. We see the same in other instances which are constituted from several principles. These things are not named from one or another of those principles alone, but from what embraces both. This is clear for flavors: sweetness is caused by the action of heat dissipating the humid, and however much heat is in this way the cause of sweetness, a body is not called sweet from the heat, but from the flavor which embraces heat and the humid. But since the principle of individuation is matter, it might seem to follow from this that the essence, which embraces form as well, is only of the particular and not the universal. From which it would follow that a universal would not have a definition, if essence is what is signified through definition. Hence it should be known that the matter which is the principle of individuation is not matter taken in any and every way, but only signate matter. And I call matter signate which is considered under definite dimensions. This matter is

not called for in the definition of man just as man; but it would be called for
in the definition of Socrates, if Socrates had a definition. In the definition of
man, non-signate matter is called for, for it is not this bone and this flesh
which is called for in the definition of man, but just bone and flesh, which
are the non-signate matter for man.

CHAPTER III

. . . The essences of genus and of species also differ with respect to signate
and non-signate, however much another manner of determination (*designa-
tionis*) might belong to each. For the determination of an individual with
respect to a species is through matter determinate in its dimensions, but
determination of a species with respect to genus is through a constitutive
difference, which is taken from the form of the thing. But this determination
or designation which is in the species with respect to the genus is not
through anything existing in the essence of the species which is in no way in
the essence of the genus. Indeed, whatever is in the species is also in the
genus, although not as determinate. . . .

Hence the basis is apparent for the analogy between genus, species, and
differentia on the one hand and matter, form, and the composite in nature on
the other, even though the latter are not the same as the former. For genus is
not matter, but is taken from matter as signifying the whole; nor is the
differentia form, but is taken from form as signifying the whole. Whence we
say man is the rational animal, but not from animal and rational in the way
we say he is from soul and body. He is said to be man from soul and body in
the way that a third thing is constituted from two things, neither of which
the third thing is. For man is not the soul nor is he the body. But if man is
said to be in some way from animal and rational, it will not be as a third
thing from two things, but as a third concept (*intellectus*) from two concepts.
For the concept of animal lacks the determination of the species-form, and it
expresses the nature of the thing through its status as matter with respect to
the final perfection. But the concept of the differentia "rational" consists in
the determination of the species-form. The concept of the species or definition is constituted from these two concepts. And so, just as a thing constituted from various things does not take the predication of those things from
which it is constituted, so neither does a concept take the predication of
those concepts from which it is constituted. For we do not say that a
definition is the genus or the differentia. . . .

As has been said, the nature of the species is indeterminate with respect to
the individual, just as the nature of the genus is with respect to the species.
Hence just as the genus, as it is predicated of the species, implies in its
signification, however indistinctly, all that is determinately in the species, so
the species, as it is predicated of the individual, must signify, though
indistinctly, all that is essentially in the individual. In this way the essence of
the species is signified by the word 'man', whence man is predicated of

Socrates. But if the nature of the species is signified as set apart from the signate matter which is the principle of individuation, it will stand as a part, and the word 'humanity' signifies it in this way. For humanity signifies that whence man is man. But signate matter is not that whence man is man, and so in no way is it contained among those from which man has it that he is man. Since, therefore, the concept of humanity includes only those from which man has it that he is man, it is obvious that signate matter is excluded or set aside from its signification. And because a part is not predicated of the whole, so it is that humanity is predicated neither of man nor of Socrates. And so Avicenna says that the quiddity of a composite is not that very composite, however much the quiddity itself is composite. Thus humanity, even though it is composite, still is not man; rather, it has to be received into signate matter.

But, as was said, the determination of a species with respect to the genus is through forms, and the determination of an individual with respect to the species is through matter. So the term signifying that from which the nature of the genus is taken, setting the determining form completing the species, has to signify that material part of the whole, just as body is the material part of man. But the term signifying that from which the nature of the species is taken, setting aside the signate matter, signifies the formal part, and so humanity is signified as a certain form. And it is called the form of the whole, but not as though it were added on to the essential parts, matter and form, as the form of a house is added to its integral parts. Rather, it is a form which is the whole, embracing both form and matter, while setting aside that through which matter is rendered determinate.

And so it is apparent that the term 'man' and the term 'humanity' each signify the essence of man, but in different ways, as has been said. For the term 'man' signifies it as a whole, in that it does not explicitly involve the determination of matter, but contains that implicitly and indistinctly, just as the genus was said to contain the differentia. Hence the term 'man' is predicated of individuals. But the term 'humanity' signifies the essence as a part, since it only contains in its signification what belongs to man as man, with all determination of matter set aside. As a result it is not predicated of individual men. On account of this, sometimes the term 'essence' is found predicated of a thing (for Socrates is said to be a certain essence) and sometimes it is denied, as when we say the essence of Socrates is not Socrates.

CHAPTER IV

Having seen what is signified by the term 'essence' in composite substances, one should see how it stands with respect to the nature of genus, species, and differentia. Since that to which the characteristic (*ratio*) of genus, species or differentia pertains is predicated of this designated singular, it is impossible for the characteristic of a universal, namely genus or species to pertain to essence signified as a part, as by the term 'humanity' or 'animality'. Hence Avicenna says that rationality is not the differentia, but the basis for the differentia; for the same reason, humanity is not the species nor is animality the genus. Likewise, it cannot be said that the characteristic of genus or species pertains to essence as a certain thing existing outside of singulars, as the Platonists maintained. For in that way, genus and species would not be predicated of this individual; it cannot be said that Socrates is what is separate from him, nor does what is separate conduce to the knowledge of this singular. What is left, then, is that the characteristic of genus or species pertains to essence as it is signified in the manner of a whole, as by the terms 'man' or 'animal', implicitly and indistinctly containing all that is in the individual.

Nature or essence taken thus can be regarded in two ways. One way is according to its own nature, and this is the absolute consideration of it. In this way, nothing is true to say of it except what pertains to it in just such a way; anything else is falsely attributed to it. For example, to man just as man there pertain rational and animal and whatever else falls into his definition. But white or black or any such not belonging to the nature of humanity does not pertain to man as man. Hence if it is asked whether this very nature can be called one or many, neither should be conceded. For either is outside of the concept of humanity, and either can accrue to it. For if plurality were of its very nature, it could never be one; yet it is one as it is in Socrates. Likewise, if unity belonged to its concept and nature, then there would be one and the same nature of Socrates and Plato, and it could not be pluralized among several instances.

Considered in the other way, essence has being in this one or that, and thus something is predicated as an accident of it by reason of that in which it is. In this way it is said that man is white, since Socrates is white, however much that does not pertain to man as man. But this nature has two-fold being, one in singulars, the other in the soul; and accidents follow upon the said nature in each. Thus in singulars it has multiple being according to the diversity of singulars. Yet for the nature itself, according to its proper, that is, absolute consideration, none of these has to be. For it is false to say that the nature of man, taken thus, has to be in this singular. For if to be in a singular pertained to man just as man, it would not ever be outside this singular. Likewise, if it pertained to man just as man not to be in this singular, it would never be in it. But it is true to say that being in this singular or that or in the soul does not belong to man just as man. It is obvious, then, that the nature of man absolutely considered abstracts from any being whatever, in a way that does not set aside any of them, and this nature so considered is what is predicated of all individuals. Yet it cannot be said that universality pertains to a nature taken thus, since unity and community belong to universality. But neither of those pertains to human nature according to its absolute consideration; for if community belonged to the concept of man, then wherever humanity were found, community would be found, and this is false. For in Socrates there is not found any community; whatever is in him is individuated. Likewise it cannot be said that the status of genus or species attaches to human nature according to the being which it has in individuals, since human nature is not found in individuals according to the unity pertaining to all, which is what the nature of universality requires.

What remains, then, is that the status of a species attaches to human nature according to the being it has in the intellect. For human nature has being in the intellect abstracted from everything individuating. It has a uniform character with regard to all individuals which are outside the soul, as it is equally the image of all and conducive to the knowledge of all insofar as they are men. And from its having such a relation to all individuals, the intellect devises and attributes to it the character of a species. Whence the Commentator says in Book I of the *De Anima* that it is the intellect which makes universality in things. Avicenna also says this in his *Metaphysics*. And however much this nature as known has the character of a universal as compared to the things which are outside the soul, since it is one likeness for all, still, according to the being it has in this or that intellect, it is a certain particular appearance (*species . . . intellecta*). Hence the mistake of the Commentator in the *De Anima* is obvious. He wished to argue the unity of the intellect from the universality of the form as known. But the universality of that form is not according to the being which it has in the intellect, but according to the way it is referred to things as their likeness, just as if there were a corporeal statue representing many men, surely the image or appearance (*species*) of the statue would have its own singular being in the way it would be in this particular matter; but it would have the character of community as commonly representative of several. . . .

Thus it is clear how essence or nature stands regarding the character of species. This character does not come from those features which pertain to it in its absolute consideration, nor from the accidents such as whiteness or blackness which accrue to it according to the being it has outside the soul; but it comes from the accidents which accrue to it according to the being it has in the intellect. It is also in this way that the character of genus or differentia pertains to it.

NOTE

Reprinted with permission of Hackett Publishing Co., Inc., Indianapolis, from *Philosophy in the Middle Ages, 2nd edition*, ed. A. Hyman and J. J. Walsh, 1973.

5 DUNS SCOTUS

Scotus relied heavily on the doctrine of the formal distinction. This doctrine states that there is a legitimate distinction that lies between the real distinction and the virtual or conceptual distinction. There is a real distinction between two or more individual things, such as between a dog and a house. A conceptual distinction pertains to different descriptions of the same thing. For example, 'the morning star' and the 'evening star' refer to the same entity—Venus. A formal distinction is one in which the mind can distinguish between two or more logically distinct characteristics (*formalitates*) that in reality are inseparable from one another.

Scotus employs the formal distinction to explain the nature of universals. He argues that the form/content distinction is a real distinction, because matter and form can undergo real separation: matter can manifest itself in different forms, although it cannot possess two different forms at the same time. This is not the case concerning the nature and the "thisness" (*haecceity*) of a thing. The thisness or individuality of a concrete entity cannot in reality be separated from its nature, although the two are formally distinct. For example, Socrates is an individual (thing) distinct from Plato. Each possesses the characteristic (nature) of humanness, which is in reality inseparable from each. However, the mind can distinguish between the individual and the nature that necessarily characterizes both Socrates and Plato. In other words, the *haecceity* of both Socrates and Plato are formally distinct from their nature.

The nature of a thing does not constitute a universal, for then there would be as many universals as there are individuals who possess that characteristic and thus universals would not be universal, but particulars. Rather, Scotus chooses to speak of universal judgments we make about individuals. Universal judgments about particulars are made possible by the objective nature of the characteristics possessed by individuals. Consequently, Scotus is not a realist in the sense of holding that universals possess a reality unto themselves such as classes (viz. Aristotle). Nor is he a conceptualist. For him, particulars are what they are by their very nature. As he says, "horseness is simply horseness" (nothing more, nothing less). This position is remarkably similar to that of Wittgenstein, who maintained that what all horses have in common is simply that they are all horses.

The Oxford Commentary on the Four Books of the Sentences: Book II, Dist. III

QUESTION 1. WHETHER MATERIAL SUBSTANCE IS INDIVIDUAL OR SINGULAR FROM ITSELF OR ITS OWN NATURE?

It seems so. The Philosopher, in Book VII of the *Metaphysics*, proves against Plato that the substance of any kind of thing is proper to it and is not in something else. Therefore, material substance from its own nature, setting aside anything else, is proper to that in which it is, such that from its own nature it cannot be in something else. Thus it is individual from its own nature.

On the contrary: Whatever is in something intrinsically, from its nature, is in it whatever it is in. Therefore, if the nature of stone is "this" of itself, in whatever there is the nature of stone, that nature would be this stone. The consequent is unsuitable in speaking about determinate singularity, which is what the question is about.

Besides, that to which an opposite belongs of itself is of itself repugnant to the other opposite. Therefore, if a nature were of itself one in number, numerical multitude would be repugnant to it of itself.

Here it is said that just as a nature is formally a nature of itself, so is a singular of itself, so that it is not necessary to seek a cause of singularity other than the cause of the nature, as though a nature were prior in time or that a nature is a nature before it is singular and then it is made singular by something added on which contracts it. Which position is proved by an analogy, since just as a nature has true existence from itself outside the soul, but only has dependent existence in the soul—that is, dependent on the soul itself (and the reason is that true existence belongs to it unqualifiedly, but existence in the soul is derived)—so universality only belongs to a thing as it has dependent existence in the soul. But singularity belongs to a thing according to true existence, and so, from itself and unqualifiedly. What is to be sought, then, is the cause whereby a nature is universal; and the intellect should be given as the cause. But a cause does not have to be sought whereby a nature is singular, other than the nature of a thing—a cause, that is, which would mediate between the nature and its singularity. But the causes of the unity of a thing are also the causes of the singularity of a thing. Therefore, etc.

Against this it is argued thus: An object insofar as it is an object is natural prior to its act; and according to you, an object as prior is singular of itself, since this always belongs to a nature not taken as dependent, or according to the existence it has in the soul. Therefore, the intellect knowing that object under a universal characteristic, knows it under a characteristic opposed to its own, for as it precedes the act, it is of itself determined to the opposite of that characteristic.

Besides, the real unity proper and sufficient to anything whatsoever is less than numerical unity; it is not of itself one with numerical unity, or it is not of itself "this." But the real unity proper or sufficient to the nature of stone existing in this stone is less than numerical unity. Therefore, etc. The major is obvious of itself, since nothing is of itself one with a unity greater than that sufficient to it. For if the unity which ought to be proper to something of itself is less than numerical unity, numerical unity does not belong to it from the nature and according to itself, lest from its nature alone it should have a greater and less unity, which are opposites concerning and according to the same thing. For a multitude opposed to a greater unity can stand together with a lesser unity without contradiction; but that multitude cannot stand together with the greater unity because it is repugnant to it. Therefore, etc. The minor premiss is proved in that if there is no real unity of a nature less than singularity, but every unity other than singular unity is merely the unity of reason, then there will be no real unity less than numerical unity. The consequent is false, which I prove in five or six ways. Therefore, etc. . . .

Besides, secondly, I prove that the consequent is false, because according to the Philosopher in Book VII of the *Physics*, an atom is compared to a species, since it is one in nature, but not to a genus, since a genus does not have such a unity. This true unity is not a unity of reason, since the concept of a genus is just as much one in the intellect as is the concept of a species. Otherwise no concept would be definitionally predicated of any species, and so no concept would be of a genus if as many concepts were predicated of species as there are concepts of species. For then in single predications the same would be predicated of itself. Likewise, whether the unity is of a concept or not of a concept is irrelevant to the intention of the Philosopher, namely, with regard to the comparison. Therefore, the Philosopher intended the specific nature there to be one with the unity of a specific nature, but he did not intend it to be one with numerical unity, since no comparison was made to numerical unity. Therefore, etc. . . .

Again, sixthly, since if every unity is numerical, then every real diversity is numerical. But the consequent is false, since every numerical diversity insofar as it is numerical is equal; and so everything would be equally distinct, and then it follows that the intellect can no more abstract something common from Socrates and Plato than from Socrates and a line, and any universal would be a pure figment. . . .

Again, seventhly, it is not by anything existing in the intellect that fire causes fire and destroys water, and that there is a certain real unity of generator to generated according to form, because of which, generation is univocal. For intellectual consideration does not make generation to be univocal; but it knows it to be univocal.

In reply to the question, therefore, I concede the conclusion of these arguments, and I say that material substance from its own nature is not of itself "this," since then, just as the first argument concluded, the intellect could not understand it under the opposite, unless it understood under a characteristic unsuited for the understanding of such an object. As the second argument also concluded with all its proofs, there is a certain real unity in a thing apart from any operation of the intellect. This unity of a nature in itself is less than numerical unity, or the unity proper to a singular. And since a nature is not of itself one with that unity, it is according to its own proper unity indifferent to the unity of singularity.

This can also be understood through the saying of Avicenna in Book V of the *Metaphysics*, where he says that "horseness is just horseness, of itself neither one nor many, universal nor particular." One should understand that a nature is not of itself one with numerical unity, nor many with a plurality opposed to that unity. Nor is it actually universal, in the way that something is made universal by the intellect; neither is it of itself particular. Although it is never really without some of these, still, of itself it is none of them; but it is naturally prior to all. And according to this natural priority it is "that which is," and is the intrinsic object of the intellect. As such, it is considered by the metaphysician and is expressed through a definition. And propositions true in the primary way are true by reason of a quiddity so accepted, since nothing is predicated in the primary way of a quiddity that is not essentially included in it insofar as it is abstracted from everything naturally posterior to it. Not only is a nature of itself indifferent to existence in the intellect and in a particular, and hence to universal and singular existence, but also, in having existence in the intellect it does not have universality primarily from itself. For although it is understood under universality, as under the mode for understanding it, still, universality is not a part of its primary concept, since that is not a concept of the metaphysician, but rather, of the logician. For according to Avicenna himself, the logician considers second intentions applied to first intentions. Thus the primary understanding is of a nature, without any mode understood with it, neither that which belongs to it in the intellect, nor that which belongs to it outside the intellect, even though the mode of it to the intellect in understanding is universality—but it is not a mode of the intellect. And just as a nature is not of itself universal according to that existence, as though universality accrued to that nature according to its primary characteristic, but rather universality accrues to it as being an object of the intellect; so also in external reality. There, a nature exists with singularity; but the nature is not of itself limited to singularity. It is naturally prior to that characteristic contracting it to that singularity. And insofar as it is naturally prior to what contracts it, it is not repugnant to it to exist without what contracts it. And just as an object in the intellect has true intelligible existence according to that being and universality; so also in things, a nature has true real existence outside the soul according to that being. And according to that being it has a unity proportional to itself which is indifferent to singularity, so that of itself it is not repugnant to that unity, which is given with every unity of singularity.

In this way, therefore, I understand a nature to have a real unity less than numerical unity. And although it does not have numerical unity of itself, so that it would be internal to the characteristic of a nature, since "horseness is just horseness," according to Avicenna in Book V of the *Metaphysics*, still that unity is an attribute proper to a nature according to its primary being. And consequently, it is not of itself internally "this," nor is it necessarily included in a nature according to its own primary being.

But against this there seem to be two objections. One, that it seems to hold that a universal is something real in a thing, which is against the Commentator, Book I of the *De Anima*, comment 8, who says that "the intellect makes universality in things," so that universality only exists through the intellect, and so is merely a being of reason. The proof of the consequence is that this nature, as it is a being in this stone, but still naturally prior to the singularity of this stone, is being said indifferently to this singular and to that. . . .

To the first objection I say that the universal in act is that which has indifferent unity, according to which it is the same in proximate power as said or whatever individual subject, since, according to the First Book of the *Posterior Analytics*, "that is universal which is one in many and of many." For nothing according to whatever unity in a thing is such that according to just that unity it is in a proximate power to whatever subject, as said of whatever subject in a predication saying "this is this." For although to be in a singularity different from that in which it is, is not repugnant to something existing in a thing, still it cannot be truly said of just any inferior that that is it. For this is only possible of an object considered by the intellect in the same indifferent act, which object as understood also has the numerical unity of an object, according to which the same is predicable of every singular, in saying that this is this.

From this appears the disproof of that saying that the agent intellect makes universality in things, through this, that it uncovers the *that which is* existing in a phantasm. For wherever it is, before it has the existence of an object of the possible intellect, whether it is in a thing or in a phantasm, it either has certain existence or is deduced by reason. And if it is not through some illumination, but is always such a nature from itself, to which it is not repugnant to exist in another, still it is not that to which as a proximate power it belongs to be said of whatever you wish, but it is only in proximate power as it is in the possible intellect. In a thing, therefore, it is common, which is not "this" of itself, and consequently to which it is not of itself repugnant not to be "this." But such a common is not a universal in act, because there is lacking to it that differentia according to which a universal is fully universal, namely, according to which the same is predicable by some identity of whatever individual, so that the individual is it. . . .

And through this the reply is obvious to the principal argument in which he disproves that fiction which he imposes upon Plato, namely, that this intrinsically existing man, which is posited as the Idea, cannot intrinsically exist universally in every man. For every intrinsically existing substance is proper to that to which it belongs. That is, it is either from itself or it is proper through something which in contracting, makes it proper, which contracting having been posited, it cannot be in another, although it is not repugnant to it from itself to be in something else.

This gloss is also true speaking of substance as it is taken for the nature. And then it follows that the Idea will not be the substance of Socrates, since it is not the nature of Socrates either. For it is of itself neither proper to nor appropriated to Socrates, as it is merely in him, but it is also in another. But if substance is taken for first substance, then it is true that any substance is proper to that to which it belongs. And then it follows much more that that idea which is posited as substance existing intrinsically in this way cannot be the substance of Socrates or Plato. But the first member suffices for the proposed position.

For the confirmation of the opinion it is obvious that commonness and singularity are not disposed to a nature as existence in the intellect and true existence outside the soul respectively, since commonness as well as singularity belong to a nature outside the intellect. And commonness belongs to a nature of itself, whereas singularity belongs to a nature through something contracting it in the thing. But universality does not belong to a thing of itself, and hence I concede that the cause of universality is to be sought. But the cause of commonness is not to be sought, other than the nature itself. And commonness having been posited in a nature in accordance with its own being and unity, it is necessary to seek the cause of singularity, which adds something to that to which the nature belongs.

QUESTION 4. WHETHER MATERIAL SUBSTANCE IS INDIVIDUAL OR SINGULAR THROUGH QUANTITY?

Here it is said that material substance is singular and individual through quantity, and the reason given is that what primarily and intrinsically belongs to something, belongs to anything else by reason of it. But substance and quantity do not make a one intrinsically, but only accidentally; and consequently, no one property belongs intrinsically to them at once and equally primarily, but rather, to one through the other. But to be divided into parts of the same character is a property which belongs intrinsically to quantity, from Book V of the *Metaphysics*. Thus it belongs to another, namely substance, through the characteristic of quantity. The division of a species into its individuals is of such a sort, since these divided individuals do not formally differ in character as do the species dividing a genus. . . .

Besides, this fire differs from that fire only because form differs from form; and form differs from form only because it is received in a part of matter different from another part. And a part of matter differs from another part only because it is under a part of quantity different from another part. Therefore, the entire distinction of this fire from that fire is reduced to quantity as what is primarily distinct. . . .

I argue against this conclusion in four ways. First, from the identity of numerical character, whether belonging to individuation or singularity. Second, from the order of substance to accident. Third, from the nature of predicational coordination. And these three ways together prove that no accident can be the intrinsic characteristic through which material substance is individuated. The fourth way will be especially against quantity, with regard to the conclusion of the opinion. And fifth, it will be argued especially against the arguments of the opinion.

As to the first way, I first explain what I understand by individuation, whether numerical unity or through singularity: not, indeed, the indeterminate unity according to which anything in a species is called one in number, but a unity demarcated as "this," so that, as was said before, it is impossible for an individual to be divided into subject-parts. And what is sought is the reason for this impossibility. So I say that it is impossible for an individual not to be a "this," demarcated by this singularity; and it is not the cause of singularity in general which is sought, but of this specially demarcated singularity, namely, as it is determinately "this." Understanding singularity thus, there is a two-fold argument from the first way:

First: a substance existing in act and not altered by some substantial transmutation cannot be turned from "this" to "not this," since this singularity (as was just said) cannot be in one thing and another with the same substance remaining the same and not substantially altered. But a substance existing in act with no substantial alteration can without contradiction be under one and another quantity, or any absolute accident. Therefore, this substance is in no such way formally demarcated by this singularity. The minor is obvious, since it is not a contradiction that God should conserve the same substance having this quantity and inform it with another quantity; nor would that substance existing in act be substantially altered because of this, since there would only be an alteration from quantity to quantity. Likewise, if it were altered in any accident without substantial alteration, possible or impossible, it would not on that account be formally "not this."

If you say that this is a miracle and hence is not conclusive against natural reason, my reply is that a miracle does not include contradictories, for which there is no power. But it is a contradiction for the same enduring substance to be two substances without substantial alteration, and this successively as well as simultaneously, which would follow if it were formally this substance through any accident. For then, with accident succeeding accident, the same unaltered substance would successively be two substances. . . .

Perhaps to escape these criticisms, the position that individuation is by quantity is held in this other way, namely, that just as the extension of matter is different from the quantity of that matter and adds nothing to the essence of the matter so demarcated, so the demarcation of matter, which it has causally by way of quantity, is different from the demarcation of its quantity and is naturally prior to the demarcation which it has through quantity. For substance as substance is naturally prior to quantity without any accident whatsoever. And the demarcation of matter is different from the demarcation of quantity, but it is not different from substance, so that just as matter does not have parts through the nature of quantity, since a part of matter is matter, so demarcated substance does not exist without substance. For demarcation only conveys a way of being disposed.

Against this: the position seems to include contradictories twice over. First, since it is impossible for anything naturally posterior and dependent to be the same as what is naturally prior, since then it would be prior and not prior. But substance is naturally prior to quantity. Therefore, nothing caused through quantity or in any way presupposing the nature of quantity can be the same as substance. This demarcation, therefore, is not the same as substance even though it is caused by quantity. The proof of the major is that where there is true and real identity, even though it is not formal, it is impossible for this to exist and that not, since then the same would really exist and not exist. But it is possible for what is naturally prior to exist without what is naturally posterior; consequently, much more without what is determined or caused by what is naturally posterior.

Besides, a necessary condition of a cause cannot have its existence from its result, since then the cause as sufficient for the causing would be caused by the result, and the result would be its own cause. But the singularity or demarcation of substance is a necessary condition for causing quantity in substance, since a singular result requires a singular cause. Therefore, it is impossible for this demarcation to be derived from what is caused by substance, insofar as it is singular.

Besides, I ask what it is to determine quantity or to cause such a mode in substance. If it precedes quantity, then demarcation is in no way through quantity. But if it is anything else, I ask how it is caused by quantity, and by what type of cause? The only type of cause that it seems possible to assign here is the efficient cause, but quantity is not an active form.

QUESTION 6. WHETHER MATERIAL SUBSTANCE IS INDIVIDUAL THROUGH SOME POSITIVE ENTITY INTRINSICALLY DETERMINING A NATURE TO SINGULARITY?

I reply "yes" to the question. I argue that just as common unity intrinsically accompanies common being, so some kind of unity intrinsically accompanies any being. Thus unqualified unity, which is the unity of an individual often described above as that to which a division into several substantial parts is repugnant and to which it is repugnant not to be a demarcated "this," if, as every opinion supposes, it exists, intrinsically accompanies some being. But it does not intrinsically accompany the being of a nature, since that has its own intrinsically real unity, as was proved in the solution to the first Question. Therefore, it accompanies some other being determining this, and together with the being of the nature making something intrinsically one which is whole and perfect of itself. . . .

This solution can be further clarified by comparing this being by which there is this perfect unity to the being from which specific difference is taken. For specific difference, or the being from which it is taken, can be compared to what is below, above, or beside it. In the first way, it is repugnant to specific difference and that specific being to be intrinsically divided into several which are essentially species or nature, and through this it is repugnant to the whole of which that entity is an intrinsic part. So it is in what is proposed: it is repugnant to this individual entity to be divided primarily into substantial parts of any kind, and through this such a division is repugnant intrinsically to the whole of which that entity is a part. And still there is a difference, in that the unity of a specific nature is less than this unity; and because of this, that unity does not exclude all division according to substantial parts, but only the division into essential parts. But the latter excludes all such division. And from this the proposed position is sufficiently confirmed, since it does not seem probable from the fact that the lesser unity has its own being which accompanies it to deny its own accompanying being to this perfect unity.

In comparison to what is above it, I say that the reality from which specific difference is taken is actual with respect to that from which the genus is taken, so that the one reality is not formally the other. Otherwise, definition would be frivolous, and the genus alone would define sufficiently, since it would indicate the entire being of the defined without the differentia. Sometimes what contracts is different from the form from which the characteristic of the genus is taken, namely, when the species adds something over and above the nature of the genus; but sometimes it is not another thing, but only another formality, or another real concept of the same thing. And following this, some specific difference does not have an irreducibly simple concept, for instance, that which is taken from the formality; some does have an irreducibly simple concept, namely that which is taken from the ultimate abstraction of the form. This distinction between specific differences has been discussed in the third distinction of Book I, where it was said how some specific differences include being, and some not. On one point, individual reality is like specific reality, since it is a sort of act determining the reality of species as though that were possible and potential. But on another point it is dissimilar, since it is never taken from an added form, but precisely from the ultimate reality of the form. On still another point it is dissimilar, since specific reality constitutes a composite in quidditative being, of which it is a part, since it is a kind of quidditative being. But individual being is fundamentally diverse from every quidditative being. This is proved from the fact that in knowing any kind of quidditative being, speaking of limited quidditative being, one does not know whence it is "this." Therefore, that being which is of itself "this" is a different being from quidditative being, and it thus cannot constitute a whole of which it is a part in quidditative being, but rather in being of a different character. . . .

And if you ask, "What is this individual being from which individual difference is taken? Is it not matter, or form, or the composite?"

I reply that every quidditative entity, whether partial or total of any kind, is of itself indifferent, as quidditative entity, to this entity and that one, so that as quidditative entity it is naturally prior to this entity as "this." And as it is naturally prior, just as being "this" does not belong to it, so the opposite is not repugnant to it from its own character. And just as the composite insofar as it is a nature does not include the being by which it is "this," so neither does matter insofar as it is a nature, nor form. Therefore, this being is not matter, nor form, nor the composite, insofar as any of these is a nature; but it is the ultimate reality of the being which is matter, or which is form, or the composite, so that anything common and yet determinable can still be distinguished, however much it is one thing, into several formally distinct realities, of which this is not formally that. But this is formally the being of a singular, and that is formally the being of a nature. And these two realities cannot be as thing and thing, as can the realities from which genus and differentia are taken, from which specific reality is taken; but in the same thing, whether part or whole, they are always formally distinct realities of the same thing. . . .

To the second objection I concede that a singular is intrinsically intelligible on its side. But if it is not intrinsically intelligible to some intellect, for instance, ours, at least this is not an impossibility on the part of the singular, just as it is not on the part of the sun that to see at night is impossible, but rather on the part of the eye.

QUESTION 9. DOES AN ANGEL HAVE A DISTINCT NATURAL KNOWLEDGE OF THE DIVINE ESSENCE?

Therefore, I reply differently to the question. First, two types of cognition should be distinguished. For there can be one cognition of an object according to what is abstracted from all actual existence, and there can be another of it according to what is existing, and according to what is present in some actual existence.

This distinction is proved by argument and by analogy. The first (type) is obvious from the fact that we can have awareness of certain quiddities; but science is of an object according to what is abstracted from actual existence. Otherwise, science could sometimes exist and sometimes not, and so it would not be perpetual; but with the thing destroyed, the science of that thing would also be destroyed—which is false. The second (type) is proved, since what there is of perfection in an inferior power seems to exist in a higher way in a superior power of the same kind. But in sense, which is a cognitive power inferior to intellect, there is the perfection of knowing a thing as existing in itself and according to what is present following its existence. Therefore, this is possible in the intellect, which is the supreme cognitive power. Therefore it can have cognition of a thing according to what is present.

And to be brief, I call the first "abstractive," which is of the quiddity as abstracted from actual existence and non-existence. The second, which is of the quiddity of a thing according to its actual existence or of what is present following such existence, I call "intuitive cognition"—not as "intuitive" is distinguished from "discursive," since in this way any abstractive would be intuitive, but unqualifiedly intuitive, in the way in which we speak of intuiting a thing just as it is in itself.

The second member (of the distinction) is through the fact that we do not await the kind of knowledge of God which could be had of Him if he were (as is impossible) non-existent, or not present through His essence; but we await intuitive cognition, which is called face-to-face, just as sensory cognition is face-to-face with a thing as it presently exists.

The second clarification of this distinction is by analogy with the sensory powers. For a particular power or sense knows an object in one way and the imagination, in another. For a particular sense is of an object according to what is through itself or existing in itself; imagination knows the same according to what is present through a species, which species can be an image of it even though it is not existent or present. So imaginative cognition is abstractive in comparison with a particular sense. And since what is dispersed in inferiors is sometimes united in the superior, these two ways of knowing which are dispersed in the sensitive powers because of the organs (for the organ that receives well is not the same as that which retains well) are united in the intellect, which as one power can perform either act.

NOTE

Reprinted by permission of Hackett Publishing Co., Inc., Indianapolis, from *Philosophy in the Middle Ages, 2nd edition*, ed. A. Hyman and J. J. Walsh, 1973.

6 OCKHAM

If universals carry with them any sort of independent status, then they must be particulars, which is contradictory. Therefore, realism of any variety is untenable. Only particulars exist *in re*. To understand the nature of universals one must consider how one thinks of and refers to particulars. Consider the word 'man'. Ockham distinguishes both the spoken and written word from the concept that he calls the natural sign of the word and that constitutes its meaning. The word 'man' is ambiguous. It can refer to either particular men or to the species of man. When 'man' is used to refer to particular men it is a term of first intention. When 'man' is used to refer to the species of man it is a term of second intention. Second intentions are natural signs of first intentions. Terms of second intention refer to features of particulars abstracted for special investigation.

Here Ockham introduces another important expression, that of *suppositio*, which means "standing for." He classifies terms under three types of *suppositio*, namely *personalis*, *materialis*, and *simplex*. When the term 'man' stands for a precise individual, it is an instance of *suppositio personalis*. When the word 'man' is mentioned (as opposed to used), that is an instance of *suppositio materialis*. When the word 'man' stands for all men, namely the species, such is an instance of *suppositio simplex*.

It is *suppositiones simplices* that stand for universals. Universals are second intentions of the simple order and can only refer to concepts. Universals do not refer to any realities. Ockham says, "no universal is anything existing in any way outside the soul; but everything which is predicable of many things is of its nature in the mind, whether subjectively or objectively; and no universal belongs to the essence or quiddity of any substance whatsoever." Universals are natural signs standing for characteristics individually possessed by two or more particulars. The universal concept arises because (1) two or more particulars possess similarities in varying degrees, and (2) the human intellect is capable of understanding (1). In other words, Socrates and Plato do not share a common characteristic or nature. Rather, the nature that is Socrates and the nature that is Plato resemble each other. A universal concept is the natural sign standing for such a resemblance. This is nominalism of a most sophisticated variety.

The Problem of Universals

First we have to treat terms of second intention; secondly, terms of first intention. It has been said that terms of second intention are those like 'universal', 'genus', 'species', etc. Hence we must say something about those which are set up as the five predicables. But first we must speak of the general term 'universal', which is predicated of every universal, and of the term 'singular', which is opposed to it.

First we must realize that 'singular' is taken in two senses. In one sense the name 'singular' signifies whatever is one thing and not several. If it is so understood, then those who hold that a universal is a certain quality of the mind predicable of many things (but standing for these many things, not for itself) have to say that every universal is truly and really a singular. For just as every word, no matter how common it may be by convention, is truly and really singular and numerically one, since it is one thing and not many, so likewise the mental content that signifies several things outside is truly and really singular and numerically one, since it is one thing and not many things, though it signifies several things.

In another sense the name 'singular' is taken for that which is one and not several things and is not of such a nature as to be the sign of several things. If 'singular' is understood in this sense, then no universal is singular, since every universal is of such a nature as to be a sign of, and to be predicated of, several things. Hence, if a universal is that which is not numerically one— a meaning attributed by many to 'universal'—then I say that nothing is a universal, unless perhaps you wish to abuse this word by saying that a population is a universal, since it is not one but many. But that would be childish.

Hence we have to say that every universal is one singular thing. Therefore nothing is universal except by signification, by being a sign of several things. This is what Avicenna says in the fifth book of the *Metaphysics*: 'One form in the intellect has reference to a multitude, and in this sense it is a universal, since the universal is a content in the intellect which is equally related to anything you take'. And later on: 'This form, though universal in reference to individuals, is nevertheless individual in reference to the particular mind in which it is impressed, for it is one of the forms in the intellect'. He wishes to say here that the universal is one particular content of the mind itself, of such a nature as to be predicated of several things; therefore, it is by the very fact that it is of such a nature as to be predicated of several things (standing not for itself, but for those many things), that it is called a 'universal'. By the fact, however, that it is one form really existing in the intellect, it is called a 'singular'. Hence 'singular' in the first sense is predicated of the universal, but not 'singular' in the second sense. In like manner, we say that the sun is a universal cause, and nevertheless it is in truth a particular and singular thing, and consequently a singular and particular cause. For the sun is called 'universal cause', because it is the cause of many things, namely of all that can be generated and corrupted here below. It is, on the other hand, called 'particular cause', because it is one cause and not several causes. Likewise the content of the soul is called 'universal', because it is a sign predicable of many, on the other hand, it is called 'singular', because it is one thing and not many things.

It must, however, be understood that there are two sorts of universal. There is one sort which is naturally universal; in other words, is a sign naturally predicable of many things, in much the same way as smoke naturally signifies fire, or a groan the pain of a sick man, or laughter an inner joy. Such a universal is nothing other than a content of the mind; and therefore no substance outside the mind and no accident outside the mind is such a universal. It is only of such a universal that I shall speak in the chapters that follow.

The other sort of universal is so by convention. In this way, an uttered word, which is really a single quality, is universal; for it is a conventional sign meant to signify many things. Therefore, just as the word is said to be common, so it can be said to be universal. But it is not so by nature, only by convention.

A UNIVERSAL IS NOT A THING OUTSIDE THE MIND

That a universal is not a substance existing outside the mind can in the first place be evidently proved as follows: No universal is a substance that is single and numerically one. For if that were supposed, it would follow that Socrates is a universal, since there is no stronger reason for one singular substance to be a universal than for another; therefore no singular substance is a universal, but every substance is numerically one and singular. For everything is either one thing and not many, or it is many things. If it is one and not many, it is numerically one. If, however, a substance is many things, it is either many singular things or many universal things. On the first supposition it follows that a substance would be several singular substances; for the same reason, then, some substance would be several men; and thus, although a universal would be distinguished from one particular thing, it would yet not be distinguished from particular things. If, however, a substance were several universal things, let us take one of these universal things and ask 'Is this one thing and not many, or is it many things?' If the first alternative is granted, then it follows that it is singular; if the second is granted, we have to ask again 'Is it many singular or many universal things?' And thus either this will go on *in infinitum*, or we must take the stand that no substance is universal in such a way that it is not singular. Hence, the only remaining alternative is that no substance is universal.

Furthermore, if a universal were one substance existing in singular things and distinct from them, it would follow that it could exist apart from them; for every thing naturally prior to another thing can exist apart from it by the power of God. But this consequence is absurd.

Furthermore, if that opinion were true, no individual could be created, but something of the individual would pre-exist; for it would not get its entire being from nothing, if the universal in it has existed before in another

individual. For the same reason it would follow that God could not annihi-
late one individual of a substance, if He did not destroy the other individuals. For if He annihilated one individual, He would destroy the whole of
the essence of the individual, and consequently he would destroy that
universal which is in it and in others; consequently, the other individuals do
not remain, since they cannot remain without a part of themselves, such as
the universal is held to be.

Furthermore, we could not assume such a universal to be something
entirely extrinsic to the essence of an individual; therefore, it would be of the
essence of the individual, and consequently the individual would be composed of universals; and thus the individual would not be more singular than
universal.

Furthermore, it follows that something of the essence of Christ would be
miserable and damned; since that common nature which really exists in
Christ, really exists in Judas also and is damned. Therefore, something is
both in Christ and in one who is damned, namely in Judas. That, however, is
absurd.

Still other reasons could be advanced which I pass over for the sake of
brevity.

The same conclusion I will now confirm by authorities. . . .

From these and many other texts it is clear that a universal is a mental
content of such nature as to be predicated of many things. This can also be
confirmed by reason. All agree that every universal is predicable of things.
But only a mental content or conventional sign, not a substance, is of such
nature as to be predicated. Consequently, only a mental content or a
conventional sign is a universal. However, at present I am not using
'universal' for a conventional sign, but for that which is naturally a universal.
Moreover, it is clear that no substance is of such nature as to be predicated;
for if that were true, it would follow that a proposition would be composed
of particular substances, and consequently that the subject could be in Rome
and the predicate in England. That is absurd.

Furthermore, a proposition is either in the mind or in spoken or written
words. Consequently, its parts are either in the mind or in speech or in
writing. Such things, however, are not particular substances. Therefore, it is
established that no proposition can be composed of substances; but a
proposition is composed of universals; hence universals are in no way
substances.

NOTE

Reprinted by permission of Thomas Nelson and Sons, Ltd., Edinburgh, from
Ockham: Philosophical Writings, trans. P. Boehner, 1957.

7 LOCKE

The significata of words are ideas. As John Locke says, "Words become general by being made the signs of general ideas: and ideas become general by separating from them the circumstances of time, and place, and any other ideas that may determine them to this or that particular existence." By means of abstraction we are thus capable of forming abstract ideas. Locke believes that a person has the capacity upon observing, for example, Peter and Paul, to isolate what is common to them. So abstracted, these common characteristics constitute an abstract idea expressed by the common noun 'man'. Upon observing men, dogs, and cats, one in turn isolates what they as species have in common and one forms the abstract idea expressed by the generic term 'mammal'. According to Locke, "It is plain . . . that general and universal belong not to the real existence of things, but are the inventions and creatures of understanding, made by it for its own use, and concern only signs, whether words or ideas."

Consequently, the content of an abstract idea is an essence, namely, the characteristic or set of characteristics without which a thing would not be the type of thing that it is. It is clear that given Locke's analysis the notions of universal and essence collapse into one.

Essay Concerning Human Understanding Book III

Chapter 2: Of the Signification of Words

1. *Words are sensible signs necessary for communication.* Man, though he have great variety of thoughts, and such from which others as well as himself might receive profit and delight, yet they are all within his own breast, invisible and hidden from others, nor can of themselves be made to appear. The comfort and advantage of society not being to be had without communication of thoughts, it was necessary that man should find out some external sensible signs, whereof those invisible ideas, which his thoughts are made up of, might be made known to others. For this purpose nothing was so fit, either for plenty or quickness, as those articulate sounds, which with so much ease and variety he found himself able to make. . . . The use, then, of words, is to be sensible marks of ideas; and the ideas they stand for are their proper and immediate signification.

2. *Words are the sensible signs of his ideas who uses them.* The use men have of these marks being either to record their own thoughts, for the

assistance of their own memory; or, as it were, to bring out their ideas, and lay them before the view of others: words, in their primary or immediate signification, stand for nothing but the ideas in the mind of him that uses them, how imperfectly soever or carelessly those ideas are collected from the things which they are supposed to represent. . . . Words being voluntary signs, they cannot be voluntary signs imposed by him on things he knows not. That would be to make them signs of nothing, sounds without signification. A man cannot make his words the signs either of qualities in things, or of conceptions in the mind of another, whereof he has none in his own.

3. This is so necessary in the use of language, that in this respect the knowing and the ignorant, the learned and the unlearned, use the words they speak (with any meaning) all alike. They, in every man's mouth, stand for the ideas he has, and which he would express by them. A child having taken notice of nothing in the metal he hears called "gold," but the bright shining yellow color, he applies the word "gold" only to his own idea of that color, and nothing else; and therefore calls the same color in a peacock's tail "gold." Another that hath better observed, adds to shining yellow great weight: and then the sound gold, when he uses it, stands for a complex idea of a shining yellow and very weighty substance. Another adds to those qualities fusibility: and then the word gold signifies to him a body, bright, yellow, fusible, and very heavy. Another adds malleability. Each of these uses equally the word gold, when they have occasion to express the idea which they have applied it to: but it is evident that each can apply it only to his own idea; nor can he make it stand as sign of such a complex idea as he has not.

4. *Words often secretly referred, first, to the ideas in other men's minds.* But though words, as they are used by men, can properly and immediately signify nothing but the ideas that are in the mind of the speaker; yet they in their thoughts give them a secret reference to two other things.

First, they suppose their words to be marks of the ideas in the minds also of other men, with whom they communicate: for else they should talk in vain, and could not be understood, if the sounds they applied to one idea were such as by the hearer were applied to another, which is to speak two languages. . . .

5. *Secondly, to the reality of things.* Secondly, because men would not be thought to talk barely of their own imagination, but of things as really they are; therefore they often suppose the words to stand also for the reality of things. . . .

6. *Words by use readily excite ideas.* Concerning words, also, it is further to be considered: first, that they being immediately the signs of men's ideas, and by that means the instruments whereby men communicate their conceptions, and express to one another those thoughts and imaginations they have within their own breasts; there comes, by constant use, to be such a connection between certain sounds and the ideas they stand for, that the

names heard, almost as readily excite certain ideas as if the objects themselves, which are apt to produce them, did actually affect the senses. Which is manifestly so in all obvious sensible qualities, and in all substances that frequently and familiarly occur to us.

7. *Words often used without signification.* Secondly, that though the proper and immediate signification of words are ideas in the mind of the speaker, yet, because by familiar use from our cradles, we come to learn certain articulate sounds very perfectly, and have them readily on our tongues, and always at hand in our memories, but yet are not always careful to examine or settle their significations perfectly; it often happens that men, even when they would apply themselves to an attentive consideration, do set their thoughts more on words than things. . . .

8. *Their signification perfectly arbitrary.* Words, by long and familiar use, as has been said, come to excite in men certain ideas so constantly and readily, that they are apt to suppose a natural connexion between them. But that they signify only men's peculiar ideas, and that by a perfect arbitrary imposition, is evident, in that they often fail to excite in others (even that use the same language) the same ideas we take them to be signs of: and every man has so inviolable a liberty to make words stand for what ideas he pleases, that no one hath the power to make others have the same ideas in their minds that he has, when they use the same words that he does. . . . But whatever be the consequence of any man's using of words differently, either from their general meaning, or the particular sense of the person to whom he addresses them; this is certain, their signification, in his use of them, is limited to his ideas, and they can be signs of nothing else.

CHAPTER 3: OF GENERAL TERMS

1. *The greatest part of words general.* All things that exist being particulars, it may perhaps be thought reasonable that words, which ought to be conformed to things, should be so too,—I mean in their signification: but yet we find quite the contrary. The far greatest part of words that make all languages are general terms: which has not been the effect of neglect or change, but of reason and necessity.

2. *For every particular thing to have a name is impossible.* First, it is impossible that every particular thing should have a distinct peculiar name. For, the signification and use of words depending on that connexion which the mind makes between its ideas and the sounds it uses as signs of them, it is necessary, in the application of names to things, that the mind should have distinct ideas of the things, and retain also the particular name that belongs to every one, with its peculiar appropriation to that idea. But it is beyond the power of human capacity to frame and retain distinct ideas of all the particular things we meet with: every bird and beast men saw; every tree and plant that affected the senses, could not find a place in the most capacious understanding. . . .

3. *And useless.* Secondly, if it were possible, it would yet be useless; because it would not serve to the chief end of language. Men could in vain heap up names of particular things that would not serve them to communicate their thoughts. Men learn names, and use them in talk with others, only that they may be understood: which is then only done when, by use or consent, the sound I make by the organs of speech, excites in another man's mind who hears it, the idea I apply it to in mine, when I speak it. This cannot be done by names applied to particular things; whereof I alone having the ideas in my mind, the names of them could not be significant or intelligible to another, who was not acquainted with all those very particular things which had fallen under my notice.

4. Thirdly, but yet, granting this also feasible (which I think is not), yet a distinct name for every particular thing would not be of any great use for the improvement of knowledge: which, though founded in particular things, enlarges itself by general views; to which things reduced into sorts, under general names, are properly subservient.

*   *   *

6. *How general words are made.* The next thing to be considered is,—how general words come to be made. For, since all things that exist are only particulars, how come we by general terms; or where find we those general natures they are supposed to stand for? Words become general by being made the signs of general ideas: and ideas become general, by separating from them the circumstances of time and place, and any other ideas that may determine them to this or that particular existence. By this way of abstraction they are made capable of representing more individuals than one; each of which having in it a conformity to that abstract idea, is (as we call it) of that sort.

7. But, to deduce this a little more distinctly, it will not perhaps be amiss to trace our notions and names from their beginning, and observe by what degrees we proceed, and by what steps we enlarge our ideas from our first infancy. There is nothing more evident, than that the ideas of the persons children converse with (to instance in them alone) are, like the persons themselves, only particular. The ideas of the nurse and the mother are well framed in their minds; and, like pictures of them there, represent only those individuals. The names they first gave to them are confined to those individuals; and the names of "nurse" and "mamma," the child uses, determine themselves to those persons. Afterwards, when time and a larger acquaintance have made them observe that there are a great many other things in the world, that in some common agreements of shape, and several other qualities, resemble their father and mother, and those persons they have been used to, they frame an idea, which they find those many particulars do partake in; and to that they give, with others, the name "man," for example. And thus they come to have a general name, and a general idea.

Wherein they make nothing new but only leave out of the complex idea they had of Peter and James, Mary and Jane, that which is peculiar to each, and retain only what is common to them all.

8. By the same way that they come by the general name and idea of man, they easily advance to more general names and notions. For observing that several things that differ from their idea of man, and cannot therefore be comprehended under that name, have yet certain qualities, wherein they agree with man, by retaining only those qualities, and uniting them into one idea, they have again another and more general idea; to which having given a name, they make a term of a more comprehensive extension: which new idea is made, not by any new addition, but only as before, by leaving out shape, and some other properties signified by the name "man," and retaining only a body, with life, sense, and spontaneous motion, comprehended under the name "animal."

9. *General natures are nothing but abstract ideas.* . . . And he that thinks general natures or notions are anything else but such abstract and partial ideas of more complex ones, taken at first from particular existences, will, I fear, be at a loss where to find them. For let any one reflect, and then tell me, wherein does his idea of "man" differ from that of "Peter" and "Paul," or his idea of "horse" from that of "Bucephalus," but in the leaving out something that is peculiar to each individual, and retaining so much of those particular complex ideas in several particular existences as they are found to agree in? Of the complex ideas signified by the names "man" and "horse," leaving out but those particulars wherein they differ, and retaining only those wherein they agree, and of those making a new distinct complex idea, and giving the name animal to it, one has a more general term, that comprehends with man, several other creatures. Leave out of the idea of "animal" sense and spontaneous motion, and the remaining complex idea, made up of the remaining simple ones of body, life, and nourishment, becomes a more general one, under the more comprehensive term, *vivens*.

* * *

11. *General and universal are creatures of the understanding.* To return to general words: it is plain, by what has been said, that general and universal belong not to the real existence of things; but are the inventions and creatures of the understanding, made by it for its own use, and concern only signs, whether words or ideas. Words are general, as has been said, when used for signs of general ideas, and so are applicable indifferently to many particular things; and ideas are general when they are set up as the representatives of many particular things: but universality belongs not to things themselves, which are all of them particular in their existence, even those words and ideas which in their signification are general. When therefore we quit particulars, the generals that rest are only creatures of our own making; their general nature being nothing but the capacity they are put into, by the

understanding, of signifying or representing many particulars. For the signification they have is nothing but a relation that, by the mind of man, is added to them.

12. *Abstract ideas are the essences of the Genera and Species.* The next thing therefore to be considered is, what kind of signification it is that general words have. For, as it is evident that they do not signify barely one particular thing; for then they would not be general terms, but proper names, so, on the other side, it is as evident they do not signify a plurality; for "man" and "men" would then signify the same; and the distinction of numbers (as the grammarians call them) would be superfluous and useless. That then which general words signify is a sort of things; and each of them does that, by being a sign of an abstract idea in the mind; to which idea, as things existing are found to agree, so they come to be ranked under that name, or, which is all one, be of that sort. Whereby it is evident that the essences of the sorts, or (if the Latin word pleases better) species of things, are nothing else but these abstract ideas. For the having the essence of any species, being that which makes anything to be of that species; and the conformity to the idea to which the name is annexed being that which gives a right to that name; the having the essence, and the having that conformity, must needs be the same thing: since to be of any species, and to have a right to the name of that species, is all one. As, for example, to be a man, or of the species man and to have right to the name "man," is the same thing. Again, to be a man, or of the species man, and have the essence of a man, is the same thing. Now, since nothing can be a man or have a right to the name "man," but what has a conformity to the abstract idea the name "man" stands for; nor anything be a man, or have a right to the species man, but what has the essence of that species; it follows, that the abstract idea for which the name stands, and the essence of the species, is one and the same. From whence it is easy to observe, that the essences of the sorts of things, and, consequently, the sorting of things, is the workmanship of the understanding that abstracts and makes those general ideas.

8 BERKELEY

Berkeley rejects the notion of an abstract idea and any doctrine that maintains that universals are abstract ideas. He tries by introspection to concentrate on what would count as an abstract idea, namely the common characteristics shared by members of the same class. He is unsuccessful in this endeavor and suggests that the content of any idea is a particular. One never has an idea (much less a mental picture), for example, of a general horse, but only of some particular horse.

However, Berkeley does not deny that there are general ideas. He does reject abstract general ideas—the notion that the content of a general idea is something general. He says, "if we will . . . speak only of what we can conceive, I believe that we shall acknowledge that an idea which, considered in itself, is particular, becomes general by being made to represent or stand for all other particular ideas of the same sort." Universality, then, turns out to be a matter of function or use. This is a proxy function of letting one's idea of a particular stand for all other particulars of the same kind. This function is successfully communicated to others by the use of general words, as Berkeley states: "a word becomes general by being made a sign, not of an abstract idea, but of several particular ideas, any one of which it indifferently suggests to the mind."

A Treatise Concerning the Principles of Human Knowledge

INTRODUCTION

1. Philosophy being nothing else but the study of wisdom and truth, it may with reason be expected that those who have spent most time and pains in it should enjoy a greater calm and serenity of mind, a greater clearness and evidence of knowledge, and be less disturbed with doubts and difficulties than other men. Yet so it is, we see the illiterate bulk of mankind that walk the highroad of plain common sense, and are governed by the dictates of nature, for the most part easy and undisturbed. To them nothing that is familiar appears unaccountable or difficult to comprehend. They complain not of any want of evidence in their senses, and are out of all danger of becoming skeptics. But no sooner do we depart from sense and instinct to follow the light of a superior principle, to reason, meditate, and reflect on the nature of things, but a thousand scruples spring up in our minds

concerning those things which before we seemed fully to comprehend. Prejudices and errors of sense do from all parts discover themselves to our view; and, endeavoring to correct these by reason, we are insensibly drawn into uncouth paradoxes, difficulties, and inconsistencies, which multiply and grow upon us as we advance in speculation, till at length, having wandered through many intricate mazes, we find ourselves just where we were, or, which is worse, sit down in a forlorn skepticism.

2. The cause of this is thought to be the obscurity of things, or the natural weakness and imperfection of our understandings. It is said the faculties we have are few, and those designed by nature for the support and comfort of life, and not to penetrate into the inward essence and constitution of things. Besides, the mind of man being finite, when it treats of things which partake of infinity it is not to be wondered at if it run into absurdities and contradictions, out of which it is impossible it should ever extricate itself, it being of the nature of infinite not to be comprehended by that which is finite.

3. But perhaps we may be too partial to ourselves in placing the fault originally in our faculties, and not rather in the wrong use we make of them. It is a hard thing to suppose that right deductions from true principles should ever end in consequences which cannot be maintained or made consistent. Upon the whole, I am inclined to think that the far greater part, if not all, of those difficulties which have hitherto amused philosophers, and blocked up the way to knowledge, are entirely owing to ourselves—that we have first raised a dust and then complain we cannot see.

4. My purpose therefore is, to try if I can discover what those principles are which have introduced all that doubtfulness and uncertainty, those absurdities and contradictions, into the several sects of philosophy; insomuch that the wisest men have thought our ignorance incurable, conceiving it to arise from the natural dullness and limitation of our faculties. And surely it is a work well deserving our pains to make a strict inquiry concerning the first principles of human knowledge, to sift and examine them on all sides, especially since there may be some grounds to suspect that those lets and difficulties, which stay and embarrass the mind in its search after truth, do not spring from any darkness and intricacy in the objects, or natural defect in the understanding so much as from false principles which have been insisted on, and might have been avoided.

*   *   *

6. In order to prepare the mind of the reader for the easier conceiving what follows, it is proper to premise somewhat, by way of introduction, concerning the nature and abuse of language. But the unraveling this matter leads me in some measure to anticipate my design, by taking notice of what seems to have had a chief part in rendering speculation intricate and perplexed, and to have occasioned innumerable errors and difficulties in almost all parts of knowledge. And that is the opinion that the mind hath a

power of framing *abstract ideas* or notions of things. He who is not a perfect stranger to the writings and disputes of philosophers must needs acknowledge that no small part of them are spent about abstract ideas. These are in a more especial manner thought to be the object of those sciences which go by the name of logic and metaphysics, and of all that which passes under the notion of the most abstracted and sublime learning, in all which one shall scarce find any question handled in such a manner as does not suppose their existence in the mind, and that it is well acquainted with them.

7. It is agreed on all hands that the qualities or modes of things do never really exist each of them apart by itself, and separated from all others, but are mixed, as it were, and blended together, several in the same object. But, we are told, the mind being able to consider each quality singly, or abstracted from those other qualities with which it is united, does by that means frame to itself abstract ideas. For example, there is perceived by sight an object extended, colored, and moved: this mixed or compound idea the mind resolving into its simple, constituent parts, and viewing each by itself, exclusive of the rest, does frame the abstract ideas of extension, color, and motion. Not that it is possible for color or motion to exist without extension; but only that the mind can frame to itself by *abstraction* the idea of color exclusive of extension, and of motion exclusive of both color and extension.

8. Again, the mind having observed that in the particular extensions perceived by sense there is something common and alike in all, and some other things peculiar, as this or that figure or magnitude, which distinguish them one from another; it considers apart or singles out by itself that which is common, making thereof a most abstract idea of extension, which is neither line, surface, nor solid, nor has any figure or magnitude, but is an idea entirely prescinded from all these. So likewise the mind, by leaving out of the particular colors perceived by sense that which distinguishes them one from another, and retaining that only which is common to all, makes an idea of color in abstract which is neither red, nor blue, nor white, nor any other determinate color. And, in like manner, by considering motion abstractedly not only from the body moved, but likewise from the figure it describes, and all particular directions and velocities, the abstract idea of motion is framed; which equally corresponds to all particular motions whatsoever that may, be perceived by sense.

9. And as the mind frames to itself abstract ideas of qualities or modes, so does it, by the same precision or mental separation, attain abstract ideas of the more compounded beings which include several coexistent qualities. For example, the mind having observed that Peter, James, and John resemble each other in certain common agreements of shape and other qualities, leaves out of the complex or compounded idea it has of Peter, James, and any other particular man, that which is peculiar to each, retaining only what is

common to all, and so makes an abstract idea wherein all the particulars equally partake; abstracting entirely from and cutting off all those circumstances and differences which might determine it to any particular existence. And after this manner it is said we come by the abstract idea of *man*, or, if you please, humanity, or human nature; wherein it is true there is included color, because there is no man but has some color, but then it can be neither white, nor black, nor any particular color, because there is no one particular color wherein all men partake. So likewise there is included stature, but then it is neither tall stature, nor low stature, nor yet middle stature, but something abstracted from all these. And so of the rest. Moreover, there being a great variety of other creatures that partake in some parts, but not all, of the complex idea of man, the mind, leaving out those parts which are peculiar to men, and retaining those only which are common to all the living creatures, frames the idea of *animal*, which abstracts not only from all particular men, but also all birds, beasts, fishes, and insects. The constituent parts of the abstract idea of animal are body, life, sense, and spontaneous motion. By body is meant body without any particular shape or figure, there being no one shape or figure common to all animals, without covering, either of hair, or feathers, or scales, etc., nor yet naked: hair, feathers, scales, and nakedness being the distinguishing properties of particular animals, and for that reason left out of the *abstract idea*. Upon the same account the spontaneous motion must be neither walking, nor flying, nor creeping; it is nevertheless a motion, but what that motion is it is not easy to conceive.

10. Whether others have this wonderful faculty of abstracting their ideas, they best can tell; for myself, I find indeed I have a faculty of imagining, or representing to myself, the ideas of those particular things I have perceived, and of variously compounding and dividing them. I can imagine a man with two heads, or the upper parts of a man joined to the body of a horse. I can consider the hand, the eye, the nose, each by itself abstracted or separated from the rest of the body. But then whatever hand or eye I imagine, it must have some particular shape and color. Likewise the idea of man that I frame to myself must be either of a white, or a black, or a tawny, a straight, or a crooked, a tall, or a low, or a middle-sized man. I cannot by any effort of thought conceive the abstract idea above described. And it is equally impossible for me to form the abstract idea of motion distinct from the body moving, and which is neither swift nor slow, curvilinear nor rectilinear; and the like may be said of all other abstract general ideas whatsoever. To be plain, I own myself able to abstract in one sense, as when I consider some particular parts or qualities separated from others, with which, though they are united in some object, yet it is possible they may really exist without them. But I deny that I can abstract from one another, or conceive separately, those qualities which it is impossible should exist so separated; or that I can frame a general notion, by abstracting from particulars in the manner aforesaid—which last are the two proper acceptations of "abstraction." And

there are grounds to think most men will acknowledge themselves to be in my case. The generality of men which are simple and illiterate never pretend to abstract notions. It is said they are difficult and not to be attained without pains and study; we may therefore reasonably conclude that, if such there be, they are confined only to the learned.

11. I proceed to examine what can be alleged in defense of the doctrine of abstraction, and try if I can discover what it is that inclines the men of speculation to embrace an opinion so remote from common sense as that seems to be. There has been a late deservedly esteemed philosopher who, no doubt, has given it very much countenance, by seeming to think the having abstract general ideas is what puts the widest difference in point of understanding betwixt man and beast.—

> The having of general ideas [saith he] is that which puts a perfect distinction betwixt man and brutes, and is an excellency which the faculties of brutes do by no means attain unto. For, it is evident we observe no footsteps in them of making use of general signs for universal ideas; from which we have reason to imagine that they have not the faculty of abstracting, or making general ideas, since they have no use of words or any other general signs.

And a little after:

> Therefore, I think, we may suppose that it is in this that the species of brutes are discriminated from men, and it is that proper difference wherein they are wholly separated, and which at last widens to so wide a distance. For, if they have any ideas at all, and are not bare machines (as some would have them), we cannot deny them to have some reason. It seems as evident to me that they do, some of them, in certain instances reason as that they have sense; but it is only in particular ideas, just as they receive them from their senses. They are the best of them tied up within those narrow bounds, and have not (as I think) the faculty to enlarge them by any kind of abstraction.—*Essay on Human Understanding*, Bk. II, chap. II, secs. 10f.

I readily agree with this learned author, that the faculties of brutes can by no means attain to abstraction. But then if this be made the distinguishing property of that sort of animals, I fear a great many of those that pass for men must be reckoned into their number. The reason that is here assigned why we have no grounds to think brutes have abstract general ideas is that we observe in them no use of words or any other general signs; which is built on this supposition—that the making use of words implies the having general ideas. From which it follows that men who use language are able to abstract or generalize their ideas. That this is the sense and arguing of the author will further appear by his answering the question he in another place puts: "Since all things that exist are only particulars, how come we by general terms?" His answer is: "Words become general by being made the signs of general ideas." (*Essay on Human Understanding*, Bk. III, chap. 3, sec. 6.) But it seems that a word becomes general by being made the sign, not of an abstract general idea, but of several particular ideas, any one of which it indifferently suggests to the mind. For example, when it is said, "the change of motion is proportional to the impressed force," or that, "whatever has extension is divisible," these propositions are to be understood of motion and extension in general; and nevertheless it will not follow that they suggest to my thoughts an idea of motion without a body moved, or any determinate direction and velocity, or that I must conceive an abstract general idea of extension, which is neither line, surface, nor solid, neither great nor small, black, white, nor red, nor of any other determinate color. It is only implied that whatever particular motion I consider, whether it be swift or slow, perpendicular, horizontal, or oblique, or in whatever object, the axiom concerning it holds equally true. As does the other of every particular extension, it matters not whether line, surface, or solid, whether of this or that magnitude or figure.

12. By observing how ideas become general we may the better judge how words are made so. And here it is to be noted that I do not deny absolutely there are general ideas, but only that there are any *abstract* general ideas; for, in the passages above quoted, wherein there is mention of general ideas, it, is always supposed that they are formed by abstraction, after the manner set forth in sections 8 and 9. Now, if we will annex a meaning to our words and speak only of what we can conceive, I believe we shall acknowledge that an idea which, considered in itself, is particular, becomes general by being made to represent or stand for all other particular ideas of the same sort. To make this plain by an example, suppose a geometrician is demonstrating the method of cutting a line in two equal parts. He draws, for instance, a black line of an inch in length: this, which in itself is a particular line, is nevertheless with regard to its signification general, since, as it is there used, it represents all particular lines whatsoever; so that what is demonstrated of it is demonstrated of all lines, or, in other words, of a line in general. And, as that *particular* line becomes general by being made a sign, so the *name* "line," which taken absolutely is particular, by being a sign is made general. And as the former owes its generality not to its being the sign of an abstract or general line, but of all particular right lines that may possibly exist, so the latter must be thought to derive its generality from the same cause, namely, the various particular lines which it indifferently denotes.

13. To give the reader a yet clearer view of the nature of abstract ideas and the uses they are thought necessary to, I shall add one more passage out of the *Essay on Human Understanding*, which is as follows:

Abstract ideas are not so obvious or easy to children or the yet unexercised mind as particular ones. If they seem so to grown men it is only because by constant and familiar use they are made so. For when we nicely reflect upon them, we shall find that general ideas are fictions and contrivances of the mind, that carry difficulty with them, and do not so easily offer themselves as we are apt to imagine. For example, does it not require some pains and skill to form the general idea of a triangle (which is yet none of the most abstract, comprehensive, and difficult); for it must be neither oblique nor rectangle, neither equilateral, equicrural, nor scalenon, but *all and none* of these at once? In effect, it is something imperfect that cannot exist, an idea wherein some parts of several different and *inconsistent* ideas are put together. It is true the mind in this imperfect state has need of such ideas and makes all the haste to them it can, for the convenience of communication and enlargement of knowledge, to both which it is naturally very much inclined. But yet one has reason to suspect such ideas are marks of our imperfection. At least this is enough to show that the most abstract and general ideas are not those that the mind is first and most easily acquainted with, nor such as its earliest knowledge is conversant about.—Bk. IV, chap. 7, sec. 9.

If any man has the faculty of framing in his mind such an idea of a triangle as is here described, it is in vain to pretend to dispute him out of it, nor would I go about it. All I desire is that the reader would fully and certainly inform himself whether he has such an idea or no. And this, methinks, can be no hard task for anyone to perform. What more easy than for anyone to look a little into his own thoughts, and there try whether he has, or can attain to have, an idea that shall correspond with the description that is here given of the general idea of a triangle, which is "neither oblique nor rectangle, equilateral, equicrural nor scalenon, but all and none of these at once"?

14. Much is here said of the difficulty that abstract ideas carry with them, and the pains and skill requisite to the forming them. And it is on all hands agreed that there is need of great toil and labor of the mind, to emancipate our thoughts from particular objects and raise them to those sublime speculations that are conversant about abstract ideas. From all which the natural consequence should seem to be, that so difficult a thing as the forming abstract ideas was not necessary for *communication*, which is so easy and familiar to all sorts of men. But, we are told, if they seem obvious and easy to grown men, "it is only because by constant and familiar use they are made so." Now, I would fain know at what time it is men are employed in surmounting that difficulty, and furnishing themselves with those necessary helps for discourse. It cannot be when they are grown up, for then it seems they are not conscious of any such painstaking; it remains therefore to be the business of their childhood. And surely the great and multiplied labor of framing abstract notions will be found a hard task for that tender age. Is it not a hard thing to imagine that a couple of children cannot prate together of their sugar plums and rattles and the rest of their little trinkets, till they have first tacked together numberless inconsistencies, and so framed in their minds abstract general ideas, and annexed them to every common name they make use of?

15. Nor do I think them a whit more needful for the *enlargement of knowledge* than for *communication*. It is, I know, a point much insisted on,

that all knowledge and demonstration are about universal notions, to which I fully agree; but then it doth not appear to me that those notions are formed by abstraction in the manner premised—*universality*, so far as I can comprehend, not consisting in the absolute, positive nature or conception of anything, but in the relation it bears to the particulars signified or represented by it; by virtue whereof it is that things, names, or notions, being in their own nature *particular*, are rendered *universal*. Thus, when I demonstrate any proposition concerning triangles, it is to be supposed that I have in view the universal idea of a triangle, which ought not to be understood as if I could frame an idea of a triangle which was neither equilateral, nor scalenon, nor equicrural, but only that the particular triangle I consider, whether of this or that sort it matters not, doth equally stand for and represent all rectilinear triangles whatsoever, and is in that sense *universal*. All which seems very plain and not to include any difficulty in it.

* * *

18. I come now to consider the *source* of this prevailing notion, and that seems to me to be language. And surely nothing of less extent than reason itself could have been the source of an opinion so universally received. The truth of this appears, as from other reasons, so also from the plain confession of the ablest patrons of abstract ideas, who acknowledge that they are made in order to naming; from which it is a clear consequence that if there had been no such thing as speech or universal signs there never had been any thought of abstraction. See Bk. III, chap. 6, sec. 39, and elsewhere of the *Essay on Human Understanding*. Let us examine the manner wherein words have contributed to the origin of that mistake: First, then, it is thought that every name has, or ought to have, one only precise and settled signification, which inclines men to think there are certain abstract, determinate ideas that constitute the true and only immediate signification of each general name; and that it is by the mediation of these abstract ideas that a general name comes to signify any particular thing. Whereas, in truth, there is no such thing as one precise and definite signification annexed to any general name, they all signifying indifferently a great number of particular ideas. All which doth evidently follow from what has been already said, and will clearly appear to anyone by a little reflection. To this it will be objected that every name that has a definition is thereby restrained to one certain signification. For example, a "triangle" is defined to be "a plane surface comprehended by three right lines," by which that name is limited to denote one certain idea and no other. To which I answer that in the definition it is not said whether the surface be great or small, black or white, nor whether the sides are long or short, equal or unequal, nor with what angles they are inclined to each other; in all which there may be great variety, and consequently there is no one settled idea which limits the signification of the word "triangle." It is one thing for to keep a name constantly to the same definition, and another

to make it stand everywhere for the same idea; the one is necessary, the other useless and impracticable.

19. But to give a further account how words came to produce the doctrine of abstract ideas, it must be observed that it is a received opinion that language has no other end but the communicating ideas, and that every significant name stands for an idea. This being so and it being withal certain that names which yet are not thought altogether insignificant do not always mark out particular conceivable ideas, it is straightway concluded that they stand for abstract notions. That there are many names in use amongst speculative men which do not always suggest to others determinate, particular ideas, or in truth anything at all, is what nobody will deny. And a little attention will discover that it is not necessary (even in the strictest reasonings) that significant names which stand for ideas should, every time they are used, excite in the understanding the ideas they are made to stand for: in reading and discoursing, names being for the most part used as letters are in algebra, in which, though a particular quantity be marked by each letter, yet to proceed right it is not requisite that in every step each letter suggest to your thoughts that particular quantity it was appointed to stand for.

20. Besides, the communicating of ideas marked by words is not the chief and only end of language, as is commonly supposed. There are other ends, as the raising of some passion, the exciting to or deterring from an action, the putting the mind in some particular disposition; to which the former is in many cases barely subservient, and sometimes entirely omitted, when these can be obtained without it, as I think does not unfrequently happen in the familiar use of language. I entreat the reader to reflect with himself and see if it does not often happen, either in hearing or reading a discourse, that the passions of fear, love, hatred, admiration, disdain, and the like, arise immediately in his mind upon the perception of certain words, without any ideas coming between. At first, indeed, the words might have occasioned ideas that were fitting to produce those emotions; but, if I mistake not, it will be found that when language is once grown familiar, the hearing of the sounds or sight of the characters is oft immediately attended with those passions which at first were wont to be produced by the intervention of ideas that are now quite omitted. May we not, for example, be affected with the promise of a *good thing*, though we have not an idea of what it is? Or is not the being threatened with danger sufficient to excite a dread, though we think not of any particular evil likely to befall us, nor yet frame to ourselves an idea of danger in abstract? If anyone shall join ever so little reflection of his own to what has been said, I believe that it will evidently appear to him that general names are often used in the propriety of language without the speaker's designing them for marks of ideas in his own, which he would have them raise in the mind of the hearer. Even proper names themselves do not seem

always spoken with a design to bring into our view the ideas of those individuals that are supposed to be marked by them. For example, when a Schoolman tells me, "Aristotle has said it," all I conceive he means by it is to dispose me to embrace his opinion with the deference and submission which custom has annexed to that name. And this effect is often so instantly produced in the minds of those who are accustomed to resign their judgment to authority of that philosopher, as it is impossible any idea either of his person, writings, or reputation should go before. Innumerable examples of this kind may be given, but why should I insist on those things which everyone's experience will, I doubt not, plentifully suggest unto him?

21. We have, I think, shown the impossibility of abstract ideas. We have considered what has been said of them by their ablest patrons, and endeavored to show they are of no use for those ends to which they are thought necessary. And lastly, we have traced them to the source from whence they flow, which appears evidently to be language. It cannot be denied that words are of excellent use, in that by their means all that stock of knowledge which has been purchased by the joint labors of inquisitive men in all ages and nations may be drawn into the view and made the possession of one single person. But at the same time it must be owned that most parts of knowledge have been strangely perplexed and darkened by the abuse of words, and general ways of speech wherein they are delivered. Since therefore words are so apt to impose on the understanding, whatever ideas I consider, I shall endeavor to take them bare and naked into my view, keeping out of my thoughts so far as I am able those names which long and constant use hath so strictly united with them; from which I may expect to derive the following advantages:

22. *First*, I shall be sure to get clear of all controversies purely verbal—the springing up of which weeds in almost all the sciences has been a main hindrance to the growth of true and sound knowledge. *Secondly*, this seems to be a sure way to extricate myself out of that fine and subtle net of *abstract ideas* which has so miserably perplexed and entangled the minds of men; and that with this peculiar circumstance, that by now much the finer and more curious was the wit of any man, by so much the deeper was he likely to be ensnared and faster held therein. *Thirdly*, so long as I confine my thoughts to my own ideas divested of words, I do not see how I can easily be mistaken. The objects I consider I clearly and adequately know. I cannot be deceived in thinking I have an idea which I have not. It is not possible for me to imagine that any of my own ideas are alike or unlike that are not truly so. To discern the agreements or disagreements there are between my ideas, to see what ideas are included in any compound idea and what not, there is nothing more requisite than an attentive perception of what passes in my own understanding.

23. But the attainment of all these advantages does presuppose an entire deliverance from the deception of words, which I dare hardly promise

myself—so difficult a thing it is to dissolve an union so early begun and confirmed by so long a habit as that betwixt words and ideas. Which difficulty seems to have been very much increased by the doctrine of *abstraction*. For, so long as men thought abstract ideas were annexed to their words, it does not seem strange that they should use words for ideas—it being found an impracticable thing to lay aside the word, and retain the *abstract* idea in the mind, which in itself was perfectly inconceivable. This seems to me the principle cause why those men who have so emphatically recommended to others the laying aside all use of words in their meditations, and contemplating their bare ideas, have yet failed to perform it themselves. Of late many have been very sensible of the absurd opinions and insignificant disputes which grow out of the abuse of words. And, in order to remedy these evils, they advise well that we attend to the ideas signified, and draw off our attention from the words which signify them. But how good so ever this advice may be they have given others, it is plain they could not have a due regard to it themselves, so long as they thought the only immediate use of words was to signify ideas, and that the immediate signification of every general name was a determinate abstract idea.

24. But these being known to be mistakes, a man may with greater ease prevent his being imposed on by words. He that knows he has no other than *particular* ideas, will not puzzle himself in vain to find out and conceive the *abstract* idea annexed to any name. And he that knows names do not always stand for ideas will spare himself the labor of looking for ideas where there are none to be had. It were therefore to be wished that everyone would use his utmost endeavors to obtain a clear view of the ideas he would consider, separating from them all that dress and encumbrance of words which so much contribute to blind the judgment and divide the attention. In vain do we extend our view into the heavens and pry into the entrails of the earth, in vain do we consult the writings of learned men and trace the dark footsteps of antiquity—we need only draw the curtain of words, to hold the fairest tree of knowledge, whose fruit is excellent and within the reach of our hand.

25. Unless we take care to clear the first principles of knowledge from the embarrassment and delusion of words, we may make infinite reasonings upon them to no purpose: we may draw consequences from consequences, and be never the wiser. The farther we go, we shall only lose ourselves the more irrecoverably, and be the deeper entangled in difficulties and mistakes. Whoever therefore designs to read the following sheets, I entreat him to make my words the occasion of his own thinking, and endeavor to attain the same train of thoughts in reading that I had in writing them. By this means it will be easy for him to discover the truth or falsity of what I say. He will be out of all danger of being deceived by my words, and I do not see how he can be led into an error by considering his own naked, undisguised ideas.

9 KANT

Kant is a conceptualist. All cognitions are either intuitions or concepts. Intuitions are singular in nature, concepts are general. "Concept . . . is a general presentation or presentation of what is common to several objects." With respect to every concept one can distinguish the matter from the form. The former is the object of the concept, whereas the latter is generality. There are three (what Kant calls logical) acts of the understanding by which the formal (i.e., general) aspect of concepts is generated: (1) comparison, (2) reflection, and (3) abstraction. The first step in the generalization process is the comparison of two or more objects. One must then reflect on the comparison, making it possible for one to abstract *from* the particulars that which they have in common. The product of this process is a concept.

Concepts are either empirical or pure. The former are abstracted from experience, whereas the latter arise "from the understanding even *as to content*." For example, the concept "man" is abstracted from our experience of several human particulars. Such is an empirical concept. The concepts of mathematics, however, are pure.

Kant understands that there is a hierarchy of concepts. This hierarchy is strictly one of comparison. "The higher concept in regard to its lower concept is called *genus*, the lower in respect of its higher, *species*." A concept may function as a genus in one relationship and as a species in a different relationship. For example, the concept "mammal" functions as a species under the genus "animal" and as a genus over the species "canine". The higher the concept, the less is understood about many things. The lower the concept, the more is understood about fewer things. Their use is of equal value.

Logic

First Section: Of Concepts

1. CONCEPT AS SUCH AND ITS DIFFERENCE FROM INTUITION

All cognitions, that is, all presentations consciously referred to an object, are either *intuitions* or *concepts*. Intuition is a *singular* presentation (*repraesentatio singularis*), the concept is a *general* (*repraesentatio per notas communes*) or reflected presentation (*repraesentatio discursiva*).

Cognition through concepts is called thinking (*cognitio discursiva*).

Note 1. Concept is opposed to intuition, for it is a general presentation or a presentation of what is common to several objects, a presentation, therefore, *so far as it may be contained in different objects.*[1]

74

Note 2. It is mere tautology to speak of general or common concepts, a mistake based on a wrong division of concepts into *general, particular,* and *singular.* Not the concepts themselves, only their use can be divided in this way.

2. MATTER AND FORM OF CONCEPTS

In every concept there is to be distinguished *matter* and *form.* The matter of concepts is the *object;* their from is *generality.*

3. EMPIRICAL AND PURE CONCEPT

The concept is either an *empirical* or a *pure* one (*vel empiricus vel intellectualis*). A pure concept is one that is not abstracted from experience but springs from the understanding even as to content.

The idea[2] is a concept of reason, whose object can be met with nowhere in experience.

Note 1. The empirical concept springs from the senses through comparison of the objects of experience and receives, through the understanding, merely the form of generality. The reality of these concepts rests on actual experience, from which they have been extracted as to their content. Whether there are *pure concepts of the understanding (conceptus puri)* which, as such, spring solely from the understanding, independent of any experience, must be investigated by metaphysics.[3]

Note 2. Concepts of reason or ideas can in no way relate to actual objects, because these must all be contained in a possible experience. But ideas nevertheless serve to guide the understanding through reason in respect of experience and use of the latter's rules to the greatest perfection, or they serve to show that not all possible things are objects of experience and that the principles of the possibility of the latter [of objects of experience] are not valid for things in themselves, neither for objects of experience as things in themselves.

The idea contains the *archetype* of the use of the understanding, e.g., the idea of the *universe,* which must be necessary, not as a *constitutive* principle of the empirical use of the understanding, but only as a *regulative* principle for the sake of the all-pervasive coherence of the empirical use of our understanding. The idea is also to be regarded as a necessary fundamental concept in order either to *complete* the subordinating acts of the understanding objectively or to regard them as *unlimited.* Nor can the idea be obtained by *composition;* for the whole is here prior to the part. Nevertheless there are ideas to which an approximation takes place. This is the case with *mathematical* ideas, or with the ideas of the *mathematical generation of a whole,* these being essentially different from *dynamic* ideas which are totally *heterogeneous* to all concrete concepts, because the [dynamic] whole differs from concrete concepts not in quantity (as does the mathematical [whole]) but in *kind.*

* * *

5. LOGICAL ORIGIN OF CONCEPTS

The origin of concepts as to *mere form* rests on reflection and abstraction from the difference of things that are designated by a certain presentation. And here the question arises: *Which acts of the understanding make up a concept,* or—which is the same—*which do belong to the generation of a concept from given presentations?*

> **Note 1.** Since general logic abstracts from all content of the cognition through concepts or from all matter of thinking, it can ponder the concept only in regard to *its form,* that is, subjectively only:[4] not how, through a characteristic, it determines an object, but only how it can be referred to several objects. Thus it is not for general logic to investigate the source of concepts, not how concepts as presentations arise, but solely how *given presentations become concepts in thinking*—whatever these concepts may contain, something taken from experience, or something thought out, or something gathered from the nature of the understanding. This *logical* origin of concepts—the origin as to their mere form—consists in reflection, whereby arises a presentation common to several objects (*conceptus communis*) as the form required for the power of judgment. In logic, *merely the difference of reflection* in the concept is considered.
>
> **Note 2.** The origin of concepts in respect of their matter, which makes a concept either empirical, or constructed, or intellectual, is pondered in metaphysics.

6. LOGICAL ACTS OF COMPARISON, REFLECTION, AND ABSTRACTION

The logical acts of the understanding by which concepts are generated as to their form are,

1) *comparison,* i.e. the likening of presentations to one another in relation to the unity of consciousness,
2) *reflection,* i.e. the going back over[5] different presentations, how they can be comprehended in one consciousness; and finally
3) *abstraction* or the segregation of everything else by which given presentations differ.

> **Note 1.** In order to make our presentations into concepts, one must thus be able to *compare, reflect,* and *abstract,* for these three logical operations of the understanding are the essential and general conditions of generating any concept whatever. For example, I see a fir, a willow, and a linden. In firstly comparing these objects, I notice that they are different from one another in respect of trunk, branches, leaves, and the like; further, however, I reflect only on what they have in common, the trunk, the branches, the leaves themselves, and abstract from their size, shape, and so forth; thus I gain a concept of a tree.
>
> **Note 2.** The expression *abstraction* is not always used correctly in logic. We must not say, to abstract *something* (*abstrahere aliquid*), but to abstract *from something* (*abstrahere ab aliquo*). If, for example, by scarlet cloth I think only the red color, then I abstract from the cloth; if I further abstract from the scarlet, and think it as a material substratum[6] generally,

I abstract from still more determinations, and my concept has thereby become even more abstract. For the more numerous the differentia of things omitted from a concept or the greater the number of determinations from which abstraction has been made, the more abstract is the concept. Abstract concepts should therefore properly be called *abstracting* concepts (*conceptus abstrahentes*), that is, concepts in which several abstractions occur. Thus, for example, the concept of *body* is, properly speaking, not an abstract concept, for from the body itself I cannot abstract, otherwise I would not have the concept of it. But I do have the abstract from size, color, hardness or liquidity; in short, from all special determinations of special bodies. The *most abstract* concept is that which has nothing in common with any concept differing from it. This is the concept of *something*, for what is different from it is *nothing*, which has nothing in common with something.

Note 3. Abstraction is only the *negative* condition under which generally valid presentations may be generated; the *positive* is comparison and reflection. For by abstraction no concept comes into being; abstraction only completes and encloses the concept within its definite limits.

7. INTENSION AND EXTENSION OF CONCEPTS

Every concept, as a *partial concept*, is contained *in* the presentation of things; as a *ground of cognition*, i.e. as a *characteristic*, it has these things contained *under* it. In the former regard, every concept has an *intension* [content]; in the latter, it has an *extension*.

Intension and extension of a concept have an inverse relation to each other. The more a concept contains under it, the less it contains in it.

Note. The generality or general validity of the concept does not rest on the concept being a *partial* concept but on its being a *ground of cognition*.

8. MAGNITUDE OF THE EXTENSION OF CONCEPTS

The more things stand under a concept and can be thought through it, the larger its extension or *sphere*.

Note. Just as one says of a *ground* generally that it contains the *consequence* under it, so one may also say of a concept that as a *ground of cognition* it contains all those things under it from which it has been abstracted, e.g., the concept of metal: gold, silver, copper, and so forth. For since every concept, as a generally valid presentation, contains what is common to several presentations of different things, all these things which in so far are contained under it, may be presented through it. And this is what makes up the *utility* of a concept. The more things there are that can be presented by a concept, the greater is its sphere. The concept of *body*, for example, has a greater extension than the concept of *metal*.

9. HIGHER AND LOWER CONCEPTS

Concepts are called *higher* (*conceptus superiores*) so far as they have other concepts under them, which in relation to them are called *lower* concepts. A characteristic of a characteristic—a *distant* characteristic—is a higher concept; the concept in reference to a distant characteristic is a lower concept.

Note. Since higher and lower concepts carry these designations only *respectively*, one and the same concept, in different relations, can be at once a higher and a lower concept. The concept *mammal*,[7] for example, is in reference to the concept *horse* a higher one, in reference to the concept *animal* a lower one.

10. GENUS AND SPECIES

The higher concept in regard to its lower concept is called *genus*, the lower in respect of its higher, *species*.

Just as higher and lower concepts, so the concepts of *genus* and species are also not different by their nature but only in respect of their relation to one another in logical subordination (*termini a quo* or *ad quod*).

11. HIGHEST GENUS AND LOWEST SPECIES

The *highest* genus is that which is no species (*genus summum non est species*), just as the *lowest* species is that which is no genus (*species quae non est genus est infima*). According to the law of continuity, however, there can be neither a *lowest* nor a *nearest* species.

Note. When we think a series of several concepts subordinated to one another, e.g., iron, metal, body, substance, thing, we can here obtain ever higher genera, for every *species* is always to be considered as a *genus* in respect of a lower concept, e.g., the concept *learned man* in respect of the concept *philosopher*—until we lastly come to a *genus* that cannot again be a *species*. And to such a one we must at last be able to come, because there must be in the end a highest concept (*conceptus summus*) from which as such no further abstraction can be made without making the entire concept disappear. But there is no lowest concept (*conceptus infimus*) or lowest species in the series of species and genera under which not yet another would be contained, because it is impossible to determine such a concept. For even if we have a concept that we apply *immediately* to individuals, there may still be present in respect of it specific differences which we either do not notice or disregard. Only *relative to use* are there lowest concepts which have received this meaning, as it were, by convention, to the extent that one has agreed to go no further down.

In respect to the determination of the concepts of genera and species, the following general law is valid: *There is a genus that can no longer be a species; but there is no species that can no longer be genus.*

12. WIDER AND NARROWER CONCEPT/RECIPROCAL CONCEPTS

The higher concept is also called a *wider* concept, the lower a *narrower* concept.

Concepts that have the same sphere are called *reciprocal concepts* (*conceptus reciproci*).

13. RELATION OF THE LOWER TO THE HIGHER—OF THE WIDER TO THE NARROWER CONCEPT

The lower concept is not contained *in* the higher, for it contains *more* in itself than the higher; but it is yet contained *under* the latter, because the higher contains the cognitive ground of the lower.

Further, a concept is not *wider* than another because it contains *more* under it—for one cannot know that—but so far as it contains under it the *other concept* and *beside it still more*.

14. GENERAL RULES WITH RESPECT TO THE SUBORDINATION OF CONCEPTS

In respect of the logical extension of concepts, the following general rules are valid:

1) What appertains to or contradicts the higher concepts, that appertains to or contradicts also all lower concepts contained under those higher ones.
2) Conversely: What appertains to or contradicts *all* lower concepts, that appertains to or contradicts also their higher concept.

Note. Because that in which things agree derives from their *general* properties and that in which they differ from their *particular* properties, one cannot conclude: What appertain to or contradicts *one* lower concept, appertains to or contradicts also *other* lower concepts belonging with the former to one higher concept. Thus, one cannot conclude, for example: *What does not appertain to man, does not appertain to angels either*.

15. CONDITIONS OF THE ORIGIN OF HIGHER AND LOWER CONCEPTS: LOGICAL ABSTRACTION AND LOGICAL DETERMINATION

By continued logical abstraction originate ever higher concepts, just as on the other hand ever lower concepts originate by continued logical determination. The greatest possible abstraction gives the highest or most abstract concept—that from which thinking can remove no further determination. The highest complete determination would give the *all-sided determination* of a concept (*conceptum omnimode determinatum*), i.e. one to which thinking can add no further determination.

Note. Since only single things or individuals are of an all-sided determination, there can be cognitions of an all-sided determination only as intuitions, not, however, as concepts; in respect of the latter, logical determination can never be considered as complete (11, Note).

16. USE OF CONCEPTS IN ABSTRACTO AND IN CONCRETO

Every concept can be used *generally* and *particularly* (*in abstracto* and *in concreto*). The lower concept is being used *in abstracto* in respect of its higher; the higher concept is being used *in concreto* in respect of its lower.

Note 1. The expressions of the *abstract* and the *concrete* thus refer not so much to the concepts in themselves—for every concept is an abstract concept—as rather to their use only. And this use again can have varying degrees, according as one treats a concept now in a more, now in a less abstract or concrete way, that is, either omits or adds a greater or smaller number of determinations. Through abstract use a concept gets nearer to the highest genus; through concrete use, however, nearer to the individual.

Note 2. Which use of concepts, the abstract or the concrete, is to be given preference over the other? On this nothing can be decided. Neither use is to be deemed less valuable than the other. By very abstract concepts we cognize *little* in *many* things, by very concrete concepts *much* in *few* things; what we therefore gain on the one hand, we lose on the other. A concept that has a large sphere is very useful in so far as one can apply it to many things; but on account of this there is the less contained *in* it. In the concept *substance*, for example, I do not think as much as in the concept *chalk*.

Note 3. The art of popularity consists in bringing about, in the same cognition, that proportion between presentation *in abstracto* and *in concreto*, of concepts and their exhibition [*in intuition*], by which the maximum of cognition is achieved both as to extension and intension.

NOTES

Reprinted by permission of Rita S. Hartman on behalf of Robert S. Hartman and Wolfgang Schwarz, trans. Immanuel Kant: *Logic*. Bobbs-Merrill Co., Inc., New York, 1974. The notes are those of the translators, R. S. Hartman and W. Schwarz.

1. *In verschiedenen*, "in different ones," which leaves the reference of the adjective open. It may refer either to objects or presentations. . . . It is equally true, however, that the concept is contained in different presentations, which are our only access to the object.
2. This is the narrower systematic meaning of "idea," for which Kant asks to reserve the word, protecting it against its indiscriminate use as a name for all kinds of presentations. In colloquial German, even recipes may call for adding to a soup "an idea" of salt.
3. As Kant has done in the *Critique of Pure Reason*. The concepts here in question, both empirical and pure, are analytic concepts. Pure concepts of the understanding, in this sense, are the unschematized categories of the *Critique of Pure Reason*.
4. Ordinarily, as Kant himself mentions in the second part of this sentence, the form of a concept is regarded as its objective rather than subjective aspect. However, here, as in other parts of the *Logic*, Kant implies his treatment in the *Critique of Pure Reason*, where the form of concepts is situated in the understanding, which is subjectively seen in reflection. In the last resort, the categories that are the source of concepts have their own source in transcendental apperception: "This pure, original, immutable consciousness."
5. *Überlegung*, "reflection," here translated by "going back over" in order to avoid repetition of the preceding "reflection," which renders the original *Reflexion* (a foreign word in German).

6. *Stoff*, "matter." In order to avoid "material matter" for *materiellen Stoff*, we translated *Stoff* by "substratum."
7. There is a clear mistake in the original version of this example which has *Mensch*, "man," where we chose "mammal" to have terms that stand in the required relation of subordination. The Akademie edition retains *Mensch*, but changes the second term to *Neger*, "negro," in line with an example found in a transcript of Kant's lectures on logic by Benno Erdmann (cf. *Göttingische gelehrte Anzeigen*, 1880, Vol. II, p. 616, which we were unable to inspect). Since a change was necessary if the faulty example was to be corrected, we felt free to make an emendation in the first term rather than in the second, thus eliminating the subordination of man to animal, a quite un-Kantian example, notwithstanding this is logic, and not metaphysics.

10 HEGEL

Hegel approaches the problem of universals from the perspective of phenomenology. Consequently, the process of perceiving/conceiving becomes logically indistinct from that which is perceived/conceived. Many factors contribute to one perceiving/conceiving and making sense of (i.e., understanding) a particular. In understanding the process one ultimately realizes that the particular is a universal.

This only appears to be contradictory. Objects are identified by their properties. Every property is unique unto itself, by which Hegel means that a property simply is what it is to the exclusion of all other properties and is therefore universal in its singularity or oneness. The property that stands by itself and constitutes the ultimate unifying (i.e., universal) principle is that of Being. All other properties are secondary. That is, every object of perception/conception presupposes the universal property of Being. Individuating properties are universals that transcend the peculiarity of the object of perception/conception. The nature of the universality of property is that of oneness, pure individuality. "But the particular quality is a property only when attached to a 'one', and determinate only by its relation to others." That relation is both positive and negative. One understands an object on the basis of what it is and what it is not. An object of perception/conception is what it is as a result of a unique combination of secondary qualities, by virtue of the unifying principle of Being. That unique combination is a unity (oneness) to the exclusion of all other objects (onenesses). Since particular (i.e., secondary) qualities are properties only when they are attached to one another to form an object (i.e., a 'one'), it follows that the object of perception/conception is the only true universal.

Perception: Or Things and Their Deceptiveness

Immediate certainty does not make the truth its own, for its truth is something universal, whereas certainty wants to deal with the This. Perception, on the other hand, takes what exists for it to be a universal. Universality being its principle in general, its moments immediately distinguished within it are also universal; *I* is a universal, and the *object* is a universal. That principle has *arisen* and come into being for *us* who are tracing the course of experience; and our process of apprehending what perception is, therefore, is no longer a contingent series of acts of apprehension, as is the case with the apprehension of sense-certainty; it is a logically necessitated process. With the origination of the principle, both the moments, which as they appear merely fall apart as happenings, have at once together come into being: the one, the process of pointing out and indicating, the other the same process, but as a simple fact—the former the process of perceiving, the latter the object perceived. The object is in its essential nature the same as the process; the latter is the unfolding and distinguishing of the elements involved; the object is these same elements taken and held together as a single totality. *For us* (tracing the process) or in itself,[1] the universal, *qua* principle, is the essence of perception; and as against this abstraction, both the moments distinguished—that which perceives and that which is perceived—are what is non-essential. But in point of fact, because both are themselves the universal, or the essence, they are both essential: but since they are related as opposites, only one can in the relation (constituting perception) be the essential moment; and the distinction of essential and non-essential has to be shared between them. The one characterized as the simple fact, the object, is the essence, quite indifferent as to whether it is perceived or not: perceiving, on the other hand, being the process, is the insubstantial, the inconstant factor, which can be as well as not be, is the non-essential moment.

This object we have now to determine more precisely, and to develop this determinate character from the result arrived at: the more detailed development does not fall in place here. Since its principle, the universal, is in its simplicity a mediated principle, the object must express this explicitly as its own inherent nature. The object shows itself by so doing to be the *thing with many properties*. The wealth of sense-knowledge belongs to perception, not to immediate certainty, where all that wealth was merely something alongside and by the way; for it is only perception that has negation, distinction, multiplicity in its very nature.

The This, then, is established as *not* This, or as superseded, and yet not *nothing* (*simpliciter*), but a determinate nothing, a nothing with a certain content, viz. *the This*. The sense-element is in this way itself still present, but not in the form of some particular that is "meant"—as had to be the case in immediate certainty—but as a universal, as that which will have the character of a *property*. Canceling, superseding, brings out and lays bare its true twofold meaning which we found contained in the negative: to supersede (*aufheben*) is at once to negate and to preserve. The nothing being a negation of the This, preserves immediacy and is itself sensuous, but a universal immediacy. Being, however, is a universal by its having in it mediation or negation. When it brings this explicitly out as a factor in its immediacy, it is a specifically *distinct determinate property*. As a result, there are many such properties set up at once, one the negation of the other. Since they are expressed in the simple form of the universal, these determinate characters—which, strictly speaking, become properties only by a further additional characteristics—are self-related, are indifferent to each other, each is by itself, free from the rest. The simple self-identical universality, however, is itself again distinct and detached from these determinate characteristics it has. It is pure self-relation, the "medium" wherein all these characteristics exist: in it, as in a bare, simple unity, they interpenetrate without affecting one another; for just by participating in this universality they are indifferent to each other, each by itself.

This abstract universal medium, which we can call "Thinghood" in general or pure essential reality, is nothing else than the Here and Now as this on analysis turned out to be, viz. a simple togetherness of many Heres and Nows. But the many (in the present case) are in their determinateness themselves simply universals. This salt is a simple Here and at the same time manifold: it is white, and *also* pungent, *also* cubical in shape, *also* of a specific weight, and so on. All these many properties exist in a simple Here, where they interpenetrate each other. None of these has a different Here from the others; each is everywhere in the same Here where the others are. And at the same time, without being divided by different Heres, they do not affect each other in their interpenetration; its being white does not affect or alter the cubical shape it has, and neither affects its tart taste, and so on: on the contrary, since each is simple relation to self, it leaves the others alone and is related to these merely by being *also* along with them, a relation of mere indifference. This "Also" is thus the pure universal itself, the "medium", the "Thinghood" keeping them together.

In this relation, which has emerged, it is merely the character of positive universality that is first noticed and developed. But there is still a side presented to view which must also be taken into account. It is this. If the many determinate properties were utterly indifferent to each other, and were entirely related to themselves alone, they would not be determinate; for they are so, merely in so far as they are *distinguished* and related to others as their opposites. In view of this opposition, however, they cannot exist together in the bare and simple unity of their "medium", which unity is just as essential to them as negation. The process of distinguishing them, so far as it does not leave them indifferent, but effectually excludes, negates one from another, thus falls outside this simple "medium". And this, consequently, is not merely an "also", an unity indifferent to what is in it, but a "one" as well, an *excluding* repelling unity.

The "One" is the moment of negation, as, in a direct and simple manner, relating itself to itself, and excluding an other: and is that by which "Thinghood" is determined *qua* Thing. In the property of a thing the negation takes the form of a specific determinateness, which is directly one with the immediacy of its being, an immediacy which, by this unity with negation, is universality. *Qua* "one", however, negation, the specific quality, takes a form in which it is freed from this unity with the object, and exists *per se* on its own account.

These moments taken together exhaust the nature of the Thing, the truth of perception, so far as it is necessary to develop it here. It is (1) a universality, passive and indifferent, the "also" which forms the sole bond of connection between the qualities, or rather constituent elements, "matters", existing together; (2) negation likewise in a simple form, or the "one", which consists in *excluding* properties of an opposite character; and (3) the many properties themselves, the relation of the two first moments—the negation, as it is related to that indifferent element and in being so expands into a manifold of differences, the focal point of particularity radiating forth into plurality within the "medium" of subsistence. Taking the aspect that these differences belong to a "medium" indifferent to what is within it, they are themselves universal, they are related merely to themselves and do not affect each other. Taking, however, the other aspect, that they belong to the negative unity, they at the same time mutually exclude one another; but do so necessarily in the shape of properties that have a separate existence apart from the "also" connecting them. The sensuous universality, the immediate unity of positive being and negative exclusion, is only then a property, when oneness and pure universality are evolved from it and distinguished from one another, and when that sensuous universality combines these with one another. Only after this relation of the unity to those pure essential moments is effected, is the "Thing" complete.

This, then, is the way the "Thing" in perception is constituted, and consciousness is perceptual in character so far as this "Thing" is its object: it has merely to "take" the object (*capio*—per*ception*) and assume the attitude of pure apprehension, and what comes its way in so doing is truth (*das Wahre*). If it did something when taking the given, it would by such supplementation or elimination alter the truth. Since the object is the true and universal, the self-same, while consciousness is the variable and non-essential, it may happen that consciousness apprehends the object wrongly and deceives itself. The percipient is aware of the possibility of deception; for, in the universality forming the principle here, the percipient is directly aware of otherness, but aware of it as null and naught, as what is superseded. His criterion of truth is therefore *self-sameness*, and his procedure is that of apprehending what comes before him as self-same. Since, at the same time, diversity is a fact for him, his procedure is a way of relating the diverse moments of his apprehension to one another. If, however, in this comparison a want of sameness comes out, this is not an untruth on the part of the object (for the object is the self-same), but on the part of perception.

Let us now see what sort of experience consciousness forms in the course of its actual perception. We, who are analyzing the process, find this experience already contained in the development (just given) of the object and of the attitude of consciousness towards it. The experience will be merely the development of the contradictions that appear there.

The object which I apprehend presents itself as purely "one" and single:

also, I am aware of the "property" (*Eigenschaft*) in it, a property which is universal, thereby transcending the particularity of the object. The first form of being, in which the objective reality has the sense of a "one", was thus not its true being; and since the *object* is the true fact here, the untruth falls on my side, and the apprehension was not correct. On account of the *universality* of the *property* (*Eigenschaft*) I must rather take the objective entity as a *community* (*Gemeinschaft*) in general. I further perceive now the property to be determinate, opposed to another and excluding this other. Thus, in point of fact, I did not apprehend the object rightly when I defined it as a "commonness" or community with others, or as continuity; and must rather, taking account of the *determinateness* of the property, isolate parts within the continuity and set down the object as a "one" that excludes. In the disintegrated "one" I find many such properties, which do not affect one another, but are indifferent to one another. Thus I did not apprehend the object correctly when I took it for something that excludes. The object, instead, just as formerly it was merely continuity in general, is now a universal common medium where many properties in the form of sense universals subsist, each for itself and on its own account, and, *qua* determinate, excluding the others. The simple and true fact, which I perceive, is, however, in virtue of this result, not a universal medium either, but the particular property by itself, which, again, in this form, is neither a property nor a determinate being, for it is now neither attached to a distinct "one" nor in relation to others. But the particular quality is a property only when attached to a "one", and determinate only by relation to others. By being this bare relation of self to self, it remains merely sensuous existence in general, since it no longer contains the character of negativity; and the mode of consciousness, which is now aware of a being of sense, is merely a way of "meaning" (*Meinen*) or "intending", i.e. it has left the attitude of perception entirely and gone back into itself. But sense existence and "meaning" themselves pass over into perception: I am thrown back on the beginning, and once more dragged into the same circuit, that supersedes itself in every moment and as a whole.

Consciousness, then, has to go over this cycle again, but not in the same way as on the first occasion. For it has found out, regarding perception, that the truth and outcome of perception is its dissolution, is reflection out of and away from the truth into itself. In this way consciousness becomes definitely aware of how its perceptual process is essentially constituted, viz. that this is not a simple bare apprehension, but in its apprehension is at the same time reflected out of the true content back into itself. This return of consciousness into itself, which is immediately involved and implicated in that pure apprehension—for this return to self has proved to be essential to perception—alters the true content. Consciousness is aware that this aspect is at the same time its own, and takes it upon itself; and by so doing consciousness will thus get the true object bare and naked.

In this way we have, now, in the case of perception, as happened in the case of sensuous certainty, the aspect of consciousness being forced back upon itself; but, in the first instance, not in the sense in which this took place in the former case—i.e. not as if the truth of perception fell within it. Rather consciousness is aware that the untruth, that comes out there, falls within it. By knowing this, however, consciousness is able to cancel and supersede this untruth. It distinguishes its apprehension of the truth from the untruth of its perception, corrects this untruth, and, so far as itself takes in hand to make this correction, the truth, *qua* truth of perception, certainly falls within its own consciousness. The procedure of consciousness, which we have now to consider, is thus so constituted that it no longer merely perceives, but is also conscious of its reflection into self, and keeps this apart from the simple apprehension proper.

To begin with, then, I am aware of the "thing" as a "one", and have to keep it fixed in this true character as "one". If in the course of perceiving something crops up contradicting that, then I must take it to be due to my reflection. Now, in perception various different properties also turn up, which seem to be properties of the thing. But the thing is a "one"; and we are aware in ourselves that this diversity, by which the thing ceases to be a unity, falls in us. This thing, then, is, in point of fact, merely white to *our* eyes, *also* tart to *our* tongue, and *also* cubical to *our* feeling, and so on. The entire diversity of these aspects comes not from the thing, but from us; and we find them falling apart thus from one another, because the organs they affect are quite distinct *inter se*, the eye is entirely distinct from the tongue, and so on. We are, consequently, the universal medium where such elements get dissociated, and exist each by itself. By the fact, then, that we regard the characteristic of being a universal medium as *our* reflection, *we* preserve and maintain the self-sameness and truth of the thing, its being a "one".

These diverse aspects, which consciousness puts to its side of the account, are, however, each by itself just as it appears in the universal medium, specifically determined. White is only in opposition to black, and so on, and the thing is a "one" just by the fact that it is opposed to other things. It does not, however, exclude others from itself, so far as it is "one"; for to be "one" is to be in a universal relation of self to self, and hence by the fact of its being "one" it is rather like all. It is through the determinate characteristic that the thing excludes other things. Things themselves are thus determinate in and for themselves; they have properties by which they distinguish themselves from one another. Since the property is the *special* and *peculiar* property [the *proper* property] of the thing, or a specific characteristic in the thing itself, the thing has *several* properties. For, in the first place, the thing is true being, is a being inherently in itself; and what is in it is so as its own essential nature, and not on account of other things. Hence, in the second place, the determinate properties are not on account of other things and *for* other things, but inherent in that thing itself. They are, however, determinate properties *in it* only by the fact that they are several, and maintain their distinction from one another. And in the third place, since they are thus within "thinghood", they are self-contained, each in and for itself, and are indifferent to one another. It is, then, in truth the thing itself which is white, and *also* cubical, and *also* tart, and so on; in other words, the *thing* is the "also", the general medium, wherein the many properties subsist externally to one another, without touching or affecting one another, and without canceling one another; and, so taken, the thing is taken as what it truly is.

Now, on this mode of perception arising, consciousness is at the same time aware that it reflects itself also into itself, and that, in perceiving, the opposite moment to the "also" crops up. This moment, however, is the unity of the thing with itself, a unity which excludes distinction from itself. It is consequently this unity which consciousness has to take upon itself; for the thing as such is the subsistence of many different and independent properties. Thus we say of the thing, "it is white, and *also* cubical, and *also* tart", and so on. But so far as it is white it is *not* cubical, and so far as it is cubical and also white it is not tart, and so on. Putting these properties into a "one" belongs solely to consciousness, which, therefore, has to avoid letting them coincide and be *one* (i.e. one and the same property) in the thing. For that purpose it introduces the idea of "in-so-far" to meet the difficulty; and by this means it keeps the qualities apart, and preserves the thing in the sense of the "also". Quite rightly consciousness at first makes itself responsible for the "oneness" in such a way that what was called a property is represented as being "free matter" (*materia libera*).[2] In this way the thing is raised to the level of a true "also", since it thus becomes a collection of component elements (materials or matters), and instead of being a "one" becomes a mere enclosure, a circumscribing surface.

If we look back on what consciousness formerly took upon itself, and now takes upon itself, what it previously ascribed to the thing, and now ascribes to it, we see that consciousness alternately makes itself, as well as the thing, into both a pure atomic many-less "one", and an "also" resolved into independent constituent elements (materials or matters). Consciousness thus finds through this comparison that not only *its* way of taking the truth contains the diverse moments of apprehension and return upon itself, but that the truth itself, the thing, manifests itself in this twofold manner. Here we find, as a result of experience, that the thing exhibits itself, in a determinate and specific manner, to the consciousness apprehending it, but *at the same time* is reflected back into itself out of that manner of presenting itself to consciousness; in other words, the thing contains within it opposite aspects of truth, a truth whose elements are in antithesis to one another.

Consciousness, then, gets away also from this second form of perceptual procedure, that, namely, which takes the thing as the true selfsame, and itself as the reverse, as the factor that leaves sameness behind and goes back into self. Its object is now the entire process which was previously shared between the object and consciousness. The thing is a "one", reflected into self; it is *for* itself; but it is also for an other; and, further, it is an other for itself *as* it is for another. The thing is, hence, for itself and *also* for another, a being that has difference of a twofold kind. But it is also "one". Its being "one", however, contradicts the diversity it has. Consciousness would, consequently, have again to make itself answerable for putting the diversity into the "one", and would have to keep this apart from the thing. It would thus be compelled to say that the thing "in-so-far as" it is for itself is not for another. But the oneness belongs to the thing itself, too, as consciousness has found out; the thing is essentially reflected into self. The "also", the distinction of elements indifferent to one another, falls doubtless within the thing as well as the "oneness", but since both are different, they do not fall within the same thing, but in different things. The contradiction which is found in the case of the objective content as a whole is assigned to and shared by two objects. The thing is, thus, doubtless as it stands (*an und für sich*) selfsame, but this unity with itself is disturbed by other things. In this way the unity of the thing is preserved, and, at the same time, the otherness is preserved outside the thing, as well as outside consciousness.

Now, although the contradiction in the object is in this way allotted to different things, yet the isolated individual thing will still be affected with distinction. The different things have a subsistence on their own account (*für sich*); and the conflict between them takes place on both sides in such a way that each is not different from itself, but only from the other. Each, however, is thereby characterized as a something distinctive, and contains *in it* essential distinction from the others; but at the same time not in such a way that this is an opposition within *its* being; on the contrary, it is by itself a simple determinate characteristic which constitutes its essential character, distinguishing it from others. As a matter of fact, since the diversity lies in it, this diversity does indeed necessarily assume the form of a *real* distinction of manifold qualities within it. But because the determinate characteristic gives the essence of the thing, by which it is distinguished from others, and has a being all its own, this further manifold constitution is something indifferent. The thing thus no doubt contains in its unity the qualifying "in-so-far" in two ways, which have, however, unequal significance; and by that qualification this oppositeness becomes not a real opposition on the part of the thing itself, but—so far as the thing comes into a condition of opposition through its absolute distinction—this opposition belongs to the thing with reference to an other thing lying outside it. The further manifoldness is doubtless necessarily in the thing too, and cannot be left out; but it is unessential to the thing.

This determinate characteristic, which constitutes the essential character of the thing and distinguishes it from all others, is now so defined that thereby the thing stands in opposition to others, but must therein preserve itself for itself (*für sich*). It is, however, a thing, a self-existent "one", only so far as it does not stand in relation to others. For in this relation, the connection with another is rather the point emphasized, and connection with another means giving up self-existence, means ceasing to have a being on its own account. It is precisely through the absolute character and its opposition that the thing relates itself to others, and is essentially this process of relation, and only this. The relation, however, is the negation of its independence, and the thing collapses through its own essential property.

The necessity of the experience which consciousness has to go through in finding that the thing is destroyed just by the very characteristic which constitutes its essential nature and its distinctive existence on its own account, may, as regards the bare principle it implies, be shortly stated thus. The thing is set up as having a being of its own, as existing for itself, or as an absolute negation of all otherness; hence it is absolute negation merely relating itself to itself. But this kind of negation is the canceling and superseding of *itself*, or means that it has its essential reality in an other.

In point of fact the determination of the object, as it (the object) has turned out, contains nothing else. It aims at having an essential property, constituting its bare existence for itself, but with this bare self-existence it means also to embrace and contain diversity, which is to be necessary, but is at the same time not to constitute its essential characteristic. But this is a distinction that only exists in words; the *non*-essential, which has all the same to be *necessary*, cancels its own meaning, or is what we have just called the negation of itself.

With this the last qualifying "in-so-far", which separated self-existence and existence for another, drops away altogether. The object is really in one and the same respect the opposite of itself—for itself "so far as" it is for another, and for another "so far as" it is for itself. It is for itself, reflected into self, one; but all this is asserted along with its opposite, with its being for another, and for that reason is asserted merely to be superseded. In other words, this existence for itself is as much unessential as that which alone was meant to be unessential, viz. the relation to another.

By this process the object in its pure characteristics, in those features which were to constitute its essential nature, is superseded, just as the object in its sensible mode of existence became transcended. From being sensible it passed into being a universal; but this universal, because derived from sense, is essentially conditioned by it, and hence is, in general, not a genuine self-identical universality, but one affected with an opposition. For that reason this universality breaks up into the extremes of singleness and universality, of the "one" of the properties and the "also" of the free constituents or "matters". These pure determinations appear to express the essential nature itself; but they are merely a self-existence which is fettered at the same time with existence for an other. Since, however, both essentially exist in a single unity, we have before us now *unconditioned absolute universality*; and it is here that consciousness first truly passes into the sphere of *Understanding*, of Intelligence.

Sensible singleness thus disappears in the dialectic process of immediate certainty, and becomes universality, but merely sensuous universality. The stage of "meaning" has vanished, and perceiving takes the object as it inherently is in itself, or, put generally, as a universal. Singleness, therefore, makes its appearance there as true singleness, as the inherent nature of the "one", or as reflectedness into self. This is still, however, a conditioned self-existence alongside which appears another self-existence, the universality opposed to singleness and conditioned by it. But these two contradictory extremes are not merely alongside one another, but within one unity; or, what is the same thing, the common element of both, self-existence, is entirely fettered to its opposite, i.e. is, at the same time, *not* an existence-for-self. The sophistry of perception seeks to save these moments from their contradiction, tries to keep them fixed by distinguishing between "aspects", by using terms like "also" and "so far as", and seeks in like manner to lay hold on the truth by distinguishing the unessential element from an essential nature opposed thereto. But these expedients, instead of keeping away deception from the process of apprehension, prove rather to be of no avail at all; and the real truth, which should be got at through the logic of the perceptual process, proves to be in one and the same "aspect" the opposite (of what those expedients imply), and consequently to have as its essential content undifferentiated and indeterminate universality.

These empty abstractions of "singleness" and its antithetic "universality", as also of "essence", that is attended with a "non-essential" element, an element which is all the same "necessary", are powers the interplay of which constitutes perceptual understanding, often called "sound common sense" (*Menschenverstand*). This "healthy common sense", which takes itself to be the solid substantial type of conscious life, is, in its process of perception, merely the sport of these abstractions; it is always poorest where it means to be richest. In that it is tossed about by these unreal entities, bandied from one to the other, and by its sophistry endeavors to affirm and hold fast alternately now one, then the exact opposite, it sets itself against the truth, and imagines philosophy has merely to do with "things of the intellect" (*Gedankendinge*), merely manipulates "ideas". As a matter of fact, philosophy does have to do with them, too, and knows them to be the pure essential entities, the absolute powers and ultimate elements. But, in doing so, philosophy knows them at the same time in their determinate and specific constitution, and is, therefore, master over them; while that perceptual understanding takes them for the real truth, and is led by them from one mistake to another. It does not get the length of being aware that there are such simple essentialities operating within it and dominating its activity; it thinks it has always to do with quite solid material and content; just as sense-certainty is unaware that its essence is the empty abstraction of pure being. But in point of fact it is these essential elements in virtue of which perceptual understanding makes its way hither and thither through every kind of material and content; they are its principle of coherence and control over its varied material; they alone are what constitutes for consciousness the essence of sensuous things, what determines their relations to consciousness; and they are that in the medium of which the process of perceiving, with the truth it contains, runs its course. The course of this process, a perpetual alternate determining of the truth and superseding of this determination, constitutes, properly speaking, the constant everyday life and activity of perceptual intelligence, of the consciousness that thinks it lives and moves in the truth. In that process it advances, without halt or stay, till the final result is reached, when these essential ultimate elements or determinations are all alike superseded; but in each particular moment it is merely conscious of one given characteristic as the truth, and then, again, of the opposite. It no doubt suspects their unessentiality; and, to save them from the impending danger, it takes to the sophistry of now asserting to be true what it had itself just affirmed to be not true. What the nature of these untrue entities really wants to force this understanding to do—viz. to bring together and thereby cancel and transcend the ideas about that "universality" and "singleness", about "also" and "one", about that "essentiality" which is necessarily connected with an "unessentiality", and about an "unessential" that is yet "necessary"—understanding strives to resist by leaning for support on the qualifying terms "in-so-far", "a difference of aspect", or by making *itself* answerable for one idea in order to keep the other separate and preserve it as the true one. But the very nature of these abstractions brings them together as they are and of their own accord. "Sound common sense" is the prey of these abstractions; they carry understanding round in their whirling circle. When understanding tries to give them truth by at one time taking their untruth upon itself, while at another it calls their deceptiveness a mere appearance due to the uncertainty and unreliability of things, and separates the essential from an element which is necessary to them, and yet is to be unessential, holding the former to be their truth as against the latter:—when understanding takes this line, it does not secure them *their* truth, but convicts *itself* of untruth.

NOTES

From Hegel, *The Phenomenology of Mind*, trans. J. B. Baillie. Originally published by George Allen and Unwin Ltd., London, 1910. Reprinted by permission of Humanities Press International, Inc., and Unwin Hyman, Ltd. The notes are those of the translator, J. B. Baillie.

1. This expression refers to the distinction already made in the Introduction, between the point of view of the *Phenomenology* and that of the actual conscious-

ness whose procedure is being analyzed in the *Phenomenology*. That is "for us" which we (i.e. the philosophical "we") are aware of by way of anticipation, but which has not yet been evolved objectively and explicitly; it is intelligible, but not yet intellectually realized. That is "in itself" (*an sich*), which is implicit, inherent, or potential, and hence not yet explicitly developed. The terms "for us" and "in itself" are thus strictly alternative: the former looks at the matter from the point of view of the philosophical subject, the latter from the point of view of the object discussed by the philosopher. The implicit nature of the object can only be "for us" who are thinking about the object: and what *we* have in mind can only be *implicitly* true of the object. The alternative disappears when the explicit nature of the object is what "we" explicitly take the object to be.

2. An expression drawn from the physics of Hegel's day.

11 HUSSERL

There are two types of acts of cognition, empirical intuition and essential intuition. Empirical intuition, or sense-experience, is awareness of an individual object. As Husserl puts it, "the datum of individual or empirical intuition is an individual object." An object of perception carries with it a primordial givenness and in that sense is genuinely individual. Concurrent with the perception of an individual object is the intuition of what it is: this is essential intuition. "The datum of essential intuition is a pure essence." Essential intuition carries with it the possibility that other individual objects can possess the same essence, but does not entail that they do in fact so possess that essence. The intuition of essence carries with it no assertion concerning facts. In that sense essential intuition entails only possibilities. The consequence is twofold: (1) individual objects partake of essences, and (2) as data of (essential) intuition, essences subsist distinct from individual objects of perception. Essences *qua* data subsist in such a way as to be the subjects of true or false predication of objects. They therefore carry with them a status distinct from the person engaged in the predicating process. This qualifies Husserl as a Platonic realist.

Ideas: General Introduction to Pure Phenomenology, Chapter I

2. FACT. INSEPARABILITY OF FACT AND ESSENCE

Sciences of experience are *sciences of "fact"*. The acts of cognition which underlie our experiencing posit the Real in *individual* form, posit it as having spatio-temporal existence, as something existing in *this* time-spot, having this particular duration of its own and a real content which in its essence could just as well have been present in any other time-spot; posits it, moreover, as something which is present at this place in this particular physical shape (or is there given united to a body of this shape), where yet the same real being might just as well, so far as its own essence is concerned, be present at any other place, and in any other form, and might likewise change whilst remaining in fact unchanged, or change otherwise than the way in which it actually does. Individual Being of every kind is, to speak quite generally, *"accidental"*. It is so-and-so, but essentially it could be other than it is. Even if definite laws of nature obtain according to which such and such definite consequences must in fact follow when such and such real

94

conditions are in fact present, such laws express only orderings that do in fact obtain, which might run quite differently, and already presuppose, as pertaining *ab initio* to the *essence* of objects of possible experience, that the objects thus ordered by them, when considered in themselves, are accidental.

But the import of this contingency, which is there called matter-of-factness (*Tatsächlichkeit*), is limited in this respect that the contingency is correlative to a *necessity* which does not carry the mere actuality-status of a valid rule of connection obtaining between temporo-spatial facts, but has the character of *essential necessity*, and therewith a relation to *essential universality*. Now when we stated that every fact could be "essentially" other than it is, we were already expressing thereby *that it belongs to the meaning of everything contingent that it should have essential being* and *therewith an Eidos to be apprehended in all its purity*; and this Eidos comes under *essential truths of varying degrees of universality*. An individual object is not simply and quite generally an individual, a "this-there" something unique; but being constituted thus and thus *"in itself"* it has *its own proper mode of being*, its own supply of *essential* predicables which much qualify it (*qua* "Being as it is in itself"), if other secondary relative determinations are to qualify it also. Thus, for example, every tone in and for itself has an essential nature, and at the limit the universal meaning-essence "tone in general", or rather the acoustic in general—understood in the pure sense of a phase or aspect intuitively derivable from the individual tone (either in its singleness, or through comparison with others as a "common element"). So too every material thing has its own essential derivatives, and at the limit the universal derivative "material thing in general", with time-determination-in-general, duration-, figure-, materiality-in-general. *Whatever belongs to the essence of the individual can also belong to another individual*, and the *broadest* generalities of essential being, of the kind we have been indicating through the help of examples, delimit *"regions"* or *"categories"* of *individuals*.

3. ESSENTIAL INSIGHT AND INDIVIDUAL INTUITION

At first "essence" indicated that which in the intimate self-being of an individual discloses to us *"what"* it is. But every such What can be "set out as Idea". *Empirical or individual intuition* can be transformed into *essential insight* (ideation)—a possibility which is itself not to be understood as empirical but as essential possibility. The object of such insight is then the corresponding *pure* essence or eidos, whether it be the highest category or one of its specializations, right down to the fully "concrete".

This insight which *gives* the essence and in the last resort in *primordial* form can be *adequate*; and as such we can easily procure it, for instance, from the essential nature of a sound; but it can also be more or less imperfect, *"inadequate"*, and that not only in respect of its greater or lesser *clearness* and *distinctness*. It belongs to the type of development peculiar to certain categories of essential being that essences belonging to them *can* be given only *"one-sidedly"*, whilst in succession more "sides", though never "all sides", can be given; so correlatively the individual concrete particularities corresponding to these categories can be experienced and represented only in inadequate "one-sided" empirical intuitions. This holds for every essence related to the *thing-like*, and indeed for all the essential components of extension and materiality respectively; it even holds good, if we look more closely (subsequent analyses will make that evident) for *all realities* generally, whereby indeed the vague expressions 'one-sidedness' and 'more-sidedness' receive determinate meanings, and different kinds of inadequacy are separated out one from the other.

Here the preliminary indication will suffice that already on grounds of principle the spatial shape of the physical thing can be given only in some single perspective aspect; also that apart from this inadequacy which clings to the unfolding of any series of continuously connected intuitions and persists in spite of all that is thereby acquired, every physical property draws us on into infinities of experience; and that every multiplicity of experience, however lengthily drawn out, still leaves the way open to closer and novel thing-determinations; and so on, *in infinitum*.

Of whatever kind the individual intuition may be, whether adequate or not, it can pass off into essential intuition, and the latter, whether correspondingly adequate or not, has the character of a dator act. And this means that—

The essence (Eidos) is an object of a new type. Just as the datum of individual or empirical intuition is an individual object, so the datum of essential intuition is a pure essence.

Here we have not a mere superficial analogy, but a radical community of nature. *Essential insight is still intuition*, just as the eidetic object is still an object. The generalization of the correlative, mutually attached concepts "intuition" and "object" is not a casual whim, but is compellingly demanded by the very nature of things.[1] Empirical intuition, more specifically sense-experience, is consciousness of an individual object, and as an intuiting agency "brings it to givenness": as perception, to primordial givenness, to the consciousness of grasping the object in "a primordial way", in its *"bodily"* selfhood. On quite similar lines essential intuition is the consciousness of something, of an "object", a something towards which its glance is directed, a something "self-given" within it; but which can then be "presented" in other acts, vaguely or distinctly thought, made the subject of true and false predications—as is the case indeed with every *"object" in the necessarily extended sense proper to Formal Logic*. Every possible object, or to put it logically, *"every subject of possibly true predications"*, has indeed its own ways, that of predicative thinking above all, of coming under a glance that presents, intuits, meets it eventually in its "bodily selfhood" and "lays hold of" it. Thus essential insight *is* intuition, and if it is insight in the pregnant sense of the term, and not a mere, and possibly a vague, representation, it is a *primordial* dator Intuition, grasping the essence in its "bodily" selfhood.[2] But, on the other hand, it is an intuition of a fundamentally *unique* and *novel* kind, namely in contrast to the types of intuition which belong as correlatives to the object-matters of other categories, and more specifically to intuition in the ordinary narrow sense, that is, individual intuition.

It lies undoubtedly in the intrinsic nature of essential intuition that it should rest on what is a chief factor of individual intuition, namely the striving for this, the visible presence of individual fact, though it does not, to be sure, presuppose any apprehension of the individual or any recognition of its reality. Consequently it is certain that no essential intuition is possible without the free possibility of directing one's glance to an individual *counterpart* and of shaping an illustration; just as contrariwise no individual intuition is possible without the free possibility of carrying out an act of ideation and therein directing one's glance upon the corresponding essence which exemplifies itself in something individually visible; but that does not alter the fact that *the two kinds of intuition differ in principle*, and in assertions of the kind we have just been making it is only the essential relations between them that declare themselves. Thus, to the essential differences of the intuitions correspond the essential relations between "existence" (here clearly in the sense of individual concrete being) and "essence", between *fact* and *eidos*. Pursuing such connections, we grasp *with intelligent insight* the conceptual essence attached to these terms, and from now on firmly attached to them, and therewith *all* thoughts *partially mystical in nature* and clinging chiefly to the concepts Eidos (Idea) and Essence remain *rigorously excluded*.

4. Essential Insight and the Play of Fancy. Knowledge of Essences Independent of All Knowledge of Facts

The Eidos, the *pure essence*, can be exemplified intuitively in the data of experience, data of perception, memory, and so forth, but just as readily *also in the mere data of fancy (Phantasie)*. Hence, with the aim of grasping an essence itself in its *primordial* form, we can set out from corresponding empirical intuitions, *but we can also set out just as well from non-empirical intuitions, intuitions that do not apprehend sensory existence, intuitions rather "of a merely imaginative order"*.

If in the play of fancy we bring spatial shapes of one sort or another to birth, melodies, social happenings, and so forth, or live through fictitious acts of everyday life, of satisfaction or dissatisfaction, of volition and the like, we can through "ideation" secure from this source primordial and even on occasion adequate insight into pure essences in manifold variety: essences, it may be, of spatial shape *in general*, of melody *as such*, of social happening *as such*, and so forth, or of the shape, melody, etc., of the relevant special *type*. It is a matter of indifference in this connection whether such things have ever been given in actual experience or not. Could free make-believe through some sort of psychological miracle lead to the imagining of something fundamentally new in kind (sensory data, for instance) which never occurred in anyone's experiences, nor ever will, that would not affect in any way the primordial givenness of the corresponding essences, although imagined data are never under any circumstances real data.

It follows essentially from all this that the *positing of the essence*, with the intuitive apprehension that immediately accompanies it, *does not imply any positing of individual existence whatsoever; pure essential truths do not make the slightest assertion concerning facts*; hence from them *alone* we are not able to infer even the pettiest truth concerning the fact-world. Just as to think a fact or to express it needs the grounding of experience (so far as the *essential relevancy* of such thinking *necessarily* demands it), so thought concerning pure essence—the unmixed thought, not that which connects essence and facts together—needs for its *grounding* and support an insight into the essences of things.

* * *

10. REGION AND CATEGORY. THE ANALYTIC REGION AND ITS CATEGORIES

If we place ourselves in imagination within any eidetic science, e.g., in the Ontology of Nature, we find ourselves directed normally, at any rate, not towards essences as objects, but towards the objects of the essences which in the case we have selected are subordinate to the Region we call Nature. But we observe thereby that "*object*" is a title for diverse though connected formations, such as "thing", "property", "relation", "substantive meaning" (fact), "group", "order" and so forth, which are clearly not equivalent but refer back at times to a type of *objectivity* which has, so to speak, the prerogative of being primarily *original*, and in respect of which all others pose in a certain sense as mere differentiations. In the instance chosen the *Thing itself* has naturally this prerogative as against the property of a thing, relation, and so forth. But this is precisely a fragment of that formal order which must be cleared up if our talk about object and object-region is not to remain in confusion. From this clarification to which we devote the following reflections, the important *concept of the category* as related to the concept of region will spontaneously emerge.

Category is a word which on the one hand and in the combination "*category of a region*" refers us precisely to the relevant region, e.g., to the region of physical nature; but on the other hand sets the material region specified in relation to the *form of region in general*, or, which comes to the same thing, to the *formal essence: object in general* and the "*formal categories*" belonging to it.

Let us first make this not unimportant remark: Formal and material ontologies appear at first sight to belong to the same series, in so far as the formal essence of an object in general and the regional essence appear on both sides to play the same part. One is therefore inclined to speak of material regions rather than of regions *simpliciter* as heretofore, and to set the *"formal region"* in alignment with them. If we adopt this form of words, we need to be a little cautious. On the one side stand the *material*, which in a certain sense are the *essences "properly so-called"*. But on the other side stands what is still eidetic but none the less fundamentally and essentially different: *a mere essential form*, which is indeed an essence, but a completely *"empty"* one, an essence which *in the fashion of an empty form fits all possible essences*, which in its formal universality has even the highest material generalities subordinated to it, and prescribes *laws* to these through the formal truths which belong to it. The so-called *"formal region"* is thus not something co-ordinate with the material regions (the regions pure and simple), *it is properly no region at all, but the pure form of region in general*; it has all regions with all their essential diversities of content *under* (though indeed only *formaliter*) rather than side by side with itself. Now this subordination of the material under the formal proclaims itself in this, that at the same time *formal Ontology conceals in itself the forms of all possible ontologies in general* (i.e., of all in the "proper", "material" sense); and that it prescribes to the material ontologies a *formal constitution common to all of them*—including therein also those which we have still to study in respect of the distinction between region and category.

We take our start from formal ontology (conceived always as pure logic in its full extension so as to cover the *mathesis universalis*), which, as we know, is the eidetic science of object in general. In the view of this science, object is everything and all that is, and truths in endless variety and distributed among the many disciplines of the *mathesis* can in fact be set down to fix its meaning. But as a whole they lead back to a small set of immediate or basic truths, which in the pure logical disciplines function as *"axioms"*. Now we define the *pure logical basic concepts* which figure in these axioms as *logical categories, or categories of the logical region, 'object-in-general'*. Through these concepts as they figure in the total system of axioms the logical essence of object-in-general is determined, and the unconditionally necessary and constitutive determinations of an object as such, a something or other—so far as it should permit of being Something at all—are expressed. Since the pure logical in the sense we have marked out with absolute precision determines the concept of the *"analytical"* as opposed to the *"synthetical"*, a concept which alone is philosophically (and indeed fundamentally) important, we are wont to designate these categories as *analytical*.

As examples of logical categories we may cite such concepts as property, relative quality, substantive meaning (fact), relation, identity, equality, group (collection), number (*Anzahl*), whole and part, genus and species, etc.

But the *"meaning-categories"* also, the fundamental concepts of the various kinds of propositions, of their elements and forms, which belong to the essence of the proposition (*apophansis*), have their proper place here, and they have it, following our definition, with reference to the essential truths which link together "object-in-general" and "meaning-in-general", and link them moreover in such a way that pure truths concerning meaning can be transformed into pure truths concerning the object. It is precisely for this reason that *"apophantic logic"*, even when its statements concern meanings exclusively, belong in the full inclusive sense to formal Ontology. None the less the meaning-categories must be separated off as a group having its own distinctive character, and the remaining ones set over against them as the *formal objective categories in the pregnant sense of the term.*[3]

We add here this further remark, that by "categories" we can understand, on the one hand, concepts in the sense of meanings, but on the other also, and to better effect, the formal essences themselves which find their expression in these meanings. For instance, the "category" substantive meaning, plurality and the like, ultimately mean the formal eidos substantive meaning generally, plurality generally and the like. The equivocation is dangerous only so long as one has not learnt to separate clearly what must here be separated on all occasions: "meaning", and that which *in virtue of* its meaning permits of being expressed; and again: meaning and objectivity meant. In the terminological interest one can expressly distinguish between *categorical concepts* (as meanings) and *categorical essences.*

*   *   *

12. Genus and Species

We now need to draw within the realm of essences as a whole a new set of categorical distinctions. Every essence, whether it has content or is empty (and therefore purely logical), has its proper place in a graded series of essences, in a graded series of *generality* and *specificity*. The series necessarily possesses two limits that never coalesce. Moving downward we reach the *lowest specific differences* or, as we also say, the *eidetic singularities*; and we move upwards through the essences of genus and species to a *highest genus*. Eidetic singularities are essences, which indeed have necessarily "more general" essences as their genera, but no further specifications in relation to which they themselves might be genera (proximate or mediate, higher genera). Likewise that genus is the highest which no longer has any genus above it.

In this sense, in the pure logical realm of meanings, "meaning in general" is the highest genus; every determinate form of proposition or of its components an eidetic singularity; proposition in general a mediating genus. Numerical quantity in general (*Anzahl*) is likewise a highest genus. Two, three, and so forth are its lowest differences or eidetic singularities. In the sphere of positive content, thing in general, for instance, or sensory quality, spatial shape, experience (*Erlebnis*) in general are highest genera; the essential elements pertaining to determinate things, determinate sensory qualities, spatial shapes, vital experiences as such, are eidetic singularities, possessing thereby positive content.

It is a mark of *these* essential relations (not class, i.e., group relations) indicated by the terms genus and species, that in the more specific essence the more general is "immediately or mediately *contained*"—in a definite sense to be understood in and through eidetic intuition and in accordance with the specific type of Being intended. For this very reason many inquiries would bring the relation of eidetic genus and species to eidetic division under the relation of the "part" to the "whole". Here "whole" and "part" bear indeed the widest conceptual meaning of "containing" and "contained", and of this the eidetic relation of kind to kind is a specification. Thus the eidetic singular implies all the generalities which lie above it, and these on their side "lie one in the other" in graded order, the higher always within the lower.

NOTES

From Edmund Husserl, *Ideas*, trans. W. R. Boyce Gibson. Originally published by George Allen and Unwin Ltd., London, 1931. Reprinted by permission of Humanities Press International, Inc., and Unwin Human, Ltd.

1. The surprising polemic of O. Kulpe against my theory of categorical intuition in the work entitled *Die Realisierung* (1912, I. p. 127) illustrates the difficulty felt by psychological experts in our time of assimilating this simple and quite fundamental insight. I regret being misunderstood by this excellent scholar. But a critical reply becomes impossible where the misconception is so complete that there remains no vestige of the *meaning* of the positions originally laid down.
2. In my *Logical Studies* I used to employ the word *Ideation* to represent the primordial dator insight into essential being, and even then chiefly of the adequate type. Yet we clearly need a more plastic concept which shall include every consciousness plainly and straightly directed to an essence which it also grasps and fixes; and in addition also includes every obscure consciousness which no longer intuits at all.
3. Concerning division of logical categories into meaning-categories and formal-ontological categories, *vide Logical Studies*, Vol. I, § 67. The whole third study of the second volume treats specifically of the categories of Whole and Part. On historical grounds I had at that time not yet dared to make use of the alienating expression Ontology, and I described their study (*loc. cit.* [*Logical Studies*], p. 222, of the first edition) as a fragment of an "*a priori theory of objects as such*", which A. V. Meinong has brought more compactly under the title "Theory of the Object" (*Gegenstandstheorie*). In opposition to this arrangement, I now hold it to be more correct, in sympathy with the changed condition of the time, to make the old expression Ontology current once again.

12 HEIDEGGER

Heidegger's overriding concern is to determine the nature of being. In the midst of that inquiry his view of the nature of universals is explored. What, for example, is the universal 'treeness' as opposed to particular trees? He says that a word like 'tree' "permits the well-known threefold differentiation; it may be considered: 1) in respect to the audible and visible form of the word; 2) in respect to the meaning of what we represent in connection with it; 3) in respect to the thing," which in this case is a particular tree. The second holds the key to the problem of universals. He argues that we would not be able to distinguish a tree from an automobile or a rabbit "unless the representation of what a tree in general is shines before us." We must have some knowledge of treeness in advance in order to be able to recognize particular trees as the things they are, namely trees, as opposed to automobiles or rabbits. What is the nature of the universal representation "tree"? It quite simply is the meaning of the word 'tree'. "[W]e must know in advance what 'tree' means in order to be able to seek and find the particulars: the tree species and the individual trees."

An Introduction to Metaphysics

CHAPTER 3: THE QUESTION OF THE ESSENCE OF BEING

We have undertaken a study of the word "being" in order to penetrate the fact under discussion and so to assign it its proper place. We do not mean to accept this fact blindly, as we accept the fact that there are dogs and cats. We intend to form an opinion of the fact itself. And this we intend to do even at the risk that this intention may give an impression of stubbornness, and be set down as a forlorn unworldliness which takes the irrelevant and unreal for reality and entangles itself in the dissection of mere words. We wish to illuminate the fact. The result of our efforts is the observation that in the process of its development language forms "infinitives," e.g. "sein," and that in the course of time language has produced a blunted, indefinite meaning of this word. This happens to *be* so. Instead of gaining an elucidation of the fact, we have merely set another fact, pertaining to the history of language, beside it or behind it.

If we now start again with these facts of the history of language and ask why they are as they are, what we perhaps may still cite as a ground of explanation becomes not clearer but more obscure. Then the fact that things stand as they do with the word "being" really congeals into its inexorable facticity. But this happened long ago. Those who follow the usual method in philosophy are indeed invoking this fact when they say at the very outset: the word "being" has the emptiest and therefore most comprehensive meaning. What is thought in connection with this word is consequently the supreme generic concept, the genus. One can still barely detect the "ens in genere" as the old ontology puts it, but just as certainly there is nothing further to be sought in that direction. To attach the crucial question of metaphysics to this empty word "being" is to bring everything into confusion. Here there is only the one possibility, to recognize the emptiness of the word and let it go at that. This we may now apparently do with a clear conscience; and all the more so since the fact is explained historically by the history of language.

Let us then get away from the empty schema of this word "being." But where to? The answer cannot be difficult. At most we may wonder why we have dwelt so long, and in such detail, on the word "being." Away from the empty, universal word "being"; let us concern ourselves with the particulars of the different realms of the essent itself. For this undertaking we have all sorts of things at our disposal. The immediately tangible things, all the things that are constantly at hand, tools, vehicles, etc. If these particular essents strike us as too commonplace, not refined and soulful enough for "metaphysics," we can restrict ourselves to the nature around us, the land, the sea, the mountains, rivers, woods, and to the particulars therein, the trees, birds, insects, grasses, and stones. If we are looking for a large, impressive essent, the earth is close at hand. Essent in the same way as the nearest mountaintop is the moon that is rising back there, or a planet. Essent is the swarming crowd of people in a busy street. Essent are we ourselves. Essent are the Japanese. Essent are Bach's fugues. Essent is the Strassburg cathedral. Essent are Hölderlin's hymns. Essent are criminals. Essent are the lunatics in the lunatic asylum.

Everywhere essents to our heart's content. But how do we know that each one of all these things that we cite and list with so much assurance is an essent? The question sounds absurd, for any normal individual can establish infallibly that this essent *is*. Yes, to be sure. [Nor is it even necessary for us to use such words, alien to our everyday speech, as "essents" and the "essent."] And actually it does not enter our heads at this moment to doubt *that* all these essents really are, basing our doubts on the supposedly scientific observation that what we experience is only our sensations and that we can never escape our body, to which all the things we have named remain related. As a matter of fact we should like to remark in advance that such considerations, with which people so easily give themselves critical and superior airs, are thoroughly uncritical.

Meanwhile we shall simply *let* the essent *be*, as it surrounds us and assails us, as it inspires us or dejects us, in our everyday lives as well as in great hours and moments. We shall let all the essent *be*, just as it is. But if we thus

hold to the course of our historical being-there, without soul searching and
as though taking it for granted; if in every case we let the essent be the essent
that it *is*, then we must know what "is" and "being" mean.

But how are we to determine whether an essent, presumed to be at some
place and time, is or is not, if we cannot clearly differentiate in advance
between being and nonbeing? How are we to make this crucial distinction
unless we definitely know the meaning of what we are differentiating:
namely nonbeing and being. How can each and every essent be an essent for
us unless we understand "being" and "nonbeing" beforehand?

But essents are always confronting us. We differentiate between their
being-so and being-otherwise, we make judgments regarding being and
nonbeing. Accordingly we know clearly what "being" means. Then it is a
superficial figure of speech and an error to say that this word is empty and
indeterminate.

Such considerations bring us into an extremely contradictory situation.
At the start we established that the word "being" tells us nothing definite.
We did not make up our minds to this in advance; no, we found out, and we
still find, that "being" has a vague and indeterminate meaning. Yet on the
other hand the investigation we have just carried through convinces us that
we clearly and surely distinguish "being" from nonbeing.

If we are to orient ourselves in this situation, we must bear in mind the
following: It may indeed be doubtful whether a particular essent, somewhere or at some time, is or is not. We can make a mistake, for example as to
whether that window there, which is after all an essent, *is* or *is not* closed.
But even in order that the doubt may arise, the definite distinction between
being and nonbeing must be present in our minds. In this case we do not
doubt that being is different from nonbeing.

Thus the word "being" is indefinite in meaning and yet we understand it
definitely. "Being" proves to be totally indeterminate and at the same time
highly determinate. From the standpoint of the usual logic we have here an
obvious contradiction. Something that contradicts itself cannot be. There is
no such thing as a square circle. And yet we have this contradiction:
determinate, wholly indeterminate being. If we decline to delude ourselves,
and if we have a moment's time to spare amid all the activities and diversions
of the day, we find ourselves standing in the very middle of this contradiction. And this "stand" of ours is more real than just about anything else that
we call real; it is more real than dogs and cats, automobiles and newspapers.

Suddenly the fact that being is an empty word for us takes on an entirely
different face. We begin to suspect that the word may not be as empty as
alleged. If we reflect more closely on the word, it ultimately turns out that
despite all the blur and mixture and universality of its meaning we mean
something definite by it. This definiteness is so definite and unique in its
kind that we must even say this:

The being which belongs to every essent whatsoever, and which is thus dispersed among all that is most current and familiar, is more unique than all else.

Everything else, each and every essent, even if it is unique, can be compared with other things. Its determinability is increased by these possibilities of comparison. By virtue of them it is in many respects indeterminate. Being, however, can be compared with nothing else. Over against being, the only other is nothing. And here there is no comparison. If being thus represents what is most unique and determinate, the word "being" cannot be empty. And in truth it never is empty. We may easily convince ourselves of this by a comparison. When we perceive the word "being," either hearing it as a phonetic unit or seeing it as a written sign, it immediately gives itself as something other than the succession of sounds and letters "abracadabra." This too is a succession of sounds, but we say at once that it is meaningless, though it may have its meaning as a magic formula. But "being" is not meaningless in this way. Similarly "being," written and seen, is at once different from "kzomil." This too is a sequence of letters but in connection with this sequence we cannot think anything. There is no such thing as an empty word; at most a word is worn out, though still filled with meaning. The name "being" retains its appellative force. "Away from this empty word 'being'; go to the particular essents," proves to be not only a hasty but also a highly questionable counsel. Let us once more think the whole matter through with the help of an example which, to be sure, like every example that we cite in dealing with this question, can never clarify the whole matter in its full scope and therefore must be taken with certain reservations.

By way of an example, we substitute for the universal concept "being" the universal concept "tree." If we wish now to say and define what the essence of tree is, we turn away from the universal concept to the particular species of tree and the particular specimens of these species. This method is so self-evident that we almost hesitate to mention it. Yet the matter is not as simple as all that. How are we going to find our famous particulars, the individual trees *as such*, *as* trees; how shall we be able even to *look for* trees, unless the representation of what a tree in general is shines before us? If this universal representation "tree" were so utterly indeterminate and blurred as to give us no certain indication for seeking and finding, we might perfectly well turn up automobiles or rabbits as our determinate particulars, as examples for tree. Even though it may be true that in order to determine the essence "tree" in every respect, we must pass through the particular, it remains at least equally true that the elucidation of essence and richness of essence is contingent on the radicalness with which we represent and know the universal essence "tree," which in this case means the essence "plant," which in turn means the essence "living things" and "life." Unless we are guided by a developed knowledge of tree-ness, which is manifestly determined from out of itself and its essential ground, we can look over thousands and thousands of trees in vain—we shall not see the tree for the trees.

Now, precisely in regard to "being," one might reply that since it is the most universal of concepts our representation cannot rise from it to anything higher. In dealing with this supreme and most universal concept reference to what is subsumed "under" it not only is advisable but is the only hope of overcoming its emptiness.

Striking as this argument may seem, it is false. Here let us give two reasons:

1. It is in general open to question whether the universality of being is a universality of genus. Aristotle already suspected this. Consequently it remains questionable whether an individual being can ever be regarded as an example of being, in the same way that oak is an example of "tree as such." It is doubtful whether the modes of being (being as nature, being as history) represent "species" in the "genus" being.

2. The word "being" is indeed a universal name and seemingly a word among others. But this appearance is deceptive. The name and what it names are unique. For this reason any illustration by examples is a distortion: in this case every example proves not too much but too little. We have pointed out above that we must know in advance what "tree" means in order to be able to seek and find the particulars: the tree species and the individual trees. This is still truer of being. Supreme and incomparable is the necessity that we understand the word "being" beforehand. Hence it does not follow from the "universality" of "being" in relation to all essents that we must hasten to turn away from it, toward the particular; no, what follows is just the opposite, that we should persevere with being and raise the uniqueness of this name and what it names to the level of knowledge.

Over against the fact that the meaning of the word "being" remains an indeterminate vapor for us, the fact that we understand being and differentiate it with certainty from nonbeing is not just another, second fact; rather, the two belong together, they are one. Meanwhile this one has altogether lost the character of a fact for us. We do not find it *also* given among many other facts. Instead we begin to suspect that some process is at work in what we have hitherto regarded as a mere fact. And the nature of this process excepts it from other "occurrences."

But before we resume our endeavor to find out what process is at work in this fact, let us make one last attempt to take it as something familiar and indifferent. Let us assume that this fact does not exist. Let us suppose that this indeterminate meaning of being does not exist and that we also do not understand what this meaning means. What then? Would there merely be a noun and a verb less in our language? No. *There would be no language at all.* No essent *as such* would disclose itself in words, it would no longer be possible to invoke it and speak about it in words. For to speak of an essent as such includes: to understand it in advance as an essent, that is, to understand its being. Assuming that we did not understand being at all, assuming that the word "being" did not even have its vaporous meaning, there would not be a single word. We ourselves could never be *speakers*. Altogether we could not be as we are. For to be a man is to speak. Man says yes and no only because in his profound essence he is a speaker, *the* speaker. That is his distinction and at the same time his burden. It distinguishes him from stones, plants, animals, but also from the gods. Even if we had a thousand eyes and a thousand ears, a thousand hands and many other senses and organs, if our essence did not include the power of language, all essents would be closed to us, the essent that we ourselves are no less than the essent that we are not.

A review of our discussion up to this point discloses the following situation: by setting down as a fact this (hitherto nameless) assumption, i.e. that being is for us an empty word of vaporous meaning, we depreciated it and deprived it of its proper rank. For our being-there, indeed, our understanding of being, even though indefinite, has the highest rank, since therein is revealed a power in which the essential possibility of our being-there is grounded. This is not a fact among other facts but something to which the highest rank should be accorded, provided that our being-there, which is always a historical being-there, does not remain indifferent to us. Yet even in order that our being-there should remain for us an indifferent essent, we should have to understand being. Without this understanding we should not even be able to say no to our being-there.

It is only by appreciating this pre-eminence of the understanding of being that we preserve it in its rank. In what way can we appreciate this rank, maintain it in its dignity? This we cannot decide arbitrarily.

Because the understanding of being resides first and foremost in a vague, indefinite meaning, and yet remains certain and definite; because, accordingly, the understanding of being, with all its rank, remains obscure, confused, and hidden, it must be elucidated, disentangled, and torn from its concealment. This can be done only if we inquire *about* this understanding of being which we at first accepted as a mere fact—if we put it in question.

Questioning is the authentic and proper and only way of appreciating what by its supreme rank holds our existence in its power. Hence no question is more worthy of being asked than that of our understanding of being, unless it be that of being itself. The more authentic our questioning, the more immediately and steadfastly we dwell on the most questionable of all questions, namely the circumstance that we understand being quite indefinitely and yet with supreme definiteness.

We understand the word "being" and with it all its inflections, even though it looks as though this understanding remained indefinite. Regarding what we understand, regarding what in *some* way *opens* itself to us in understanding, we say: it has a meaning. Insofar as it is in any way understood, being has a meaning. To experience and understand being as the most worthy of problems, to inquire specially after being, means then nothing other than to ask after the meaning of being.

In *Sein und Zeit* the question of the meaning of being is raised and developed *as a question* for the first time in the history of philosophy. It is also stated and explained in detail what is meant by meaning (namely the disclosure of being, not only of the essent as such; see *Sein und Zeit*, §§ 32, 44, 65).

Why may we no longer call what we have just mentioned a fact? Why was this term misleading from the very start? Because this circumstance that we understand being does not just occur among other circumstances in our lives, as, for example, the circumstance that we possess ear lobes of such and such form. Instead of these ear lobes, some other structure might serve as part of our hearing organ. That we understand being is not only real; it is also necessary. Without such a disclosure of being we could not be "the human race." To be sure, it is not absolutely necessary that we should be. There is the pure possibility that man might not be at all. After all there was a time when man was not. But strictly speaking we cannot say: There was a time when man *was* not. At all *times* man was and is and will be, because time produces itself only insofar as man is. There is no time when man was not, not because man was from all eternity and will be for all eternity but because time is not eternity and time fashions itself into a time only as a human, historical being-there. But a necessary condition for his being-there is that he understand being. Insofar as this is necessary, man is historically real. Therefore we understand being and not only, as it may appear at first sight, in the manner of the vague meaning of the word. No, the determinateness with which we understand the indeterminate meaning can be unambiguously delimited, and not after the fact, but as a determinateness which, unbeknownst to us, governs us from out of our very foundations. In order to show this, we start again from the word "being." But here it should be recalled that, in line with the basic metaphysical question set forth in the beginning, we take the word in the widest sense: it finds its limit only at nothing. Everything that is not simply nothing *is*, and for us even nothing "belongs" to "being."

In the present discussion we have taken a decisive step. In a lecture everything depends on such steps. Occasional questions that have been submitted to me about this lecture have shown me over and over again that most people listen in the wrong direction and become entangled in details. True, even in lectures on the special sciences, it is the context that counts. But for the sciences the context is determined directly by the object, which for the sciences is always in some way present. For philosophy on the other hand, the object is not present; what is more, philosophy has no object to begin with. It is a process which must at all times achieve being (in *its* appropriate manifestness) anew. Only in this process can philosophical truth disclose itself. For this reason it is crucial that the listener should take the different steps in the process after and with the lecturer.

What step have we taken? What step must we take over and over again?

First we considered the following proposition as a fact: The word "being" has a vague meaning; it is almost an empty word. Closer discussion of this fact revealed: the vagueness of this meaning finds its explanation: 1) in the blurring characteristic of the infinitive, 2) in the mixture into which all three of the original stem meanings entered.

We designated the fact thus explained as the unshaken point of departure of all the traditional metaphysical questioning about "being." It starts from the *essent* and is oriented toward it. It does *not* start from being and does not enter into the questionable nature of *its* manifestness. Because the meaning and concept of "being" have supreme universality, meta-physics as "physics" cannot go higher to define them more closely. It has only one way left, from the universal to the particular essent. In this way, it is true, it fills in the emptiness of the concept of being, namely with the essents. Yet the admonition "Away from being; go to the particular essents," shows that metaphysics is mocking itself without knowing it.

For the much vaunted particular essent can only disclose itself as such insofar as we already understand being in *its* essence.

Some light has been thrown on this essence. But it has not yet been drawn into the area of questioning.

Now let us recall the question we asked in the beginning: Is "being" only an empty word? Or are being and the asking of the question of being the crux of the spiritual history of the West?

Is being merely the last cloudy streak of evaporating reality; is the only possible attitude for us to let it evaporate into complete indifference? Or is being the worthiest of all questions?

Thus inquiring, we take the decisive step from an indifferent fact, from the supposed meaninglessness of the word "being," to the supremely problematic phenomenon that being necessarily discloses itself in our understanding.

The seemingly unshakable bald fact so blindly trusted by meta-physics has been shaken.

Thus far in our inquiry about being we have striven primarily to grasp the word according to its form and meaning. Now it becomes clear that the question of being is not a matter of grammar and etymology. If in spite of this we again take language as our starting point, a special status must, here and in general, be accorded to the relation between being and language.

Ordinarily language, the word, is regarded as an expression of experience, which follows in the wake of experience. Insofar as things and occurrences are experienced in these experiences, language is indeed an expression, a copy as it were, of the experienced essent. The word "watch" for example, permits the well-known threefold differentiation; it may be considered: 1) in respect to the audible and visible form of the word; 2) in respect to the meaning of what we represent in connection with it; 3) in respect to the thing: a watch, this particular watch. Here 1) is a sign for 2) and 2) is an indication of 3).

Thus presumably we may do the same with the word "being," that is, differentiate word form, word meaning, and thing. And we easily see that as long as we dwell on the word form and its meaning we have not yet come to the "thing," to the point as it were of our question about being. If we expect to apprehend the essence of the thing, here of being, by mere discussions of the word and its meaning, we shall obviously be making a mistake. We are hardly likely to fall into such an error, for it would be like trying to investigate the phenomena of motion in the ether, in matter, to determine the atomic processes, by grammatical studies of the words "atom" and "ether" rather than by the necessary physical experiments.

Thus, regardless of whether the word "being" has an indefinite or a definite meaning, or, as we have seen, both at once, we must, beyond the factor of signification, come to the thing itself. But is "being" a thing like watches, houses, or any essent whatsoever? We have already run into the troublesome circumstance that being is not an essent and not an essent component of the essent. The being of the building over there is not just *another* thing of the *same* kind as the roof or the cellar. No thing corresponds to the word and the meaning "being."

But from this we cannot infer that being consists only of the word and its meaning. The meaning of the word does not, as a meaning, constitute the essence of being. If it did, this would mean that the being of the essent, of our building for example, consisted in a word meaning. It would obviously be absurd to suppose any such thing. No; in the word "being," in its meaning, we pass through word and meaning and aim at being itself, except that it is not a thing, if by thing we mean something that is in any way essent.

From this it follows that in respect to the word "being" and its inflections, and all the words lying within its sphere, word and meaning are more profoundly dependent on what is meant than in the case of other words. But the converse is also true. Being itself is dependent on the word in a totally different and more fundamental sense than any essent.

In each of its inflections the word "being" bears an essentially different relation to being itself from that of all other nouns and verbs of the language to the essent that is expressed in them.

From this it may be inferred that the foregoing considerations regarding the word "being" are of greater import than other remarks about words and linguistic usage in connection with things of any sort whatsoever. But even though we have here a very special and fundamental connection between word, meaning, and being, in which so to speak the thing is missing, we must not suppose that it will be possible to sift out the essence of being itself from a characterization of the word meaning.

After regarding the peculiar phenomenon that the question of being remains intimately bound up with the question of the word, we resume the course of our questioning. We must show that our understanding of being has a determinateness of its own, ordained by being itself. Now when we start from discourse about being, because in a certain sense we are always and essentially compelled to take this as our starting point, we shall try to bear in mind the being itself of which the discourse speaks. We select a simple and familiar and almost careless kind of discourse where being is uttered in a word form whose use is so frequent that we scarcely notice it.

We say: "God is." "The earth is." "The lecture is in the auditorium." "This man is from Swabia." "The cup is of silver." "The peasant is to the fields." "The book is mine." "Red is the port side." "There is famine in Russia." "The enemy is in retreat." "The plant louse is in the vineyard." "The dog is in the garden." "Über allen Gipfeln/ ist Ruh."

In each case the "is" is meant differently. Of this we may easily convince ourselves, particularly if we take this utterance of the "is" as it really occurs, i.e. spoken in each case out of a definite situation, purpose, and mood, and not as a mere sentence or stale example in a grammar.

"God is"; he is *really present*. "The earth is"; i.e. we experience and believe it to be *permanently there*; "the lecture is in the auditorium"; i.e. it *takes place*. "The man is from Swabia"; i.e. *he comes from there*. "The cup is of silver"; i.e. *it is made of* . . . "The peasant is to the fields"; he has gone to the fields and is *staying there*. "The book is mine"; i.e. it *belongs to me*. "Red is the port side"; i.e. it *stands for* port. "The dog is in the garden"; i.e. he is *running around* the garden. "Over all the summits/ is rest"; that is to say ??? Does the "is" in these lines mean is situated, is present, takes place, abides? None of these will fit. And yet it is the same simple "is." Or does the verse mean: Over all the summits peace *prevails*, as quiet prevails in a classroom? No, that won't do either. Or perhaps: Over all the summits lies rest—or holds sway? That seems better, but it also misses the mark.

"Über allen Gipfeln/ ist Ruh"; the "ist" cannot be paraphrased and yet it is only this "ist," tossed off in those few lines that Goethe wrote in pencil on the window frame of a mountain hut near Ilmenau (cf. his letter to Zelter of September 4, 1831). Strange how we hesitate in our attempted paraphrase and in the end drop it altogether, not because the understanding is too complicated or difficult but because the line is spoken so simply, even more simply and uniquely than any of the other familiar "ises" that are forever dropping unnoticed into our everyday speech.

Regardless of how we interpret these examples, they show one thing clearly: in the "is" being discloses itself to us in a diversity of ways. Once again the assertion, which at first seemed plausible, that being is an empty word is shown—more compellingly than ever—to be untrue.

But—it might here be argued—granted that the "is" is meant in many different ways. This springs not from the "is" itself but solely from the diverse content of the statements, each of which applies to a different essent: God, earth, cup, peasant, book, famine, peace over the summits. Only because the "is" remains intrinsically indeterminate and devoid of meaning can it lie ready for such diverse uses, can it fulfill and determine itself "as the circumstances require." The diversity of definite meanings cited above proves the contrary of what was to be shown. It offers the clearest proof that in order to be determinable being must be indeterminate.

What shall we say in reply to this? Here we come into the area of a decisive question: Does the "is" become manifold on the strength of the content brought to it in the different sentences, i.e. by virtue of the realms concerning which they speak, or does the "is," i.e. being, conceal within itself the multiplicity whose concentration <Faltung, lit. "folding" in contrast to "unfolding"> enables us to make manifold essents accessible to us, each *as* it is? For the present I merely throw out this question. We are not yet equipped to develop it further. What cannot be argued away—and this is the only point we wish to make for the moment—is that the "is" in our discourse manifests a rich diversity of meanings. In each one of these meanings we say the "is" without, either before or afterward, effecting a special exegesis of "is," let alone reflecting on being. The "is," meant now so and now so, simply wells up as we speak. Yet the diversity of its meanings is not arbitrary diversity. Let us now convince ourselves of this.

We run through the different meanings that we have interpreted by paraphrase. The "being" uttered in "is" means: really present, permanently there, takes place, come from, belongs to, is made of, stays, succumbs to, stands for, has entered upon, has appeared. It remains difficult, perhaps impossible, because contrary to the essence of being, to pick out a common meaning as a universal generic concept under which all these modes of "is" might be classified as species. Yet a single determinate trait runs through them all. It directs our contemplation of "being" to a definite horizon, in which understanding is effected. The limitation of the meaning of "being" remains within the sphere of actuality and presence, of permanence and duration, of abiding and occurrence.

All this points in the direction of what we encountered when we characterized the Greek experience and interpretation of being. If we retain the usual interpretation of being, the word "being" takes its meaning from the unity and determinateness of the horizon which guided our understanding. In short: we understand the verbal substantive "Sein" through the infinitive, which in turn is related to the "is" and its diversity that we have described. The definite and particular verb form "is," the *third person singular of the present indicative*, has here a pre-eminent rank. We understand "being" not in regard to the "thou art," "you are," "I am," or "they would be," though all of these, just as much as "is," represent verbal inflections of "to be." "To be" <sein> is for us the infinitive of "is." And involuntarily, almost as though nothing else were possible, we explain the infinitive "to be" to ourselves through the "is."

Accordingly, "being" has the meaning indicated above, recalling the Greek view of the essence of being, hence a determinateness which has not just dropped on us accidentally from somewhere but has dominated our historical being-there since antiquity. At one stroke our search for the definition of the meaning of the word "being" becomes explicitly what it is, namely a reflection on the source of our hidden history. The question "How does it stand with being?" must itself remain within the history of being if it is, in turn, to unfold and preserve its own historical import. In pursuing it we, in turn, shall hold to the discourse of being.

NOTE

From Martin Heidegger, *An Introduction to Metaphysics*, trans. Ralph Manheim, 1959. Reprinted by permission of Yale University Press, New Haven, Conn.

13 RUSSELL

Russell is an admitted Platonic realist in the most literal sense of the term. It is important to note that he stresses the importance of universals expressed by verbs and prepositions over and above those named by substantives and adjectives. Universals of the latter type are qualities. Those of the former class are relations. Whereas one may not be able to prove that there are qualities, one can prove that there must be relations. Furthermore, since relations are essential components of facts, universals are not mental constructs. They are as real as the facts of which they are a part. However, they exist in a timeless manner known as subsistence.

The Problems of Philosophy

THE WORLD OF UNIVERSALS

At the end of the preceding chapter we saw that such entities as relations appear to have a being which is in some way different from that of physical objects, and also different from that of minds and from that of sense data. In the present chapter we have to consider what is the nature of this kind of being, and also what objects there are that have this kind of being. We will begin with the latter question.

The problem with which we are now concerned is a very old one, since it was brought into philosophy by Plato. Plato's 'theory of ideas' is an attempt to solve this very problem, and in my opinion it is one of the most successful attempts hitherto made. The theory to be advocated in what follows is largely Plato's, with merely such modifications as time has shown to be necessary.

The way the problem arose for Plato was more or less as follows, Let us consider, say, such a notion as justice. If we ask ourselves what justice is, it is natural to proceed by considering this, that, and the other just act, with a view to discovering what they have in common. They must all, in some sense, partake of a common nature, which will be found in whatever is just and in nothing else. This common nature, in virtue of which they are all just, will be justice itself, the pure essence the admixture of which with facts of ordinary life produces the multiplicity of just acts. Similarly with any other word which may be applicable to common facts, such as 'whiteness' for example. The word will be applicable to a number of particular things because they all participate in a common nature or essence. This pure essence is what Plato calls an 'idea' or 'form'. (It must not be supposed that 'ideas', in

114

his sense, exist in minds, though they may be apprehended by minds.) The 'idea' *justice* is not identical with anything that is just: it is something other than particular things, which particular things partake of. Not being particular, it cannot itself exist in the world of sense. Moreover it is not fleeting or changeable like the things of sense: it is eternally itself, immutable and indestructible.

Thus Plato is led to a supra-sensible world, more real than the common world of sense, the unchangeable world of ideas, which alone gives to the world of sense whatever pale reflection of reality may belong to it. The truly real world, for Plato, is the world of ideas; for whatever we may attempt to say about things in the world of sense, we can only succeed in saying that they participate in such and such ideas, which, therefore, constitute all their character. Hence it is easy to pass on into a mysticism. We may hope, in a mystic illumination, to *see* the ideas as we see objects of sense; and we may imagine that the ideas exist in heaven. These mystical developments are very natural, but the basis of the theory is in logic, and it is as based in logic that we have to consider it.

The word 'idea' has acquired, in the course of time, many associations which are quite misleading when applied to Plato's 'ideas'. We shall therefore use the word 'universal' instead of the word 'idea', to describe what Plato meant. The essence of the sort of entity that Plato meant is that it is opposed to the particular things that are given in sensation. We speak of whatever is given in sensation, or is of the same nature as things given in sensation, as a *particular*; by opposition to this, a *universal* will be anything which may be shared by many particulars, and has those characteristics which, as we saw, distinguish justice and whiteness from just acts and white things.

When we examine common words, we find that, broadly speaking, proper names stand for particulars, while other substantives, adjectives, prepositions, and verbs stand for universals. Pronouns stand for particulars, but are ambiguous: it is only by the context or the circumstances that we know what particulars they stand for. The word 'now' stands for a particular, namely the present moment; but like pronouns, it stands for an ambiguous particular, because the present is always changing.

It will be seen that no sentence can be made up without at least one word which denotes a universal. The nearest approach would be some such statement as 'I like this'. But even here the word 'like' denotes a universal, for I may like other things, and other people may like things. Thus all truths involve universals, and all knowledge of truths involves acquaintance with universals.

Seeing that nearly all the words to be found in the dictionary stand for universals, it is strange that hardly anybody except students of philosophy ever realizes that there are such entities as universals. We do not naturally dwell upon those words in a sentence which do not stand for particulars; and if we are forced to dwell upon a word which stands for a universal, we naturally think of it as standing for some one of the particulars that come under the universal. When, for example, we hear the sentence, 'Charles I's head was cut off', we may naturally enough think of Charles I, of Charles I's head, and of the operation of cutting off *his* head, which are all particulars; but we do not naturally dwell upon what is meant by the word 'head' or the word 'cut', which is a universal. We feel such words to be incomplete and insubstantial; they seem to demand a context before anything can be done with them. Hence we succeed in avoiding all notice of universals as such, until the study of philosophy forces them upon our attention.

Even among philosophers, we may say, broadly, that only those universals which are named by adjectives or substantives have been much or often recognized, while those named by verbs and prepositions have been usually overlooked. This omission has had a very great effect upon philosophy; it is hardly too much to say that most metaphysics, since Spinoza, has been largely determined by it. The way this has occurred is, in outline, as follows: Speaking generally, adjectives and common nouns express qualities or properties of single things, whereas prepositions and verbs tend to express relations between two or more things. Thus the neglect of prepositions and verbs led to the belief that every proposition can be regarded as attributing a property to a single thing, rather than as expressing a relation between two or more things. Hence it was supposed that, ultimately, there can be no such entities as relations between things. Hence either there can be only one thing in the universe, or, if there are many things, they cannot possibly interact in any way, since any interaction would be a relation, and relations are impossible.

The first of these views, advocated by Spinoza and held in our own day by Bradley and many other philosophers, is called *monism*; the second, advocated by Leibniz but not very common nowadays, is called *monadism*, because each of the isolated things is called a *monad*. Both these opposing philosophies, interesting as they are, result, in my opinion, from an undue attention to one sort of universals, namely the sort represented by adjectives and substantives rather than by verbs and prepositions.

As a matter of fact, if any one were anxious to deny altogether that there are such things as universals, we should find that we cannot strictly prove that there are such entities as *qualities*, i.e. the universals represented by adjectives and substantives, whereas we can prove that there must be *relations*, i.e. the sort of universals generally represented by verbs and prepositions. Let us take in illustration the universal *whiteness*. If we believe that there is such a universal, we shall say that things are white because they have the quality of whiteness. This view, however, was strenuously denied by Berkeley and Hume, who have been followed in this by later empiricists. The form which their denial took was to deny that there are such things as 'abstract ideas'. When we want to think of whiteness, they said, we form an image of some particular white thing, and reason concerning this particular, taking care not to deduce anything concerning it which we cannot see to be equally true of any other white thing. As an account of our actual mental processes, this is no doubt largely true. In geometry, for example, when we wish to prove something about all triangles, we draw a particular triangle and reason about it, taking care not to use any characteristic which it does not share with other triangles. The beginner, in order to avoid error, often finds it useful to draw several triangles, as unlike each other as possible, in order to make sure that his reasoning is equally applicable to all of them. But a difficulty emerges as soon as we ask ourselves how we know that a thing is white or a triangle. If we wish to avoid the universals *whiteness* and *triangularity*, we shall choose some particular patch of white or some particular triangle, and say that anything is white or a triangle if it has the right sort of resemblance to our chosen particular. But then the resemblance required will have to be a universal. Since there are many white things, the resemblance must hold between many pairs of particular white things; and this is the characteristic of a universal. It will be useless to say that there is a different resemblance for each pair, for then we shall have to say that these resemblances resemble each other, and thus at last we shall be forced to admit resemblance as a universal. The relation of resemblance, therefore, must be a true universal. And having been forced to admit this universal, we find that it is no longer worth while to invent difficult and unplausible theories to avoid the admission of such universals as whiteness and triangularity.

Berkeley and Hume failed to perceive this refutation of their rejection of 'abstract ideas', because, like their adversaries, they only thought of *qualities*, and altogether ignored *relations* as universals. We have therefore here another respect in which the rationalists appear to have been in the right as against the empiricists, although, owing to the neglect or denial of relations, the deductions made by rationalists were, if anything, more apt to be mistaken than those made by empiricists.

Having now seen that there must be such entities as universals, the next point to be proved is that their being is not merely mental. By this is meant that whatever being belongs to them is independent of their being thought of or in any way apprehended by minds. We have already touched on this subject at the end of the preceding chapter, but we must now consider more fully what sort of being it is that belongs to universals.

Consider such a proposition as 'Edinburgh is north of London'. Here we have a relation between two places, and it seems plain that the relation subsists independently of our knowledge of it. When we come to know that Edinburgh is north of London, we come to know something which has to do only with Edinburgh and London: we do not cause the truth of the proposition by coming to know it, on the contrary we merely apprehend a fact which was there before we knew it. The part of the earth's surface where

Edinburgh stands would be north of the part where London stands, even if there were no human being to know about north and south, and even if there were no minds at all in the universe. This is, of course, denied by many philosophers, either for Berkeley's reasons or for Kant's. But we have already considered these reasons, and decided that they are inadequate. We may therefore now assume it to be true that nothing mental is presupposed in the fact that Edinburgh is north of London. But this fact involves the relation 'north of', which is a universal; and it would be impossible for the whole fact to involve nothing mental if the relation 'north of', which is a constituent part of the fact, did involve anything mental. Hence we must admit that the relation, like the terms it relates, is not dependent upon thought, but belongs to the independent world which thought apprehends but does not create.

This conclusion, however, is met by the difficulty that the relation 'north of' does not seem to *exist* in the same sense in which Edinburgh and London exist. If we ask 'Where and when does this relation exist?' the answer must be 'Nowhere and nowhen'. There is no place or time where we can find the relation 'north of'. It does not exist in Edinburgh any more than in London, for it relates the two and is neutral as between them. Nor can we say that it exists at any particular time. Now everything that can be apprehended by the senses or by introspection exists at some particular time. Hence the relation 'north of' is radically different from such things. It is neither in space nor in time, neither material nor mental; yet it is something.

It is largely the very peculiar kind of being that belongs to universals which has led many people to suppose that they are really mental. We can think *of* a universal, and our thinking then exists in a perfectly ordinary sense, like any other mental act. Suppose, for example, that we are thinking of whiteness. Then *in one sense* it may be said that whiteness is 'in our mind'. We have here the same ambiguity as we noted in discussing Berkeley in Chapter IV. In the strict sense, it is not whiteness that is in our mind, but the act of thinking of whiteness. The connected ambiguity in the word 'idea', which we noted at the same time, also causes confusion here. In one sense of this word, namely the sense in which it denotes the *object* of an act of thought, whiteness is an 'idea'. Hence, if the ambiguity is not guarded against, we may come to think that whiteness is an 'idea' in the other sense, i.e. an act of thought; and thus we come to think that whiteness is mental. But in so thinking, we rob it of its essential quality of universality. One man's act of thought is necessarily a different thing from another man's; one man's act of thought at one time is necessarily a different thing from the same man's act of thought at another time. Hence, if whiteness were the thought as opposed to its object, no two different men could think of it, and no one man could think of it twice. That which many different thoughts of whiteness have in common is their *object*, and this object is different from all of them. Thus universals are not thoughts, though when known they are the objects of thoughts.

We shall find it convenient only to speak of things *existing* when they are in time, that is to say when we can point to some time *at* which they exist (not excluding the possibility of their existing at all times). Thus thoughts and feelings, minds and physical objects *exist*. But universals do not exist in this sense; we shall say that they *subsist* or *have being*, where 'being' is opposed to 'existence' as being timeless. The world of universals, therefore, may also be described as the world of being. The world of being is unchangeable, rigid, exact, delightful to the mathematician, the logician, the builder of metaphysical systems, and all who love perfection more than life. The world of existence is fleeting, vague, without sharp boundaries, without any clear plan or arrangement, but it contains all thoughts and feelings, all the data of sense, and all physical objects, everything that can do either good or harm, everything that makes any difference to the value of life and the world. According to our temperaments, we shall prefer the contemplation of the one or of the other. The one we do not prefer will probably seem to us a pale shadow of the one we prefer, and hardly worthy to be regarded as in any sense real. But the truth is that both have the same claim on our impartial attention, both are real, and both are important to the metaphysician. Indeed no sooner have we distinguished the two worlds than it becomes necessary to consider their relations.

NOTE

From Bertrand Russell, *The Problems of Philosophy*. Originally published by Clarendon Press, London, 1912. Reprinted by permission of Oxford University Press.

14 RAMSEY

Russell argues that there is a fundamental difference between particulars and universals. This difference is verified by the feeling one gets by comparing the referent of a (particular) subject, for example, Socrates, and the referent of a (universal) predicate, for example, wise. In the proposition "Socrates is wise" one understands the subject to be an independent entity, whereas the predicate is incomplete because it is a quality of something else. Ramsey argues that this observation demonstrates no fundamental difference between particulars and universals because the proposition "wisdom is a characteristic of Socrates" has the same meaning as the proposition "Socrates is wise." However, in the former proposition, wisdom functions as the subject. The difference, Ramsey concludes, is not one of logical significance. It is a subjective difference and is due to what a person wants to emphasize; in this case either Socrates or wisdom. Consequently, the difference depends upon human interest and needs.

The comparative convenience of the functional notation of the second edition of Russell's *Principia Mathematica* justifies the conclusion that it corresponds most closely to the facts, that there is a genuine difference between particulars and universals. Ramsey observes, however, that within the functional notation of the *Principia* a variable, for example, ϕ, can (1) stand for a name (corresponding to a particular) or (2) function as an incomplete symbol (corresponding to a universal). In either case, the symbol ϕ impartially refers to classes and in that sense fails to distinguish between (1) and (2). In other words, the theory fails to distinguish between particulars and universals. If, as Russell maintained, his notation most closely corresponds to the facts, then there must be no difference between particulars and universals—contrary to what Russell initially maintained.

Universals

The purpose of this paper is to consider whether there is a fundamental division of objects into two classes, particulars and universals. This question was discussed by Mr. Russell in a paper printed in the Aristotelian Society's proceedings for 1911. His conclusion that the distinction was ultimate, was based upon two familiar arguments, directed against the two obvious methods of abolishing the distinction by holding either that universals are collections of particulars, or that particulars are collections of their qualities. These arguments, perfectly sound as far as they go, do not however seem to me to settle the whole question. The first, which appears again in "The Problems of Philosophy," shows as against the nominalists that such a proposition as "This sensedatum is white" must have as one constituent something, such as whiteness or similarity, which is not of the same logical type as the sensedatum itself. The second argument, also briefly expounded in McTaggart's "Nature of Existence," proves that a man cannot be identified with the sum of his qualities. But although a man cannot be one of his own qualities, that is no reason why he should not be a quality of something else. In fact, material objects are described by Dr. Whitehead as "true Aristotelian adjectives"; so that we cannot regard these two arguments as rendering the distinction between particular and universal, secure against all criticism.

What then, I propose to ask, is the difference between a particular and a universal? What can we say about one which will not also be true of the other? If we follow Mr. Russell, we shall have to investigate three kinds of distinction, psychological, physical and logical. First we have the difference between a percept and a concept, the objects of two different kinds of mental acts; but this is unlikely to be a distinction of any fundamental importance, since a difference in two mental acts may not correspond to any difference whatever in their objects. Next we have various distinctions between objects based on their relations to space and time; for instance, some objects can only be in one place at a time, others, like the color red, can be in many. Here again, in spite of the importance of the subject, I do not think we can have reached the essence of the matter. For when, for instance, Dr. Whitehead says that a table is an adjective, and Mr. Johnson that it is a substantive, they are not arguing about how many places the table can be in at once, but about its logical nature. And so it is with logical distinctions that our inquiry must mainly deal.

According to Mr. Russell the class of universals is the sum of the class of predicates and the class of relations; but this doctrine has been denied by Dr. Stout. But Dr. Stout has been already sufficiently answered. So I shall only discuss the more usual opinion to which Mr. Russell adheres.

According to him terms are divided into individuals or particulars, qualities and relations, qualities and relations being grouped together as universals; and sometimes qualities are even included among relations as one-termed relations in distinction from two- , three- or many-termed relations. Mr. Johnson also divides terms into substantives and adjectives, including relations as transitive adjectives; and he regards the distinction between substantive and adjective as explaining that between particular and universal. But between these authorities, who agree so far, there is still an important difference. Mr. Johnson holds that although the nature of a substantive is such that it can only function in a proposition as subject and never as predicate, yet an adjective can function either as predicate, or as a subject of which a secondary adjective can be predicated. For example in "unpunctuality is a fault" the subject is itself an adjective, the quality of unpunctuality. There is thus a want of symmetry between substantives and adjectives, for while a predicate must be an adjective, a subject may be either a substantive or an adjective, and we must define a substantive as a term which can only be a subject, never a predicate.

Mr. Russell, on the other hand, in his lectures on Logical Atomism,[1] has denied this. He says that about an adjective there is something incomplete, some suggestion of the form of a proposition; so that the adjective symbol can never stand alone or be the subject of a proposition, but must be completed into a proposition in which it is the predicate. Thus, he says, the appropriate symbol for redness is not the word "red" but the function "x is red," and red can only come into a proposition through the values of this function. So, Mr. Russell would say, "unpunctuality is a fault" really means something like "for all x, if x is unpunctual, x is reprehensible"; and the adjective unpunctuality is not the subject of the proposition but only comes into it as the predicate of those of its parts which are of the form "x is unpunctual". This doctrine is the basis of new work in the second edition of *Principia Mathematica*.

Neither of these theories seems entirely satisfactory, although neither could be disproved. Mr. Russell's view does, indeed, involve difficulties in connection with our cognitive relations to universals, for which reason it was rejected in the first edition of *Principia*; but these difficulties seem to me, as now to Mr. Russell, by no means insurmountable. But I could not discuss them here without embarking upon innumerable questions irrelevant to the main points which I wish to make. Neither theory, then, can be disproved, but to both objections can be raised which may seem to have some force. For instance, Mr. Russell urges that a relation between two terms cannot be a third term, which comes between them, for then it would not be a relation at all, and the only genuinely relational element would consist in the connections between this new term and the two original terms. This is the kind of consideration from which Mr. Bradley deduced his infinite regress, of which Mr. Russell apparently now approves. Mr. Johnson might reply that for him the connectional or structural element is not the relation but the characterizing and coupling ties; but these ties remain most mysterious objects. It might also be objected that Mr. Johnson does not make particulars and universals different enough, or take into account the peculiar incompleteness of adjectives which appears in the possibility of prefixing to them the auxiliary "being"; "being red," "being a man," do not seem real things like a chair and a carpet. Against Mr. Russell it might be asked how there can be such objects as his universals, which contain the form of a proposition and so are incomplete. In a sense, it might be urged, all objects are incomplete; they cannot occur in facts except in conjunction with other objects, and contain the forms of propositions of which they are constituents. In what way do universals do this more than anything else?

Evidently, however, none of these arguments are really decisive, and the position is extremely unsatisfactory to any one with real curiosity about such a fundamental question. In such cases it is a heuristic maxim that the truth lies not in one of the two disputed views but in some third possibility which has not yet been thought of, which we can only discover by rejecting something assumed as obvious by both the disputants.

Both the disputed theories make an important assumption, which, to my mind, has only to be questioned to be doubted. They assume a fundamental antithesis between subject and predicate, that if a proposition consists of two terms copulated, these two terms must be functioning in different ways, one as subject, the other as predicate. Thus in "Socrates is wise," Socrates is the subject, wisdom the predicate. But suppose we turn the proposition round and say, "wisdom is a characteristic of Socrates," then wisdom formerly the predicate is now the subject. Now it seems to me as clear as anything can be in philosophy, that the two sentences "Socrates is wise," "wisdom is a characteristic of Socrates" assert the same fact and express the same proposition. They are not, of course, the same sentence, but they have the same meaning, just as two sentences in two different languages can have the same meaning. Which sentence we use is a matter either of literary style, or of the point of view from which we approach the fact. If the center of our interest is Socrates we say "Socrates is wise," if we are discussing wisdom we may say "wisdom is a characteristic of Socrates"; but whichever we say we mean the same thing. Now of one of these sentences "Socrates" is the subject, of the other "wisdom"; and so which of the two is subject, which predicate, depends upon what particular sentence we use to express our proposition, and has nothing to do with the logical nature of Socrates or wisdom, but is a matter entirely for grammarians. In the same way, with a sufficiently elastic language any proposition can be so expressed that any of its terms is the subject. Hence there is no essential distinction between the subject of a proposition and its predicate, and no fundamental classification of objects can be based upon such a distinction.

I do not claim that the above argument is immediately conclusive; what I claim is that it throws doubt upon the whole basis of the distinction between particular and universal as deduced from that between subject and predicate, and that the question requires a new examination. It is a point which has often been made by Mr. Russell, that philosophers are very liable to be misled by the subject-predicate construction of our language. They have supposed that all propositions must be of the subject-predicate form, and so have been led to deny the existence of relations. I shall argue that nearly all philosophers, including Mr. Russell himself, have been misled by language in a far more far-reaching way than that; that the whole theory of particulars and universals is due to mistaking for a fundamental characteristic of reality, what is merely a characteristic of language.

Let us, therefore, examine closely this distinction of subject and predicate, and for simplicity let us follow Mr. Johnson and include relations among predicates and their terms among subjects. The first question we have to ask is this; what propositions are they that have a subject or subjects and a predicate? Is this the case with all propositions or only with some? Before, however, we go on to answer this question let us remind ourselves that the task on which we are engaged is not merely one of English grammar; we are not school children analyzing sentences into subject, extension of the subject, complement and so on, but are interested not so much in sentences themselves, as in what they mean, from which we hope to discover the logical nature of reality. Hence we must look for senses of subject and predicate which are not purely grammatical, but have a genuine logical significance.

Let us begin with such a proposition as "Either Socrates is wise, or Plato is foolish". To this, it will probably be agreed, the conception of subject and predicate is inapplicable; it may be applicable to the two parts "Socrates is wise," "Plato is foolish," but the whole "Either Socrates is wise or Plato is foolish" is an alternative proposition and not one with a subject or predicate. But to this someone may make the following objection: In such a proposition we can take any term we please, say Socrates, to be the subject. The predicate will then be "being wise unless Plato is foolish" or the propositional function "$\hat{x}$ is wise, or Plato is foolish". The phrase "being wise unless Plato is foolish" will then stand for a complex universal which is asserted to characterize Socrates. Such a view, though very frequently held, seems to me nevertheless certainly mistaken. In order to make things clearer let us take a simpler case, a proposition of the form "aRb"; then this theory will hold that there are three closely related propositions; one asserts that the relation R holds between the terms a and b, the second asserts the possession by a of the complex property of "having R to b," while the third asserts that b has the complex property that a has R to it. These must be three different propositions because they have different sets of constituents, and yet they are not three propositions, but one proposition, for they all say the same thing, namely that a has R to b. So the theory of complex universals is responsible for an incomprehensible trinity, as senseless as that of theology. This argument can be strengthened by considering the process of definition, which is as follows. For certain purposes "aRb" may be an unnecessarily long symbol, so that it is convenient to shorten it into ϕb. This is done by definition, $\phi x = aRx$, signifying that any symbol of the form ϕx is to be interpreted as meaning what is meant by the corresponding symbol aRx, for which it is an abbreviation. In more complicated cases such an abbreviation is often extremely useful, but it could always be dispensed with if time and paper permitted. The believer in complex universals is now confronted with a dilemma; is "ϕ," thus defined, a name for the complex property of x which consists in a having R to x? If so, then ϕx will be the assertion that x has this property; it will be a subject-predicate proposition whose subject is

x and predicate ϕ; which is not identical with the relational proposition aRx. But as ϕx is by hypothesis defined to be short for aRx this is absurd. For if a definition is not to be interpreted as signifying that the definiendum and definiens have the same meaning, the process of definition becomes unintelligible and we lose all justification for interchanging definiens and definiendum at will, on which depends its whole utility. Suppose on the other hand "ϕ," as defined above, is not a name for the complex property; then how can the complex property ever become an object of our contemplation, and how can we ever speak of it, seeing that "ϕ," its only possible name, is not a name for it at all but short for something else? And then what reason can there be to postulate the existence of this thing?

In spite of this *reductio ad absurdum* of the theory, it may still be worth while to inquire into its origin, and into why it is held by so many people, including formerly myself, without its occurring to them to doubt it. The chief reason for this is I think to be found in linguistic convenience; it gives us one object which is "the meaning" of "ϕ". We often want to talk of "the meaning of 'ϕ'" and it is simpler to suppose that this is a unique object, than to recognize that it is a much more complicated matter, and that "ϕ" has a relation of meaning not to one complex object but to the several simple objects, which are named in its definition. There is, however, another reason why this view is so popular, and that is the imaginary difficulty which would otherwise be felt in the use of a variable propositional function. How, it might be asked, are we to interpret such a statement as "a has all the properties of b," except on the supposition that there are properties? The answer is that it is to be interpreted as being the logical product of all propositions which can be constructed in the following way; take a proposition in which a occurs, say ϕa, change a into b and obtain ϕb, and then form the proposition $\phi b \,.\, \supset \,.\, \phi a$. It is not really quite so simple as that, but a more accurate account of it would involve a lot of tiresome detail, and so be out of place here; and we can take it as a sufficient approximation that "a has all the properties of b" is the joint assertion of all propositions of the form $\phi b \,.\, \supset \,.\, \phi a$, where there is no necessity for ϕ to be the name of a universal, as it is merely the rest of a proposition in which a occurs. Hence the difficulty is entirely imaginary. It may be observed that the same applies to any other case of apparent variables some of whose values are incomplete symbols, and this may explain the tendency to assert that some of Mr. Russell's incomplete symbols are not really incomplete but the names of properties or predicates.

I conclude, therefore, that complex universals are to be rejected; and that such a proposition as "either Socrates is wise or Plato foolish" has neither subject nor predicate. Similar arguments apply to any compound proposition, that is any proposition containing such words as "and," "or," "not," "all," "some"; and hence if we are to find a logical distinction between subject and predicate anywhere it will be in atomic propositions, as Mr. Russell calls them, which could be expressed by sentences containing none of the above words, but only names and perhaps a copula.

The distinction between subject and predicate will then arise from the several names in an atomic proposition functioning in different ways; and if this is not to be a purely grammatical distinction it must correspond to a difference in the functioning of the several objects in an atomic fact, so that what we have primarily to examine is the construction of the atomic fact out of its constituents. About this three views might be suggested; first there is that of Mr. Johnson according to whom the constituents are connected together by what he calls the characterizing tie. The nature of this entity is rather obscure, but I think we can take it as something which is not a constituent of the fact, but represented in language by the copula "is"; and we can describe this theory as holding that the connection is made by a real copula. Next there is the theory of Mr. Russell that the connection is made by one of the constituents; that in every atomic fact there must be one constituent which is in its own nature incomplete or connective and, as it were, holds the other constituents together. This constituent will be a universal, and the others particulars. Lastly there is Mr. Wittgenstein's theory that neither is there a copula, nor one specially connective constituent, but that, as he expresses it, the objects hang one in another like the links of a chain.

From our point of view, it is the second of these theories that demands most attention; for the first and third do not really explain any difference in the mode of functioning of subject and predicate, but leave this a mere dogma. Only on Mr. Russell's theory will there be an intelligible difference between particular and universal, grounded on the necessity for there to be in each fact a copulating term or universal, corresponding to the need for every sentence to have a verb. So it is Mr. Russell's theory that we must first consider.

The great difficulty with this theory lies in understanding how one sort of object can be specially incomplete. There is a sense in which any object is incomplete; namely that it can only occur in a fact by connection with an object or objects of suitable type; just as any name is incomplete, because to form a proposition we have to join to it certain other names of suitable type. As Wittgenstein says: "The thing is independent, in so far as it can occur in all *possible* circumstances, but this form of independence is a form of connection with the atomic fact, a form of dependence. (It is impossible for words to occur in two different ways, alone and in the proposition.)" And Johnson "ultimately a universal means an adjective that may characterize a particular, and a particular means a substantive that may be characterized by a universal." Thus we may admit that "wise" involves the form of a proposition, but so does "Socrates," and it is hard to see any ground for distinguishing between them. This is the substance of Mr. Johnson's criticism, that Mr. Russell will not let the adjective stand alone, and in treating "*s* is *p*" as a function of two variables takes the arguments to be not *s* and *p*, but *s* and "$\hat{x}$ is *p*".

In reply to this criticism Mr. Russell would, I imagine, use two lines of argument whose validity we must examine. The first would dwell on the great convenience in mathematical logic of his functional symbolism, of which he might say there was no explanation except that this symbolism corresponded to reality more closely than any other. His second line of argument would be that everyone can feel a difference between particulars and universals; that the prevalence of nominalism showed that the reality of universals was always suspected, and that this was probably because they did in fact differ from particulars by being less independent, less self-contained. Also that this was the only account of the difference between particulars and universals, which made them really different kinds of objects, as they evidently were, and not merely differently related to us or to our language. For instance, Mr. Johnson describes the particular as presented to thought for its character to be determined in thought, and others might say a particular was what was meant by the grammatical subject of a sentence; and on these views what was particular, what universal would depend on unessential characteristics of our psychology or our language.

Let us take these lines of argument in reverse order, beginning with the felt difference between particular and universal, and postponing the peculiar symbolic convenience of propositional functions. Anyone, it may be said, sees a difference between Socrates and wisdom. Socrates is a real independent entity, wisdom a quality and so essentially a quality of something else. The first thing to remark about this argument, is that it is not really about objects at all. "Socrates is wise" is not an atomic proposition, and the symbols "Socrates" and "wise" are not the names of objects but incomplete symbols. And according to Wittgenstein, with whom I agree, this will be the case with any other instances that may be suggested, since we are not acquainted with any genuine objects or atomic propositions, but merely infer them as presupposed by other propositions. Hence the distinction we feel is one between two sorts of incomplete symbols, or logical constructions, and we cannot infer without further investigation that there is any corresponding distinction between two sorts of names or objects.

We can, I think, easily obtain a clearer idea of the difference between these two sorts of incomplete symbols (Wittgenstein calls them "expressions") typified by "Socrates" and "wise". Let us consider when and why an expression occurs, as it were, as an isolated unit. For instance "*aRb*" does not naturally divide into "*a*" and "*Rb*," and we want to know why anyone should so divide it, and isolate the expression "*Rb*". The answer is that if it were a matter of this proposition alone, there would be no point in dividing it in this way, but that the importance of expressions just arises, as Wittgenstein points out, in connection with generalization. It is not "*aRb*" but

"$(x) . xRb$" which makes Rb prominent. In writing $(x) . xRb$ we use the expression Rb to collect together the set of propositions xRb, which we want to assert to be true; and it is here that the expression Rb is really essential because it is that which is common to this set of propositions. If now we realize that this is the essential use of expressions, we can see at once what is the difference between Socrates and wise. By means of the expression "Socrates" we collect together all the propositions in which it occurs, that is, all the propositions which we should ordinarily say were about Socrates, such as "Socrates is wise," "Socrates is just," "Socrates is neither wise nor just". These propositions are collected together as the values of "ϕ Socrates," where ϕ is a variable.

Now consider the expression "wise"; this we use to collect together the propositions "Socrates is wise," "Plato is wise," and so on, which are values of "x is wise". But this is not the only collection we can use "wise" to form; just as we used "Socrates" to collect all the propositions in which it occurred, we can use "wise" to collect all those in which it occurs, including not only ones like "Socrates is wise" but also ones like "neither Socrates nor Plato is wise," which are not values of "x is wise," but only of the different function "ϕ wise," where ϕ is variable. Thus whereas Socrates gives only one collection of propositions, wise gives two; one analogous to that given by Socrates, namely the collection of all propositions in which wise occurs; and the other a narrower collection of propositions of the form "x is wise".

This is obviously the explanation of the difference we feel between Socrates and wise, which Mr. Russell expresses by saying that with wise you have to bring in the form of a proposition. Since all expressions must be completed to form a proposition, it was previously hard to understand how wise could be more incomplete than Socrates. Now we can see that the reason for this is that whereas with "Socrates" we only have the idea of completing it in any manner into a proposition, with "wise" we have not only this but also an idea of completing it in a special way, giving us not merely any proposition in which wise occurs but one in which it occurs in a particular way, which we may call its occurrence as predicate, as in "Socrates is wise".

What is this difference due to? and is it a real difference at all? That is to say, can we not do with "Socrates" what we do with "wise" and use it to collect a narrower set of propositions than the whole set in which it occurs? Is this impossible? or is it merely that we never in fact do it? These are the questions we must now try to answer. The way to do it would seem to be the following. Suppose we can distinguish among the properties of Socrates a certain subset which we can call qualities; the idea being roughly that only a simple property is a quality. Then we could form in connection with "Socrates" two sets of propositions just as we can in connection with "wise". There would be the wide set of propositions, in which "Socrates" occurs at all, which we say assert properties of Socrates, but also there would be the narrower set which assert qualities of Socrates. Thus supposing justice and wisdom to be qualities, "Socrates is wise," "Socrates is just" would belong to the narrower set and be values of a function "Socrates is q". But "Socrates is neither wise nor just" would not assert a quality of Socrates but only a compound characteristic or property, and would only be a value of the function "ϕ Socrates," not of "Socrates is q".

But although such a distinction between qualities and properties may be logically possible, we do not seem ever to carry it out systematically. Some light may be thrown on this fact by a paragraph in Mr. Johnson's logic in which he argues that whereas "we may properly construct a compound adjective out of simple adjectives, yet the nature of any term functioning as substantive is such that it is impossible to construct a genuine compound substantive". Thus from the two propositions "Socrates is wise," "Socrates is just" we can form the proposition "Neither is Socrates wise, nor is Socrates just" or, for short, "Socrates is neither wise nor just"; which still, according to Mr. Johnson, predicates an adjective of Socrates, is a value of "ϕ Socrates" and would justify "$(\exists\phi) . \phi$ Socrates," or "Socrates has some property". If, on the other hand, we take the two propositions "Socrates is wise," "Plato is wise" and form from them "Neither Socrates is wise nor Plato is wise"; this is not a value of "x is wise" and would not justify "$(\exists x) . x$ is wise," or "someone is wise". So in as much as "Socrates is neither wise nor just" justifies "Socrates has some adjective" we can say that "neither wise nor just" is a compound adjective; but since "Neither Socrates nor Plato is wise" does not justify "something is wise," "neither Socrates nor Plato" cannot be a compound substantive, any more than nobody is a compound man.

If, however, we could form a range of qualities, as opposed to properties, "Socrates is neither wise nor just" would not justify "Socrates has some quality" and "neither wise nor just" would not be a quality. Against this Mr. Johnson says that there is no universally valid criterion by which we can distinguish qualities from other properties; and this is certainly a very plausible contention, when we are talking, as we are now, of qualities and properties of logical constructions such as Socrates. For the distinction is only really clear in connection with genuine objects; then we can say that ϕ represents a quality when ϕa is a two termed atomic proposition, and this would distinguish qualities from other propositional functions or properties. But when the subject a is a logical construction and ϕa a compound proposition of which we do not know the analysis, it is hard to know what would be meant by asking if ϕ were simple, and calling it, if simple, a quality. It would clearly have to be a matter not of absolute but of relative simplicity.

Yet it is easy to see that, in theory, an analogous distinction can certainly be made for incomplete symbols also. Take any incomplete symbol "a"; this will be defined not in isolation but in conjunction with any symbol of a certain sort x. Thus we might define ax to mean aRx. Then this incomplete symbol "a" will give us two ranges of propositions, the range ax obtained by completing it in the way indicated in its definition; and the general range of propositions in which a occurs at all, that is to say all truth functions of the propositions of the preceding range and constant propositions not containing a. Thus in the two famous cases of descriptions and classes, as treated in *Principia Mathematica*, the narrower range will be that in which the description or class has primary occurrence, the wider range that in which it has any sort of occurrence primary or secondary, where the terms "primary" and "secondary" occurrence have the meanings explained in *Principia*. In brief with regard to any incomplete symbol we can distinguish its primary and secondary occurrences, and this is fundamentally the same distinction which we found to be characteristic of the adjective. So that any incomplete symbol is really an adjective, and those which appear substantives only do so in virtue of our failing whether through inability or neglect to distinguish their primary and secondary occurrences. As a practical instance let us take the case of material objects; these we are accustomed to regard as substantives, that is to say we use them to define ranges of propositions in one way only, and make no distinction between their primary and secondary occurrences. At least no one made such a distinction until Dr. Whitehead declared that material objects are adjectives of the events in which they are situated, so that the primary occurrence of a material object A is in a proposition "A is situated in E". From such propositions as this we can construct all other propositions in which A occurs. Thus "A is red" will be "for all E, A is situated in E implies redness is situated in E," in which A has secondary occurrence. So the distinction between primary and secondary occurrence is not merely demonstrated as logically necessary, but for this case effected practically.

The conclusion is that, as regards incomplete symbols, the fundamental distinction is not between substantive and adjective but between primary and secondary occurrence; and that a substantive is simply a logical construction between whose primary and secondary occurrences we fail to distinguish. So that to be a substantive is not an objective but a subjective property, in the sense that it depends not indeed on any one mind but on the common elements in all men's minds and purposes.

This is my first conclusion, which is I think of some importance in the philosophy of nature and of mind, but it is not the conclusion which I most want to stress, and it does not answer the question with which I began my paper. For it is a conclusion about the method and possibility of dividing certain logical constructions into substantives and adjectives, it being in connection with these logical constructions that the idea of substantive and adjective traditionally originated. But the real question at issue is the possibility of dividing not logical constructions but genuine objects into particulars and universals, and to answer this we must go back and pick up the thread of the argument, where we abandoned it for this lengthy digression about logical constructions.

We saw above that the distinction between particular and universal was derived from that between subject and predicate, which we found only to occur in atomic propositions. We then examined the three theories of atomic propositions or rather of atomic facts, Mr. Johnson's theory of a tie, Mr. Russell's that the copulation was performed by universals, of which there must be one and only one in each atomic fact, and Mr. Wittgenstein's that the objects hung in one another like the links of a chain. We observed that of these theories only Mr. Russell's really assigned a different function to subject and predicate and so gave meaning to the distinction between them, and we proceeded to discuss this theory. We found that to Mr. Johnson's criticisms Mr. Russell had two possible answers; one being to argue that his theory alone took account of the difference we feel there to be between Socrates and wisdom, the other that his notation was far more convenient than any other, and must therefore correspond more closely to the facts. We then took the first of these arguments, and examined the difference between Socrates and wisdom. This we found to consist in the fact that whereas Socrates determined only one range of propositions in which it occurred, wise determined two such ranges, the complete range "f wise," and the narrower range "x is wise". We then examined the reason for this difference between the two incomplete symbols Socrates and wise, and decided that it was of a subjective character and depended on human interests and needs.

What we have now to consider is whether the difference between Socrates and wise, has any such bearing on the composition of atomic facts, as Mr. Russell alleges it to have. This we can usefully combine with the consideration of Mr. Russell's other possible argument from the superior convenience of his symbolism. The essence of this symbolism, as Mr. Johnson has observed, consists in not letting the adjective stand alone, but making it a propositional function by attaching to it a variable x. A possible advantage of this procedure at once suggests itself in terms of our previous treatment of the difference between substantive and adjective; namely that attaching the variable x helps us to make the distinction we require to make in the case of the adjective, but not in the case of the substantive, between the values of ϕx, and those of $f(\phi\hat{z})$ where f is variable. Only so, it might be said, can we distinguish $(x) \cdot \phi x$ from $(f) \cdot f(\phi\hat{z})$. But very little consideration is required to see that this advantage is very slight and of no fundamental importance. We could easily make the distinction in other ways; for instance by determining that if the variable came after the ϕ it should mean what we now express by ϕx, but if before the ϕ what we express by $f(\phi\hat{z})$; or simply by deciding to use the letters "x," "y," "z," in one case, "f," "g," "h," in the other.

But, although this supposed advantage in the functional symbolism is imaginary, there is a reason which renders it absolutely indispensable. Take such a property as "either having R to a, or having S to b"; it would be absolutely impossible to represent this by a simple symbol "ϕ". For how then could we define ϕ? We could not put $\phi = Ra$. v . Sb because we should not know whether the blanks were to be filled with the same or different arguments, and so whether ϕ was to be a property or relation. Instead we must put ϕX . $= .$ xRa . v. xSb; which explains not what is meant by ϕ by itself but that followed by any symbol x it is short for xRa . v . xSb. And this is the reason which makes inevitable the introduction of propositional functions. It simply means that in such a case "ϕ" is not a name but an incomplete symbol and cannot be defined in isolation or allowed to stand by itself.

But this conclusion about xRa . v . xSb will not apply to all propositional functions. If ϕa is a two termed atomic proposition, "ϕ" is a name of the term other than a, and can perfectly well stand by itself; so, it will be asked, why do we write "ϕx" instead of "ϕ" in this case also? The reason for this lies in a fundamental characteristic of mathematical logic, its extensionality, by which I mean its primary interest in classes and relations in extension. Now if in any proposition whatever we change any individual name into a variable, the resulting propositional function defines a class; and the class may be the same for two functions of quite different forms, in one of which "ϕ" is an incomplete symbol, in the other a name. So mathematical logic being only interested in functions as a means to classes, sees no need to distinguish these two sorts of functions, because the difference between them, though all-important to philosophy, will not correspond to any difference between the classes they define. So, because some ϕ's are incomplete and cannot stand alone, and all ϕ's are to be treated alike in order to avoid useless complication, the only solution is to allow none to stand alone.

Such is the justification of Mr. Russell's practice; but it is also the refutation of his theory, which fails to appreciate the distinction between those functions which are names and those which are incomplete symbols, a distinction which, as remarked above, though immaterial for mathematics is essential for philosophy. I do not mean that Mr. Russell would now deny this distinction; on the contrary, it is clear from the second edition of *Principia* that he would accept it; but I think that his present theory of universals is the relic of his previous failure to appreciate it.

It will be remembered that we found two possible arguments for his theory of universals. One was from the efficiency of the functional notation; this clearly lapses because, as we have seen, the functional notation merely overlooks an essential distinction which happens not to interest the mathematician, and the fact that some functions cannot stand alone is no argument that all cannot. The other argument was from the difference we feel between Socrates and wise, which corresponds to a difference in his logical system between individuals and functions. Just as Socrates determines one range of propositions, but wise two, so a determines the one range ϕa, but

$\phi\hat{z}$ the two ranges ϕx, and $f(\phi\hat{z})$. But what is this difference between individuals and functions due to? Again, simply to the fact that certain things do not interest the mathematician. Anyone who was interested not only in classes of things, but also in their qualities, would want to distinguish from among the others, those functions which were names; and if we called the objects of which they are names qualities, and denoted a variable quality by q, we should have not only the range ϕa, but also the narrower range qa and the difference analogous to that between "Socrates" and "wisdom" would have disappeared. We should have complete symmetry between qualities and individuals; each could have names which could stand alone, each would determine two ranges of propositions, for a would determine the ranges qa and ϕa, where q and ϕ are variables, and q would determine the ranges qx and fq, where x and f are variables.

So were it not for the mathematician's biased interest he would invent a symbolism which was completely symmetrical as regards individuals and qualities; and it becomes clear that there is no sense in the words individual and quality; all we are talking about is two different types of objects, such that two objects, one of each type, could be sole constituents of an atomic fact. The two types being in every way symmetrically related, nothing can be meant by calling one type the type of individuals and the other that of qualities, and these two words are devoid of connotation.

To this, however, various objections might be made which must be briefly dealt with. First it might be said that the two terms of such an atomic fact must be connected by the characterizing tie and/or the relation of characterization, which are asymmetrical, and distinguish their relata into individuals and qualities. Against this I would say that the relation of characterization is simply a verbal fiction. "q characterizes a" means no more and no less than "a is q," it is merely a lengthened verbal form; and since the relation of characterization is admittedly not a constituent of "a is q" it cannot be anything at all. As regards the tie, I cannot understand what sort of a thing it could be, and prefer Wittgenstein's view that in the atomic fact the objects are connected together without the help of any mediator. This does not mean that the fact is simply the collection of its constituents but that it consists in their union without any mediating tie. There is one more objection suggested by Mr. Russell's treatment in the new edition of *Principia*. He there says that all atomic propositions are of the forms $R_1(x)$, $R_2(x,y)$, $R_3(x,y,z)$ etc., and can so *define* individuals as terms which can occur in propositions with any number of terms; whereas of course an n-termed relation could only occur in a proposition with $n + 1$ terms. But this assumes his theory as to the constitution of atomic facts, that each must contain a term of a special kind, called a universal; a theory we found to be utterly groundless. The truth is that we know and can know nothing whatever about the forms of atomic propositions; we do not know whether some or all objects can occur in more than one form of atomic proposition;

and there is obviously no way of deciding any such question. We cannot even tell that there are not atomic facts consisting of two terms of the same type. It might be thought that this would involve us in a vicious circle contradiction, but a little reflection will show that it does not, for the contradictions due to letting a function be its own argument only arise when we take for argument a function containing a negation, which is therefore an incomplete symbol not the name of an object.

In conclusion let us describe from this new point of view the procedure of the mathematical logician. He takes any type of objects whatever as the subject of his reasoning, and calls them individuals, meaning by that simply that he has chosen this type to reason about, though he might equally well have chosen any other type and called them individuals. The results of replacing names of these individuals in propositions by variables he then calls functions, irrespective of whether the constant part of the function is a name or an incomplete symbol, because this does not make any difference to the class which the function defines. The failure to make this distinction has led to these functional symbols, some of which are names and some incomplete, being treated all alike as names of incomplete objects or properties, and is responsible for that great muddle the theory of universals. Of all philosophers Wittgenstein alone has seen through this muddle and declared that about the forms of atomic propositions we can know nothing whatever.

NOTES

From *Mind* 34, no. 136 (1925). Reprinted by permission of Oxford University Press.

1. *Monist*, Oct., 1918–July, 1919.

15 LAZEROWITZ

Lazerowitz states very clearly the problem of universals. He says, "the philosophical controversy is not about what everyone knows very well, that such [general] words have correct use in the language; it is a controversy over the purported discovery that *in addition* to their having an ordinary use they *also* stand for entities philosophers have called 'universals'." What might these additional entities be and why would anyone be persuaded they exist? Whatever universals are, they are expressed by general words such as whiteness and horseness. General words are abstract words. When universals are believed to be entities, they are the referents of abstract words. In effect, abstract words function as the proper names for the entities they represent. The question, of course, is just what sort of entities? Universals are common properties shared by members of the same class. That sounds all well and good. However, Lazerowitz demonstrates that when one tries to ascertain just what the universal horseness is by isolating the property that all horses have in common, the result is nothing at all. To put it another way, it is impossible by a process of successive elimination of properties to determine the precise point at which a horse ceases to be a horse. "The fact that there are no sharp lines of demarcation shows that there is no property common and unique to all things, actual or imaginable, to which the word 'horse' is applicable." So what is a universal if it is not a common property referred to by an abstract term? Clearly, abstract words have meaning. That is the key to the problem. It is the meaning of an abstract word that is the universal.

The test for acquaintance with a given universal is the proper use of the relevant abstract word. In other words, "knowing the meaning of a word is the same as knowing its proper use." What is the basis for the correct use of an abstract word? Lazerowitz says, "The *fact* with regard to abstract words is that they are applicable to each of a number of things because the things resemble each other more or less, without there being anything common to all of them to set exact boundaries which would mark off correct from incorrect applications of the words." This analysis of universals is obviously and purely Wittgensteinean in nature.

The Existence of Universals

Many philosophers have claimed that in addition to objects met with in sense-experience there exist entities of an entirely different and more esoteric kind, technically designated as "universals". According to this claim, there are, in addition to such things as tables and white sheets of paper, the utterly different and less well-known objects tableness and whiteness. Universals, in contrast to the changing and passing phenomena perceived with our senses, have been described by many philosophers as being timeless, unchangeable, and exact. But perhaps more important than this, they are intangible to the senses; they cannot be seen with our eyes nor felt with our hands. They are "intelligible" objects which can be apprehended only in thought. As Plato expressed it: ". . . these, unlike objects of sense, have no separate organ, but that the mind, by a power of her own, contemplates the universals in all things."[1] Legend has it that Diogenes remarked he could see tables but not tableness, to which Plato retorted that although Diogenes had eyes he had no intelligence.

As is well known, philosophers are by no means in agreement on the problem of the nature of universals. Endless controversies have been carried on about their nature without a theory being arrived at acceptable to all competent philosophers. This lack of a generally accepted view may seem surprising, inasmuch as research in the problem has been carried on for so many hundreds of years. What is even more strange, however, is that philosophers have been unable to reach a unanimous opinion about the existence of universals. And in the present paper, it will be my purpose to consider the theory that there are universals, not with the object of estab-lishing or refuting it, but in order to make as clear as possible the nature of the view. For the most part I shall make use of material from the writings of Bertrand Russell, because they seem to me to contain the clearest and most forthright statements of the view in philosophical literature.

It can easily be appreciated that anyone who for the first time comes upon the theory that there are such things as universals will receive the impression that philosophers have discovered a new, hitherto unknown, realm of objects, "the supra-sensible world of universals",[2] that they have made a discovery comparable in general respects to the scientific discovery of microscopic forms of life. Philosophers themselves seem to have thought this. Thus Russell once wrote: "Seeing that nearly all the words to be found in the dictionary stand for universals, it is strange that hardly anybody except students of philosophy ever realizes that there are such entities as universals."[3] Many philosophers who have held the theory that there are such entities have done two things. They have claimed, for one thing, having direct knowledge of them. Russell, for example, has said: "In addition to our acquaintance with particular existing things, we also have acquaintance with what we shall call *universals* . . .";[4] and Moore has claimed having made analyses of some of them.[5] For another thing, they have offered proofs of their existence, if not to strengthen their own convictions, to convince those who are ignorant of the theory and to defend their view against philosophers like Berkeley and James Mill, who have denied that there are any abstract ideas.

All this, the form of words in which the theory is expressed, and the manner in which philosophers have conducted their dispute with regard to it, creates the impression that the theory is about *objects*, of which ordinary people are unaware and the existence of which is in dispute amongst philosophers. One would gather from Plato's remark that those, like Diogenes, who have been instructed in the theory and persist in denying that they ever have the experience of contemplating a universal, suffer from some sort of mental deficiency, a psychological blindness comparable to ordinary blindness. And in the same way, one would gather from Diogenes' statement the skeptical hint that philosophers who claim having contemplated universals have somehow been deluded. An outsider would naturally be led to think that some sort of process of mental looking has convinced many philosophers that the entities in dispute exist while it has led others to deny this. He would quite naturally think that philosophers were engaged in an empirical dispute, one with regard to matter of fact, which some sort of mental looking has not so far been able to settle.

His impression would be further strengthened by Russell's explanation of how it happens that people fail to notice universals.

"We do not naturally dwell upon those words in a sentence which do not stand for particulars; and if we are forced to dwell upon a word which stands for a universal, we naturally think of it as standing for some one of the particulars that come under the universal. When, for example, we hear the sentence, 'Charles I.'s head was cut off', we may naturally enough think of Charles I., of Charles I.'s head, and of the operation of cutting off *his* head, which are all particulars; but we do not naturally dwell upon what is meant by the word 'head' or the word 'cut', which is a universal. We feel such words to be incomplete and insubstantial; they seem to demand a context before anything can be done with them. Hence we succeed in avoiding all notice of universals as such, until the study of philosophy forces them upon our attention."[6]

The impression created by these words is that, like a retiring guest at a party where everyone else boisterously clamors for attention, universals have been overlooked by people who understand the words for which they stand. The explanation is expressed in the language of empirical description, in language which purports to describe how it happens that we fail to notice the presence of certain objects.

Now, in the case of the boisterous party, if the attention of people is called to the modest guest, they will see him and acknowledge his presence; they will not, except as a bad joke, get into a dispute about his existence. Similarly, if philosophers are asked to disregard disturbing imagery and the like which may come up when they consider a sentence like "Charles I's head was cut off", and are directed to contemplate the universals symbolized by "head" and "cut", it is to be expected that they will become aware of them. It is to be expected that if some such request is made as "Disregard A's head and B's and concentrate on the *meaning* of 'head'", philosophers will think of what is meant by the word and will without exception acknowledge the existence of the universal. But this is not what happens. Instead, what happens is that philosophers get into a *serious* dispute over the existence of universals. Their difference of opinion is unquestionably sincere, and is expressed in language which makes it look to be of such a kind that to its resolution some sort of process of examining the meanings of general words is relevant and should be conclusive, though, strange to say, this does not serve to resolve the disagreement.

A further and unexpected complication has been introduced into this dispute by other philosophers, who have declared the problem to be without literal sense. Thus, for example, in contradistinction to philosophers who have held the theory that there are such objects as universals to be *false*, Mr. Ayer has maintained that it is a pseudo-view, one which, contrary to what it appears to be, is really *nonsensical*.[7] According to him, those who assert the existence of universals, and even devise ingenious arguments to demonstrate this, are not really asserting that anything exists, but are only pronouncing nonsensical combinations of words; and those who deny their existence are not really denying the existence of anything but are likewise pronouncing nonsense. The controversy does not involve a difference of opinion with regard to a theory and is not, therefore, genuine.

Is the dispute empirical, one with regard to whether universals exist, or is it a pseudo-dispute in which no opposing views are really expressed but only nonsense is uttered? How is the theory and the dispute with regard to it to be understood?

It is possible, in the first place, to side at least partly with Mr. Ayer and argue that the supposed dispute is only a pseudo-disagreement, one not constituted by any actual difference of opinion between those philosophers who appear to take sides on the problem: that those philosophers who affirm the existence of universals, those who deny their existence, and even those who pronounce the theory nonsensical, are not actually disagreeing, despite the fact that their language and behavior are appropriate to an actual divergence of beliefs. It is possible to argue, with good reason, that philosophers have not discovered, and are not stating the existence of, entities of a new kind, that the layman is not unaware of the existence of these entities but rather also has knowledge by acquaintance of them, and that those philosophers who deny that universals exist are not disputing the claim of those who assert that there are universals.

For consider how the term "universal" is used in philosophy. Russell wrote that "we 'conceive' whenever we understand the meaning of an abstract word, or think of that which is in fact the meaning of the word. If you see a white patch of snow, or recall it by means of images, you do not have a concept; but if you think about whiteness, you have a concept. . . . The object of your thought in such a case, is a *universal* or a Platonic idea."[8]

This, quite clearly, is an explanation of how the word "universal" is used by philosophers. It tells us the term is so used that to say an abstract word, for example, a general name or a verb or an adjective, has a meaning is the same thing as to say it expresses a universal. The meaning of an abstract word is a universal, so that the expression "the universal for which a word stands" translates into the expression "the meaning of an abstract word", e.g., "the universal for which 'lion' stands" means the same as what is meant by "the meaning of 'lion'". In order, then to know whether there are universals it is only necessary to know the meaning of a general name like "lion" or the meaning of some other abstract word. And since everyone, layman as well as philosopher, who can understand ordinary conversation knows the meanings of some such words, it follows that *everyone* knows that there are universals.

Philosophers who think that laymen are unaware of the fact that universals exist must be supposed, therefore, to be thinking that laymen are unaware of the fact that abstract words have meanings. But this they *know* to be false, and it is not easy to see how they ever could come to think it. The "theory" which is expressed by the words "Universals exist" is also expressed by the words "Abstract words have meanings". But no one who understood the sentence "Prepositions, adjectives, etc., have meanings" would imagine that it expressed a *theory*; and it is difficult to see what happened that could have led anyone to think that "Universals exist" expressed one, or that philosophers at one time had *discovered* the "suprasensible world of universals", which implies that they had discovered that abstract words have meanings.

The idea that there actually is a dispute over whether universals exist becomes completely incomprehensible. For what is asserted by the statement "There are no universals" is also asserted by the statement "General names, adjectives, etc., have no meanings". The further statement "'There are universals' is literally meaningless" expresses what is also expressed by "It makes no sense to say 'Adjectives, general names, etc. have meanings'". But it is plain, I think, that no one would dream of denying that verbs, etc. had meanings, or of maintaining that it makes no sense to say that they do. All philosophers, those who pronounce the view that there are universals to be without sense, those who merely contend it is false, as well as those who hold it, *know* that abstract words have meanings. They all, therefore, know that there are universals. There is no difference of opinion over whether abstract words have meanings. How then could there be a difference of opinion over whether there are universals? Seen in this light, it becomes plausible to say that, although there appears to be a controversy, there really is none.

Nevertheless, although there is good reason for arriving at the conclusion that there is no divergence of belief, and hence no actual dispute amongst philosophers, and that there is no problem about the existence of universals, to assert this is to deny the obvious. Undeniably philosophers are in intelligible disagreement *of some sort* over universals, even though there is none over whether abstract words have meaning. And unquestionably they are sincere; they are not pretending a dispute. To consider any other possibility would be to explore fantasy rather than fact. The problem, rather, is to find an explanation which will be an explanation of *both* facts: both that there is a dispute about universals and that there is none over whether abstract words have meanings. One may, of course, stop short and take the dispute as merely showing a "strange thing" about the psychology of philosophers, namely, that they are able to hold ". . . sincerely, as part of their philosophical creed, propositions inconsistent with what they themselves *know* to be true".[9] But this is not satisfactory. It is psychologically possible, to be sure, for a person to believe what he knows to be false. And it is conceivable that many philosophers, regardless of what they know perfectly well, are nevertheless expressing contrary opinions which they believe. Something strange, psychologically, could have happened to philosophers to arouse beliefs which in normal circumstances they would not have. One is reminded of the man who *knows* his love is untrue to him, has seen her in another man's arms, sees the lie in her face when she denies his accusations, but nevertheless believes her: "I know she is false to me, and yet I believe her. I *must*."[10] Something like what happened to this man could, conceivably, have also happened to philosophers, but there is no reason for thinking so. There is no good reason for thinking that any philosophers suffer from some sort of emotional conflict with regard to the fact that words have meanings. The dispute over universals has to be explained in some other way; so far we have not rightly understood it.

The problem is to arrive at an explanation of the theory of universals which will at the same time allow for and be an explanation of the dispute, i.e., will tell us whether the dispute is factual or whether no facts are in dispute but something else is and what it is. Russell has drawn a distinction on the basis of which such an explanation could, perhaps, be constructed. He writes:

> "General words such as 'man' or 'cat' or 'triangle' are said to denote 'universals', concerning which, from the time of Plato to the present day, philosophers have never ceased to debate. Whether there are universals, and, if so, in what sense, is a metaphysical question, which need not be raised in connection with the use of language. The only point about universals that needs to be raised at this point is that the correct use of general words is no evidence that a man can think about universals. It has often been supposed that, because we can use a word like 'man' correctly, we must be capable of a corresponding 'abstract' idea of man, but this is quite a mistake. . . . Consequently there is no need to suppose that we ever apprehend universals, although we use general words correctly."[11]

According to the distinction here implied between the correct use of general words and their standing for universals or abstract ideas, it follows that the statement which is asserted by some philosophers and controverted by others, that an abstract word, say "chair", stands for a universal, expresses something new and in addition to the undisputed fact that the word has a correct use in the language. The sentence "The word 'chair' stands for the universal chairness" says something new and in addition to what would be said by a statement explaining the proper use of "chair" in English, so that in learning the second statement a person would not at the same time be learning what was expressed by the first. The distinction thus seems to provide an explanation of how the layman, who knows how to use abstract words like "cheese", "walk", and "not" correctly, could be unaware of the existence of universals, and of how it has happened that even philosophers have disagreed over whether there are any. For we are told that knowing how to use a word correctly, e.g., "cheese" or "not", is not the same as, nor does it imply, being able to frame the abstract idea of cheese or of not, or to have acquaintance with the universal it denotes. A person who behaved appropriately on hearing the request, "Please pass the cheese to me", who knew how to make his own wants known in similar words; and could even talk at length on the differences between cheeses, might not know the abstract idea of cheese, although we should say he knew the correct use of "cheese" in the language. Similarly, with regard to words like "five", "not", "between", "white", "walk", the fact that he has used them correctly on numerous occasions and in different circumstances is not to be counted as any evidence whatever for thinking he knows the universals they denote, or even that there are any such objects. And the philosophical controversy is not about what everyone knows perfectly well, that such words have correct use in the language; it is a controversy over the purported discovery that *in addition* to their having an ordinary use they *also* stand for entities philosophers have called "universals". The possibility of a genuine difference of opinion arising seems to be explained; since those philosophers, who have failed to apprehend abstract ideas, even though they know verbal usage, may think the claim that there are universals false, or even that it is senseless. Thus, although Diogenes could apply the word "horse" to the right animals, knew the correct use of "horse", he was incapable of framing the abstract idea of horse, and so was led to deny that there were universals.

Another thing that would seem to follow from Russell's distinction is that there are two different processes connected with learning a word: one, of learning its correct use, and the other, a *further* process, of framing an abstract idea, or becoming acquainted with the universal for which the word stands: one process of learning to what animals "horse" is applicable and another process of framing the abstract idea of horse. The first process is, of course, familiar to all of us; admittedly those of us who know word usage were subjected to it. But what is this further process? What, in addition to teaching us how to use correctly the words in a language, for instance, in the usual, ostensive ways in which children are taught them, is necessary in order to make us *also* know the universals they symbolize?

Russell appears to have answered this question too, to have described the further process: "When we see a white patch, we are acquainted, in the first instance, with the particular patch; but by seeing many white patches, we easily learn to abstract the whiteness which they all have in common, and in learning this we are learning to be acquainted with whiteness. A similar process will make us acquainted with any other universal of the same sort."[12] One may suppose that "learning to abstract the whiteness which particular white things have in common or the horseness which particular horses have in common" describes something which has to be gone through in addition to the process of learning the proper use of "white" or "horse", so that a person who has learnt to apply "white" to things that are white and to withhold applying it to things having another color, and has learnt to apply "horse" to animals that are horses and to withhold applying it to other animals, could not, merely because he has this knowledge, be said to have gone through the process of abstracting whiteness and horseness, and thereby to have become acquainted with the universals. The description of the process of abstraction gives rise to the idea that becoming acquainted with a universal requires, so to speak, some mysterious sort of mental distillation in which, e.g., whiteness, a non-visual, abstract idea, is derived from visual, concrete objects. The attempts in chemistry to obtain a pure substance may come to mind as analogous.

But what would be a test for ascertaining whether a person has achieved acquaintance with a universal? What is to be reckoned as evidence for a person's being acquainted, say, with whiteness or tableness? Philosophers do not explicitly tell us, and Russell denies that the correct use of a word is to be considered as any evidence whatever. Their omission, in conjunction with Russell's denial, is important because, by putting them in a position comparable to that of an explorer who claims to have discovered a strange, new land but has brought back nothing which could serve as evidence for his claim, some philosophers get the idea that the theory of universals is false while others think it is unverifiable and therefore nonsensical.

Nevertheless, there is an ordinary way at hand of finding out whether a person has acquaintance with a universal. In accordance with the philosophical explanation of the word "universal" to the effect that the meaning of a general word is a universal, it will be plain that knowledge of the meaning of a word is identical with or at least implies acquaintance with a universal. Thus, from the fact that a person knows the meaning of "white" or of "table" it follows that he has acquaintance with whiteness or tableness. And we do, of course, have a test, which is the only one, for ascertaining whether he knows the meaning of a word. We find out whether a person knows the meaning of "white" or "table" by observing how he uses the word. If he continues to use it properly, i.e., in the way in which it is ordinarily used, applies it only to the right things, uses it correctly in assertions and questions, etc., we say he knows its meaning. We take the correct use of "white" and "table" as evidence that a person knows their meaning. It follows, then, contrary to what Russell holds, that we do count their correct use as evidence that the person has acquaintance with the universals whiteness and tableness. And what could ever have made anyone deny this, is not easy to see; though we can, perhaps, see a reason why philosophers should have omitted explicitly stating a test for ascertaining whether a person has acquaintance with universals, since no procedure in addition to the usual one for finding out that people know the meanings of words is necessary.

Furthermore, it will be clear that knowing the meaning of a word is the same as knowing its proper use. The test for each is exactly the same; it consists in each case of observing how the word is used and what the responses to its use in statements made by others are. There is no test which is a test of one and not of the other; and this is because the expressions "knows its use but does not know its meaning", "knows its meaning but does not know its use" are self-contradictory. "Knows its meaning as well as its use" says nothing different from "knows its use", because it makes no sense to ask "Which did you learn first, the meaning of the word or its correct use?". It will be clear, too, that it is not merely false to say that there are two processes connected with learning a word, one of learning its correct use, and a further one, not involved in the first, of learning to abstract a universal, but it makes no sense to say this. Learning to abstract the universal for which a word stands is the same as learning to use the word properly. There is nothing more mysterious about the one than there is about the other.

The attempt to understand the theory of universals by way of the distinction between a general word having a correct use and standing for a universal has not been enlightening. It only leads back to the former unacceptable idea that the dispute about universals is a disagreement over whether general words have meanings. The distinction no doubt has point, however; though what it is remains obscure. Russell would not deny that the correct use of a general word like "white" is evidence that a person knows its meaning. His denial, which I find hard to think is just a mistake, that it is evidence for a person's being acquainted with the universal for which it stands raises the suspicion that there is a problem about universals which there is not about the meanings of words, that the theory that general words stand for universals does not reduce to the statement that general words have meanings.

Having learned words in the usual ways in which words are learned seems to leave many people unsatisfied. It leaves them with the feeling, apparently, that it is not enough, that the ordinary ways have not given them knowledge of what the words really mean. Moore has given explicit expression to this dissatisfaction: "What, *after all*, is it that we mean to say of an action when we say that it is right or ought to be done?"[13] And in the attempt to answer this question Moore, who knows the ordinary use of the word, thought it necessary to try to *discover* a property common and exclusive to all right actions. Again, as in the case of Russell's distinction of which the present expression of dissatisfaction is a continuation, knowing how to apply "right" to actions to which the word is commonly applied is not to be taken for knowing its meaning. In order to know what the word means it is necessary to know a property, one that is common and exclusive to all actions to which the word would ordinarily be applied. The meaning of "right" is a common property, which a person may not know even though he knows the ordinary use of the word. In general with regard to abstract words, Plato tells us: "Whenever a number of individuals have a common name, we assume them to have also a corresponding form or idea."[14] And from Russell we have the statement: "Let us consider, say, such a notion as 'justice'. If we ask ourselves what justice is, it is natural to proceed by considering this, that, and the other just act, with a view to discovering what they have in common. They must all, in some sense, partake of a common nature, which will be found in whatever is just and in nothing else. This common nature, in virtue of which they are all just, will be justice itself, the pure essence the admixture of which with facts of ordinary life produces the multiplicity of just acts. Similarly with any other word which may be applicable to common facts, such as 'whiteness', for example. The word will be applicable to a number of particular things because they all participate in a common nature or essence."[15]

The idea that the meanings of abstract words, or universals, are common properties is one which seems natural and invites ready acceptance. It seems to account for the difference between proper names and general names, etc., e.g., between "Edward" and "boy". And it provides us with an explanation of how it is that after having had pointed out to him a number of things to each of which the same word is applied a person can go on by himself to apply the word correctly to new things: of how it is that after having been shown applications of a word W to a, b, c he can go on by himself and apply it correctly to d, e, etc. If in the course of being taught ostensively the use of W, all he learned were the *separate facts* that a was called W and that b also was called W, he would not have learned anything which would enable him to proceed independently to new applications, i.e., to applications which had not been explicitly made for him, any more than after being told that this boy was called "Edward" and that boy, too, he would have been told anything which would justify him in calling other boys "Edward". If, however, we suppose that W is applied to a, b, and c in virtue of their having a given property ϕ in common, we can understand how a person who has learned this, namely that W is applicable to a, b, c because they have ϕ in common, can go on by himself to make further applications of W to *d*, *e*, etc. What enables him to make independently the new applications is knowledge of the *general fact* that W is applicable to anything which has φ: he applies W to *d* and *e*, etc., by noting that in common with *a*, *b*, and *c* they have φ. The general fact that W is applicable to anything which has φ, which he learns from the separate applications of W, is equivalent to the fact that φ is the meaning of W, so that in knowing the meaning of W he knows to what it is applicable. It is natural, thus, to think that "the meaning of the term will be what is common to the various examples pointed out as meant by it".[16]

Despite the naturalness of this account of the meanings of words, some philosophers have disagreed with the theory that the meanings of words are common properties. Locke's well-known challenge may be recalled: "For I demand, what are the alterations which may or may not be in a horse or lead, without making either of them to be of another species? . . . he will never be able to know when anything precisely ceases to be of the species of a horse or lead."[17] This challenge is unanswerable. Imagine a horse changing by imperceptible gradation into a swan. Clearly, we can distinguish three stages in the process of transformation: one with regard to which everyone would say the animal was a horse, another with regard to which everyone would say it was neither a horse nor a swan, and still a third with regard to which everyone would say it was a swan. But these stages, which themselves involve an undetermined amount of latitude, are connected by imperceptible gradation with each other, so that there is no sharp line of division between any of the stages and no way of ascertaining where one ends and the other begins. Like a person going from one army to another facing it and separated from it by No-Man's Land, one can imaginatively proceed from the horse to an animal which is neither horse nor swan, and finally to the swan without being able to know where precisely he left one and arrived at the other. If, on the other hand, there were a property φ, simple or complex, in virtue of having which the animal was a horse and in virtue of failing to have which the animal ceased to be a horse, and another property φ', on the possession of which depended whether a thing was a swan or not, it would be possible to know at *exactly* what point in the process of transformation the animal ceased to be a horse, at what point *exactly* it became neither a horse nor a swan, and at what point *exactly* it became a swan. It would cease to be a horse at precisely the point when it lost φ, and it would become a swan precisely at the point of transformation when it acquired φ'. But this is made impossible by the fact that the change proceeds by imperceptible gradation. The fact that there are no sharp lines of demarcation shows that there is no property common and unique to all things, actual or imaginable, to which the word "horse" is applicable and the failure to have which makes the word inapplicable. The meaning of the word is not an essence, a common property.

Without instancing other words to illustrate the point, it can be seen that with regard to any abstract word W there are things which we should

correctly and without hesitation call "W"; there are things from which we
should correctly and without hesitation withhold application of "W"; and
there are things, actual or easily imaginable, with regard to which a person
who knew all there was to be known about the ordinary, actual use of "W",
would not know what to do, whether to apply it or withhold it. His
knowledge of actual usage would be of no help to him. This is not, as Prof.
Broad seemed to think,[18] due to inadequate knowledge of the rules for the
use of "W", but obtains in spite of knowing all there is to be known about
the actual use of the word. And to search for *exact* rules, or what is
equivalent to this, to search for a common property in virtue of which a
word is applied and in the absence of which application is withheld, would
be like trying to discover rules for a game in addition to the well-known
ones, while knowing perfectly well that the usual rules were all the rules that
had ever been invented for the game. There are no sharply defined criteria
for the use of a word, in the sense that if we knew the criteria we could never
conceivably be in the position of not knowing whether it is correct or
incorrect to apply the word, given also that we knew all the relevant facts
concerning the thing to which the word is to be applied, so that further
observation would be of no help.

It is worth while to bring out Locke's point somewhat differently. If
Russell's account is the right explanation of the condition under which a
general name like "horse" is applicable to each of a number of things, it is to
be supposed that anyone who has applied the word correctly and continues
to use it properly under a variety of circumstances will know the common
property in virtue of which it is correct to apply it. If the reason why each of
a number of animals is called "horse" is that they have a common property
ϕ, it would be a miracle if in continuing correctly to call more of the right
animals "horse" we nevertheless did not know ϕ. It would be as if a person
in his everyday transactions made purchases with dollar bills, never accepted
the wrong change in coins, etc., but, in spite of this, did not know the
monetary value of dollar bills. The fact, however, that philosophers think a
search for common properties is necessary, and that finding one in any
particular case will constitute a *discovery*, implies exactly this. It implies that,
at least frequently, and perhaps always, we do not know the common
properties which make it correct for us to apply words to each of a class of
individuals. It becomes difficult in such cases to see what the explanation of
continued correct application could be. The Mormons once thought, when a
person in a state of religious exaltation suddenly began to speak in strange
syllables, that he was divinely inspired and talked sense; and when someone
else in the congregation began to translate his words to the others, they
thought that he too was divinely inspired and understood the words. Their
explanation of what happened was intelligible, though undoubtedly false.
And one might hold, in explanation of what happens in the case of the
continued correct application of a word, that this is due to divine assistance

or to a mysterious influence the property exerts over our pens and tongues, or that it just happens that we continue to use the word correctly while remaining in ignorance of the property which makes our use correct. It is hardly to be supposed, however, that philosophers would offer any such explanation or find it acceptable. The only remaining possible explanation of continued correct use of a word, on the Platonic assumption, is that those who use the word know the property for which it stands.

But then the idea that a word is applicable to each of a number of things because they participate in a common essence, together with the idea that some sort of search is necessary in order to discover the essence symbolized by the word, which we already are able to use in everyday life, leads to a paradox. If in knowing how to use the word correctly we must know the property ϕ in virtue of which it is applied to things, there can be no problem of searching for or discovering ϕ: to know the correct use of the word is the same as knowing that ϕ is its meaning. If, on the other hand, *a search* for a supposedly unknown property is necessary, then *there is no common property for which the word stands*, no property which is its meaning. Even if an examination of all the things to which the word is applicable were to end in the discovery of a property ϕ, common and unique to the things to which the word is applicable, ϕ could not have been the property in virtue of the possession of which by each of a number of things the word was applicable to them.

In sum, if a word is applicable in virtue of ϕ, ϕ must be known; and if, *in knowing its use*, we don't know of any common property in virtue of which the word is applicable, we do then *know* that it is not because the things have such a property that it is applicable to them. In neither case is a search sensible, or a relevant discovery possible. It is a paradox, in view of this fact, that philosophers have thought a search was necessary and that after so many years they apparently have failed to realize that it is not a genuine search but is rather a pseudo-search. By asserting both that abstract words stood for common properties and that the properties were unknown and had to be discovered as things in addition to what we get to know when we learn the use of words, philosophers have, to all appearances, held a view according to which *words had meanings which they were never given by anyone nor were known by anyone to have*. It is difficult to suppose that philosophers have really thought anything of this sort; and more directly with regard to the dispute over whether the meanings of words are common properties, it is difficult to see why Locke's familiar challenge should have had so little influence on other philosophers.

The *fact* with regard to abstract words is that they are applicable to each of a number of things because the things resemble each other more or less, without there being anything common to all of them to set exact boundaries which would mark off correct from incorrect applications of the words. And it is entirely reasonable to think that if the dispute concerned whether the

things to which a word was applicable all had something in common, or
were exactly similar in some respect or set of respects, it would have been
resolved long ago in favor of Locke and others, instead of ending in a
stalemate. It is to be expected as a *normal* thing that philosophers would
come in time to see and admit the facts. How, then, is the apparent failure on
the part of many philosophers over a long period of years to see and admit
the facts to be understood? In only one way: as not actually constituting any
such failure at all. In order to reach an understanding of what philosophers
are saying, we must take into consideration the fact, which we have to take
seriously, that they persist in apparently not seeing, what seems plain to us,
that the adduced facts are inconsistent with their theory. When continued
confrontation with plain fact does not make philosophers give up their
theory, it is safest to proceed on the assumption, not that their intelligence is
weak, but that somehow the facts do not count against the theory. Their
behavior clearly shows that they do not reckon the facts as constituting a
reason for giving up the view that *they* are holding. Hence we are driven to
conclude that the view which has naturally been attributed to these philosophers because of the manner in which they have expressed themselves, the
view against which the facts do count, is *not* the view that they are holding.
Their words have to be reconstrued in such a way that the facts do not refute
what they are intended to express.

When philosophers assert that a word W is applicable to each of a number
of things because they have a property in common, and continue to insist on
this in face of the fact that the things to which W is applicable only resemble
each other more or less without there being anything common to all of them
in virtue of which W is applicable to each, they do not by their words wish
to controvert fact. They mean, rather, to tell us something about their use of
an expression, although they do this in an indirect and misleading way. A
fuller statement of what they assert is the following: A word is applicable to
each of a number of things because it stands for the property which they all
have in common. This tells us that to say a word is applicable to each of a
number of things is the same as to say it stands for a common property. And
now we can see what they are doing: they wish, regardless of the facts to *use*
"stands for a common property" to mean the same as "is applicable to each
of a number of things". This explains why the facts do not count against
what they are saying, and why the dispute over common properties ends in a
stalemate. Some philosophers wish to use, and in their philosophical writings do use, "stands for a common property" synonymously with, so that it
means no more than, "is applicable to each of a number of things", while
other philosophers, like Locke, are opposed to their use of the expression.
And since matter of fact is not in dispute, neither can win, and each can go
his own way.

Now, also, we are in a better position to see what the dispute over the
existence of universals comes to. There is no controversy, no divergence of

opinion, with regard to whether words have meanings, and there is no factual controversy over whether the meanings of words are common properties. But the tendency of many philosophers to use "stands for a common property" synonymously with "is applicable to each of a number of things" throws some light, as will later be seen, on the nature of the view that there are universals, and the dispute regarding it.

Connected with the philosophical idea that the meanings of abstract words are common properties is the idea that common properties, or universals, are *entities*, different in kind from the things they are said to "characterize" and such that they could exist even when characterizing nothing. It is not by an accidental use of language or merely for the purpose of expressing themselves more colorfully that some philosophers have asserted: "Universals can be in many places" is not merely an unusual way of expressing the commonplace fact that there are many white things; it serves to bring out the point that, though they are very queer, universals are entities. By way of parenthetical observation, it may be remarked that philosophers like Stout, who seem to have been outraged by what they took to be a flagrant misuse of the word "entity", a misuse in violation of the necessary proposition that nothing can be in several places at the same time and according to which we should have to say that there were self-contradictory entities, have argued that no object could be in "local separation" from itself. It is self-contradictory to say "Jones is now in two different parts of the world", and, as "entity" is ordinarily used, it is self-contradictory to say "The *entity* whiteness is now in a number of different parts of the world". Thus, Prof. Stout let himself be governed by the ordinary, non-contradictory use of "entity" and proposed a view according to which characters are particular.[19] Other philosophers, however, have not felt the force of the objection from the logical impossibility of "local separation". This, I think, is noteworthy. For if "Some entities can be in many places at one time", rightly understood, were self-contradictory, one would expect that philosophers who have asserted it would give it up. Read in terms of ordinary usage, it is self-contradictory; and there is no particular difficulty in seeing this, no complicated chain of reasoning is involved. There is, therefore, some reason for thinking that it is *not* self-contradictory, that philosophers mean something different by it from what a literal interpretation of the words would make one think.

The theory that there are such entities as universals implies that the meanings of abstract words, i.e., the meanings of general names, adjectives, etc., are entities. Since it is not to be supposed that the fact that abstract words have meanings is being asserted as a theory or is in question among philosophers, it may be gathered that what some philosophers have intended to convey is the theory that the meanings of such words are *entities*. Accordingly, what now would seem to be in dispute is not whether there are universals, but whether universals are entities, or to include Mr. Ayer, whether it makes sense to say they are objects. It would appear to be a factual dispute about the nature of the meanings of words.

Is this a possible construction? Have some philosophers really claimed having discovered a further fact, unknown by most people and disputed by others, the fact, namely, that the meanings of abstract words are objects? There is, in the first place, an air of absurdity about supposing that any philosopher has actually meant to hold this. No philosopher, or group of philosophers, would think of saying, "Jones, like most men, knew his wife for thirty years but never did know that she was not just a shadow, never did know that she was made of flesh and bones and had a temper". And it is not easy to think that philosophers have ever held a theory of such a sort that they might naturally be imagined as saying, "Like most men, Jones knew the meaning of 'horse' for thirty years or more, but, oddly enough, he never did know it was an entity". Were Diogenes alive we could hardly imagine him refraining from remarking that after thirty years and better of assurance based on knowledge by acquaintance Russell himself has become uncertain: "I conclude, therefore, though with hesitation, that there are universals, and not merely general words."[20] One might very appropriately ask what happened that an assurance based on *acquaintance* with universals, similar to acquaintance with sense-data, should have dissolved into uncertainty. Without laboring the point, it becomes justifiable to suspect that the view that universals are objects is not an empirical theory about the nature of the meanings of words. Berkeley and others, who appear to have placed a straightforward interpretation on the words philosophers have used to express this view, made the *Gedankenexperiment* of attempting to envisage "abstract ideas", and came to the conclusion that there were no such entities, that is, that the meanings of words are not objects, over and above the tangible things, etc., to which the words are applicable. It would be absurd to think that what Russell has called a natural oversight could not be corrected by a serious effort. But it is a mistake to take the theory as empirical, to be established or refuted by some sort of examination of the meanings of words. "Coming to know that universals are entities" describes no conceivable process of learning anything about the meanings of words.

This, and at the same time what the theory comes to, can be seen if we keep in mind both the connection of the idea that universals are entities with the contention, which is also the main source of the idea, that the meanings of general words are common properties, and also the form of speech philosophers sometimes use to express the relation between words and their meanings, *viz.*, general words *stand for* universals. The view that universals, and therefore common properties, are entities of an abstract sort, when considered in conjunction with this form of speech, is readily seen to lead to the further statement that "General words stand for abstract entities". Nevertheless, in spite of their description of universals as being less tangible than the concrete things they characterize, as being non-sensuous, abstract objects to be gazed on only with the mind's eye, philosophers so use the phrase "stands for a common property", or (to call attention to another of Russell's expressions) "denotes a universal", that a word that is said to stand for or denote a common property does not stand for anything in addition to the things or events, etc., to which it applies. Also, thus, to say that a general word stands for an abstract entity does not mean that it denotes anything other than the concrete, particular things to which it is applicable.

It can now be seen that "Universals are entities" does not, nor is it intended to, express a theory about the nature of the meanings of words, any more than to assert that general words stand for common properties or for abstract entities is to state a theory about the meanings of words. "Universals are entities" means no more and no less than the expression it naturally brings to mind, namely, "General words stand for abstract entities", which itself is only an alternative form of words for "General words are applicable to each of a number of things". But the intermediate expression has a further point.

"Abstract words stand for abstract entities" leads to "Abstract words are the *proper names* of abstract entities". Thus Russell speaks of universals as being *named* by words.[21] In effect philosophers may be construed as arguing: A word that is applicable to each of a number of things, events, etc., *stands for* the property they have in common; it therefore stands for an abstract entity; consequently, in addition to being the general name of each of the things, etc., to which it is applicable, it is also a proper name, the proper name of an abstract object.[22] And since to be the proper name of an *abstract object* is not to be the name of an *object*, in any ordinary sense, we can see that in an indirect way what philosophers are saying is that abstract words are proper names, without their being the proper names of any things. Philosophers whom we may suppose to be saying this know, of course, that words like "white", "horse", "running", "similarity" are not commonly classified with proper names like "Plato" and "London"; and it is therefore natural to suppose that they are recommending, for various reasons, such a classification. By asserting that universals are entities, they are not, in an indirect way, making the obviously false statement that abstract words, as a matter of ordinary classification of parts of speech, are proper names. Rather, to put the matter provisionally, they are making in concealed form the *linguistic proposal*, "Let us classify such words with proper names". The statement "Universals are entities" hides the linguistic proposal to reclassify, formally, abstract words with proper names.

The theory I am here stating, or some modification of it, will not, I expect, impress itself with any great amount of favor on most philosophers. Nevertheless, with the help of this hypothesis a number of puzzling things connected with the philosophical view, which otherwise remain unexplained, can be cleared up. For one thing, it is completely puzzling to think what could have happened that should have made anyone *think* that universals have been discovered or that hardly anybody except students of philosophy know that there are universals. On the theory that the philosophical view is a linguistic proposal to reclassify abstract words with proper names it is not difficult to see what the "discovery" refers to. Philosophers have actually discovered a new *possible* way of classifying words, and those people who are unaware of the existence of universals are merely unaware of this possibility. In a similar way it is possible to explain anyone's *thinking* that knowledge of the correct use of an abstract word does not imply knowledge of a universal; what he thinks but expresses in a misleading manner is that knowledge of the correct use of "horse", for example, does not imply that a person sees the possibility of classifying the word "horse" with "Dobbin", say. Also we can now understand why the controversy over universals should have continued without resolution for so many hundreds of years, which if it had been empirical or *a priori* would be astonishing beyond belief. If the dispute consists of counter-proposals with regard to altering linguistic conventions, then we can understand why the dispute should continue without resolution, although, it must be admitted, this does not explain the intense and recurrent interest in the problem. Perhaps further investigation following Wisdom's hint that philosophical views are the vehicles for expressing "unconscious fantasies", will lead to an understanding of this point also. Furthermore, an increasing hesitation, after years of certainty about the existence of universals, like that in the case of Russell, can be made intelligible as an uncertainty about the appropriateness of the proposed verbal reclassification, induced by the fact that the *differences* between abstract words and proper names have come, for some reason, to impress themselves more on his mind; indecision would be reached when both the differences and similarities between abstract words and proper names impress themselves with equal force.

Finally, to cut matters short, we can understand why philosophers who hold that universals exist should be unmoved by the argument from the logical impossibility of an entity being in local separation from itself. The necessary proposition that no entity can be in more than one place at any given time does not deny the physical possibility of something happening which can be imagined or conceived as happening. If "No entity can be in several places at one time" denied the possibility of a situation *described* by "Entity *a* is in several places now", it would not express a necessary proposition, one which could not be false under any conceivable or describable circumstance. We make it express a necessary proposition by preventing "Entity *a* is now in several places" from describing anything. Its import, if not its form, is thus verbal, to the effect that as "entity" is actually used it makes no sense to say with regard to a named or described object that it is in several places at a given time: it tells us that such a sentence as "Moore is now in Cambridge and also in Northampton" describes no state of affairs, makes no sense. Now, the merely *formal* reclassification of abstract words with proper names, without depriving them of their ordinary use as abstract words, carries with it the possibility of sensibly writing such sentences as "Whiteness is now in many places", which are only bizarre expressions for familiar sentences like "There are now many white things". But the necessary proposition that no entity can be in several places at one time together with the philosophical proposition that universals can be in several places at the same time implies that universals are not entities. And one thing, although not the only one, which those who raise the objection from the logical impossibility of local separation are doing, is to point out that since the substitution of the proper name of an entity, e.g., a name like Russell, for x in "x is now in many places" results in nonsense, whereas the substitution of "whiteness", "chairness", etc. does not, these words are not proper names of entities. They are not proper names at all, as "proper name" is ordinarily used. Philosophers who make the reclassification proposal know, of course, that abstract words are not proper names. Their indifference to the objection is therefore to be construed as indicating an academic willingness to give up a necessary proposition for the sake of their proposal. They wish to classify abstract words with proper names without converting them into proper names of *entities*. And doing this involves changing the meaning of "proper name" in such a way that from the fact that a word is a proper name it no longer follows that it is the name of an object; that is, the philosophical use of "proper name" is no longer determined by the prevailing use of "entity". Berkeley's *Gedankenexperiment* can be seen as coming to nothing more than pointing out that abstract words are not proper names of entities, which fact he urges against the formal reclassification of abstract words with proper names, against *calling* them proper names.

The fact that on the reclassification proposal hypothesis it becomes possible to explain a number of otherwise puzzling features connected with the philosophical theory of universals is a positive reason in its favor. What Wisdom has pointed out about typical linguistic proposals,[23] however, shows that it is an *exaggeration* to characterize the theory as a proposal. For one thing, a philosopher who holds the theory of universals does not say "*Let us* classify abstract words with proper names". Instead he uses the language of assertion; "There are such entities as universals", which masks the *assertion* "Abstract words are proper names". In view of this, it is undoubtedly closer to the facts to describe him as stating the notational classification of abstract words with proper names to be a fact, i.e., as actually asserting that abstract words *are* proper names, though in a subtly disguised way. His classification is not to be thought incorrect or improper,[24] as not corresponding to the prevailing classification, but is to be viewed as a classification which, for some reason, he prefers. That is, it is not based on a mistake; it is based on a preference, perhaps, to use Wisdom's phrase, with a hidden purpose, or for convenience in the development of a uniform notation for logic. It will be obvious that the preceding explanations of the various puzzling features connected with the view remain, with slight modifications, the same.

For one thing, in the usual case of a person making a verbal recommendation the intention is that the change be adopted for ordinary use as a regular thing. This, in the present case, the philosopher undoubtedly does not intend; he is not interested in having grammar books or the grammatical structure of ordinary sentences changed. We could then say that he is making an academic proposal, for esoteric adoption only. Again, however, it seems closer to the facts to describe what he does as making or maintaining an actual though academic reclassification of abstract words with proper names. And what he does is concealed from himself as well as from others. The view is an instance of linguistic magic, which, if we are to take seriously the panegyric expressions of philosophers over universals, gives rise to feelings which are appropriate to objects more wonderful and satisfying than those met with in sense-experience.

Wisdom also points out that it is usual in the case of an ordinary recommendation to give a reason for the proposed change. But this, in the present instance, is done in the form of "proofs" advanced for the theory. These are actually statements which call attention to analogies that obtain between the use of expressions, on the basis of which philosophers feel justified in making the reclassification. The following brief argument will serve to illustrate this point. The meaning of a word is something different from the word. For instance, the meaning of "horse" in English is the same as the meaning of the different word "cheval" in French, i.e., the two different words have one and the same meaning, so that two people, each of whom knows one word and not the other, will know the same meaning. It must therefore be something over and above the words which express it. Like the case of a person who is called "Jacques" by his French friends and "James" by his English friends, the meaning of a word in English is an object named by the word, and either is or could be named by other words in different languages. What this proof *actually* shows is, not that the meaning of a word is an entity or, what comes to the same thing, that "meaning" is a substantive the grammatical use of which bears some resemblance to the use of general names denoting things. The argument calls attention to a linguistic similarity which is used by some philosophers to justify their classification of "meaning" with general names of objects. In turn, this regulates the further reclassification of other abstract words with proper names.

The view expressed in this paper concerning the nature of the theory that there are such entities as universals is, of course, an interpretation which had been arrived at indirectly, by inference from certain assumptions that seemed to me to be reasonable but which may not impress others in the same way. It is, therefore, of interest to find independent confirmation in the form of a statement[25] from a philosopher which, except for the fact that it is combined with the Platonic theory, is a linguistically unconcealed expression of the reclassification view set out in this paper: "It is convenient, however, to regard such general terms ['wise', 'city'] as names on the same footing as 'Socrates' and 'Paris': names each of a single specific entity, though a less tangible entity than the man Socrates or the town Boston."[26]

NOTES

From *Mind* 60, no. 217 (1946). Reprinted by permission of Oxford University Press.

1. [Plato,] *Theaetetus*, 185. Jowett translation, third edition. [New York: Random House, 1937].
2. [B. Russell,] *The Problems of Philosophy* [London: Oxford University Press, 1912], p. 144.
3. *Ibid.*, p. 146.
4. *Ibid.*, p. 81.
5. *The Philosophy of G. E. Moore* [3rd ed. (La Salle, Ill.: Open Court Publishing Co., 1968)], pp. 664–665.
6. *The Problems of Philosophy*, pp. 146–147.
7. [A. J. Ayer,] *Language, Truth and Logic* [New York: Dover Publications, Inc., 1952], p. 36.
8. *Philosophy*, p. 203.
9. G. E. Moore, "A Defence of Common Sense", *Contemporary British Philosophy*, Vol. II, p. 203. [Also *Philosophical Papers* (New York: Collier Books, 1962), pp. 32–59.]
10. I cannot recall the novel from which this is taken.
11. *Philosophy*, pp. 53–54.
12. *The Problems of Philosophy*, pp. 158–159; see also the following paragraph.
13. [G. E. Moore,] *Ethics*, p. 8. Italics my own. See also C. D. Broad, *Scientific Thought*, Introduction [London: Routledge and Kegan Paul, 1923].
14. [Plato,] *Republic*, Book X, 596. [Trans. B. Jowett (New York: Random House, 3rd ed., 1937), vol. 1, p. 852.]
15. *The Problems of Philosophy*, p. 143.
16. C. I. Lewis, *Mind and the World-Order* [New York: Dover Publications, Inc., 1929], p. 78.
17. [J. Locke, *An Essay Concerning*] *Human Understanding*, Book III, Chap. III, 13.
18. [C. D. Broad,] *Scientific Thought*, Introduction [London: Routledge & Kegan Paul, 1923].
19. "Are Characteristics Universal or Particular?", *Proc. Arist. Soc.* Supp. Vol. 3 [1923].
20. *An Inquiry into Meaning and Truth*, p. 436.
21. *The Problems of Philosophy*, p. 147.
22. See C. I. Lewis, "The Modes of Meaning", *Philosophy and Phenomenological Research*, Vol. IV, No. 2, pp. 238–239.
23. "Philosophy, Anxiety and Novelty", *Mind*, April 1944, p. 173.
24. For a different point of view see Norman Malcolm's paper, "Moore and Ordinary Language", in *The Philosophy of G. E. Moore*.
25. Pointed out to me by Prof. Alice Ambrose.
26. W. V. Quine, *Mathematical Logic* [Cambridge, Mass.: Harvard University Press, 1940], pp. 119–120.

16 QUINE

Quine approaches the problem of universals from the standpoint of (1) one's interest and (2) the simplicity of description of that which is dictated to exist as a result of one's interest. One's interest dictates the framework by which one approaches the problem of being. That framework constitutes the "game" to which one is committed, e.g., the science game, the math game or, for that matter, the epistemological game. The nature of being is determined by the game one chooses to play. However, it is not quite as capricious as that. There is an iron-clad manner by which one can ferret out, within a chosen game, the entities to which one must necessarily be committed. That way is properly determined by Russell's theory of descriptions.

Russell's theory is one by which being and nonbeing are determined and has the advantage of preserving the meanings of pronouns, as well as nouns, without at the same time committing one to abstract entities (namely, universals), which are the (supposed) referents of those units of language. This is accomplished by the means of bound variables. By this method one can dispose of such illusive (universal) entities as redness by analyzing the claim that there is a red car as "there is an X such that X is a car and X is red"; one thereby avoids any commitment to the universal redness that otherwise carries with it an existence over and above the car, which is red. The word 'red' is preserved of meaning without at the same time committing one to a universal redness. There is, in this case, simply a car that is red. Quine understands, however, that there is meaningful predication of nouns that "denote" species, that is, general words such as cars in general. It turns out to be the case that regardless of the game one wishes to play, one cannot avoid making reference to classes of things. Quine would prefer it otherwise, namely, that the game one chooses to play ultimately determines one's ontological commitments. However, regardless of the game one chooses to play it seems inevitable that sooner or later one must be committed to classes. Consequently, his analysis of universals results in a commitment to classes, much as does Aristotle's analysis of the problem.

On What There Is

A curious thing about the ontological problem is its simplicity. It can be put in three Anglo-Saxon monosyllables: 'What is there?' It can be answered, moreover, in a word—'Everything'—and everyone will accept this answer as true. However, this is merely to say that there is what there is.

There remains room for disagreement over cases; and so the issue has stayed alive down the centuries.

Suppose now that two philosophers, McX and I, differ over ontology. Suppose McX maintains there is something which I maintain there is not. McX can, quite consistently with his own point of view, describe our difference of opinion by saying that I refuse to recognize certain entities. I should protest, of course, that he is wrong in his formulation of our disagreement, for I maintain that there are no entities, of the kind which he alleges, for me to recognize; but my finding him wrong in his formulation of our disagreement is unimportant, for I am committed to considering him wrong in his ontology anyway.

When *I* try to formulate our difference of opinion, on the other hand, I seem to be in a predicament. I cannot admit that there are some things which McX countenances and I do not, for in admitting that there are such things I should be contradicting my own rejection of them.

It would appear, if this reasoning were sound, that in any ontological dispute the proponent of the negative side suffers the disadvantage of not being able to admit that his opponent disagrees with him.

This is the old Platonic riddle of nonbeing. Nonbeing must in some sense be, otherwise what is it that there is not? This tangled doctrine might be nicknamed *Plato's beard*; historically it has proved tough, frequently dulling the edge of Occam's razor.

It is some such line of thought that leads philosophers like McX to impute being where they might otherwise be quite content to recognize that there is nothing. Thus, take Pegasus. If Pegasus *were* not, McX argues, we should not be talking about anything when we use the word; therefore it would be nonsense to say even that Pegasus is not. Thinking to show thus that the denial of Pegasus cannot be coherently maintained, he concludes that Pegasus is.

McX cannot, indeed, quite persuade himself that any region of space-time, near or remote, contains a flying horse of flesh and blood. Pressed for further details on Pegasus, then, he says that Pegasus is an idea in men's minds. Here, however, a confusion begins to be apparent. We may for the sake of argument concede that there is an entity, and even a unique entity (though this is rather implausible), which is the mental Pegasus-idea; but this mental entity is not what people are talking about when they deny Pegasus.

McX never confuses the Parthenon with the Parthenon-idea. The Parthenon is physical; the Parthenon-idea is mental (according anyway to McX's version of ideas, and I have no better to offer). The Parthenon is visible; the Parthenon-idea is invisible. We cannot easily imagine two things more unlike, and less liable to confusion, than the Parthenon and the Parthenon-idea. But when we shift from the Parthenon to Pegasus, the confusion sets in—for no other reason than that McX would sooner be deceived by the crudest and most flagrant counterfeit than grant the nonbeing of Pegasus.

The notion that Pegasus must be, because it would otherwise be nonsense to say even that Pegasus is not, has been seen to lead McX into an elementary confusion. Subtler minds, taking the same precept as their starting point, come out with theories of Pegasus which are less patently misguided than McX's, and correspondingly more difficult to eradicate. One of these subtler minds is named, let us say, Wyman. Pegasus, Wyman maintains, has his being as an unactualized possible. When we say of Pegasus that there is no such thing, we are saying, more precisely, that Pegasus does not have the special attribute of actuality. Saying that Pegasus is not actual is on a par, logically, with saying that the Parthenon is not red; in either case we are saying something about an entity whose being is unquestioned.

Wyman, by the way, is one of those philosophers who have united in ruining the good old word 'exist'. Despite his espousal of unactualized possibles, he limits the word 'existence' to actuality—thus preserving an illusion of ontological agreement between himself and us who repudiate the rest of his bloated universe. We have all been prone to say, in our common-sense usage of 'exist', that Pegasus does not exist, meaning simply that there is no such entity at all. If Pegasus existed he would indeed be in space and time, but only because the word 'Pegasus' has spatio-temporal connotations, and not because 'exists' has spatio-temporal connotations. If spatio-temporal reference is lacking when we affirm the existence of the cube root of 27, this is simply because a cube root is not a spatio-temporal kind of thing, and not because we are being ambiguous in our use of 'exist'.[1] However, Wyman, in an ill-conceived effort to appear agreeable, genially grants us the nonexistence of Pegasus and then, contrary to what we meant by nonexistence of Pegasus, insists that Pegasus is. Existence is one thing, he says, and subsistence is another. The only way I know of coping with this obfuscation of issues is to give Wyman the word 'exist'. I'll try not to use it again; I still have 'is'. So much for lexicography; let's get back to Wyman's ontology.

Wyman's overpopulated universe is in many ways unlovely. It offends the aesthetic sense of us who have a taste for desert landscapes, but this is not the worst of it; Wyman's slum of possibles is a breeding ground for disorderly elements. Take, for instance, the possible fat man in that doorway; and, again, the possible bald man in that doorway. Are they the same possible man, or two possible men? How do we decide? How many possible men are there in that doorway? Are there more possible thin ones than fat ones? How many of them are alike? Or would their being alike make them one? Are no two possible things alike? Is this the same as saying that it is impossible for two things to be alike? Or, finally, is the concept of identity simply inapplicable to unactualized possibles? But what sense can be found in talking of entities which cannot meaningfully be said to be identical with themselves and distinct from one another? These elements are well-nigh incorrigible. By a Fregean therapy of individual concepts, some effort might be made at rehabilitation; but I feel we'd do better simply to clear Wyman's slum and be done with it.

Possibility, along with the other modalities of necessity and impossibility and contingency, raises problems upon which I do not mean to imply that we should turn our backs. But we can at least limit modalities to whole statements. We may impose the adverb 'possibly' upon a statement as a whole, and we may well worry about the semantical analysis of such usage; but little real advance in such analysis is to be hoped for in expanding our universe to include so-called *possible entities*. I suspect that the main motive for this expansion is simply the old notion that Pegasus, for example, must be because otherwise it would be nonsense to say even that he is not.

Still, all the rank luxuriance of Wyman's universe of possibles would seem to come to naught when we make a slight change in the example and speak not of Pegasus but of the round square cupola on Berkeley College. If, unless Pegasus were, it would be nonsense to say that he is not, then by the same token, unless the round square cupola on Berkeley College were, it would be nonsense to say that it is not. But, unlike Pegasus, the round square cupola on Berkeley College cannot be admitted even as an unactualized *possible*. Can we drive Wyman now to admitting also a realm of unactualizable impossibles? If so, a good many embarrassing questions could be asked about them. We might hope even to trap Wyman in contradictions, by getting him to admit that certain of these entities are at once round and square. But the wily Wyman chooses the other horn of the dilemma and concedes that it is nonsense to say that the round square cupola on Berkeley College is not. He says that the phrase 'round square cupola' is meaningless.

Wyman was not the first to embrace this alternative. The doctrine of the meaninglessness of contradictions runs away back. The tradition survives, moreover, in writers who seem to share none of Wyman's motivations. Still, I wonder whether the first temptation to such a doctrine may not have been substantially the motivation which we have observed in Wyman. Certainly the doctrine has no intrinsic appeal; and it has led its devotees to such quixotic extremes as that of challenging the method of proof by *reductio ad absurdum*—a challenge in which I sense a *reductio ad absurdum* of the doctrine itself.

Moreover, the doctrine of meaninglessness of contradictions has the severe methodological drawback that it makes it impossible, in principle, ever to devise an effective test of what is meaningful and what is not. It would be forever impossible for us to devise systematic ways of deciding whether a string of signs made sense—even to us individually, let alone other people—or not. For it follows from a discovery in mathematical logic, due to Church, that there can be no generally applicable test of contradictoriness.

I have spoken disparagingly of Plato's beard, and hinted that it is tangled. I have dwelt at length on the inconveniences of putting up with it. It is time to think about taking steps.

Russell, in his theory of so-called singular descriptions, showed clearly how we might meaningfully use seeming names without supposing that there be the entities allegedly named. The names to which Russell's theory directly applies are complex descriptive names such as 'the author of *Waverley*', 'the present King of France', 'the round square cupola on Berkeley College'. Russell analyzes such phrases systematically as fragments of the whole sentences in which they occur. The sentence 'The author of *Waverley* was a poet', for example, is explained as a whole as meaning 'Someone (better: something) wrote *Waverley* and was a poet, and nothing else wrote *Waverley*'. (The point of this added clause is to affirm the uniqueness which is implicit in the word 'the', in '*the* author of *Waverley*'.) The sentence 'The round square cupola on Berkeley College is pink' is explained as 'Something is round and square and is a cupola on Berkeley College and is pink, and nothing else is round and square and a cupola on Berkeley College'.

The virtue of this analysis is that the seeming name, a descriptive phrase, is paraphrased *in context* as a so-called incomplete symbol. No unified expression is offered as an analysis of the descriptive phrase, but the statement as a whole which was the context of that phrase still gets its full quota of meaning—whether true or false.

The unanalyzed statement 'The author of *Waverley* was a poet' contains a part, 'the author of *Waverley*', which is wrongly supposed by McX and Wyman to demand objective reference in order to be meaningful at all. But in Russell's translation, 'Something wrote *Waverley* and was a poet and nothing else wrote *Waverley*', the burden of objective reference which had been put upon the descriptive phrase is now taken over by words of the kind that logicians call bound variables, variables of quantification, namely, words like 'something', 'nothing', 'everything'. These words, far from purporting to be names specifically of the author of *Waverley*, do not purport to be names at all; they refer to entities generally, with a kind of studied ambiguity peculiar to themselves. These quantificational words or bound variables are, of course a basic part of language, and their meaningfulness, at least in context, is not to be challenged. But their meaningfulness in no way presupposes there being either the author of *Waverley* or the round square cupola on Berkeley College or any other specifically preassigned objects.

Where descriptions are concerned, there is no longer any difficulty in affirming or denying being. 'There *is* the author of *Waverley*' is explained by Russell as meaning 'Someone (or, more strictly, something) wrote *Waverley* and nothing else wrote *Waverley*'. 'The author of *Waverley* is not' is explained, correspondingly, as the alternation 'Either each thing failed to write *Waverley* or two or more things wrote *Waverly*'. This alternation is false, but meaningful; and it contains no expression purporting to name the author of *Waverley*. The statement 'The round square cupola on Berkeley College is not' is analyzed in similar fashion. So the old notion that statements of nonbeing defeat themselves goes by the board. When a statement of being or nonbeing is analyzed by Russell's theory of descriptions, it ceases to contain any expression which even purports to name the alleged entity whose being is in question, so that the meaningfulness of the statement no longer can be thought to presuppose that there be such an entity.

Now what of 'Pegasus'? This being a word rather than a descriptive phrase, Russell's argument does not immediately apply to it. However, it can easily be made to apply. We have only to rephrase 'Pegasus' as a description, in any way that seems adequately to single out our idea; say, 'the winged horse that was captured by Bellerophon'. Substituting such a phrase for 'Pegasus', we can then proceed to analyze the statement 'Pegasus is', or 'Pegasus is not', precisely on the analogy of Russell's analysis of 'The author of *Waverley* is' and 'The author of *Waverley* is not'.

In order thus to subsume a one-word name or alleged name such as 'Pegasus' under Russell's theory of description, we must, of course, be able first to translate the word into a description. But this is no real restriction. If the notion of Pegasus had been so obscure or so basic a one that no pat translation into a descriptive phrase had offered itself along familiar lines, we could still have availed ourselves of the following artificial and trivial-seeming device: we could have appealed to the *ex hypothesi* unanalyzable, irreducible attribute of *being Pegasus*, adopting, for its expression, the verb 'is-Pegasus', or 'pegasizes'. The noun 'Pegasus' itself could then be treated as derivative, and identified after all with a description: 'the thing that is-Pegasus', 'the thing that pegasizes'.

If the importing of such a predicate as 'pegasizes' seems to commit us to recognizing that there is a corresponding attribute, pegasizing, in Plato's heaven or in the minds of men, well and good. Neither we nor Wyman nor McX have been contending, thus far, about the being or nonbeing of universals, but rather about that of Pegasus. If in terms of pegasizing we can interpret the noun 'Pegasus' as a description subject to Russell's theory of descriptions, then we have disposed of the old notion that Pegasus cannot be said not to be without presupposing that in some sense Pegasus is.

Our argument is now quite general. McX and Wyman supposed that we could not meaningfully affirm a statement of the form 'So-and-so is not', with a simple or descriptive singular noun in place of 'so-and-so', unless so-and-so is. This supposition is now seen to be quite generally groundless, since the singular noun in question can always be expanded into a singular description, trivially or otherwise, and then analyzed out *à la* Russell.

We commit ourselves to an ontology containing numbers when we say there are prime numbers larger than a million; we commit ourselves to an ontology containing centaurs when we say there are centaurs; and we commit ourselves to an ontology containing Pegasus when we say Pegasus is. But we do not commit ourselves to an ontology containing Pegasus or the author of *Waverley* or the round square cupola on Berkeley College when we say that Pegasus or the author of *Waverley* or the cupola in question is *not*. We need no longer labor under the delusion that the meaningfulness of a statement containing a singular term presupposes an entity named by the term. A singular term need not name to be significant.

An inkling of this might have dawned on Wyman and McX even without benefit of Russell if they had only noticed—as so few of us do—that there is a gulf between meaning and naming even in the case of a singular term which is genuinely a name of an object. The following example from Frege will serve. The phrase 'Evening Star' names a certain large physical object of spherical form, which is hurtling through space some scores of millions of miles from here. The phrase 'Morning Star' names the same thing, as was probably first established by some observant Babylonian. But the two phrases cannot be regarded as having the same meaning; otherwise that Babylonian could have dispensed with his observations and contented himself with reflecting on the meanings of his words. The meanings, then, being different from one another, must be other than the named object, which is one and the same in both cases.

Confusion of meaning with naming not only made McX think he could not meaningfully repudiate Pegasus; a continuing confusion of meaning with naming no doubt helped engender his absurd notion that Pegasus is an idea, a mental entity. The structure of his confusion is as follows. He confused the alleged *named object* Pegasus with the *meaning* of the word 'Pegasus', therefore concluding that Pegasus must be in order that the word have meaning. But what sorts of things are meanings? This is a moot point; however, one might quite plausibly explain meanings as ideas in the mind, supposing we can make clear sense in turn of the idea of ideas in the mind. Therefore Pegasus, initially confused with a meaning, ends up as an idea in the mind. It is the more remarkable that Wyman, subject to the same initial motivation as McX, should have avoided this particular blunder and wound up with unactualized possibles instead.

Now let us turn to the ontological problem of universals: the question whether there are such entities as attributes, relations, classes, numbers, functions. McX, characteristically enough, thinks there are. Speaking of attributes, he says: "There are red houses, red roses, red sunsets; this much is prephilosophical common sense in which we must all agree. These houses, roses, and sunsets, then, have something in common; and this which they have in common is all I mean by the attribute of redness." For McX, thus, there being attributes is even more obvious and trivial than the obvious and trivial fact of there being red houses, roses, and sunsets. This, I think, is characteristic of metaphysics, or at least of that part of metaphysics called ontology: one who regards a statement on this subject as true at all must regard it as trivially true. One's ontology is basic to the conceptual scheme by which he interprets all experiences, even the most commonplace ones. Judged within some particular conceptual scheme—and how else is judgment possible?—an ontological statement goes without saying, standing in need of no separate justification at all. Ontological statements follow immediately from all manner of casual statements of commonplace fact, just as—from the point of view, anyway, of McX's conceptual scheme—'There is an attribute' follows from 'There are red houses, red roses, red sunsets'.

Judged in another conceptual scheme, an ontological statement which is axiomatic to McX's mind may, with equal immediacy and triviality, be adjudged false. One may admit that there are red houses, roses, and sunsets, but deny, except as a popular and misleading manner of speaking, that they have anything in common. The words 'houses', 'roses', and 'sunsets' are true of sundry individual entities which are houses and roses and sunsets, and the word 'red' or 'red object' is true of each of sundry individual entities which are red houses, red roses, red sunsets; but there is not, in addition, any entity whatever, individual or otherwise, which is named by the word 'redness', nor, for that matter, by the word 'househood', 'rosehood', 'sunsethood'. That the houses and roses and sunsets are all of them red may be taken as ultimate and irreducible, and it may be held that McX is no better off, in point of real explanatory power, for all the occult entities which he posits under such names as 'redness'.

One means by which McX might naturally have tried to impose his ontology of universals on us was already removed before we turned to the problem of universals. McX cannot argue that predicates such as 'red' or 'is-red', which we all concur in using, must be regarded as names each of a single universal entity in order that they be meaningful at all. For we have seen that being a name of something is a much more special feature than being meaningful. He cannot even charge us—at least not by *that* argument—with having posited an attribute of pegasizing by our adoption of the predicate 'pegasizes'.

However, McX hits upon a different stratagem. "Let us grant," he says, "this distinction between meaning and naming of which you make so much. Let us even grant that 'is red', 'pegasizes', etc., are not names of attributes. Still, you admit they have meanings. But these *meanings*, whether they are named or not, are still universals, and I venture to say that some of them might even be the very things that I call attributes, or something to much the same purpose in the end."

For McX, this is an unusually penetrating speech; and the only way I know to counter it is by refusing to admit meanings. However, I feel no reluctance toward refusing to admit meanings, for I do not thereby deny that words and statements are meaningful. McX and I may agree to the letter in our classification of linguistic forms into the meaningful and the meaning-less, even though McX construes meaningfulness as the *having* (in some sense of 'having') of some abstract entity which he calls a meaning, whereas I do not. I remain free to maintain that the fact that a given linguistic utterance is meaningful (or *significant*, as I prefer to say so as not to invite hypostasis of meanings as entities) is an ultimate and irreducible matter of fact; or, I may undertake to analyze it in terms directly of what people do in the presence of the linguistic utterance in question and other utterances similar to it.

The useful ways in which people ordinarily talk or seem to talk about meanings boil down to two: the *having* of meanings, which is significance, and *sameness* of meaning, or synonomy. What is called *giving* the meaning of an utterance is simply the uttering of a synonym, couched, ordinarily, in clearer language than the original. If we are allergic to meanings as such, we can speak directly of utterances as significant or insignificant, and as synonymous or heteronymous one with another. The problem of explaining these adjectives 'significant' and 'synonymous' with some degree of clarity and rigor—preferably, as I see it, in terms of behavior—is as difficult as it is important. But the explanatory value of special and irreducible intermediary entities called meanings is surely illusory.

Up to now I have argued that we can use singular terms significantly in sentences without presupposing that there are the entities which those terms purport to name. I have argued further that we can use general terms, for example, predicates, without conceding them to be names of abstract enti-ties. I have argued further that we can view utterances as significant, and as synonymous or heteronymous with one another, without countenancing a realm of entities called meanings. At this point McX begins to wonder whether there is any limit at all to our ontological immunity. Does *nothing* we may say commit us to the assumption of universals or other entities which we may find unwelcome?

I have already suggested a negative answer to this question, in speaking of bound variables, or variables of quantification, in connection with Russell's theory of descriptions. We can very easily involve ourselves in ontological commitments by saying, for example, that *there is something* (bound vari-able) which red houses and sunsets have in common; or that *there is something* which is a prime number larger than a million. But this is, essentially, the *only* way we can involve ourselves in ontological commit-ments: by our use of bound variables. The use of alleged names is no criterion, for we can repudiate their namehood at the drop of a hat unless the assumption of a corresponding entity can be spotted in the things we affirm in terms of bound variables. Names are, in fact, altogether immaterial to the ontological issue, for I have shown, in connection with 'Pegasus' and 'pegasize', that names can be converted to descriptions, and Russell has shown that descriptions can be eliminated. Whatever we say with the help of names can be said in a language which shuns names altogether. To be assumed as an entity is, purely and simply, to be reckoned as the value of a variable. In terms of the categories of traditional grammar, this amounts roughly to saying that to be is to be in the range of reference of a pronoun. Pronouns are the basic media of reference; nouns might better have been named propronouns. The variables of quantification, 'something', 'nothing', 'everything', range over our whole ontology, whatever it may be; and we are convicted of a particular ontological presupposition if, and only if, the alleged presuppositum has to be reckoned among the entities over which our variables range in order to render one of our affirmations true.

We may say, for example, that some dogs are white and not thereby commit ourselves to recognizing either doghood or whiteness as entities. 'Some dogs are white' says that some things that are dogs are white; and, in order that this statement be true, the things over which the bound variable 'something' ranges must include some white dogs, but need not include doghood or whiteness. On the other hand, when we say that some zoological species are cross-fertile we are committing ourselves to recognizing as entities the several species themselves, abstract though they are. We remain so committed at least until we devise some way of so paraphrasing the statement as to show that the seeming reference to species on the part of our bound variable use an avoidable manner of speaking.

Classical mathematics, as the example of primes larger than a million clearly illustrates, is up to its neck in commitments to an ontology of abstract entities. Thus it is that the great medieval controversy over universals has flared up anew in the modern philosophy of mathematics. The issue is clearer now than of old, because we now have a more explicit standard whereby to decide what ontology a given theory or form of discourse is committed to: a theory is committed to those and only those entities to which the bound variables of the theory must be capable of referring in order that the affirmations made in the theory be true.

Because this standard of ontological presupposition did not emerge clearly in the philosophical tradition, the modern philosophical mathematicians have not on the whole recognized that they were debating the same old problem of universals in a newly clarified form. But the fundamental cleavages among modern points of view on foundations of mathematics do come down pretty explicitly to disagreements as to the range of entities to which the bound variables should be permitted to refer.

The three main medieval points of view regarding universals are designated by historians as *realism*, *conceptualism*, and *nominalism*. Essentially these same three doctrines reappear in twentieth-century surveys of the philosophy of mathematics under the new names *logicism*, *intuitionism*, and *formalism*.

Realism, as the word is used in connection with the medieval controversy over universals, is the Platonic doctrine that universals or abstract entities have being independently of the mind; the mind may discover them but cannot create them. *Logicism*, represented by Frege, Russell, Whitehead, Church, and Carnap, condones the use of bound variables to refer to abstract entities known and unknown, specifiable and unspecifiable, indiscriminately.

Conceptualism holds that there are universals but they are mind-made. *Intuitionism*, espoused in modern times in one form or another by Poincaré, Brouwer, Weyl, and others, countenances the use of bound variables to refer to abstract entities only when those entities are capable of being cooked up individually from ingredients specified in advance. As Fraenkel has put it, logicism holds that classes are discovered while intuitionism holds that they are invented—a fair statement indeed of the old opposition between realism and conceptualism. This opposition is no mere quibble; it makes an essential difference in the amount of classical mathematics to which one is willing to subscribe. Logicists, or realists, are able on their assumptions to get Cantor's ascending orders of infinity; intuitionists are compelled to stop with the lowest order of infinity, and, as an indirect consequence, to abandon even some of the classical laws of real numbers. The modern controversy between logicism and intuitionism arose, in fact, from disagreements over infinity.

Formalism, associated with the name of Hilbert, echoes intuitionism in deploring the logicist's unbridled recourse to universals. But formalism also finds intuitionism unsatisfactory. This could happen for either of two opposite reasons. The formalist might, like the logicist, object to the crippling of classical mathematics; or he might, like the *nominalists* of old, object to admitting abstract entities at all, even in the restrained sense of mind-made entities. The upshot is the same: the formalist keeps classical mathematics as a play of insignificant notations. This play of notations can still be of utility—whatever utility it has already shown itself to have as a crutch for physicists and technologists. But utility need not imply significance, in any literal linguistic sense. Nor need the marked success of mathematicians in spinning out theorems, and in finding objective bases for agreement with one another's results, imply significance. For an adequate basis for agreement among mathematicians can be found simply in the rules which govern the manipulation of the notations—these syntactical rules being, unlike the notations themselves, quite significant and intelligible.

I have argued that the sort of ontology we adopt can be consequential—notably in connection with mathematics, although this is only an example. Now how are we to adjudicate among rival ontologies? Certainly the answer is not provided by the semantical formula "To be is to be the value of a variable"; this formula serves rather, conversely, in testing the conformity of a given remark or doctrine to a prior ontological standard. We look to bound variables in connection with ontology not in order to know what there is, but in order to know what a given remark or doctrine, ours or someone else's, *says* there is; and this much is quite properly a problem involving language. But what there is is another question.

In debating over what there is, there are still reasons for operating on a semantical plane. One reason is to escape from the predicament noted at the beginning of this essay: the predicament of my not being able to admit that there are things which McX countenances and I do not. So long as I adhere to my ontology, as opposed to McX's, I cannot allow my bound variables to refer to entities which belong to McX's ontology and not to mine. I can, however, consistently describe our disagreement by characterizing the statements which McX affirms. Provided merely that my ontology countenances linguistic forms, or at least concrete inscriptions and utterances, I can talk about McX's sentences.

Another reason for withdrawing to a semantical plane is to find common ground on which to argue. Disagreement in ontology involves basic disagreement in conceptual schemes; yet McX and I, despite these basic disagreements, find that our conceptual schemes converge sufficiently in their intermediate and upper ramifications to enable us to communicate successfully on such topics as politics, weather, and, in particular, language. In so far as our basic controversy over ontology can be translated upward into a semantical controversy about words and what to do with them, the collapse of the controversy into question-begging may be delayed.

It is no wonder, then, that ontological controversy should tend into controversy over language. But we must not jump to the conclusion that what there is depends on words. Translatability of a question into semantical terms is no indication that the question is linguistic. To see Naples is to bear a name which, when prefixed to the words 'sees Naples', yields a true sentence; still there is nothing linguistic about seeing Naples.

Our acceptance of an ontology is, I think, similar in principle to our acceptance of a scientific theory, say a system of physics: we adopt, at least insofar as we are reasonable, the simplest conceptual scheme into which the disordered fragments of raw experience can be fitted and arranged. Our ontology is determined once we have fixed upon the over-all conceptual scheme which is to accommodate science in the broadest sense; and the considerations which determine a reasonable construction of any part of that conceptual scheme, for example, the biological or the physical part, are not different in kind from the considerations which determine a reasonable construction of the whole. To whatever extent the adoption of any system of scientific theory may be said to be a matter of language, the same—but no more—may be said of the adoption of an ontology.

But simplicity, as a guiding principle in constructing conceptual schemes, is not a clear and unambiguous idea; and it is quite capable of presenting a double or multiple standard. Imagine, for example, that we have devised the most economical set of concepts adequate to the play-by-play reporting of immediate experience. The entities under this scheme—the values of bound variables—are, let us suppose, individual subjective events of sensation or reflection. We should still find, no doubt, that a physicalistic conceptual scheme, purporting to talk about external objects, offers great advantages in simplifying our over-all reports. By bringing together scattered sense events and treating them as perceptions of one object, we reduce the complexity of our stream of experience to a manageable conceptual simplicity. The rule of simplicity is indeed our guiding maxim in assigning sense data to objects: we associate an earlier and a later round sensum with the same so-called penny, or with two different so-called pennies, in obedience to the demands of maximum simplicity in our total world-picture.

Here we have two competing conceptual schemes, a phenomenalistic one and a physicalistic one. Which should prevail? Each has its advantages; each has its special simplicity in its own way. Each, I suggest, deserves to be developed. Each may be said, indeed, to be the more fundamental, though in different senses: the one is epistemologically, the other physically, fundamental.

The physical conceptual scheme simplifies our account of experience because of the way myriad scattered sense events come to be associated with single so-called objects; still there is no likelihood that each sentence about physical objects can actually be translated, however deviously and complexly, into the phenomenalistic language. Physical objects are postulated entities which round out and simplify our account of the flux of experience, just as the introduction of irrational numbers simplifies laws of arithmetic. From the point of view of the conceptual scheme of the elementary arithmetic of rational numbers alone, the broader arithmetic of rational and irrational numbers would have the status of a convenient myth, simpler than the literal truth (namely, the arithmetic of rationals) and yet containing that literal truth as a scattered part. Similarly, from a phenomenalistic point of view, the conceptual scheme of physical objects is a convenient myth, simpler than the literal truth and yet containing that literal truth as a scattered part.[2]

Now what of classes or attributes of physical objects, in turn? A platonistic ontology of this sort is, from the point of view of a strictly physicalistic conceptual scheme, as much a myth as that physicalistic conceptual scheme itself is for phenomenalism. This higher myth is a good and useful one, in turn, in so far as it simplifies our account of physics. Since mathematics is an integral part of this higher myth, the utility of this myth for physical science is evident enough. In speaking of it nevertheless as a myth, I echo that philosophy of mathematics to which I alluded earlier under the name of formalism. But an attitude of formalism may with equal justice be adopted toward the physical conceptual scheme, in turn, by the pure aesthete or phenomenalist.

The analogy between the myth of mathematics and the myth of physics is, in some additional and perhaps fortuitous ways, strikingly close. Consider, for example, the crisis which was precipitated in the foundations of mathematics, at the turn of the century, by the discovery of Russell's paradox and other antinomies of set theory. These contradictions had to be obviated by unintuitive, *ad hoc* devices; our mathematical myth-making became deliberate and evident to all. But what of physics? An antinomy arose between the undular and the corpuscular accounts of light; and if this was not as out-and-out a contradiction as Russell's paradox, I suspect that the reason is that physics is not as out-and-out as mathematics. Again, the second great modern crisis in the foundations of mathematics—precipitated in 1931 by Godel's proof that there are bound to be undecidable statements in arithmetic—has its companion piece in physics in Heisenberg's indeterminacy principle.

In earlier pages I undertook to show that some common arguments in favor of certain ontologies are fallacious. Further, I advanced an explicit standard whereby to decide what the ontological commitments of a theory are. But the question what ontology actually to adopt still stands open, and the obvious counsel is tolerance and an experimental spirit. Let us by all means see how much of the physicalistic conceptual scheme can be reduced to a phenomenalistic one; still, physics also naturally demands pursuing, irreducible *in toto* though it be. Let us see how, or to what degree, natural science may be rendered independent of platonistic mathematics; but let us also pursue mathematics and delve into its platonistic foundations.

From among the various conceptual schemes best suited to these various pursuits, one—phenomenalistic—claims epistemological priority. Viewed from within the phenomenalistic conceptual scheme, the ontologies of physical objects and mathematical objects are myths. The quality of myth, however, is relative; relative, in this case, to the epistemological point of view. This point of view is one among various, corresponding to one among our various interests and purposes.

NOTES

From *Review of Metaphysics* 2, no. 1 (1948). Reprinted by permission of the editor of *Review of Metaphysics*.

1. The impulse to distinguish terminologically between existence as applied to objects actualized somewhere in space-time and existence (or subsistence or being) as applied to other entities arises in part, perhaps, from an idea that the observation of nature is relevant only to questions of existence of the first kind. But this idea is readily refuted by counterinstances such as 'the ratio of the number of centaurs to the number of unicorns'. If there were such a ratio, it would be an abstract entity, viz. a number. Yet it is only by studying nature that we conclude that the number of centaurs and the number of unicorns are both 0 and hence that there is no such ratio.

2. The arithmetical analogy is due to [Phillip] Frank, [*Modern Science and Its Philosophy* (Cambridge, Mass.: Harvard University Press, 1949)], pp. 108f.

17 PEARS

David Pears is a particularist. He is in agreement with Joseph Butler, who maintained that "everything is what it is and not another thing." In support of this position Pears argues that the historical positions of realism, conceptualism, and nominalism rest on circular reasoning. The problem of universals inevitably involves naming things. How are we to justify naming things the way we do? The realist, for example, maintains that there is a universal that particulars share or have in common. It is the universal that justifies the naming process.

Pears suggests that we are faced with two, and only two, alternatives. The first, to justify the naming process by the use of other words, is inevitably circular—it is tantamount to going to a dictionary to learn the meaning of the word 'X'. 'X' is defined by the word 'Y', 'Y' by the word 'Z', and 'Z' is, in turn, defined by 'X'. In the end one ends up justifying the naming process in somewhat the following way: "'We are able to call things red because they are red' which is too obviously circular even to look informative." The second alternative Pears suggests is that the only way to avoid this circularity is to break out of the vicious cycle of words by ostension. However, when one justifies the naming process by ostensive definition one is not denoting a universal; rather one is denoting a particular (thing). We understand, therefore, that there are no universals.

Universals

'Do universals exist?' This question was debated so long and vehemently because it was mistaken for a factual question about some airy realm of being. But why was this mistake made? One diagnosis is that general words were tacitly assimilated to proper names,[1] and that when this practice is exposed, it becomes harmless but pointless.[2] But this is a description of what happened rather than an explanation; it gives something more like a symptom than a cause. Could so many philosophers have been so silly in such a simple way? Even moderate skepticism on this point would lead to an attempt to supplement this suggestion. This article is such an attempt.

'Universals exist' has a deceptive logic. Realists offer it as the conclusion of many arguments: but unlike the premises of these arguments, it cannot be understood as a verifiable statement of fact. On the other hand, if it is taken merely as an esoteric way of stating those premises over again, the vehemence of the controversy becomes inexplicable. Faced with this difficulty of interpretation, some modern philosophers suggest that it is no good puzzling about its literal meaning, just as it is no good puzzling about the literal meaning of dreams. For traditional philosophy provided a small set of possible conclusions to arguments about the generality of thought and language, and tradition was strong. If a tribe educated its children to dream according to a tradition which restricted their manifest dream contents within narrow limits, it would be difficult to discover their much more varied latent dream contents.[3] Similarly, although realists are argumentative, it is difficult to answer the question why they maintain that universals exist. Any answer must be based on a selection from among the many reasons which they themselves proffer: and a good selection will be diagnostic; it will successfully explain the doctrine. There is no sharp boundary here between descriptions of the premises of philosophical arguments and diagnoses of their conclusions: because success in explaining, which is the criterion of a diagnosis, is a matter of degree, and because the reasons which philosophers themselves give for their doctrines sometimes completely explain why they held them. Quine's remark, that realists find a universal for every property which can be existentially generalized,[4] is an extremely brief description. The thesis of Berkeley and Mill was more than this: it was a diagnosis, but an inadequate one. I shall try to provide a less inadequate diagnosis.

'Because universals exist' is the answer to at least two general questions: 'Why are things what they are'?[5] and 'Why are we able to name things as we do'? Though Plato and Aristotle sometimes distinguished these two questions, it was characteristic of Greek thought to confuse them. Yet they can be clearly distinguished, the first requiring a dynamic answer from scientists, and the second a static answer from logicians. Now philosophy has often staked premature claims in the territory of science by giving quick comprehensive answers to questions which really required laborious detailed answers. And clearly this is what happened to the first of the two questions. When detailed causal answers were provided to it, the comprehensive answer 'Because universals exist' was no longer acceptable or necessary.[6] But what would detailed answers to the second question be like? Presumably they would be explanations of the meanings of words. But philosophers are easily led to neglect such detailed progressive answers to the second question, and to seek instead a comprehensive and ultimate explanation of naming. For, though comprehensive answers to the first question are clearly futile, there are no obvious penalties attached to answering the second question in a comprehensive way. Yet, I shall argue—and this will be my first thesis—that any comprehensive explanation of naming is necessarily circular: and that philosophers think that, in spite of this disadvantage, such explanations have some point largely because they wrongly assimilate naming to natural processes. Yet surely naming cannot be utterly artificial? My second thesis will be that the desire to understand naming leads to a hunt for a completely satisfactory analogy: but that all other processes either already contain the very feature of naming which was puzzling, or else are too natural or too artificial to be really analogous; and that it was the inevitable oscillation between these three points which prolonged the controversy about universals.

It is unnecessary to produce evidence that philosophers who proposed the existence of universals thought that they were explaining the unity of classes and hence the possibility of naming. What is debatable is whether this was an important motive, and this can be decided only in the sequel. My first thesis, which I must now try to establish, is that realism is necessarily a circular explanation of naming. Now the answer to the question 'Why are we able to name things as we do?' is 'The reason varies'. For it is always possible with more or less ingenuity, depending on the degree of atomicity of the name, to give a detailed informative reason; and this reason will vary with the name. But ultimately there must be some exit from the maze of words, and, wherever this exit is made, it will be impossible to give an informative reason except by pointing. For the only other way of giving an informative reason is to give a new word, and this would prevent the exit from the maze of words from being made at this place.[7] Still at the place where the exit is made it is always possible to give a detailed reason like 'We are able to call things red because they are red', which is too obviously circular even to look informative. Or alternatively it is possible to say "We are able to call things φ because they are φ, and this is a general reason which is almost as obviously circular and uninformative. What philosophers who propose the existence of universals do is to propose a general reason which looks informative because it shifts to another level, but unfortunately is not. It merely marks time: but marking time can look very like marching if only the movements of the performers are watched, and not the ground which they profess to be covering. Yet this ground could not be covered. For the reason could not be informative even if it were detailed; since there could be a non-circular answer to the question 'What universal?' only if the exit from the maze of words were made at some different point, which would merely put off the moment of embarrassment from which in the end neither speech nor thought can be saved. Thus realism fails to escape the limitations of all explanations of naming; that they can be informative only if they are not general but detailed, and then only if they are not given at the point where an exit is made from the maze of words.

Uninformative answers have their point. They are silencing. What is wrong with realism is not this, but that it masquerades as an answer which advances knowledge one step further. The analytic machine acquires a momentum which carries it beyond the point where it ought to stop. And there is an inveterate philosophical habit which strengthens the tendency to go beyond this point, or rather to think that one has gone beyond it. 'A thing is called by a certain name because it instantiates a certain universal' is obviously circular when particularized, but it looks imposing when it is left in this general form. And it looks imposing in this general form largely because of the inveterate philosophical habit of treating the shadows cast by words and sentences as if they were separately identifiable. Universals, like facts and propositions, are such shadows; and too often philosophers by appealing to them in general terms have produced in their readers a feeling of satisfaction which ought to have been produced only by specifying them.[8] But universals are specifiable only by reference to words. Similarly facts may be brute and propositions may be definite, but what exactly it is about them which is brute or definite can be specified only by reference to the sentences which were the unacknowledged starting-points. In all these cases it is tacit reduplication which makes philosophers think that they can enjoy the benefits of specifying without actually specifying. Yet the explanation of naming is incomplete until a particular universal is specified, and, when it is specified, the explanation immediately fails through circularity. Naming is hazardous,[9] and any attempt to make it foolproof by basing it on an independent foundation must fail in this way. It is impossible to cross the gap between language and things without really crossing it.[10]

Since the failure of realism to perform this feat is inevitable, its rivals fail too. Nominalism, conceptualism and imagism,[11] in so far as they are rivals of realism, are attempts to provide a unity which will explain naming. Nominalism says that a name is merely connected with a multitude of things, sometimes adding that these things are similar. Conceptualism says that the name is not directly connected with the things but only via a concept, thus changing the nodal point. Imagism says that the nodal point is an image. And realism says that there is really no nodal point, since a name, though it appears to be connected with a multitude of things is all the time connected with only one thing, a universal. This is an over-simplification of what these theories say about the One and the Many; but it is enough for my next purpose, which is to show that these rivals of realism cannot produce a non-circular explanation of naming at those points where an exit is made from the maze of words.

The two psychological theories say that one word can apply to many things only because of the mediation of a concept or of an image. Locke's abstract general idea is 'the workmanship of the understanding, but has its foundation in the similitudes of things'.[12] And Berkeley replaces it by an idea which 'considered in itself is particular but becomes general by being made to represent or stand for all other particular ideas of the same sort'.[13] But what similitudes, and what representation? In the end both Locke's concept and Berkeley's image are completely identifiable only by their use.[14] Of course we can partly identify images by describing their features: and in this way we may even almost completely identify them, since certain images most naturally stand for certain things. And the same could be said of concepts, if they were not merely philosophers' reifications of mental processes. But this will not completely identify either of them, since thought may not follow the most natural course; nor is it always clear which is the most natural course. It is not so much that thinking is speaking as that thinking is like speaking in the only way that matters: it uses one thing as a symbol to stand for many things. And the only tool which could not be used differently is the use. Even something which had its use written on it could be used differently.[15] And, if the psychological tool, whether concept or image, can be completely identified only by the things on which it is used, it cannot explain naming without circularity. For, unless we point, the use can be specified only by backward reference to the name. Nor is this circularity surprising. For psychological tools have no advantage over words: they are like them in being symbols, and unlike them only in being shadowy symbols.

The type of nominalism which says that a name is applied to a number of things which are similar immediately falls into the same circularity. For 'similar' is an incomplete predicate, anything being similar to anything in some way, perhaps a negative way.[16] And in the end the kind of similarity which is meant can be specified only by a backward reference to the name. Equally the type of nominalism which merely says that a name is applied to a class of things cannot say which class without a backward reference to the name. Here the circularity is so obvious and there is so little to cushion the shock of the realization that naming is naming that this type of nominalism seems hardly tenable. For, however strongly nominalists react against realism, they can never quite escape its influence: once somebody had said that universals exist it could never be quite the same again. Surely, one wants to protest, there must be some way of giving the class besides reference to the name? Well there is, of course, enumeration. But this answer seems to fail to allow for the possibility of ever using the name correctly in any synthetic sentence. For, if the class is given by enumeration, surely every use of the name must be either incorrect or analytic? Since, if to call a thing 'ϕ' is to include it in the class of things called 'ϕ', then surely either it is incorrect to call it 'ϕ' or else the class cannot be given without reference to it? It is the example of realism which encourages these protests. But it is a bad example. Such neatness is not to be had. For, first of all, these classes cannot be given by enumeration of all their members, since, except for words belonging to dead languages, they are never complete. Nor is it true even that each member must either contribute or not contribute towards giving a class; since a name may be applied to the same thing twice, once analytically and once synthetically, and even a single use of a name may be synthetic for the speaker and analytic for the hearer. In fact the disjunction 'Analytic or Synthetic' cannot be applied simply to the addition of a member to a class without further caveats. But this in itself is not enough to remove the difficulty; it only makes it reappear in a new form. For if the addition of a member to a class can be synthetic for the speaker and analytic for a subsequent lexicographer, then to what class was the member added? Surely we now have two classes on our hands instead of one? An analogy will help us to deal with this new form of the difficulty. Naming is like electing the sort of member who makes a difference to a club. Strictly we cannot say without qualification to what club he was elected, since it was one club before he was elected and another club after he was elected. The club building might be pointed out, and of course there is no parallel move in the case of naming, although realism pretends that there is. But, even if there were no building or anything else of that kind, the puzzle about the two clubs would not be very perplexing. Similarly, when we reject the simple application of the dichotomy 'Analytic or Synthetic' the resulting puzzle about two classes is not very perplexing. All that is necessary is to point out that a class is incompletely given by a changing quorum. This may be untidy, but why not? There is something radically wrong with a request to be given a class which is not satisfied either with a reference to the name or with progressive enumeration. It is a request to be given something without being given it; as if somewhere, if only philosophers searched long enough, there could be found something which possessed all the advantages of a word and none of its disadvantages, an epistemological vehicle which carried all its destinations.

I now turn to my second thesis, that nothing is sufficiently like naming without being too like naming. Defenders of realism, like defenders of the other theories of naming, might object that the criticism contained in my first thesis is obvious, superficial and directed against a man of straw. For realism does not offer a non-circular detailed explanation of naming— how could it?—but simply gives a general characterization of the sort of unity which makes naming possible. But notice how very like a dream realism is. Taken literally it seems to be of little importance. But, if it is taken as the expression of a doctrine which, if *per impossibile* it were true, would give it great importance, the suggestion is immediately repudiated. Yet it does express such a doctrine, even if its exponents intermittently deny that it does; and it is to the devious expression of this doctrine that it owes most of its attractiveness. Its manifest content is little more than a harmless caprice, but its latent content is a serious error.

But has realism no point when it is taken simply as a general characterization of the sort of unity which makes naming impossible? One might answer that it has no point and that it succeeds in appearing to have some point only by the device of inventing a new comprehensive term; and that this device is considered effective only in philosophy, since outside philosophy it is too obviously like making an impressive gesture in the direction of the interesting object, opening one's mouth and saying absolutely nothing. But such a denial would be tantamount to a denial that any general characterization of the sort of unity which makes naming possible could have a point. And surely such a denial would be wrong, since something can be done towards explaining the general possibility of naming by finding analogous processes? For instance, what makes naming possible is one thing which is in many things as an ingredient.[17] But does this analogy throw much light on naming? Any feature of logical mixing which is at all interesting seems to distinguish it from all other sorts of mixing. The values of an unrestricted variable are strange receptacles. What prevents contrary ingredients from being put in together, or an implicant from appearing without its implicate, is never the causal consequences. And anyway the whole notion of mixing ingredients which were not there before the mixing is peculiar. Could there be a logical conjuring trick?

Here defenders of realism might object that a new misunderstanding had replaced the old one. For, if realism is to be understood, not only must a general characterization of naming be allowed, but also the verification principle must not be applied too crudely. And anyway, if mixing is not a good analogy, this only means that some better analogy must be sought. This objection might lead to a tolerant examination of other analogies.[18] But fortunately it also opens up a short cut to the heart of the matter, which I shall soon take. Now it would be taking too short a cut to repeat the platitude that naming is *sui generis*. For it is natural to seek an analogy even if the search can never be completely successful. And anyway Butler's truism applies to everything. What is needed in order to explain the peculiar persistence of the debate about universals is something slightly longer, a demonstration that no analogy can be sufficiently close to satisfy philosophers without being too close.

It is most natural to seek a visible process as an analogy to naming, particularly for the Greeks who began this controversy.[19] Now previously I insisted that it is impossible in the end to give a detailed non-circular description of what makes it possible to name anything. Here, however, it would be unfair to object that, if naming in general is compared to a visible process, still that process itself must be named. For this sort of circularity is the inevitable result of the philosopher's predicament. However, it is dangerous to begin speaking at all where so little can be said. For it is fatally easy to think that one has separate access to what makes a name applicable just because one has separate access to whatever stands for this in the analogy. But, waiving this, let us now take the short cut and ask what sort of visible process could be analogous to naming. Let us try a rough analogy and say that one word is connected with many objects in the same way that the estuary of a river is connected with its many sources. But this analogy fails because this connection just happens naturally. We might then try to mend the analogy by saying that water follows the easiest course. But this could be called choice only anthropomorphically, in an extended and weak sense of 'choice'. In order to introduce choice in a restricted, strong sense, it is necessary to alter the analogy and say that people by directing the streams choose which sources shall feed the river. But, if the first process was too natural to be like naming, the second is too artificial, since, for the analogy to work, the sources ought to have something in common besides the fact that the river is fed from them. And it is difficult to find an analogy which is neither too natural nor too artificial. The characteristic of naming which is difficult to match is that the objects have something in common besides being called by one name, but nothing in common which counts except that in virtue of which they are called by one name. And this characteristic can be matched only by allowing that something makes it convenient but not absolutely necessary for people to canalize streams into the river in the way they do, and that whatever it is which makes this choice convenient is the only thing common to the sources which counts. But this compromise between the two extremes introduces into the analogy the very feature which it was intended to explain. For just how something works in influencing usage was what was to be explained. Nor is there a fourth alternative. So after all even general analogical characterizations of naming do fall into a circularity which is closely related to the type of circularity which my first thesis exposed. Neither in detail nor in general is it possible to step outside language.

This short way with analogies looks too superficial. For suppose that it is granted that one of the things that metaphysicians do is to seek the unattainable: that they hunt for definitions which would in no way involve their definienda,[20] and for analogies which would in no way involve what they were intended to explain. Yet even so metaphysics is a natural and inevitable pursuit, since the easiest way to discover how far one can go is to try to go one stage farther. And anyway there is a difference between complete failure and partial success; since, so long as analogies do not reach the point of self-frustration they get better and better as they approach it. These two qualifications are just but they only serve to strengthen my thesis that it was oscillation between the three points which prolonged the controversy about universals. For unless the possible analogies are mapped out in this simple way, it seems always conceivable that some altogether better analogy might lurk in an unexplored corner.

And what more are the rival theories of naming doing than seeking a completely satisfactory analogy? It is only jargon which makes them appear to be doing something more. The type of nominalism which suggests that things which are called by one name have only their name in common represents the extreme of artificiality.[21] It suggests that there are never any ways of telling even approximately whether a word is used in one sense or two senses. At the other extreme stands the type of realism which suggests that there is always one method of getting a precise answer to this question. In between are all the other theories of naming, which allow that it is neither impossible for the lexicographer to succeed in answering this question nor impossible for him to fail. None of these middle theories is really wrong, since of course we do bestow common names on certain chosen groups of things which exhibit certain similarities (else why should we do it?) or instantiate certain universals (why else were they invented?). But on the other hand none of them goes deep enough to satisfy the true metaphysician who is in all of us; since though they take us to the bottom of naming, we were in a simpler way already there, and they do not succeed in showing us how naming is founded on something else which lies even deeper. Hence each of these middle theories (except imagism, which says something empirical which seems to be false) develops its own thesis with embarrassing success up to a point, and can discredit its rivals only by accusing them of not going beyond that point. But, since naming cannot be explained by anything which really goes beyond a reasoned choice of usage, this is an unfair accusation. And its unfairness is concealed from those who make it only because each tacitly and wrongly assumes that his own theory alone does go beyond this point. Thus moderate nominalists maintain that similarity is a better explanation of the unity of a class than the presence of a universal. (But why should people not *just* recognize the presence of universals?) And moderate realists retort that this admits the existence of at least one universal, similarity. (But why should the presence of a universal explain the recognition of similarity if it cannot explain the recognition of anything else? Why should people not *just* recognize similarity?) Really these are not two arguments but two bare assertions of superiority. They are manoeuvres which are carried out in a way which suggests that they are difficult and that they must be advances: but both these suggestions are false. Yet these theories do seem to be striving towards something. And they are. Their goal is the unattainable completely satisfactory explanation of naming. And, as so often happens in metaphysics, progress is measured by distance from the starting-point and not by proximity to the goal whose unattainability each uses against its rivals without allowing it to deter itself.

Thus theories of naming, which seem to flout the verification principle without therefore saying nothing, can be interpreted as disguised analogies. And, though there is a common limit beyond which they cannot go, the success with which they stealthily approach this limit, camouflaged in the technical terms of epistemology, varies. But if this almost mechanical oscillation is avoided what else can be said about naming? Certainly as the first part of this article showed, detailed answers to the question why we name things as we do will in the end be circular. Only the trick of giving a general answer as if it were a detailed one cloaks their failure. If a word is explained ostensively, then however difficult this process may be it really is explained ostensively. It is no good trying to combine the concreteness of ostensive definition with the clarity of verbal definition. Verbal definitions have such an easy task just because ostensive definitions have such a difficult task. Surveyors find it easier to fix the positions of points which they can visit than to fix the positions of points which they cannot visit. Similarly it is easy to fix the relative positions of words: but the points in things to which words are related are in the end inaccessible to logicians.

Then what else can be said about naming? How *does* the lexicographer tell when a word is used in two senses rather that in one sense? Surely there must be something in common to all well constructed series of things? Yes, just that they *are* well constructed. For this question already contains the equivalent of any possible comprehensive answer which could be given to it. And, though in one way it is hard to see what detailed answers could be given to it, in another way it is only too easy to see. For we never reach a point where an exit *must* be made from the maze of words. Admittedly, if a verbal explanation is given at one point, it is only successful if at some other point a connection with things is already understood; and at some points it is more natural not to offer more words. But at no point is an exit obligatory. So, if detailed reasons why we call a thing what we do are required, it is easy to give them; but never ultimately or in the end, since here *ex vi termini* it is impossible to give them. But philosophers tend to ignore this kind of detailed answer and press on. But where to? Perhaps to experimental psychology, in order to discover how changes in the sense organs, in training and in interests alter the ways in which people group things. But this sort of investigation only gives the varying tests of the good construction of a series, and not its essence. But what could its essence be? When general analogical characterizations of naming have been mentioned, and detailed reasons why we call particular things by particular names, and the psychological background of all this, what is left? The desire to go on explaining naming is to some extent the result of the way these three fields have been confused, and to some extent the result of a natural feeling that in such a vast territory there might be something which lies outside these three fields. But above all it is the result of the Protean metaphysical urge to transcend language.

NOTES

From *Philosophical Quarterly* 1 (1951). Reprinted by permission of the author and the editor of *Philosophical Quarterly*.

1. Cf. J. S. Mill, *Examination of Sir William Hamilton's Philosophy* (5th edn., London, 1878) chap. XVII, p. 381, and Berkeley, [*A Treatise Concerning the*] *Principles of Human Knowledge*, Introduction § 18.
2. Cf. M. Lazerowitz, 'The Existence of Universals' (*Mind*, 1946, pp. 1 ff.).
3. Cf. Freud, *The Interpretation of Dreams*, tr. A. A. Brill (London, 1913), p. 166.
4. Cf. 'Designation and Existence' in Feigl and Sellars, *Readings in Philosophical Analysis* (New York, 1949), p. 48.
5. Aristotle criticized Plato's theory largely as an inadequate answer to this question.

6. Socrates in the *Phaedo* (100 d) says that it is the only acceptable answer to the first question. But the advance of science has undermined this thesis more thoroughly than the advance of logic has undermined the thesis that it is an acceptable answer to the second question.
7. Cf. the view sketched by Socrates in the *Theaetetus* 201e–202c, and Antisthenes' view given by Aristotle in *Met [Metaphysics]*. H, 1043 b 23–32; also L. Wittgenstein, *Tractatus* 5; M. Schlick, *Grundzüge der Naturphilosophie* (Vienna, 1948), p. 21; and A. J. Ayer, *Thinking and Meaning* (London, 1947), p. 28.
8. The same trick is played by those who say that laws of nature exhibit connections between universals. This gives the impression that we could independently know the eternal framework in which temporal things move and change, rather as we independently know how a piston must move by looking at a cylinder: cf. what Kohler says about Aristotle's astronomy and Descartes' neurology (*Gestalt Psychology*, London, 1930, pp. 82–86).
9. Cf. Bradley, *Appearance and Reality* [Oxford: The Clarendon Press, 1893], p. 22 and p. 533; and C. S. Peirce, *Collected Papers* (vol. I, para. 145): 'Direct experience is neither certain nor uncertain, because it affirms nothing—it just is.'
10. Cf. Stuart Hampshire, 'Skepticism and Meaning' (*Philosophy*, July 1950, p. 245).
11. Cf. H. H. Price, *Thinking and Representation* (British Academy Lecture, 1946).
12. Locke, *Essay Concerning Human Understanding*, Bk. III, Chap. III, § xiii.
13. Berkeley, *Principles of Human Knowledge*, Introduction, para. 12.
14. This is due to Wittgenstein: cf. e.g. *Tractatus*, 3.326, 'In order to recognize the symbol in the sign we must consider the significant use'.
15. W. T. Stace in 'Russell's Neutral Monism' in *The Philosophy of Bertrand Russell*, pp. 381–83, complains that neither Berkeley's precise image nor Russell's vague image (in *An Inquiry into Meaning and Truth* [London: Allen and Unwin, 1940]) succeeds in explaining the generality of thought. But no description of any item of mental furniture which included only its momentary properties and not its habitual use could possibly explain the generality of thought.
16. Hence the point of many riddles. Cf. Stuart Hampshire, 'Skepticism and Meaning' (*Philosophy*, July 1950, p. 238). Also Plato, *Protagoras* 331 d. The Platonic theory avoids the 'similarity' difficulty, but not of course the general difficulty of which this is only one form. Speusippus, who abandoned the Platonic theory, seems to have held that, since every species is like every other species in some way, it is impossible to define one species without defining every other species. Cf. Aristotle, *Post. An. [Posterior Analytics]* 97 a 6–11. Cf. H. Cherniss, *Aristotle's Criticism of Plato and the Academy* (I. 60), quoted by W. D. Ross in his note on this passage. J. Stenzel, in Pauly-Wissowa *Real-Encyclopädie*, s.v. Speusippus, pp. 1650 and 1655, brings out the affinity between Speusippus' view and Post-Kantian idealism. Cf. Brand Blanshard on individuals (not species). 'One never gets what is fully particular until one has specified its relations of every kind with everything else in the universe', *The Nature of Thought* (London, 1939), vol. I, p. 639. Curiously enough N. R. Campbell arrives independently at a similar conclusion about species, when he is discussing the definition of such substances as silver, mercury or lead (*Physics. The Elements*, Cambridge, 1920, p. 50). All attempts to explain the unity of a species by similarity—whether by similarity of the individuals to one another, or by similarities and differences between the species and other species—suffer from the same incompleteness.
17. Cf. A. N. Whitehead, *Science and the Modern World* (Cambridge, 1928), pp. 197 ff. For a criticism of this analogy, cf. Bentham, *Works*, vol. VIII, p. 335.

18. Metaphors must not be dismissed just because they are metaphors, as, e.g., 'copying' and 'participation' are by Aristotle, *Met.* 991 a 20.
19. Cf. J. Stenzel, *Plato's Method of Dialectic* (Oxford, 1940), p. 37.
20. Cf. J. Wisdom, 'Metaphysics and Verification' (*Mind*, 1938, pp. 465 ff.).
21. There are traces of such an extreme form of nominalism in Hobbes. Cf. *Leviathan*, Pt. I, Chap. IV, p. 13 (Everyman edition).

18 BAYLIS

Baylis observes at the outset that "The existence of communicable knowledge requires shared meanings. Such knowledge, in its simplest form, is knowledge of the common characters exhibited by various objects and events." Since knowledge depends on the existence of universals it is important to determine their nature. Only the extreme nominalist rejects the existence of universals, and Baylis dismantles recent nominalist arguments. He then proceeds to demonstrate that there are three kinds of universals, namely "(1) *characteristics*, those universal characters which are exemplified whether thought or not, (2) *concepts*, those universal characters which are conceived whether exemplified or not, and (3) *pure concepts*, or those abstract characters which are neither exemplified nor conceived." The ontology of Baylis is as rich as it gets and qualifies him as an extreme realist.

Universals, Communicable Knowledge, and Metaphysics

Except for an extreme skeptic the "problem of universals" can, I think, be formulated as follows. The existence of communicable knowledge requires shared meanings. Such knowledge, in its simplest form, is knowledge of the common characters exhibited by various objects and events. In the more advanced form of scientific knowledge it is knowledge of the interrelations of these characters in all their possible instances. If we call such potentially exemplifiable and conceivable common characters "universals," our problem is to explain their nature and their function in knowledge in terms that are neither mystical nor false to the facts of conscious communication. The extreme nominalist who denies the existence of such common characters seems unable to account for the knowledge we appear to share. On the other hand the speculative metaphysician who hypostatizes them tends toward mystification and eulogy rather than knowledge-yielding explanation. How can we avoid these opposite errors and present a straightforward account of universals that will explain the facts and yet not go beyond the evidence?

Scientific knowledge, whether empirical, as in a natural science like biology, or *a priori*, as in a rational science like logic or mathematics, depends on knowledge of the interrelations of specifiable characters. Even classification requires grouping by means of some character or group of characters. Empirical scientific study often begins with the discovery and examination of the properties of objects or events, e.g., of magnetic fields or

182

of electric currents. The discovery of empirical laws rests on knowledge of the interrelations of such characters. Neo-Humeans describe the crucial relationship as one of uniform concomitance. Others, in growing numbers, remain dissatisfied until their evidence reveals a "real" or "natural" connection between such conjoined characters. But in either case knowledge of sharable qualities, properties, or relations constitutes the basis of scientific generalization.

That such knowledge is fundamental also in logic and mathematics is readily indicated. We study the relations between implication and logical consistency and between implication and truth values. Our knowledge of the interrelations of logical properties enables us to organize whole fields into deductive systems, of arithmetic, of geometry, of logic itself. In these fields, instead of concentrating attention on the primary characteristics of particular objects and events we study secondary and high-order properties. And in many cases, of course, we study defined properties of these higher orders without regard—at least for the time being—as to whether or not there are first-order objects which have the characters which in turn these higher-order properties might characterize. In any case, however, in the rational as well as in the empirical sciences, our knowledge rests on discernment of specifiable characters or universals. What is the nature of such universal characters? What kind of being do they have? How is knowledge of them possible?

That we can discriminate common characteristics in objects and events is admitted by all save extreme nominalists. Some describe the process as abstraction, others as focusing our attention on certain features of our experience and neglecting others. Even those determined would-be nominalists, Berkeley and Hume, were led to admit that by a "distinction of reason" we could notice, for example, the respects in which they differ.

There are perhaps three main types of extreme nominalists. One group confuses concepts with images. Finding that all images are particular, they deny the possibility of "abstract ideas." Their error can be indicated by pointing out that in many cases we know with great clarity the connotative meaning of a term without being able to form an image of that meaning. Thus we know precisely that a chiliagon is a plane polygon with a thousand angles, though psychologists assure us that we cannot imagine anywhere near that many angles at once. Again, if we accept something like Russell's and Whitehead's analysis of the meaning of the expression "cardinal number three" we realize that our meaning is not identical with any image we can form. Even where a relevant image can be formed, it cannot correctly be identified with our meaning. Berkeley and Hume have shown quite adequately that no image of a triangle is limited to precisely those properties which define triangularity.

It is easy to explain why some behaviorists are nominalists, for of course, since they shun introspection, they are not likely to meet a concept directly.

Much credit is due those behaviorists who recognize that universals, at least in the sense of common characteristics, turn up even in nature.

A third class of extreme nominalists is composed of those logical positivists who, from admirable motives of logical economy and metaphysical clarity, deny the existence of universals. But their denial is inconsistent with their practice as long as they make use of variable symbols. For variable symbols are precisely such as can be replaced by any member of a certain class of constant symbols, and whether this class be specified by a class property or by enumeration, all of its members will have certain characteristics in common—in the first case, the class property, and in the second, the characteristic of having just been enumerated.

The denial by extreme nominalists[1] that particulars have common characteristics leads them to affirm that no two things can be precisely alike in any respect. This has the *prima facie* absurd consequence that, for example, no two books can be precisely alike in containing exactly 232 pages. The extreme nominalist tries to avoid this absurdity by urging that there is no one property of having 232 pages which is shared or exemplified by two or more books, but rather that there are two or more unique particular properties which, though not alike in any respect, are nevertheless similar. As Russell and others have pointed out, such a nominalist, to be consistent, must then go on to insist that all relations of similarity are also particulars, not alike in any respect, but only similar in some still different sense of "similar." Such a nominalist has at his disposal only particulars and names of particulars. This appears to make it impossible for him, without inconsistency, to make any descriptive statements, for all such statements assert or deny that something has, i.e., exemplifies, some character.

It seems likely that nominalism in the extreme form in which I have been discussing it is one of those views which C. D. Broad has suggested we call "silly"; that is, it is a view which only an extremely able philosopher would even try to hold. Let us turn from it, then, to a less extreme nominalism such as is represented by the position which W. V. Quine seems to take.[2]

Quine appears to admit general terms, e.g., "square," which often apply correctly to a number of particulars. But he wants at least to try to construct a language in which such terms do not designate or name anything. This involves, he agrees, giving up terms as substituends, save as an eliminable notational abbreviation.

He believes he has shown how by a contextual definition he can treat statements and statement variables as a mere abridged manner of speaking, translatable at will back into an idiom which uses no statement variables and hence presupposes no propositions.[3] He has worked also in the direction of providing contextual definitions of this kind for terms which would otherwise designate concepts,[4] but this task is incomplete. He adds that until the nominalist can supply the relevant contextual definitions his plea that his apparent abstract entities are merely convenient fictions "is no more than incantation."[5]

Should Quine be able to overcome the difficulties which now block completion of his linguistic attempt to avoid all variables whose values would be abstract entities, his success would show only that a nominalistic language is possible. It would furnish no evidence as to whether or not universals exist. For evidence as to that we must seek to determine whether or not our abstract terms have clear and specifiable intensional meanings. Let us, then, ask what manner of entity universals are or would be, and what is involved in affirming that there are some. Perhaps a theory can be constructed which at once does justice to the facts of common concepts and communicable knowledge and also respects our desires for clarity and economy of ontological hypothesis.

Let us start with the common characters of particular things which moderate nominalists seem to admit. Such characters, as embodied or exemplified, we can call *characteristics*. We notice the resemblances between things and events and classify on the basis of them. We then go further and observe some of the relations which hold between these abstract, though not abstracted, characteristics. On such knowledge the empirical sciences are based.

It is an easy next step to think of abstract characters which might characterize but which as a matter of fact do not. We can safely assume that zoologists know and can specify the set of characters that any animal must have to be an American bison or buffalo. This knowledge, combined with knowledge of botany and biochemistry, makes it possible to know that some types of prairie flora will in general prove nutritious for buffaloes and other types will prove poisonous. Now, suppose that buffaloes become quite extinct. It will still be possible to think of those characters which are definitive of buffaloes even though nothing exemplifies all of them. And experts in such matters will still know the relation between possession of these characters and the suitability for food of certain prairie vegetation. Such knowledge is not destroyed by the death of all the creatures whose existence gave rise to it and made it applicable. We can still think or conceive of the characters that once characterized buffaloes and we still know what any creature which possessed such characters should and should not eat. Let us call abstract characters which are conceived but are not exemplified *concepts*.

Another way of bringing out these points is through the traditional distinction between denotation and connotation. Some such distinction becomes imperative where a meaningful symbol has no denotation. The words "hundred-dollar bill now in my pocket" convey a clear meaning to me, though I know that no such bill is there. The expression has significance, connotation though no denotation. In this sense the connotation of a term consists precisely of those characters whose possession is necessary and sufficient for anything to be denoted by it. Again, in the case of many terms, there must be some sense in which we are acquainted with their connotation before we can determine whether or not there are things denoted by them. Thus, for example, we must know what is meant by the expression "white crow" before we can search intelligently to see if there are any. We must know in terms of income what we mean by the phrase "rich man" before a study of income tax returns would be rewarding in identifying some.

These are trivial and obvious examples. But something like them seems needed in the face of persistent denials that there are concepts. These examples indicate that we are often aware of the connotative meaning of terms that denote nothing. But to be aware of such connotative meanings is to conceive abstract characters that are unexemplified, namely, concepts. We can select as a concept any character we wish, and we can limit this concept by stipulation to just that character or set of characters we choose. This ability is essential to classification and to the discovery of empirical laws.

At a second stage of abstraction we notice that concepts themselves exemplify characters which can in turn be conceived. Thus relations, a species of concepts, can themselves be classified as symmetric, asymmetric, or non-symmetric, transitive, intransitive, non-transitive, and so on. It is knowledge of second and higher-level concepts which makes logic and mathematics possible.

One way in which we can combine concepts to obtain more complex concepts is by simple conjunction. Since we can conceive of the concept *old* and the concept *man*, we can think of the concept *old man*. By conjoining *creature having the body of a horse and creature having the chest and head of a man*, we can conceive the defining characteristics of a centaur. Walt Disney goes us one better and by a happy modification conceives that titillating conjunction of characters possessed by every centaurette.

Unless we limit the principle that the conjunct of any two concepts is itself a concept, it follows further that there are self-inconsistent concepts such as round-square-ness. Though startling at first, a little reflection convinces us that there is nothing alarming in this. The elements of the concept round-square-ness are mutually incompatible in the sense that nothing can at once exemplify both these concepts. But the concept round-square-ness does not violate the principle of contradiction. It is neither round nor square, let alone both. It is composed of, but does not have in the sense commonly symbolized by ϵ, two incompatible characters which nothing whatever can possess. Round-square-ness is an unfamiliar concept but a harmless one. We are guaranteed that it can have no instances. To avoid such concepts one would have to complicate logic unduly by limiting the principle of conjunction to mutually compatible concepts. This would have as one unfortunate consequence the fact that in dealing with complicated concepts, for example, some of those of mathematics, we may not know whether we can conjoin certain pairs or not. Such a limitation would be analogous to forbidding statement conjuncts of p and q unless they are mutually consistent. This can indeed be done but our pragmatic interests in simplicity, like those of Quine and Lewis, militate against it.

Thus far we have distinguished two sub-classes of universals: (1) *characteristics*, those universal characters which are exemplified whether thought of or not, and (2) *concepts*, those universal characters which are conceived whether exemplified or not. There is, I think, a third sub-class, (3) *pure universals*, or those abstract characters which are neither exemplified nor conceived. Here it is, of course, impossible to give examples, save by indirection. As Russell has remarked, we know that the product of any two positive integers which have never been thought of is more than 100, although by hypothesis these numbers have not themselves been conceived. We have knowledge about them but no acquaintance with them. Again, it has always been true, and always will be, that were there to be a plane triangle in the sense prescribed by Euclid, the sum of its interior angles would be 180°. The geometrical characters which Euclid had studied had exactly the interrelations he noted before he remarked them. And they will continue to have those relations even when all knowledge of Euclidean geometry fades away. Or consider the empirical laws mentioned earlier about nutritional foods for buffaloes. When all buffaloes are dead and all buffalo experts also, these laws, though unknown and unexemplified, will still be true in the sense that if there were buffaloes certain plants would nourish them and others would not. To be sure, the relations between characters which these laws state would probably not have been known unless buffaloes had existed and their essential characters had been conceived, but neither such existence nor such conception is necessary for these relations to hold.

What are the criteria which distinguish universals, of whatever kind, from particulars? They can be stated in terms either of the relation of exemplification or embodiment, whose converse is characterization, or of logical implication. Universals are the sort of entity which, except for conjuncts of mutually incompatible characters,[6] can characterize, that is, can be embodied or exemplified. If they are thus embodied we call them characteristics of that which exemplifies them. Universals also have characteristics. Particulars, on the other hand, though they have many characteristics, do not and cannot characterize anything.

Strict implication between concepts, which is the intensional counterpart of the relation of logical inclusion between classes, also serves to distinguish universals from particulars. Any concept either implies or is implied by some other concept. When a concept, A, strictly implies a concept, B, nothing *could* be a member of the class determined by A and fail to be a member of the class determined by B. But no particular thus implies any other particular. Either characterization, then, or logical implication, will serve to distinguish particulars from universals. Particulars can neither characterize nor imply, universals can do both.

Are universals as thus described independent of being thought of and independent of being exemplified? That exemplification is extrinsic to the nature of universals is shown by the fact that often we first conceive of a set of characters and then look around to see if that set is exemplified. Thus mathematicians have conceived of Riemannian geometry and also of Euclidean geometry. Though we do not know with certainty whether our world is Euclidean, Riemannian, or neither, the nature of each of these geometries, since it has been completely specified, is independent of exemplification.

That universal characters can exist as embodied in things though they have not yet been thought of, is indicated by every new discovery of a scientific law. Presumably the law of gravitation held before it was first thought of, let alone confirmed. Or again, suppose a time in the course of evolution when paramecia existed, but no human or other species capable of mathematical thought. Even then, when two paramecia swam over to two other paramecia there were four paramecia gathered together. Universals may be embodied without being thought of and in this sense, at least, they are independent of being conceived.

But further, pure universals are independent simultaneously of both conception and embodiment. To take one more example, let us suppose that Leonardo da Vinci was the first man who ever thought of airplaneness, that set of characteristics which anything must have to be an airplane and which, if anything has it, makes that thing an airplane. Yet airplaneness had at least this minimal sort of being before Leonardo thought of it, that many propositions were true about it. Though no one then knew it, we now know that it was true just before Leonardo's birth that airplaneness would be thought of within the next century. And if some mischance had killed Leonardo before he thought of it then it might well have been true that airplaneness would not have been thought of until some time later. In this minimal sense, then, that some propositions are true and others are false about characters or sets of characters that are neither exemplified nor thought of, the nature of such pure universals is independent both of exemplification and of conception.

It seems not unnatural to say of universals that are embodied that they exist as characteristics, and of universals that are conceived that they exist as concepts. Whether we want to say of pure universals that they exist or not seems largely a matter of verbal usage. If we use the term "exist" as many mathematicians do, we would say that they do exist, just as we would say that the thousandth decimal of "pi" exists even though what number it is has not yet been discovered. But if we wish to restrict application of the word "exist" to entities which have spatial and temporal properties, then we shall need some other term such as "subsist" to describe the kind of being that pure universals have.

Perhaps one reason why pure universals have been discounted and even denied in some quarters is their relative uselessness. We cannot discover instances of universals which are not embodied. And we cannot use in our thinking universals which have not yet been thought of. But is uselessness a sound reason for denying to pure universals the minimal being specified?

If it be urged against universals that they "clutter up" the universe in infinitely chaotic fashion, the answer is obvious. It is those who raise this objection, not proponents of such an ontologically modest theory as this, who hypostatize. Universals occupy no space and because of their fixed relations they are more neatly and precisely ordered than anything else in our experience. Furthermore, their number does not surpass the bounds of the characteristics which are exemplified, the concepts which are conceived, and the characters which could be conceived if we but turned our attention to them.

Nor are the unchanging or, if you like, eternal characteristics of universals at all incompatible with our changing interests and our changing language. Characters which once were usefully conceived are no longer so and are neglected. But if we wished, they could be used again because their relations with other characters are still what they have always been. Though the same character may be signified now by one term, now by another, and though different characters may be signified by the same term, these facts about the way in which characters are described do not alter their defining characteristics and relations.

Beyond the account of the minimal characteristics described here which universals must possess if we are to justify scientific knowledge, it is of course possible to construct elaborate metaphysical theories. Some may wish to think of universals as being more "real" than particulars; others prefer to judge them less "real." Some may wish to distinguish between the types of "reality" possessed by pure universals, by concepts, and by characteristics. But such addenda are not necessary for purposes of explaining common meanings and communicable knowledge. They are, I suspect, purely speculative undertakings. Even if their usually undefined terms, such as "real" and "reality," can be given explicit meaning, the result tends to be only a number of unverifiable though mutually incompatible metaphysical theories. From their rivalries we can safely remain detached.

The discussion of this paper justifies, I think, the following conclusion: There are unchanging characters or universals at least in the sense that the same characters can be thought of again and again, that they can be exemplified repeatedly, and that certain relations obtain among these characters whether they are exemplified or not and whether they are thought of or not.

NOTES

From *Journal of Philosophy* 48, no. 21 (1951). Reprinted by permission of the author and the editor of *Journal of Philosophy*.

1. E.g., E. B. McGilvery, "Relations in General and Universals in Particular," *Journal of Philosophy*, Vol. XXXVI (1939), pp. 5–15, 29–40.
2. [W. V. Quine,] "Designation and Existence," *Journal of Philosophy*, Vol. XXXVI (1939), pp. 701–9, and "Identity, Ostension, and Hypostasis," ibid., Vol. XLVII (1950), pp. 621–33.
3. [W. V. Quine,] "A Logistical Approach to the Ontological Problem," *The Journal of Unified Science*, Vol. 9.
4. [W. V. Quine,] "A Theory of Classes Presupposing No Canons of Type," *Proceedings, National Academy of Science*, Vol. 22 (1936), pp. 320–26.
5. "Designation and Existence," p. 709.
6. The constituent characters of such conjuncts can characterize.

19 PRICE

Price maintains that thinking would not be possible unless there were recurrences in the natural world. Specifically, there must be recurrent characteristics in the world. There are at least two types of characteristics: qualities, and relations. These are understood to be universals. That universals recur in nature is an essentially Aristotelean position. The commitment to *universalia in rebus* is the first view Price examines. He calls this the Philosophy of Universals, which "says that when A resembles B, this is *because* they are both instances of the same universal." The problem with this view is that it requires the resemblance between A and B to be exact. In other words, the Philosophy of Universals is too restrictive in its view of universals. This is the point at which the Philosophy of Resemblances enters upon the scene. This is the position that resemblance is not the result of the presence of a universal, but is itself ultimate or underivative.

We get our idea of red as a result of the resemblance of several red objects compared to one or more paradigmatic red objects. There is no universal common to all members of a class, no *universalia in rebus*. What is common to the members of a class are resemblances *inter res*. Resemblances are objective, and in that sense the Philosophy of Resemblances is as realistic as the Philosophy of Universals. However, Price rebuffs the argument that a resemblance is itself a universal. They are nothing of the kind; yet they are ultimate and underivative. Interestingly enough, on the other hand, he demonstrates that the Philosophy of Universals can, in the end, accommodate inexact resemblances that gave rise to the Philosophy of Resemblances. Where does that leave us with respect to these two philosophies? From an ontological point of view, they are equally acceptable. "[T]here is only a (systematic) difference of terminology between these two philosophies." Each has misleading features, "and when we are in danger of being misled by the one, we may save ourselves by changing over to the other."

Thinking and Experience

UNIVERSALS AND RESEMBLANCES

When we consider the world around us, we cannot help noticing that there is a great deal of recurrence or repetition in it. The same color recurs over and over again in ever so many things. Shapes repeat themselves likewise. Over and over again we notice oblong-shaped things, hollow things, bulgy things. Hoots, thuds, bangs, restlings occur again and again.

191

There is another and very important sort of recurrence which we also notice. The same pattern or mode of arrangement is found over and over again in many *sets* of things, in many different pairs of things, or triads, or quartets, as the case may be. When A is above B, and C is above D, and E is above F, the above-and-below pattern or mode of arrangement recurs in three pairs of things, and in ever so many other pairs of things as well. Likewise, we repeatedly notice one thing inside another, one preceding another, one thing between two others.

These recurrent features sometimes recur singly or separately. The same color recurs in this tomato, that sunset sky, and this blushing face; there are few other features, if any, which repeat themselves in all three. But it is a noteworthy fact about the world that there are *conjoint* recurrences as well as separate ones. A whole group of features recurs again and again as a whole in many objects. Examine twenty dandelions, and you will find that they have many features in common; likewise fifty cats have very many features in common, or two hundred lumps of lead. In such cases as these there is conjoint recurrence of many different features. Again and again they recur together in a clump or block. This is how it comes about that many of the objects in the world group themselves together into Natural Kinds. A Natural Kind is a group of objects which have *many* (perhaps indefinitely many) features in common. From observing that an object has some of these features, we can infer with a good deal of probability that it has the rest.

These constant recurrences or repetitions, whether separate or conjoint ones, are what make the world a dull or stale or boring place. The same old features keep turning up again and again. The best they can do is to present themselves occasionally in new combinations, as in the black swan or the duck-billed platypus. There is a certain *monotony* about the world. The extreme case of it is found where the same old feature repeats itself in all parts of a single object, as when something is red all over, or sticky all through, or a noise is uniformly shrill throughout its entire duration.

Nevertheless, this perpetual repetition, this dullness or staleness, is also immensely important, because it is what makes conceptual cognition possible. In a world of incessant novelty, where there was no recurrence at all and no tedious repetitions, no concepts could ever be acquired; and thinking, even of the crudest and most primitive kind, could never begin. For example, in such a world nothing would ever be recognizable. Or again, *in so far as* there is novelty in the world, non-recurrence, absence of repetition, so far the world cannot be thought about, but only experienced.

Hitherto I have been trying to use entirely untechnical language, so that we may not commit ourselves unawares to any philosophical theory. But it is at any rate not unnatural, it is not a *very* wild piece of theorizing, to introduce the word 'quality' and 'relation' for referring to those facts about the world to which I have been trying to draw the reader's attention. A *quality*, we say, is a recurrent feature of the world which presents itself in individual objects or events taken singly. Redness or bulginess or squeakiness are examples. A *relation*, on the other hand, is a recurrent feature of the world which presents itself in complexes of objects or events, such as this beside that, this preceding that, or B between A and C. It is also convenient sometimes to speak of *relational properties*. If A precedes B, we may say that A has the relational property of preceding B, and B has the converse relational property of succeeding A.

One further remark may be made on the distinction between qualities and relations. I said just now that a quality presents itself in individual objects or events taken singly, and a relation in complexes of objects or events. But it must not be forgotten that an individual object or event usually (perhaps always) has an *internal* complexity. In its history there is a plurality of temporal phases, and often it has a plurality of spatial parts as well. And there are relations between these parts, or these phases, which it has. Such relations *within* an individual object or event are sometimes said to constitute the 'structure' of the object or event. For scientific purposes, and even for purposes of ordinary common sense prediction, what we most need to know about any object or process is its structure. And from this point of view the chief importance of qualities, such as color or hardness or stickiness, is that they often enable us to infer the presence of a structure more minute than our unaided senses would reveal. It has often been maintained that sensible qualities are 'subjective'. But subjective or not, they have a most important function. They give us a clue to what the minute structure of objects and events is. If a gas smells like rotten eggs, we can infer that it is sulphuretted hydrogen.

The terms 'quality' and 'relation' enable us to give a simple analysis of *change*. The notion of change has puzzled some philosophers greatly, ever since Heracleitus, or some disciple of his, remarked long ago that πάντα ῥεῖ, 'all things flow'. Indeed, it has sometimes led them to suppose that this world *is* a world of perpetual novelty after all, and not the tedious or boring or repetitious world which it has to be, if conceptual cognition is to be possible. They have, therefore, concluded—rightly, from their premises—that all conceptual cognition is radically erroneous or illusory, a kind of systematic distortion of Reality; so that *whatever* we think, however intelligent or however stupid we may be, we are in error. On this view, only non-conceptual cognition—immediate experience or direct intuition—can be free from error.

These conclusions are so queer that we suspect something is wrong with the premises. We can now see what it is. The notion of Change, as Plato pointed out, has itself to be analyzed in terms of the notions of Quality and Relation. In qualitative change, as when an apple changes from being green to being red, an object has quality q_1 at one time and a different quality q_2 at a later time. In relational change, an object A has a relation R_1 to another object B at one time, and a different relation R_2 to B at a later time. At

12 o'clock, for example, it is six inches away from B, at 12.5 it is a mile away from B; at one time the relation it has to B is the relation 'hotter than', at another the relation 'as hot as', at another the relation 'cooler than'.

It is not necessary for our present purposes to enquire whether there are other recurrent features of the world which are neither qualities nor relations nor analyzable in terms of these. Some philosophers have thought, for instance, that causality (in its various determinate forms, hitting, bending, pushing, pulling, attracting, repelling, etc.) was such an ultimate and irreducible feature of the world, recurring or repeating itself in many situations. Others have undertaken to give a purely relational analysis of causality (the 'Regularity' theory). For our present purpose, however—which is merely to explain why philosophers have thought it worth while to talk about recurrent features of the world at all—it is not necessary to decide how many irreducibly different types of recurrents there might be. It will be enough to consider just qualities and relations.

We may now sum up the results of this ontological discussion so far by introducing another technical term, again not so *very* technical, the term 'characteristic'. Characteristics, we say, are of at least two different types, qualities and relations. What has been said so far then comes to this: there are *recurrent characteristics* in the world, which repeat themselves over and over again in many different contexts. Is it not just an obvious fact about the world, something we cannot help noticing whether we like it or not, that there *are* recurrent characteristics? Now these recurrent characteristics have been called by some philosophers *universals*. And the line of thought we have been pursuing leads very naturally to the traditional Aristotelian doctrine of *universalia in rebus*, 'universals in things'. (To provide for universals of relation, 'things' must be understood to cover complexes as well as individuals. The *res* which the universal 'beside' is in is not this, nor that, but this-and-that.)

I do not propose to discuss the Platonic doctrine of *universalia ante rem*, 'universals anterior to (or independent of) things'. This is not because I think it uninteresting or unimportant, but merely because it is more remote from common sense and our ordinary everyday habits of thought than the Aristotelian theory of *universalia in rebus*. It is a sufficiently difficult task in these days to convince people that there is any sense in talking of universals at all, even in the mild and moderate Aristotelian way.

The doctrine of *universalia in rebus* may, of course, be mistaken, or gravely misleading. There certainly are objections to it, as we shall find presently. But I cannot see that it is in the least absurd or silly, as the most approved thinkers nowadays seem to suppose. Nor can I see that it arises entirely from erroneous views about language, as the same thinkers seem to suppose; for example, from the superstition that all words are names, from which it would follow that general or abstract words must be names of general or abstract entities. On the contrary, this philosophy seems to me to be the result, and the very natural result, of certain *ontological* reflections. It seems to me to arise from reflections about the world; from consideration of what things are, and not—or certainly not merely—from consideration of the way we talk about them. On the contrary, it could be argued that we talk in the way we do, using general terms and abstract terms, because of what we find the world to be; because we find or notice *recurrences* in it.

Let us now consider how the doctrine of *universalia in rebus* might mislead us, although it arises in this natural and plausible way from the ontological considerations which we have been discussing. One danger of it obviously is that universals may be regarded as a sort of *things* or entities, over and above the objects or situations in which they recur. We may indeed emphasize the word 'in'. We may insist that universals are *in* things, and not apart from them as the doctrine of *universalia ante rem* maintains. But is the danger of supposing that they are themselves things or quasi-things entirely removed? Does it not arise over again as soon as we reflect upon the implications of the word 'in' itself?

If it is our profession to be misled—as, of course, it *is* the profession of philosophers—we shall be liable to suppose that redness is in the tomato somewhat as juice is in it, or as a weevil is in it. And if so, what can be meant by saying that redness is recurrent? How can it be *in* thousands of other tomatoes as well, or hundreds of post boxes, or dozens of blushing faces? It does not make sense to say that a weevil is in many places at once. Again, when the tomato begins to decay and turns brown, where has the redness gone to, which used to be in it? (The weevil has gone somewhere else; you will find him in the potato basket.) Likewise, where has the brownness come from?

If we prefer to say that the tomato *has* redness, rather than 'redness is in it', we shall again mislead these literal-minded persons, and in the same sort of way. Does the tomato *have* redness as Jones *has* a watch? If so, how can millions of other things have it too?

I confess that I do not think much of these difficulties. The meaning of 'in' and 'have' in this context can be quite easily exhibited by examples, just as their literal meaning can, when we say that there is a weevil in the tomato, or I have a watch. Surely we all know quite well what is being referred to when two things are said to *have* the same color? And is it really so very difficult to recognize what is meant by saying that the same color is *in* them both? It is true, no doubt, that the words 'in' and 'have' are here being used in a metaphorical sense, though not, I think, extravagantly metaphorical. But we must use metaphorical words, or else invent new and technical terms (which are themselves usually metaphorical words taken from a dead language, Greek or Latin). Our ordinary language exists for practical ends, and it has to be 'stretched' in one way or other if we are to use it for purposes of philosophical analysis. And if our metaphors can be cashed quite easily by examples, as these can, no harm whatever is done.

It could, however, be argued that the terminology of 'characteristics', which was current in the last philosophical epoch, some twenty years ago, is better than the more ancient terminology of 'universals'. A characteristic is pretty obviously a characteristic of something or other, and cannot easily be supposed to be an independent entity, like the weevil. Nor can we be easily misled into supposing that when something 'has' a characteristic, i.e. is characterized by it, this is at all analogous to the having of a watch. In the technical symbolism of Formal Logic, the most appropriate expression for referring to one of these recurrent features of the world is not a single letter, such as ϕ or R, which might possibly be mistaken for the name of an entity, but a propositional function, such as ϕx, or xRy, or $R(x,y,z)$. Here the x,y and z are variables, so that the propositional function is an overtly *incomplete* expression. To complete it, one must replace the variable by a constant, denoting some object which satisfies the function; or if there are several variables, as in xRy or $R(x,y,z)$, each of these must be replaced by a constant. The terminology of characteristics is an approximate equivalent in words to the non-verbal symbolism of propositional functions, and has much the same advantages; whereas if we use the more traditional terminology of universals, there is some danger (though not, I think, unavoidable) that we may be led to speak of them as though they were in themselves complete and independent entities.

Henceforth, the Aristotelian theory of *universalia in rebus* will be called 'the Philosophy of Universals' for short. If our argument so far has been correct, the Philosophy of Universals is drawing our attention to certain important facts about the world. Yet it is at the same time proposing an analysis of those facts. We cannot dispute the facts, nor can we dispute their fundamental importance. We cannot deny that something which may be called 'the recurrence of characteristics' is genuinely there. We must also admit that if it were not there, conceptual cognition could not exist. If the world were not like this, if there were no recurrence in it, it could be neither thought about nor spoken about. We could never have acquired any concepts; and even if we had them innately (without needing to acquire them) they could never have been applied to anything.

But though we cannot dispute the facts, nor their importance, we may, nevertheless, have doubts about the analysis of them which the Philosophy of Universals proposes. At any rate, another and quite different analysis of them appears to be possible. It is the analysis offered by what one may call the Philosophy of Ultimate Resemblances. (Henceforth I shall call this 'the Philosophy of Resemblances' for short.) This is the analysis which most contemporary philosophers accept, so far as they consider the *ontological* side of the Problem of Universals at all. It is also accepted by Conceptualists, like Locke. The Philosophy of Resemblances is more complicated than the Philosophy of Universals, and more difficult to formulate. It involves one in long and cumbrous circumlocutions. Yet it claims, not unplausibly, that it keeps closer to the facts which have to be analyzed. The unkind way of putting this, the one its critics prefer, is to say that it is 'more naturalistic'. Let us now consider the Philosophy of Resemblances in more detail.

When we say that a characteristic, e.g. whiteness, *recurs*, that it presents itself over and over again, that it characterizes ever so many numerically different objects, what we say is admittedly in some sense true. But would it not be clearer, and closer to the facts, if we said that all these objects resemble each other in a certain way? Is not this the rock-bottom fact to which the Philosophy of Universals is drawing our attention, when it uses this rather inflated language of 'recurrent characteristics'? The Philosophy of Universals of course agrees that all the objects characterized by whiteness do resemble one another. But according to it, resemblance is always derivative, and is just a *consequence* of the fact that the very same characteristic—whiteness, in this case—characterizes all these objects. To use more traditional language, it says that when A resembles B, this is *because* they are both instances of the same universal.

Now this is all very well where the resemblance is exact, but what are we to say when it is not? Let us consider the following series of examples: a patch of freshly fallen snow; a bit of chalk; a piece of paper which has been used for wrapping the meat in; the handkerchief with which I have been dusting a rather dirty mantelpiece; a full evening dress bow tie which has been left lying about for several years on the floor. All these, we say, are white objects. But are they exactly alike in their color, if white may be counted as a color for the purpose of this discussion? Clearly they are not. They are, of course, more or less alike. In fact there is a very considerable degree of color-likeness between them. But certainly they are not exactly alike in color. And yet if the very same characteristic, whiteness, is present in them all (as the Philosophy of Universals, apparently, says it is) ought it not to follow that they are exactly alike in color?

To make quite clear what the point at issue is, we shall have to distinguish, rather pedantically perhaps, between *exact* resemblance in this or that respect and *total* or *complete* resemblance. To put it in another way, resemblance has two dimensions of variation. It may vary in intensity; it may also vary in extent. For example, a piece of writing paper and an envelope, before one has written on either of them, may be exactly alike in color, and perhaps also in texture. These likenesses between them have the maximum degree of intensity. But the two objects are not completely or totally alike. For one thing, they are unlike in shape. Moreover, the envelope is stuck together with gum and has gum on its flap, while the piece of writing paper has no gum on it. It might perhaps be thought that two envelopes from the same batch are completely alike; and certainly they come nearer to it than the envelope and the piece of notepaper. All the same, there is unlikeness in respect of place. At any given time, envelope A is in one place and envelope B is in a different place. On the Relational Theory of Space, this is equivalent to saying that at any given time A and B are related in unlike ways to something else, e.g. the North Pole, or Greenwich Observatory.

According to Leibniz's Principle of the Identity of Indiscernibles, complete or total likeness is an ideal limit which can never quite be reached, though some pairs of objects (the two envelopes, for example) come closer to it than others. For if *per impossibile* two objects were completely alike, place and date included, there would no longer be two objects, but only one. Whether Leibniz's Principle is correct, has been much disputed. But we need not concern ourselves with this dispute. It is sufficient to point out that if there were two objects which resembled each other completely, in date and place as well as in all other ways, and this complete resemblance continued throughout the whole of the histories of both, there could not possibly be any evidence for believing there were two of them. So in this discussion we need not concern ourselves any more with complete or total resemblance, though it is of course an important fact about resemblances that they vary in extent, as well as in degree of intensity.

What does concern us is intensity of resemblance. The maximum intensity of it is what I called 'exact resemblance in this or that respect'. Now some people appear to think that even this is an ideal limit. They seem to think that no two objects are ever *exactly* alike even in one way (e.g. color, or shape) though, of course, many objects are closely alike in one way or in several. I do not see what evidence we could have for believing such a sweeping negative generalization. It is true that sometimes, when we thought at first that there was an exact likeness in one or more respects between two objects, we may find on more careful examination that there was not. We may have thought that two twins were exactly alike in the conformation of their faces. We look more closely, and find that John's nose is a millimeter longer than William's. But still, there are many cases where there is no discoverable inexactness in a resemblance. We often find that two pennies are indistinguishable in shape, or two postage stamps indistinguishable in color. And we should not confine ourselves to cases where two or more objects are being compared. There is such a thing as monotony or uniformity within a single object. For example, a certain patch of sky is blue, and the same shade of blue, all over. It is monotonously ultramarine. In other words, all its discernible parts are exactly like each other in color; at any rate, we can discover no unlikeness of color between them. Again, there is often no discoverable unlikeness of pitch between two successive phases of the same sound. Will it be said that such monotony is only apparent, not real? But what ground could we have for thinking that no entity is ever really 'monotonous' in this sense, not even in the smallest part of its extent, or throughout the smallest phase of its duration? Thus there is no good ground for maintaining that resemblance of maximum intensity never occurs at all, still less for maintaining that it never *could* occur. Nevertheless, it is not so very common for two objects to be exactly alike even in one way, though monotony within a single object or event is more frequent. What we most usually find in two or more objects which are said to be 'alike' is *close* resemblance in one respect or in several.

We can now return to the controversy between the Philosophy of Resemblances and the Philosophy of Universals. It is argued that if the Philosophy of Universals were right, exact resemblance in one or several respects (resemblance of maximum intensity) ought to be much more common than it is; indeed, that *in*exact resemblance in a given respect, say color or shape, ought not to exist at all. Of course, there could still be incomplete or partial resemblance, resemblance between two objects in one respect or in several, and lack of resemblance in others. But whenever two objects do resemble each other in a certain respect, it would appear that the resemblance ought to be exact (of maximum intensity), if the Philosophy of Universals were right; either it should be exact, or else it should not exist at all. The Philosophy of Universals tells us that resemblance is derivative, not ultimate; that when two objects resemble each other in a given respect, it is because the very same universal is present in them both. This seems to leave no room for inexact resemblance.

Now if we consider the various white objects I mentioned before—the whole series of them, from the freshly fallen snow to the unwashed bow-tie—how can anyone maintain that the very same characteristic, whiteness, recurs in all of them? Clearly it does not. If it did, they must be exactly alike in their color; and quite certainly they are not. If we are to use the language of universals or characteristics, shall we not have to say that each of the objects in this series, from the snow to the unwashed tie, is characterized by a *different* characteristic, or is an instance of a *different* universal? In this case, then, the resemblance seems to be ultimate and underivative, *not* dependent on the presence of a single universal in all these objects, although they certainly do resemble each other.

Let us consider another example. Two pennies may be exactly alike in their shape. If so, one may plausibly say that the very same characteristic, roundness, is present in both of them, and that their resemblance is depen-dent on this. But what about a penny and a sixpence? They certainly *are* alike in shape; but not exactly, because the sixpence has a milled edge and the penny a smooth one. So here again, it would seem, there is no *single* characteristic present in them both, upon which the resemblance could be dependent. This resemblance again seems to be ultimate and underivative.

Thus the Philosophy of Universals, when it makes all resemblance derivative, appears to forget that resemblances have degrees of intensity. Resemblance is treated as if it were degreeless, either present in its maximum degree or else not present at all. In practice, the Philosopher of Universals concentrates his attention on *close* resemblances, and averts his attention from the awkward circumstance that few of them are exact; and resemblances of a lower degree than this (small or moderate ones, not intense enough to be called 'close') are just neglected altogether. But is it not a glaringly obvious fact that resemblances do differ in degree or intensity?

That being so, shall we not be inclined to *reverse* this alleged dependence-relation between 'being alike' and 'being characterized by'? Surely we shall be inclined to say that it is resemblance which is more fundamental than characterization, rather than the other way round. We shall, of course, be willing to go on using terms like 'characteristic' and 'characterized by'; they are part of ordinary language, and everyone has a sufficient understanding of them. But we shall define 'characteristic' in terms of resemblance, and not conversely. Where a number of objects do happen to resemble each other exactly in one respect or three or fifteen, there, and in consequence, we shall be quite willing to say that they have one, or three, or fifteen 'characteristics in common'. But in other cases, where the resemblance is less than exact, we shall not be willing to say this. We shall just say that they resemble each other in such and such a degree, and stop there. In a given set of objects there is whatever degree of resemblance there is. Let us be content to take the facts as we find them.

Turning for a moment to the epistemological side of the matter, surely it is obvious that the applicability of concepts does *not* require an exact resemblance in the objects which a concept applies to? Of course there does have to be a considerable degree of resemblance between all the objects which 'satisfy' a given concept. As we say, there has to be a sufficient likeness between them, e.g. between all the objects to which the concept White applies. What degree of likeness is sufficient, and where the borderline comes between something which falls just within the concept's sphere of application and something else which just falls outside it, is often difficult to decide. For instance, one may wonder whether the *very* dirty bow-tie is white at all. Indeed, it is difficult to see how such a question can be definitely answered, at least in the case of whiteness and many other familiar concepts. The right way to tackle it, perhaps, is to refuse to answer it as it stands. Perhaps we should rather say that a concept may be 'satisfied' in many different degrees; or, in more commonsensical language, that there are good instances and bad instances, better and worse ones, and some so bad that it is arbitrary whether one counts them as instances or not. Thus the piece of chalk is a *better* instance of whiteness than the rather dirty handkerchief is. The patch of freshly fallen snow is a better instance still, perhaps a perfect one. We may give it the mark (+). Then $\alpha\beta$ is about the right mark for the piece of chalk, and we will give the unwashed bow-tie $y=$, to denote that it is just on the borderline between 'pass' and 'failure'.

It is not easy to see how the doctrine of *universalia in rebus* can make any room for this important and familiar notion of degrees of instantiation. But there is plenty of room for it in Conceptualism, which is the epistemological counterpart of the ontological Philosophy of Resemblances. We must add, in fairness, that there is also plenty of room for it in the Platonic doctrine of *universalia ante rem*. Indeed Plato, or perhaps Socrates, was the first philosopher who noticed that there are degrees of instantiation. This is one of the points, and a good point, which Conceptualism and Platonic Realism have in common.[1]

In the last few pages, I have been discussing the difficulties which the Resemblance Philosophers find in the Philosophy of Universals. But the Philosophy of Resemblances has its difficulties too. The most important ones are concerned with resemblance itself. I shall discuss two of them, and the solutions proposed for them. The first arises from the phrase 'resemblance in respect of. . . .'

It is obvious that we must distinguish between *different* resemblances. Objects resemble each other in different respects, as well as in different degrees. Red objects resemble each other in one respect, round objects in another respect. The members of a natural kind, for instance cats or oak trees, resemble each other in many respects at once. Thus it would be much too vague if we said that red objects, for example, are just a set of objects which resemble one another, or sufficiently resemble each other. That would not distinguish them from blue objects, or round objects, or any other class of objects one cares to name. We must specify what resemblance it is. Red objects are those which resemble each other 'in a certain respect'. But in *what* respect? And now it looks as if we should have to introduce universals again. Our first answer would probably be that they resemble each other in respect of color; and this looks very like saying that they are all instances of the universal Coloredness. That is bad enough; but we shall be driven to go farther, because we have not yet said enough to distinguish red objects from blue ones or green ones. Can we stop short of saying that red objects are just those objects which resemble each other in respect of *redness*? And here we seem to be admitting the very point which the Philosophy of Universals is so anxious to maintain; namely that the resemblance between these objects is after all derivative, dependent upon the presence of a single universal, Redness, in them all. To generalize the argument: whenever we say that A, B, and C resemble each other in a certain respect, we shall be asked 'In *what* respect?' And how can we answer, except by saying 'in respect of being instances of the universal ф' or 'in respect of being characterized by the characteristic ф'? We may try to get round the difficulty by saying that they resemble each other in a certain *way* (avoiding the word 'respect'), or that there is a certain *sort* of resemblance between them. But when we are asked to specify in *what* way they resemble each other, or what sort of resemblance there is between them, surely we shall still have to answer by mentioning such and such a universal or characteristic? 'The way in which red objects resemble each other is that all of them are instances of the universal Redness, or all of them are characterized by the characteristic Redness.'

This is one of the classical objections to the Philosophy of Resemblances. The argument purports to show that resemblance is not after all ultimate or underivative, but is dependent on the presence of a universal or characteristic which is common to the things which resemble each other. There is something about this objection which arouses our suspicions. It comes perilously near to the tautology 'red things are the things which are red'. The Resemblance philosophers were not undertaking to deny this tautology. They do not deny that x is red entails x is red. They are only concerned to offer an analysis of x is red itself.

Let us now consider the answer they might make to this celebrated objection. Roughly, it consists in substituting 'resemblance *towards* . . .' for 'resemblance in respect of . . .' Resemblance towards what? Towards certain standard objects, or *exemplars* as I shall call them—certain standard red objects, or standard round objects, or whatever it may be.

It is agreed by both parties that there is a *class* of red objects. The question is, what sort of a structure does a class have? That is where the two philosophies differ. According to the Philosophy of Universals, a class is so to speak a promiscuous or equalitarian assemblage. All its members have, as it were, the same status in it. All of them are instances of the same universal, and no more can be said. But in the Philosophy of Resemblances a class has a more complex structure than this; not equalitarian, but aristocratic. Every class has, as it were, a nucleus, an inner ring of key-members, consisting of a small group of standard objects or exemplars. The exemplars for the class of red things might be a certain tomato, a certain brick and a certain British post-box. Let us call them A, B and C for short. Then a red object is any object which resembles A, B and C as closely as they resemble one another. The resemblance between the exemplars need not itself be a very close one, though it is of course pretty close in the example just given. What is required is only that every other member of the class should resemble the class-exemplars as closely as they resemble one another. Thus the exemplars for a class might be a summer sky, a lemon, a post-box, and a lawn. These do resemble one another, though not very closely. Accordingly there is a class consisting of everything which resembles these four entities *as* closely as they resemble each other. It is the class of colored things, whereas the previous one was the class of red things.

It may be thought that there is still a difficulty about the resemblance between the exemplar objects themselves. In *what respect* do the tomato, the brick and the post-box resemble each other? Surely this question still arises, even though it does not arise about the other members of the class? And how can one answer it, except by saying that these three objects resemble each other in respect of being red, or of being characterized by redness?

But this assumes that we know beforehand what 'being red' is, or what 'being characterized by redness' amounts to. And this begs the question against the Resemblance Philosophy. The Resemblance Philosophers maintain that our knowledge of what it is for something to be red just consists in a capacity to compare any particular object X with certain standard objects, and thereby to discover whether X does or does not resemble these standard objects as closely as they resemble each other. It does not make sense to speak of comparing the standard objects *with themselves*, or to ask whether *they* resemble one another as closely as they do resemble one another. Yet that is just what we should be trying to do, if we tried to say 'in what respect' they are alike. To say that *they* are red, or are characterized by redness, would not be an informative statement, but a tautology.

This objection does however draw our attention to an important point. According to the Philosophy of Resemblances, there cannot be a class unless there are exemplar objects to hold the class together. Nevertheless, the same class may have *alternative* sets of exemplars. The class of red things, we said, consists of everything which resembles the post-box, the tomato and the brick as closely as they resemble each other. It could equally be said to consist of everything which resembles a certain bit of sealing wax, a certain blushing face and a certain sunset sky as closely as *they* resemble each other. In that case, it does make sense to ask whether the post-box, the tomato and the brick are red, or are characterized by redness. And the answer 'Yes, they are' is now no longer tautologous. We are no longer trying, absurdly, to compare them with themselves. We are comparing them with three other things, and discovering that they do all have a sufficient degree of resemblance to these other things. But because there are (within limits) alternative sets of standard objects for the same class, we are led to suppose, erroneously, that a class can exist without any standard objects at all. This or that set of standard objects can be deposed from its privileged position without destroying the unity of the class; and we then suppose, by a process of illegitimate generalization, that the class would still remain what it is if privilege were abolished altogether. There must be a set of standard objects for each class, though within limits its does not matter which set of objects have this status.

Thus in the Philosophy of Resemblances, as well as the Philosophy of Universals, there does after all have to be something which holds a class together, if one may put it so. Where the two philosophies differ is, in their view of what that something is. In the Philosophy of Universals, what holds a class together is a universal, something of a different ontological type from the members. In the Philosophy of Resemblances there is no question of different ontological types. There are just particular objects, and there is nothing non-particular which is 'in' them, in the way that a universal is supposed to be 'in' the particulars which are its instances. What holds the class together is a set of nuclear or standard members. Anything which has a sufficient degree of resemblance to these is thereby a member of the class; and 'resembling them sufficiently' means 'resembling them as closely as they resemble each other'.

Again, to turn for a moment to epistemological considerations, it is their relationship to the standard objects or exemplars which enables all these objects to satisfy the same concept, e.g. the concept Red, and likewise enables the same word or other symbol, e.g. the word 'red', to apply to them all. But this is to anticipate. The Philosophy of Resemblances is an *ontological* doctrine, though it may be used as the starting point for certain epistemological theories (Conceptualism, Imagism and Nominalism), just as the Philosophy of Universals may be used as the starting-point of a Realist epistemology. If the Philosophy of Resemblances is true at all, it might still have been true even if there had been no thinkers and no speakers. As it happens, there are thinkers and speakers too. But there may be many classes in the world, which do exist (because the requisite resemblances do happen to be there) although no mind happens to have formed the corresponding class-concepts, and no speaker has acquired the habit of using the corresponding class-symbols. Thus there is nothing subjectivist or anthropocentric about the Philosophy of Resemblances. It denies that there are universals *in rebus*, but it asserts that there are resemblances *inter res*. Certain objects really are as like the objects A, B and C as these are to one another, whether anyone notices the fact or not. Known or not, spoken of or not, the relationship is there; just as in the Philosophy of Universals objects are instances of universals whether they are known to be so or not. In this respect, both these philosophies are equally 'realistic'.

We must now turn to the second of the classical objections against the Philosophy of Resemblances, an objection so familiar that one might almost call it notorious. It is concerned with resemblance itself. Surely resemblance is itself a universal, present in many pairs or groups of resemblant objects? It is of course, a universal of relation. The instances of it are not individual objects taken singly, but complexes, and each of these complexes is composed of two objects or more. In their attempt to 'get rid of universals', the Philosophers of Resemblance seem to concentrate their attention on universals of *quality* (e.g. redness, color, shape) and say little or nothing about universals of relation. Hence they have failed to notice that resemblance itself is one of them. But if we are obliged to admit that resemblance at any rate is a genuine universal, a relation which does literally recur in many different situations or complexes, what ground have we for denying that there are other *universalia in rebus* as well?

It may seem audacious to question this formidable argument, which has convinced many illustrious men. But is it as strong as it looks? The Resemblance philosophers might very well reply that it begs the question at issue, that it just assumes what it purports to prove. For after all, what reason is given for the crucial assertion that resemblance is a universal? Apparently none. It is not enough just to say 'surely resemblance at any rate is a universal'. Could any reason be given? We might perhaps try to find one by starting from the linguistic side of the matter. The word 'resemblance', we might say, is an *abstract* word, like the words 'redness' and 'proximity'; therefore it must stand for a universal or characteristic (a relational one, of course). But if this is the argument, it seems to beg the question. For if one does start from a linguistic point of view, the very question at issue is whether abstract words and general words do stand for universals. And if the argument is to be cogent, it ought to be an argument about the noun 'resemblance' in particular, or about the verb 'to resemble' in particular. We ought to be shown that it is somehow peculiarly obvious that *this* word at any rate (or this pair of words) stands for a universal, even though it may be less obvious that other general words do.

Perhaps it will be said, the peculiar obviousness consists in this, that even the people who try to get rid of universals have to use *this* general word at least, or equivalent general words such as 'similar', 'like'. True enough, one cannot speak in a language consisting entirely of proper names and demonstratives. One cannot say anything at all without using some general words. As an observation about the nature of language, this is perfectly indisputable. But the question is, what are its implications? Does it follow that because we must use general words, there are, therefore, general somethings in *rerum natura* which they stand for? That is just the point at issue. One cannot just assume that the answer is 'Yes'. Of course the Philosophy of Resemblances admits that we do use general words, and cannot avoid using them if we are to speak at all. It does not at all deny the fact. But it does deny the conclusion which the Philosophy of Universals draws from it—namely that because we use general words, there must be *general somethings* (universals) which they mean. Has anything been done to show that this denial is mistaken? Nothing. The Philosophy of Universals has just repeated over again the principle which has to be proved, the principle that every general word stands for a universal; adding—what is obvious—that *if* this principle is true, the word 'resemblance' is an illustration of it. Of course. But *is* the principle true?

If the Philosopher of Resemblances is asked to explain how the general word 'resemblance' is used, or what kind of meaning it has, he will presumably point out that there are resemblances of *different orders*. Two cats, A and B, resemble each other, and two sounds, C and D, also resemble each other. These are first-order resemblances. But it is also true that the two-cat situation resembles the two-sound situation, and resembles many other situations too. This is a second-order resemblance. The A-B situation and the C-D situation really are alike, though the constituents of the one are unlike the constituents of the other. In virtue of this second-order likeness (a likeness *between* likeness-situations) we may apply the same general word to both of them; and the word we happen to use for this purpose is the word 'resemblance', in a second-order sense. There is nothing wrong or unintelligible in the notion of second-order resemblance. Or if it be said that there is, we can reply with the *tu quoque* argument that universality must itself be a universal. When it is said that 'cathood is a universal' the word 'universal' is itself a general word, just as 'cat' is when we say 'Pussy is a cat'. So according to the Philosophy of Universals, there must be a universal called 'universality'. And if it is a universal, universality must accordingly be an instance of itself. But this is a contradiction. For according to this Philosophy, anything which is an *instance* of a universal is *ipso facto* a particular, and not a universal. To get out of this difficulty, the Philosophy of Universals must introduce the notion of 'different orders' too. The word 'universal', it has to say, stands for a second-order universal, whereas 'green' or 'cat' or 'in' stand for first-order ones. This is equivalent to saying that the expression 'a universal', or the propositional function 'ϕ is a universal', can occur only in a metalanguage.

This suggests another way in which the Philosophy of Resemblances might reply to the objection that 'resemblance is itself a universal'. The objection assumes that resemblance is just one relation among others: a relation of the same type as 'on top of', or 'near to', or 'side by side with'. But according to the Philosophy of Resemblances, resemblance is not just one relation among others. Indeed, according to this philosophy, it would be misleading to call it 'a relation' at all. It is too fundamental to be called so. For what we *ordinarily* call 'relations' (as well as what we call 'qualities') are themselves founded upon or analyzable into resemblances. For example, the relation 'being inside of' is founded upon the resemblance between the Jonah-whale complex, the room-house complex, the match-matchbox complex, etc. Moreover, the Philosophy of Universals itself does not really hold that resemblance is just one relation among others, and in pretending that it does, it is abandoning one of its own fundamental principles; indeed it is abandoning the very one which this argument ('resemblance is itself a universal') is ultimately intended to establish, the principle, namely, that all resemblance is derivative. In the Philosophy of Universals itself, resemblance has a status quite different from relations like 'side by side with' or 'on top of'. Resembling is connected with *being an instance of* ... in a way that ordinary relations are not. When A resembles B and C, this is supposed to be a direct consequence of the fact that A, B and C are all instances of the same universal; and not only when A, B and C are individual objects (in which case the universal is a universal of quality) but also when they are complexes, so that the universal they are instances of is a relational one, such as 'being inside of'. If resemblance, in the Philosophy of Universals, is to be called a relation at all, it is a relation of a very special sort, quite different from anything to which the word 'relation' is *ordinarily* applied. We should have to say that it is a 'formal' or 'metaphysical' relation (as opposed to a 'natural' or empirical one) just as the relation of instantiation is, if that can be called a relation at all.

So much for the reply the Philosophy of Resemblances might make to this celebrated argument that 'resemblance is itself a universal'. First, it might be objected that the argument begs the question, by just assuming (what it ought to prove) that because 'resemblance' is admittedly a general word, it must stand for a universal. Secondly, the argument overlooks the fact that there are resemblances of different orders. Thirdly, it treats resemblance as one relation among others, parallel in principle to 'side by side with' or 'on top of', whereas the Philosophy of Resemblances maintains that it is too fundamental to be called a relation at all, in the ordinary sense of the word 'relation'. Fourthly, the Philosophy of Universals itself admits, in its own way, that resemblance does *not* have the same status as other relations, in spite of maintaining in this argument that it has.

Thus the Philosophy of Resemblances has an answer to these two classical objections, the one about 'resemblance in respect of' and the one we have just discussed 'that resemblance is itself a universal'. But the Philosophy of Universals also has an answer to the objection about inexact resemblances, and to the complaint that it ignores the different degrees of intensity which resemblances may have.[2] We must consider this answer if we are to do justice to both parties.

The first step is to distinguish between *determinable* and *determinate* characteristics. Universals or characteristics, it is said, have different degrees of determinateness. The adjectives 'determinable' and 'determinate' are too fundamental to be defined. But their meaning can be illustrated. Thus the characteristic of being colored is a determinable, and the characteristic of being red is a determinate of it. Being red is again a sub-determinable, and has under it the determinates being scarlet, being brick-red, being cherry-red, etc. Likewise, being a mammal is a determinable characteristic, a highly complex one this time. There are many different ways of being a mammal. Being a dog, being a whale, being a man are some of the determinates of this determinable.

Now whenever two objects resemble each other with less than the maximum intensity (i.e. whenever they have what was called an 'inexact' resemblance) we can always say that the same *determinable* characteristic characterizes them both, though not the same determinate one. Two objects may each have a different shade of red. A is scarlet, and B is brick-red. They resemble each other fairly closely, but by no means exactly. That is because redness itself is a determinable characteristic, a sub-determinable falling under the higher determinable coloredness. The two objects do have this determinable characteristic in common, though each of them has a different determinate form of it. So we can still maintain that this resemblance, though inexact, is derivative, dependent on the presence of the same determinable universal in both objects.

Let us apply these considerations to the two examples given on pp. 197 and 199: (1) the various white objects; (2) the penny and the sixpence. It may

now be maintained that all my different white objects—from the freshly
fallen snow at one end of the series to the unwashed bow-tie at the
other—do have a *determinable* characteristic in common; though 'whitish',
rather than 'white', would be the appropriate word for it. 'White' might be
taken to mean pure white. And pure white is only one determinate of the
determinable *whitish*. We certainly should not say that all the objects in this
series are pure white. At the most, only the freshly fallen snow is pure white,
but not the piece of chalk, or the rather messy bit of paper, or the rather
dirty handkerchief, or the very dirty unwashed bow-tie. But we should
admit that all of them are 'whitish'.

Let us now consider my other example, the penny and the sixpence,
which resemble each other in shape, but inexactly. The penny with its
smooth edge and the sixpence with its milled (slightly serrated) edge have
different determinate shapes. How is it, then, that they do still resemble each
other in shape, though inexactly, and both would be called 'round coins' in
ordinary speech? Because the same *determinable* shape—we might more
appropriately call its 'roundish'—characterizes both of them; and it characterizes many other things as well, e.g. slightly buckled bicycle wheels,
cogwheels with not too large teeth, which resemble each other a good deal
less closely than the penny and the sixpence do.

By this expedient the Philosophy of Universals is able to maintain its
thesis that all resemblances, inexact ones too, are derivative, and not ultimate, as the Philosophy of Resemblances would have them. Inexact resemblance, we are invited to say, depends upon or is derived from the presence
of the same *determinable* characteristic in a number of objects; exact
resemblance (resemblance of maximum intensity) depends upon their being
characterized by the same *determinate* characteristic.

Perhaps this will also enable us to dispense with the notion of 'degrees of
instantiation' which was mentioned on p. 200 above. It was not easy to see
what could be meant in the Philosophy of *universalia in rebus* by saying that
one object is a *better* instance of so-and-so than another, though this notion
fits well enough into the Platonic theory of *universalia ante rem*, and into
Conceptualism too. Perhaps it could now be suggested that the determinates
of some determinables, e.g. 'whitish', 'roundish', are serially ordered. Thus
the various determinates of whitishness which characterize the patch of
snow, the piece of chalk, the paper, etc., may be arranged in a series
beginning with 'pure white'. After this comes 'nearly pure white' (the color
the piece of chalk has), then 'farther from pure white' and then 'farther still
from pure white', until we come to a characteristic which is as far from pure
whiteness as it can be without ceasing to be a determinate of whitishness at
all. The system of marking ($\alpha+$, α, $\alpha-$, $\beta+$, etc.) which we suggested for
indicating the 'goodness' or 'badness' of instances can still be used: only it is
now applied not to the objects themselves, but to the determinate character-

istics by which they are respectively characterized.

Thus this objection to the Philosophy of Universals, that it can make no room for inexact resemblances (resemblances of less than the maximum intensity), turns out after all to be indecisive, although it looked so convincing at first sight. The facts to which this argument draws our attention are of course perfectly genuine, and important too. It is, for example, an important fact about language that most of our general words apply to sets of objects which inexactly resemble one another; and it is an important fact about thinking that the various objects which 'satisfy' a given concept, e.g. the concept of Crow, do not have to be exactly alike. Nevertheless, this argument does not at all refute the Philosophy of Universals, as it is often supposed to do. All it does is to point out what was lacking in our first rough-and-ready formulation of that philosophy. Certainly the Philosophy of Universals would be quite unworkable *without* the distinction between determinable and determinate universals. The doctrine that universals or characteristics have different degrees of determinacy is an indispensable part of it. But the distinction between determinables and determinates is perfectly consistent with the contention that there are recurrent characteristics in the world, and with the accompanying doctrine that resemblances are derivative, not ultimate. Indeed, it could be argued, the fact that recurrent characteristics do differ in their degree of determinateness is just as obvious as the fact of recurrence itself.

Finally, it is worth repeating that the phrases 'inexact resemblance' 'not exactly alike' are sometimes used in another way, to mean *incomplete* or *partial* resemblance. If A and B are closely alike in a large number of respects, but unlike or not closely alike in one or two, we sometimes say that they are very like each other but not exactly like each other. For example, within the same species of bird we often find that there are slight differences of size or coloring between two individual specimens, although they also resemble each other closely in very many ways. It is obvious that if the phrase 'inexact resemblance' is used in *this* sense, the Philosophy of Universals has no difficulty at all about inexact resemblances. We merely have to say that many universals are common to the two birds, or recur in both of them; and consequently the two individuals resemble each other in a great many respects. We then add that bird A is also an instance of a certain universal φ, while bird B is not an instance of this, but of a certain other universal ψ; and consequently there is a respect in which they are *not* alike. (It may be found, of course, and in this example it almost certainly will be, that though φ and ψ are different determinate universals, they are determinates of the same determinable universal, say 'mottled'). It must not be forgotten that every individual object is an instance of several universals at once, and often of very many at once. When we compare it with another object, we may easily find that some universals are common to both of them,

and other universals are not. It would be a strange misunderstanding of the
Philosophy of Universals to suppose that in this philosophy every particular
is held to be an instance of only *one* universal. When we say that something
is a cat, we are saying that it is an instance of many universals conjointly, and
not just of one.

Our discussion has been long and complicated. What conclusion shall we
draw from it? It would seem that there is nothing to choose between these
two philosophies, the Philosophy of Universals or characteristics (*universalia in rebus*)[3] on the one hand, and the Philosophy of Ultimate Resemblances
on the other. At any rate, it would seem that there is nothing to choose
between them so long as they are considered as purely ontological doctrines,
which is the way we have been considering them in this chapter. Both seem
to cover the facts, though only when both are stated with sufficient care.
Moreover, they both cover the *same* facts. This strongly suggests that they
are two different (systematically different) terminologies, two systematically
different ways of saying the same thing. It does not follow that both alike are
just pieces of solemn and elaborate trifling. On the contrary, the thing which
they both say is of the first importance, and we do need a way of saying it.
The efforts which each party has made to provide us with a systematic
terminology for saying it have not been a waste of time. For if there were no
recurrent characteristics, *or* no resemblances between different objects—
whichever way you choose to put it—there could be no conceptual cognition, and no use of general symbols either.

Now if there is only a (systematic) difference of terminology between
these two philosophies, it is well to be familiar with both. Each of them may
have its misleading features; and when we are in danger of being misled by
the one, we may save ourselves by changing over to the other.

The danger of the terminology of Universals has been pointed out
already. If we can only do our philosophizing in this terminology, we may
be led to regard universals as *things* or *entities*. We reduce this danger by
using the word 'characteristic' instead; or by using phrases like 'being red'
'being a cat' 'being side by side with . . .' instead of noun-substantives like
'redness', 'cathood', 'side-by-sideness', which do look like *names* for entities; or by using the propositional function notation ϕx, xRy, $R(x,y,z)$, etc.,
where 'x', 'y' and 'z' are variables. But perhaps we do not avoid the danger
altogether, especially when we make very general statements, as we have to
in philosophy; for example 'characteristics are divided into two sorts,
qualities and relations' or even 'the characteristic of being red entails the
characteristic of being colored'. Such statements may mislead us into supposing that 'there are' characteristics in the sense in which 'there are' dogs,
or planets.

We can avoid these dangers by changing over to the terminology of
Resemblances, and by recalling that everything which can be said in the

language of Universals or Characteristics can also be said (though usually less elegantly) in the language of Resemblances.

Perhaps there is another danger as well. The Philosophy of Universals may tend to make us think that the world is a more neat and tidy place than it is. If one may say so, there is sometimes a certain air of infallibility or omnicompetence about its exponents, as if the basic structure of the universe were perfectly clear to them, and only a few rather unimportant details remained to be settled. The Philosophy of Resemblances delivers us from this danger, by reminding us that most of the resemblances we think and talk of are by no means exact ones. It restores to human thought and language that fuzziness or haziness, that absence of hard and fast boundaries, which do belong to them, and even in a way to the world itself.

On the other hand, the terminology of Resemblances has its defects too. It is clumsy, complicated, and difficult to handle. Moreover, it tends to make us too much preoccupied with the inexactitude of resemblances; and so we may come to forget the vastly important fact that after all they *are* resemblances, and some of them pretty close ones too. There is such a thing as too much attention to 'marginal cases'. Attention to them is a philosophical virtue, but exclusive preoccupation with them is a philosophical vice. If that is our temptation, we may escape it by changing over to the terminology of Universals. In this terminology, we remind ourselves, there are determinable characteristics and not only determinate ones; so that even where objects resemble each other inexactly, there is still *recurrence*.

NOTES

From H. H. Price, *Thinking and Experience*. Originally published by Hutchinson University Press, London, 1953. Reprinted by permission of Unwin Hyman, Ltd.

1. In Christian Platonism, where Plato's transcendent 'forms' become concepts in the mind of God, the differences between Platonic Realism and Conceptualism are still further diminished, though they do not disappear altogether.
2. See pp. 197–99 above.
3. It may be worth while to remind the reader that the phrase 'the Philosophy of Universal', as it has been used in this chapter, is *not* intended to cover the Platonic doctrine of *universalia ante rem*.

20 STRAWSON

At the outset Strawson attempts to ascertain the difference between particulars and universals. He demonstrates that the traditional means of doing so break down. He then offers what he believes to be three kinds of universals. They are (1) materials named by partitive nouns (e.g., 'gold' and 'snow'), (2) substances named by articulative nouns (e.g., '(a) man' and '(an) apple'), and (3) qualities or properties named by abstract nouns (e.g., 'redness' and 'anger').

He then develops a procedure whereby one can adequately distinguish between a particular and a universal. More specifically, he wants a scheme by which one can understand the difference between a particular and a universal when the former is an instance of the latter. His analysis leads to the conclusion that

> it is a necessary condition for a thing's being a general thing that it can be referred to by a singular substantival expression, a unique reference for which is determined solely by the meaning of the words making up that expression; and it is a necessary condition of a thing's being a particular thing that it cannot be referred to by a singular substantival expression, a unique reference for which is determined solely by the meaning of the words making up that expression.

In other words, a universal can be understood solely on the basis of the meaning of a singular substantival expression that describes (that is, denotes) that universal. A particular, to be a particular, requires more than the meaning of a singular substantival expression. Particulars are instances of universals as a result of what Strawson calls placing, that is, making specific reference to a context as part of the description of the particular. Placing is what makes something particular and not general.

It is clear from the quotation above that Strawson is a realist. His concern is not with the existence of universals, but with the relationship between universals and particulars.

Particular and General[1]

1. There is a certain philosophical question which, if antiquity confers respectability, is as respectable as any. It was not long ago discussed by Ramsey in the form "What is the difference between a particular and a universal?",[2] and more recently by Ayer in the form "What is the difference between properties and individuals?"[3] Ramsey decided that there was no

ultimate difference; but perhaps he set the standard for an ultimate difference higher than we should wish to, or drew it from a theory we no longer wish to hold. Ayer, after some interesting suggestions, changed the subject, and discussed instead two other questions: viz., what is the difference in function between indicator words and predicates, and could we in principle say what we want to say without using the former?[4] It may be that the original question is made easier to start on, and more difficult to settle, by an initial failure to make even fairly clear what types or classes of things are to be included in the two general categories between which a satisfying difference is sought. The words of the questions I quoted are not very helpful. Universals are said to include qualities and relations. But if, for example, we take the words "quality," "relation" and "property" in their current uses, much that we should no doubt wish to include on the side of the general, as opposed to the particular, would be left out; and if we do not take them in their current uses, it is not clear how we are to take them. Thus snow, gold and clothing are not properties; nor is man, nor any other species; nor is chess nor furniture; nor is the Union Jack—by which I mean, not the tattered specimen the porter keeps in a drawer, but the flag designed in the 19th century, examples of which are taken from drawers by porters and hung from windows. But all these are things which we might well wish to classify with properties correctly so-called, like inflammability, or with qualities correctly so-called, like prudence, when we contrast these latter with individuals or particulars. For there are individual flakes or drifts or falls of snow, pieces of gold, articles of clothing or furniture, games of chess,[5] members of species, and there are hundreds of Union Jacks. These are all (are they not?) particular instances of the general things named in *their* names. Sometimes the unlikeness of these general things to properties or qualities correctly so-called is masked by the introduction of expressions like "being (a piece of) gold," "being snow," "being a man," "being a Union Jack," "being a chair," "being a game of chess"—phrases like these being said to name properties. Now such expressions no doubt have a participial use; and some (*e.g.*, "being a man") may have a use as noun-phrases, as singular terms. But it is dubious whether many of them have a use as singular terms; and it is dubious whether any of them can be regarded as names of properties. And however we resolve these doubts in different cases, the following dilemma arises in each. Either these verbal nouns (where they are nouns) have the same use as the general names they incorporate—and in that case they may as well be discarded in favor of those general names, which are more familiar, and about the use of which we are consequently less liable to be misled; or they have a different use from those general names—and in this case we still have on our hands, to be differentiated, like properties correctly so-called, from particulars, the general things designated by those familiar general names.

2. This initial unclarity about the limits of the two great categories of general and particular shows itself also in that arbitrary narrowing of the field which must be presumed to occur whenever certain answers to our question seem plausible. I shall consider again some of these answers, which were dismissed by Ayer or Ramsey or both, not so much on the ground that they thought them false as on the ground that they did not think them fundamental. There is, for example, the suggestion that general, unlike particular, things cannot be perceived by means of the senses; and this seems most plausible if one is thinking of the things designated by certain abstract nouns. It is not with the eyes that one is said to see hope. But one can quite literally smell blood or bacon, watch cricket, hear music or thunder; and there are, on the other hand, certain particulars which it makes dubious sense to say one perceives. Then there is the suggestion that general, unlike particular, things, can be in several places at once. There can be influenza in London as well as in Birmingham, and gold in Australia as well as in Africa. But then so can many particulars be scattered over the surface of the table or the globe. Moreover, it makes dubious sense to say of some general things (e.g., solubility) that they are in any place, let alone in many; and equally dubious sense to say of some particular things (a sudden thought, a mental image, the constitution of France) that they have a particular spatial location. It may be said that I have missed the point of both these theories; that, first, when we say we perceive general things, what we really perceive is individual instances of them, not the general things themselves; and, second, to say that general things can be in several places at once is to say that they may have different instances, differently located; whereas it makes no sense to speak of different instances of individuals. But so to explain these theories is to give them up. It is to fall back on saying that general things may have instances, and individual instances of general things may not. This is, perhaps, an unexceptionable statement of the general distinction between the two categories, but scarcely seems to count as an explanation of it.

A third suggestion is that individual things, unlike general things, have dates or histories. But similar objections apply to this. We may speak of the history of dress or engineering, the origins of civilization, the invention of golf and the evolution of man. This theory, like the others (when taken at their face value), may draw a logically interesting distinction; but, like them, does not draw one that coincides with the categorical line between particular and general.

A doctrine which might appear more promising, because more general, than these, is that individuals can function in propositions only as subjects, never as predicates, whereas general things can function as both. But it is not clear what this doctrine amounts to. Suppose, first, it is a grammatical point. Then if it says that the names of individuals never have adjectival or verbal forms, whereas names of general things do, it is false. If it says that individual names never form parts of grammatical predicates, or alternatively, never stand by themselves after the word "is" in a grammatical predicate, it is equally false. In any case, a grammatical point could scarcely be fundamental, since it is easy to imagine the elimination of those distinctions upon which such points must rely, in favor of the device of merely coupling names of appropriate types, in any order, in a singular sentence. We should not, by so doing, eliminate the category-distinction. For we might imagine changing the language once more, requiring that our names should stand on one side or the other of the phrase "is an instance of," and then simply distinguishing the individual names as those that could never stand on the right of this phrase.[6] So I think we must conclude that the point misleadingly made in the languages of grammar is simply once more the point that individuals, unlike general things, cannot have instances. To say that general things, unlike individuals, can be predicated of other things, is simply to paraphrase this; and neither expression seems more perspicuous than the other.

3. But will the word "instance" itself really bear the weight of this distinction? Of course, as a philosopher's word, understood in terms of that distinction, it cannot fail to bear it; but then it ceases to explain the distinction for us. If we ask what expressions we actually use to refer to or describe an individual thing as an instance of a general thing, we find that they are many; and that perhaps none of them is appropriate in every case. They include: "a case of," "an example of," "a specimen of," "a member of," "a piece of," "a quantity of," "a copy of," "a performance of," "a game of," "an article of," and so on. Though each can be followed by the name of a general thing, many can also be followed by expressions we should hesitate to regard as the names of general things. This is true of the phrase "an instance of" itself. We may speak of a signal instance of generosity; but we may also speak of a signal instance of Smith's generosity. Similarly we may speak not only of a piece of gold and an article of clothing, but of a piece of Smith's gold and an article of Smith's clothing. So if we seek to draw our distinction in terms of the words actually used to play the part of the philosopher's word "instance"—including the word "instance" itself—then it will not be enough to say that general things may have instances. For so may non-general things.

The point here may be put roughly as follows. We are tempted to explain the distinction between two types of things, T_1 and T_2 by means of a certain relation R; by saying, that is, that only things belonging to T_2 can appear as the second term of this relation, whereas both things belonging to T_2 and things belonging to T_1 can appear as its first term. R is something like, but more general than, *is characterized by* or *is a member of* or the converse of *is predicated of*. But then it appears that we really have no notion of R except one which is useless for explanatory purposes since it is itself to be explained in terms of the difference between T_1 and T_2; this is what I called the philosopher's notion of "an instance of." What we have instead is a lot of notions which are either too restricted to serve our purpose (*e.g.*, "has the property of"), or fail to be restricted in precisely the way in which we want them to be, or both. As a member of this set of notions, preeminent for its abstract character, we may take the logician's idea of class-membership. The difficulty is, roughly, that we can form closed classes on what principle we please; we could count almost any particular we are likely to mention as such a class, and hence as the second term of our relation. (These remarks are very rough and schematic; but they serve, I hope, to make the point in a general form). Consequently, we shall have to give up the idea of explaining the difference between the particular and the general in terms of such a relation. This will not lead us, as it perhaps led Ramsey, to despise the philosopher's notion of an instance, and to think that there is nothing in it; for it is easy enough to teach anyone the application of it, without precise explanations. But it will lead us to look further for such explanations.

4. To begin with, I want to draw a rough distinction between three classes of nouns, all of which would traditionally be regarded either as themselves the names of universals (general things) or—in the case of the nouns of group (2)—as closely linked to such names. The distinctions are indicated only by examples; and the three classes are by no means exhaustive of the field. But this does not matter for my purpose.

(1) Examples of the first class are such partitive nouns as "gold," "snow," "water," "jam," "music." These I shall call *material-names* and what they name, *materials.*

(2) Examples of the second are certain articulative nouns such as "(a) man," "(an) apple," "(a) cat." These I shall call *substance-names*, and what they apply to, *substances.*

(3) Examples of the third are such abstract nouns as "redness," (or "red"), "roundness," "anger," "wisdom." These I shall call *quality-* or *property-names*, and what they name, *qualities* or *properties.*[7]

These three classes of nouns may be compared and contrasted with one another in a number of ways. But the contrast on which I wish to lay most emphasis is

(i) The contrast between the nouns of group (3) and those of groups (1) and (2). The nouns of group (3) are the most sophisticated and the most dispensable. They are derived from adjectives and the general things they name usually enter our talk by way of the adjectives from which their names are derived. When we consider the things which philosophers are prepared to count as individual instances of these general things, we find a considerable latitude in the categories of the things to which these instances may belong. Thus an instance of wisdom may be a man, a remark or an action. An instance of the color red may be a material thing like a pillar-box, an event like a sunset, or a mental thing like an image. A word, a gesture, an expression, a man may all be instances of anger. In contrast, unsystematic ambiguities aside, there is no latitude at all about what category of thing can be an individual instance of a cat or an apple. There is some latitude, but one would often hesitate to call it a category-latitude, about what can be an individual instance of the general things named by the nouns of group (1). An instance of gold may be a vein, a piece or a quantity of gold; an instance of snow may be a drift, an expanse, a piece, and even a fall, of snow.

(ii) Next I want to emphasize a respect in which the nouns of group (2) differ from those of groups (1) and (3). Philosophers may speak of "an individual (particular) instance (example, specimen) of φ," where "φ" is replaced by a noun from any of these three groups. Suppose the noun is drawn from group (2). Then we have such phrases as "an instance of a horse" or "an instance of an apple." It is to be noticed that what follows the expression "an instance of" is a phrase which can and does *by itself* function as an indefinite designation of an individual instance. (An instance of a horse is the same as a horse.) This is not the case if the nouns are drawn from groups (1) or (3). (Gold is not the same as a piece of gold). It seems as if, when we say that x is an instance of y, then when y is such that there is no choice about the sort of thing we can count as an instance of it, we feel no need of a true general-thing name for y, *i.e.*, of a name differing from an indefinite designation of an individual instance of y. (It is true that we have the expressions "*the* horse," "*the* apple," etc., names of species or kinds, obvious collectors of homogeneous individuals; but these follow less naturally after the expression "an instance of" than does the phrase containing the indefinite article.) Philosophers have felt this difference, and tried to blur it with the invention of such expressions as "horseness" (*cf.* "being a horse"). But it should rather be treated as a clue until proved an anomaly.

(iii) Finally, I want to note the existence of a special class of individual instances of general things whose names belong to group (3). The simplest, though not the only recipe, for forming the names of members of this class is as follows: in the formula "the . . . of . . . ," fill the first gap with the property-name in question and the second gap with the definite designation of a suitable individual. Thus we may speak of *the wisdom of Socrates* as an instance of wisdom; of *the redness of Smith's face* as an instance of redness; and we may also speak of *Jones' present mental state* as an instance of anger. This class of individual instances of properties, or property-like things, will include the "particular qualities" which Stout defended. And an analogy may be found between referring to a horse as "an instance of a horse" and referring to Jones' present stage of anger as "an instance of anger."

5. Next, I want to make some general, and still propaedeutic, remarks about the notion of an individual or particular.

(1) The idea of an individual is the idea of an individual instance *of* something general. There is no such thing as a pure particular. (This truth is too old to need the support of elaboration.)

(2) The idea of an individual instance of φ is the idea of something which we are able in principle

(a) to distinguish from other instances of φ; and
(b) to recognize as the same instance at different times (where this notion is applicable).

So, to have the idea of a particular instance of φ, we need (in general)

(a) criteria of distinctness,
(b) criteria of identity

for a particular instance of φ. On the need for these criteria the following comments must be made:

(i) It might be supposed that the distinction between the two kinds of criteria is a mistake; that there is no such distinction. For identity and difference are two sides of the same coin. It is possible, however, at least in some cases, to consider separately the criteria by which we distinguish and enumerate objects of the same sort, in a situation in which the question of identifying any one of them as, or distinguishing it from, the one which had such-and-such a history, does not arise or is not considered. It is to criteria of this kind that I give the name "criteria of distinctness". They might also be called "criteria of enumeration".[8]

(ii) What the criteria of distinctness and identity for instances of φ may be is obviously closely connected with what φ is; but is not wholly determined by it in every case. That it is not so determined is obvious in the case of properties, qualities, states, etc.; we have already seen how wide a range of categories their instances may be drawn from (4 (i)). It is less obvious, but still true, in the case of general things named by material-names. The *general* question of the criteria of distinctness and identity of individual instances of snow or gold cannot be raised or, if raised, be satisfactorily answered. We have to wait until we know whether we are talking of *veins, pieces or quantities* of gold, or of *falls, drifts* or *expanses* of snow. There are cases, however, where this indeterminateness regarding the criteria of identity and distinctness does not seem to exist, where it seems that once φ is given, the criteria are given, too. And among these cases are those where "φ" is a substance-name (4(ii)). It should once more be noted that these are the cases where we do not find a true name of a general thing following the phrase "an instance of," but instead an expression which can by itself function as an indefinite designation of an individual instance (*e.g.*, "a horse").

(3) When it has been said that a particular must be an instance of something general, and that there must be criteria of distinctness and (where applicable) of identity for individual instances of a general thing, something of central importance still remains unsaid. In giving the relevant criteria—or sets of criteria—for individual instances of a certain general thing, we do not indicate how such particulars are brought into our discourse. Nor do we bring a particular into our discourse by mentioning these criteria. (To

mention them is still to talk *in general*.) We bring a particular into our discourse only when we determine, select, *a point of application* for such criteria, only when we mention, refer to, something to which these criteria are to be applied; and no theory of particulars can be adequate which does not take account of the means by which we determine such a point of application *as* a point of application of these criteria.

6. In the rest of this paper I shall try to do two things. First, I shall try to show how in the case of *certain kinds* of particulars (particular instances of *certain kinds* of general things), the notion of a particular may be seen as something logically complex in relation to other notions (a kind of compound of these notions). That is, I shall try to produce a partial explanation (analysis) of the notion of an individual instance, for certain cases; and then I shall try to show how this notion, as explained for these cases, may be used in the explanation of the notion of individual instances of *other* sorts of general things, and in the explanation of the notions of those other types of general things themselves. So in this part of the paper (sections 6–9), no general account is offered of the distinction we are concerned with. The procedure is essentially one of indicating, step by step, how certain types of notion can be seen as depending upon others; and it makes no claim at all to completeness. Second (section 12), this procedure is found to suggest a possible general account of the distinction we are concerned with; though the acceptability or otherwise of this general account seems to be independent of that of the step-by-step schema of explanation.

Now it might seem that the difficulty of finding an explanation of the notion of an individual instance arises from the fact that the category distinction between general and individual is so fundamental that there is nothing logically simpler, or more fundamental, in terms of which this notion could be explained. But I think this view can be challenged for a certain range of important cases, which can then perhaps serve as the basis for the explanation of others. To challenge it successfully we have to envisage the possibility of making statements which (a) do not make use of the notion of individual instances, and (b) do not presuppose the existence of statements which do make use of this notion. The second condition may be held to rule out general statements, for though many general statements make no direct mention of individuals, they have often and plausibly been held in some sense to presuppose the existence of statements which do. So what we have to consider is the possibility of singular statements which make no mention of (*i.e.*, contain no names for, or other expressions definitely or indefinitely referring to) individual instances of general things. Now there certainly does exist, in ordinary use, a range of empirical singular statements answering to this description. I suggest, as examples, the following:—

It is (has been) raining
Music can be heard in the distance
Snow, is falling
There is gold here
There is water here.

All these sentences contain either the material-name of a general thing ("music," "snow") or a corresponding verb; but none contains any expression which can be construed as serving to make a definite or indefinite mention of individual instances of those general things (*i.e.*, falls or drops of rain, pieces of gold, pools of water and so on). Of course, when these sentences are used, the combination of the circumstances of their use with the tense of the verb and the demonstrative adverbs, if any, which they contain, provides an indication of the incidence of the general thing in question. Such an indication must be provided somehow, if empirical singular statements are to be made at all. But it is important that it can be provided by means of utterance-centered indications which do not include noun-expressions referring definitely or indefinitely to individual instances. *Such sentences as these do not bring particulars into our discourse.*

Languages imagined on the model of such sentences are sometimes called "property-location" languages. But I think the word "property" is objectionable here because (a) the general things which figure in my examples are not properties, and (b) the idea of a property belongs, with the idea of an individual instance itself to a level of logical complexity we are trying to get below. So I propose to substitute the less philosophically committed word "feature"; and to speak of feature-placing sentences.

Though feature-placing sentences do not introduce particulars into our discourse, they provide the materials for this introduction. Suppose we compare a feature-placing *sentence* ("There is snow here") with a *phrase* ("This (patch of) snow") in the use of which an individual instance of the feature is mentioned. It seems possible, in this case, to regard the notion of the individual instance as something logically complex in relation to the two simpler notions of the feature and of placing. The logical complexity may be brought out in the following way. In making the feature-placing statement, we utter a completed sentence without mentioning individuals. If we *merely* mention the individual without going on to say anything about it, we fail to utter a completed sentence; yet what the feature-placing sentence does explicitly is, in a sense, implicit in this mere mention. So, as the basic step in an explanatory schema, we may regard the notion of a particular instance of *certain sorts* of general things as a kind of logical compound of the simpler notions of a feature and of placing.

But what about the criteria of distinctness and identity which were said in general to be necessary to the notion of an individual instance of a general thing? The *basis* for the criteria of distinctness can already be introduced at the feature-placing level, without yet introducing particulars. For where we can say "There is snow here" or "There is gold here," we can also, perhaps, more exactly, though not more correctly, say "There is snow (gold) *here*—and *here*—and *here*." And when we can say "It snowed to-day," we can also, perhaps, more exactly, but not more correctly, say "It snowed twice to-day." The considerations which determine multiplicity of placing become, when we introduce particulars, the criteria for distinguishing this *patch of* snow from that, or the first *fall of* snow from the second. Of criteria of identity I shall say more in general later.

It might be objected that it is absurd to speak of an imagined transition from feature-placing sentences to substantival expressions definitely designating particular instances of features as the *introduction* of particulars, that it is absurd to represent this imagined transition as part of a possible analysis of the notion of a particular instance, even for these simple cases of material-names which seem the most favorable; and that at most what is achieved is the indication of a possible way of looking at certain *designations* of certain particulars. For are not the particulars as much a relevant part of the situation in which a feature-placing sentence is employed as they are of a situation in which a substantival particular-designation is employed? To this I would reply by asking what philosophical question there would be about particulars if we did not designate them, could not make lists of them, did not predicate qualities of them and so on. What we have to explain is a certain mode of speech.

7. When we turn from material-names to substance-names, the attempt to provide an analogous explanation of the notion of an individual instance seems much harder. But though it is harder, it is perhaps worth making; for if it succeeds, we may find we have then an adequate basis for the explanation of the notion of an individual instance in other cases, and for the explanation of further kinds of general things. In order for the attempt to succeed, we must be able to envisage a situation in which, instead of operating with the notion of an individual instance of a cat or an apple, we operate with the notions of a corresponding feature and of placing. Ordinary language does not seem to provide us, in these cases, with feature-placing sentences. And it might be argued that the idea of such sentences was, in these cases, absurd. For (1) it might be pointed out that an all-important difference between such things as snow and such things as cats lay in the fact that different instances of snow are, in a sense, indefinitely additive, can be counted together as one instance of snow; while this is not true in the case of instances of cats; and it might be suggested that herein lay a reason for the possibility of feature-placing sentences in the case of snow and for their impossibility in the case of cats. And (2) it might be added that we have no name for a general thing which could count as the required feature in the case of cats. It is true that we speak of *the cat* in general; but "the cat" ranks as a species-name, and the notion of a species as surely presupposes the

notion of individual members as the notion of a property involves that of individual things to which the property belongs or might belong. It is also true that we may speak of an instance (specimen) of *a* cat, as we may speak of an instance of gold; but here what follows the phrase "an instance of" is not, as "gold" is, a general-thing name which could figure in a merely feature-placing sentence, but an expression which also serves as an indefinite designation of an individual. Does not all this strongly suggest that there *could* be no concept of the "cat-feature" such as would be required for the analysis to work, that any general idea of cat must be the idea of a cat, *i.e.*, must involve criteria of identity and distinctness for cats as individuals and hence the notion of an individual instance?

These objections have great force and importance; but I do not think them decisive. For they do not show that it is logically absurd to suppose that we might recognize the presence of cat or signs of the past or future presence of cat, without ever having occasion to distinguish one cat from another as the cat on the left, or identify a cat as ours or as Felix.[9] The second argument merely reminds us that the resources of our language are such that on any actual occasion of this kind we in fact use, not a partitive noun, but the indefinite forms ("cats" or "a cat") of the articulative noun. But this fact can be explained in a way consistent with the advocated analysis (see section 10). Nevertheless, these arguments show something. The point about the species-name, for example, is sound; the notion of a species, like that of a property, belongs to a level of logical complexity we are trying to get below. Second, and more immediately important, the first argument shows that if there is to be a general concept of the cat-feature, corresponding in the required way to the notion of an individual instance, it must already include in itself the *basis* for the criteria of *distinctness* which we apply to individual cats. (Roughly, the idea of cat, unlike that of snow, would include the idea of a characteristic shape.) But to concede this is not to concede the impossibility of the analysis. It is worth adding that sometimes we do find verbal indications of our use of feature-concepts such as those we are trying to envisage; as, *e.g.*, when we speak of "smelling cat" or "hunting lion," using the noun in the singular without the article.

There might seem to exist a more general objection to this whole procedure. For it seems that it would always be possible in practice to paraphrase a given feature-placing sentence in use, by means of a sentence incorporating *indefinite* designations of particular instances; e.g., "There is gold here" by "There is a *quantity of* gold here"; "Snow has fallen twice" by "There have been *two falls of* snow"; "There is snow here—and here" by "There are *patches (expanses) of* snow here and here"; and so on. And if sentences incorporating definite or indefinite designations of particular instances bring particulars into our discourse; and if statements made by the use of feature-placing sentences are *equivalent* to statements made by the use of sentences incorporating indefinite designations of particular instances; then do not feature-placing sentences themselves bring particulars into our discourse? But this argument can be turned in favor of the explanation it is directed against. Suppose there is a statement S made by means of a feature-placing sentence; and an equivalent statement S' made by means of a sentence incorporating an indefinite particular-designation; and a statement T made by means of a sentence incorporating a definite designation of the particular indefinitely designated in S'. *Now only if a language admits of statements like T can it admit of statements correctly described as I have described S'.* (There are no *indefinite* designations of particulars where there are no *definite* designations of particulars.) But a language might admit of statements like S without admitting of statements like T. So the existence of statements like S', in a language which admits of both statements like S and statements like T, is not destructive of the analysis, but is a proof of its correctness.

8. If the argument so far is acceptable, then at least in the case of some materials and some substances, we can regard the notion of an individual instance as partially explained in terms of the logical composition (of the two notions of a feature and of placing). When we turn to properties and qualities, we may make use of a different kind of explanation which is also, in a sense, the completion of the first kind. I shall not, that is to say, try to explain the notion of individual instances of anger or wisdom or red in terms of the logical composition of a feature, such as *anger* or *red*, and placing. But nor shall I maintain that it would be wrong or impossible to do so. We *might* think of such general things as anger (or red) *not* primarily as qualities, properties, states or conditions of persons or things, but primarily as instantiated in, say, situations (or patches) which acquired their status as individuals from just such a logical composition. But though this is how we might think, it is not, for the most part, how we do think. It is natural, rather, to regard those general things which are properly called qualities, conditions, etc., as belonging at least to the same level of logical complexity as the idea of individual instances of the kinds we have so far been concerned with; to regard them, that is, as feature-*like* things, the incidence of which, however, is primarily indicated, not by placing, but by their *ascription* to individual instances of material or substantial features the incidence of which *is* primarily indicated by placing.[10] We have seen that the notion of an individual instance of some materials and substances can be regarded as a logical compound of the notions of a feature and of placing. We have now to see the ascription of a quality (etc.) to such an individual as an operation *analogous* to the placing of a feature. Indeed, we may find in the possibility of this operation the point—or one important point—of that logical composition which yields us the particular. The individual instance of the simply placeable feature emerges as a possible location-point for general things other than the feature of which it is primarily an instance, and hence as also

an individual instance of *these* general things, its properties or qualities or states. One might exaggeratedly say: the *point* of having the idea of individual instances of material or substantial features is that they may be represented as individual instances of property-like features. The individuals are distinguished as individuals in order to be contrasted and compared.

Other notions call for other treatment. I consider two more.

(a) I mentioned, at 4 (iii), a rather special class of individual instances of properties or property-like things. We form the notion of such an instance when, for example, we speak not of a man or an action as an instance of wisdom or anger, but of the wisdom of Socrates as an individual (a case of wisdom) or of Jones' present mental state as an individual instance of anger. Here the notion of the individual instance can be seen as a new kind of logical compound, namely, a compound which includes as elements both the notion of the general thing (property) in question and that of the material or substantial individual which is an instance of it; it may sometimes include a further element of temporal placing (*cf.* "his *present* state of anger").

(b) Instances of events, processes and changes I have so far scarcely mentioned. Most of our most familiar words for happenings strike us essentially as names for the actions and undergoings of individual instances of material or substantial features. But there is a difference between these happening words and quality or state-words. A wise man is an instance of wisdom, but a dead or dying man is not an instance of death. Only a death is that. As regards such happening-words as these, then, we have to see the idea of an individual instance as reached by a kind of logical composition analogous to that considered in the paragraph immediately above: an individual instance of a material or substantial feature is an element in the compound. But these, though perhaps the most important, are not the only kinds of happening-words.

9. The general form of these explanations may be roughly indicated as follows. The notion of placing a feature is taken as basic, as consisting of the logically simplest elements with which we are to operate. It is pointed out that neither of these elements involves the notion of an individual instance, nor therefore the notions of certain types of general things, such as properties and species; and it is shown that the idea of operating solely with these simplest elements can be made intelligible for certain cases. (Features in fact of course belong to the class of general things; but so long as we remain at the feature-placing level, they cannot be assigned to it; for there is nothing to contrast the general with.) From this basis we proceed by composition and analogy. The designations of individual instances of (some) material and substantial features are first introduced, as expressions, not themselves complete sentences, which include placing-indications; and, complementarily, certain types of general things (*e.g.*, properties and types of happening) are introduced as items the designations of which do not include placing-

indications and which are ascribed to material or substantial individuals. The ascription of such a thing as a property to a substantial individual is represented simply as an operation analogous to the placing of a feature; so no circularity attends the word "ascription." Individuals of certain other types (*e.g.*, events happening to substances, states of substances and "particularized" qualities) are then introduced as the designata of expressions which include the designations of individuals of earlier types, and hence indirectly include the notion of placing.

There are many types of individual and of general thing besides these here considered. Some may admit of analogous treatment; and it might be possible to introduce others, on the basis already provided, by other methods of construction and explanation. But every introduction of a particular, in terms of such a schema, will either directly contain the notion of placing or will preserve, by way of individuals already introduced, the original link with this notion. Of course the value of this suggestion, as it stands, is small. For the notion of an individual instance extends itself indefinitely, by way of far more complicated connections than I have so far indicated; and the limits of plausibility for the kinds of construction-procedure I have used would, no doubt, soon be reached, if they are not already overpassed. Nevertheless, I think this sketch of a procedure has certain merits:

(1) Some of the difficulties which attend any attempt to elucidate the category-distinction between the particular and the general arise from the fact that these two classes include so many different category-distinctions within themselves. This fact creates a dilemma for the theorist of the distinction. On the one hand, he is tempted, in a way illustrated at the beginning of this paper, into drawing distinctions which indeed separate one or more sub-categories of one class from one or more sub-categories of the other, but which fail to yield the desired result if applied over the whole field. Or, on the other hand, in the effort to escape from this domination by irrelevant category differences, he is tempted by the prospect of a purely formal distinction, drawing for this purpose on the terms and concepts of grammar or of formal logic. But distinctions so drawn can only seem to succeed by forfeiting their formal character and silently incorporating the problematic category-distinction. The present procedure offers at least a hope of escape from this difficulty. For it fully allows for the differences between types of general thing and of individual; and instead of producing one single explanation, the same for every case, it offers a serial method of explaining later types of general or particular things on the basis of earlier ones, while preserving a continuous general differentiation between the two major categories in the course of the explanation. Too much must not be claimed for the suggested procedure, however; in particular, it must not be thought that it has been so described as to provide a *criterion* for the distinction we are concerned with.

(2) Another characteristic of the schema of explanation is that it accords a central place to the notion of an individual instance of certain kinds of general things, viz., of material and substantial features. This (see section 8) is not an essential characteristic; it could be modified. But there is reason to think that it corresponds to our actual way of thinking; that these individuals *are* the "basic particulars." Why this should be so, and whether it might not be otherwise, are questions which I shall not now consider.

(3) Finally, while not itself providing a criterion of general and particular, the schema points the way to a possible general distinction which might be defensible even if the procedure which suggests it should prove unsatisfactory. This general distinction I shall outline in section 12. Before I do so, some further points remain to be considered.

10. Something further must first be said on the subject of criteria of identity for individual instances of a general thing. We saw (5 (2)) how in many cases the question of the criteria of distinctness and identity of an individual instance of a general thing was incompletely determined when the general thing was named. This was particularly evident in the case of some properties and was evident also in the case of materials. Where substance-names were concerned, however, this indeterminateness seemed not to exist; when the name was given, the criteria were fixed. And this was connected with the fact that in these cases there seemed to exist no true general-thing name, apart from expressions which ranked as species-names and obviously presupposed certain definite criteria of identity for individual members. As far as criteria of distinctness are concerned, this raises no particular difficulty. We saw, for example, how the idea of a simply placeable feature might include—might indeed *be*—the idea of a characteristic shape, and in this way provide a basis for criteria of distinctness for individual instances of the feature. But it is not so easy to account for the apparent determinateness of criteria of identity. The explanatory schema advanced required that we should theoretically be able to form concepts of some substance-features which were logically prior to, and independent of the corresponding concepts of an individual instance of such features; and this requirement seems to clash with the apparent determinateness of the criteria of identity for such individuals. A parallel answer to that given in the case of criteria of distinctness is theoretically available, but is unattractively unplausible. If we reject this answer, and cannot find an alternative, then we must at least radically revise, though in a not unfamiliar direction, the basis of the explanatory schema. (The difficulty is essentially a more specific form of that encountered already in section 7.)

I think, however, that an acceptable alternative can be found. For in all cases where a feature-concept can be assumed to be possible, the criteria of identity (and of distinctness) for an instance of the general thing in question—or the sets of such criteria, where there is more than one set—can be seen as determined by a *combination* of factors, viz., the nature of the feature itself, the ways in which the feature empirically manifests itself in the world, and—to adopt a possibly misleading mode of expression—the kind of incentives[11] that exist for having a notion of an individual instance of the feature in question. The relevance of this third factor even, perhaps, gives us the right to say that there is something arbitrary about the criteria we adopt, something which, given the other two factors is—in at any rate a stretched sense—a matter of choice. In extreme cases this is obvious. Even those who had witnessed the whole of the affair under discussion might, for example, give varying answers to such a question as: Is this the same quarrel going on now as was going on when I left? The answer we choose may depend on just what distinctions we are interested in; and one can imagine many situations for this example, and many different things which might influence us. There may, on the other hand, be very many cases of features where the adoption of a certain particular set of criteria of identity (and distinctness) for their instances is so utterly natural that it would seem to be stretching the phrase "matter of choice" intolerably to apply it to them. But, even in these cases, the naturalness may still be seen as depending on the combination of factors I mentioned; and, if we bear this in mind, we can sometimes imagine the possibility of alternatives. (Here is a question which might with advantage be explored for many different types of case.)

It seems reasonable to view substantial features as cases of this kind. If this view is acceptable, we can find in it an explanation of that difference between substance-names and certain other true general-thing names to which I have several times referred. Given a true general-thing name, like "gold" or "wisdom," the question of the criteria of identity of its instances cannot be answered until the kind of instance is specified, by such a phrase as "a *piece* of gold" or "a wise *action*". But where one set of criteria of identity is peculiarly dominant, its adoption peculiarly compelling, we find no such non-committal general name in current, adult, unsophisticated use. All that we might wish to do with it, we can equally well do without it, by the use of the indefinite singular or plural forms of the ordinary substance-name (*e.g.*, "a horse" or "horses").

11. It is, perhaps, necessary to guard briefly against a misunderstanding. Of course, I am not denying that we can very well use individual-designations as such without being, or ever having been, in a position to make a relevant placing of some feature which, in terms of the explanatory schema I have defended, is immediately or ultimately relevant to the explanation of the type of instance concerned. To deny this would be absurd. It would be to deny, for example, that when we talk about remoter historical characters, we are really talking about individuals. But the view I am defending does not require such a denial. For this view seeks merely to explain the notion of an individual instance of a general thing in terms,

ultimately, of feature-placing. It does not at all imply that we cannot make use of this notion in situations other than those in terms of which it is explained. In fact, of course, the expansiveness of our talk about individuals is in marked contrast with the restrictedness of our contacts with them. Both the possibility of, and the incentives to, this expansiveness have an empirical ground; in the variousness of individuals, the non-repetitiveness of situations. But this fact may nevertheless mislead us, may make the theoretical problem of individuation look more difficult than it is by distracting our attention from an essential element in the notion of an individual instance. The problem would scarcely seem difficult for the case of an imagined universe in which all that happened was the repetition of a single note, varying, perhaps, in volume. Individual instances could then be described only as, say, "the third before now" or "the next one to come". But in such a universe the incentives to forming the notion of an individual instance would be small. We might say that, in general, what is essential to the notion of an individual instance is not what is interesting about individuals.

12. To conclude, I remarked earlier that the explanatory schema I have sketched points the way to a possible general distinction between the two major categories we are concerned with. To recall, first, some vague, figurative and unsatisfactory terms I have already used: the schema suggests that the notion of a particular individual always includes, directly or indirectly, that of placing, whereas the notion of a general thing does not. Now placing is characteristically effected by the use of expressions the *reference* of which is in part determined by the context of their use and not by their *meaning*, if any, alone. And this suggests the possibility of formulating a general distinction in a more satisfactory way. We may say: *it is a necessary condition for a thing's being a general thing that it can be referred to by a singular substantival expression, a unique reference for which is determined solely by the meaning of the words making up that expression; and it is a necessary condition of a thing's being a particular thing that it cannot be referred to by a singular substantival expression, a unique reference for which is determined solely by the meaning of the words making up that expression.* This specification of mutually exclusive necessary conditions could be made to yield definitions by stipulating that the conditions were not only necessary, but also sufficient. But there is point in refraining from doing so. For as we consider substantival expressions increasingly remote from the simplest cases, there may be increasing reluctance to apply the distinction at all. Nor is this reluctance quite irrational; for the simplest cases are those which form the basis of the general distinction. (Hence roughly, the association of particularity with concreteness.) We may admit that the traditional distinction was vague as well as unclear, and respect its well-founded vagueness in this way.

To elucidate this quasi-definition of particular and general, I add some miscellaneous comments of varying degrees of importance.

(1) It might be objected to the conditions given that expressions like "The third tallest man who ever lived or lives or will live" answer to the specifications for a general-thing designation. If they did, it would perhaps not be difficult to legislate them out, by suitable amendments of those specifications. But in fact they do not. For their meaning does not suffice to determine for them a unique object of reference. It is, if true, contingently true that there is a single thing answering to such a description. This case, however, does raise a problem about how the words "expression a unique reference for which is determined solely by the meaning" are to be construed. If we construe them as "expression the *existence* of just one object of reference for which is *guaranteed* by the meaning," we may find ourselves in (possibly circumventable) trouble over, *e.g.*, "phlogiston" and "the unicorn." Yet this is the construction at first suggested by the present case.[12] It will be better, therefore, to construe them as follows: "expression the (or a) meaning of which is such that it is both logically impossible for it to refer to more than one thing (in that meaning)[13] and logically impossible for the expression to fail to have reference because of the existence of competing candidates for the title". And the sense of "competing candidates" can be explained as follows: x, y and z are competing candidates (and the only competing candidates) for the title D if, if any two of them had not existed, D would apply to the third.

(2) It may seem, perhaps, a more troublesome fact that the names we commonly employ for certain *types*, like Beethoven's Fifth Symphony, do not answer to the specifications given for a general-thing designation, although we may be more than half inclined to count such types as general things; for these names include, as a part of themselves or of their explanation, proper names like "Beethoven." We have, however, an easy remedy here. We can regard the pattern of sounds in question as a general thing for which there might (perhaps does) exist a general description the meaning of which uniquely determines its reference; and then it will appear as the contingent truth it is that Beethoven stands to the general thing so designated in a certain special relation. This does not commit us to saying that it is a contingent truth that Beethoven's Fifth Symphony was composed by Beethoven; but the necessity here is simply a consequence of the fact that we ordinarily and naturally refer to the general thing in question by means of an expression which incorporates a reference to a particular individual who stands in a special relation to it. Analogous considerations apply to many other types. Of course, the alternative is always open to us of declining to apply the criterion in such cases.

(3) It is clear that numbers, if we apply our criterion to them, will emerge as general things. But this is a result which will disturb few, and will

certainly disturb no one who continues to feel the charm of the class-of-classes analysis.

(4) If we choose to apply the test to facts, we get the not wholly unappealing result that, e.g., the facts that $2 + 2 = 4$, that all crows are black and that crows exist (in one use of "exist") are general things, while the facts that Brutus killed Caesar and that all the people in this room are philosophers are particular things. For propositions, of course, the result is similar. The distinction will correspond roughly to the old distinction between those propositions (or facts) which are "truly universal" and those which are not. In the case of facts and propositions, however, we may well feel a *very* strong reluctance to classify in this way at all; and, if we do, there is no reason why we should struggle to overcome it.[14]

Some points of more general significance remain.

(5) As historical evidence for the general correctness of this doctrine, we may note that Russell who, for so large a part of his philosophical life, showed an anxiety to equate meaning and reference in the case of *names*, finally inclined to the conclusion that the only true names are those of universals.[15] We do not, of course, need to adopt his idiosyncratic use of the word "name," in acknowledging the correctness of his implied view of universals.

(6) It will be clear that the quasi-definition I am suggesting has points of contact with some of those more familiar ways of marking the distinction which turn out to be more or less unsatisfactory. For instance, it will not do to say that general things do not have spatio-temporal positions and limits, whereas particular things do. Some general things, those of appropriate categories, like gold, do have spatial distribution; and some may have temporal limits. It is rather that when we refer to general things, we abstract from their actual distribution and limits, if they have any, as we cannot do when we refer to particulars. Hence, with general things, meaning suffices to determine reference. And with this is connected the tendency, on the whole dominant, to ascribe superior reality to particular things. Meaning is not enough, in their case, to determine the reference of their designations; the extra, contextual element is essential. They are, in a quite precise sense, less abstract; and we are, on the whole, so constituted as to count the less abstract as the more real.

(7) Finally, we may, if we choose, revert to the original philosophical way of marking the distinction in terms of the concept of an instance, and give it a sense in terms of the final definition. Instantiability, in the philosophers' sense, ends precisely at the point at which contextual dependence of referring expressions begins, or where referring expressions, as being proper names of individuals, have meaning only in a sense in which it is altogether divorced from reference. So general things may have instances, while particular things may not.

NOTES

From the *Proceedings of the Aristotelian Society* 54 (1953–54). Reprinted by courtesy of the editor of the *Proceedings of the Aristotelian Society*.

1. I am much indebted to Mr. H. P. Grice for his criticisms of an earlier version of this paper; and I owe much to the stimulus of an unpublished paper by Mr. Michael Dummett. For the errors and obscurities which remain in the present paper I am alone responsible.
2. Ramsey. *[The] Foundations of Mathematics [and Other Logical Essays*, ed. by R. B. Braithwaite (Totowa, N.J.: Littlefield, Adams, & Co., 1965)], pp. 112–134.
3. Ayer, *Individuals*, "Mind," 1952.
4. To the second question Ayer's answer was affirmative; and, things being as they are, this is no doubt correct as a matter of what is theoretically practicable. Ayer also acknowledges (a) that in actual practice we could scarcely dispense with indicator words, and (b) that the attempt to do so would always involve a theoretical failure to individuate, since no elaboration of predicates rules out the theoretical possibility of reduplication. But I doubt if the original question can be answered unless we take these two facts more seriously than he does.
5. But a game of chess *may* be something which itself has instances.
6. Ramsey seems to suggest that this would simply be to manufacture an empty verbal distinction. (Cf. *Foundations of Mathematics*, pp. 132–133). But it would not. For it would not be an arbitrary matter to decide which names to put on which side of the coupling phrase.
7. The terminology, evidently, is not to be taken too seriously. Anger is a state, not a property or quality.
8. It might be true, if intelligible, that *if* we had so time-indifferent a perspective of things as to see them as four-dimensional objects in space-time, then there would be no point in giving separate consideration to criteria of distinctness. But we do not have such a perspective.
9. Cf. Price, *Thinking and Experience* [London: Hutchinson University Press, 1953], pp. 40–41, on identity of individuals and of characteristics.
10. These remarks, of course, apply only to some of the things correctly called properties, states, qualities, etc.
11. What I mean by "incentives" here may be illustrated from the convenience of the institution of property. Suppose there is a general feature, ϕ, which human beings wish to make use of. Even if there is enough ϕ for all, friction may be avoided if criteria are used for distinguishing my ϕ from yours. ("Mine" is indeed one of the earliest individuating words used by children.)
12. This difficulty was pointed out to me by Mr. H. P. Grice.
13. This qualification allows for the possible case where there is no convenient unambiguous designation of the general thing in question; but is not strictly necessary since an unambiguous designation could always be framed.
14. What I have said here of facts and propositions must not lead us to suppose that we should obtain a similar result for *sentences*. These, and expression-*types* generally, will emerge as general things (*e.g.*, in virtue of the conventions for the use of inverted commas, the expression "the word 'and'" may be said to determine, by meaning alone, a unique object of reference).
15. See [B. Russell,] *Enquiry into Meaning and Truth* [London: Allen and Unwin, 1940] and *Human Knowledge: Its Scope and Limits* [New York: Simon and Schuster, 1948].

21 CARNAP

Carnap is suspicious of such questions as, "Are there properties as such?" or "Are there numbers as such?" That questions as these have been thought to be legitimate has made possible the controversy over universals historically formulated as realism versus nominalism. Carnap maintains that the above are pseudo-questions. He explains this by suggesting that we use different linguistic frameworks to explain phenomena. For example, the "thing" language or linguistic framework has proved expedient for that which lends itself to empirical investigation. Alternatively the "number" language or linguistic framework is particularly accommodating to logical analysis.

A given linguistic framework dictates the rules of acceptable play (i.e., ontological commitments) within the game. At this point Carnap draws a distinction between internal and external questions. An internal question is always a question as to whether "object X" is compatible with the rules of a given linguistic framework. Therefore, the question, "Do properties exist within the 'thing' linguistic framework?" is an internal question. The answer is yes. The question, "Do numbers exist within the linguistic framework of logical analysis?" is an internal question. Once again, the answer is yes. In both cases the answer is yes because the rules of those linguistic frameworks allow a commitment to properties and numbers respectively. However, to ask if properties or numbers exist independently of their respective linguistic frameworks is to ask an external question, and consequently, a pseudo-question. In other words, ontological commitments are meaningful only within a linguistic framework. The realist-nominalist debate has persisted because philosophers have mistakenly thought it meaningful to ask external questions. To ask if there are properties or numbers *per se* is a demonstration of philosophical confusion only to be rectified by appreciating the distinction between internal and external questions.

Meaning and Necessity

EMPIRICISM, SEMANTICS, AND ONTOLOGY[1]

Empiricists are in general rather suspicious with respect to any kind of abstract entities like properties, classes, relations, numbers, propositions, etc. They usually feel much more in sympathy with nominalists than with realists (in the medieval sense). As far as possible they try to avoid any reference to abstract entities and to restrict themselves to what is sometimes called a nominalistic language, i.e., one not containing such references.

However, within certain scientific contexts it seems hardly possible to avoid them. In the case of mathematics, some empiricists try to find a way out by treating the whole of mathematics as a mere calculus, a formal system for which no interpretation is given or can be given. Accordingly, the mathematician is said to speak not about numbers, functions, and infinite classes, but merely about meaningless symbols and formulas manipulated according to given formal rules. In physics it is more difficult to shun the suspected entities, because the language of physics serves for the communication of reports and predictions and hence cannot be taken as a mere calculus. A physicist who is suspicious of abstract entities may perhaps try to declare a certain part of the language of physics as uninterpreted and uninterpretable, that part which refers to real numbers as space-time coordinates or as values of physical magnitudes, to functions, limits, etc. More probably he will just speak about all these things like anybody else but with an uneasy conscience, like a man who in his everyday life does with qualms many things which are not in accord with the high moral principles he professes on Sundays. Recently the problem of abstract entities has arisen again in connection with semantics, the theory of meaning and truth. Some semanticists say that certain expressions designate certain entities, and among these designated entities they include not only concrete material things but also abstract entities e.g., properties as designated by predicates and propositions as designated by sentences.[2] Others object strongly to this procedure as violating the basic principles of empiricism and leading back to a metaphysical ontology of the Platonic kind.

It is the purpose of this article to clarify this controversial issue. The nature and implications of the acceptance of a language referring to abstract entities will first be discussed in general; it will be shown that using such a language does not imply embracing a Platonic ontology but is perfectly compatible with empiricism and strictly scientific thinking. Then the special question of the role of abstract entities in semantics will be discussed. It is hoped that the clarification of the issue will be useful to those who would like to accept abstract entities in their work in mathematics, physics, semantics, or any other field; it may help them to overcome nominalistic scruples.

LINGUISTIC FRAMEWORKS

Are there properties, classes, numbers, propositions? In order to understand more clearly the nature of these and related problems, it is above all necessary to recognize a fundamental distinction between two kinds of questions concerning the existence or reality of entities. If someone wishes to speak in his language about a new kind of entities, he has to introduce a system of new ways of speaking, subject to new rules; we shall call this procedure the construction of a linguistic *framework* for the new entities in question. And now we must distinguish two kinds of questions of existence:

first, questions of the existence of certain entities of the new kind *within the framework*; we call them *internal questions*; and second, questions concerning the existence or reality *of the system of entities as a whole*, called *external questions*. Internal questions and possible answers to them are formulated with the help of the new forms of expressions. The answers may be found either by purely logical methods or by empirical methods, depending upon whether the framework is a logical or a factual one. An external question is of a problematic character which is in need of closer examination.

The world of things. Let us consider as an example the simplest kind of entities dealt with in the everyday language: the spatio-temporally ordered system of observable things and events. Once we have accepted the thing language with its framework for things, we can raise and answer internal questions; e.g., "Is there a white piece of paper on my desk?," "Did King Arthur actually live?," "Are unicorns and centaurs real or merely imaginary?," and the like. These questions are to be answered by empirical investigations. Results of observations are evaluated according to certain rules as confirming or disconfirming evidence for possible answers. (This evaluation is usually carried out, of course, as a matter of habit rather than a deliberate, rational procedure. But it is possible, in a rational reconstruction, to lay down explicit rules for the evaluation. This is one of the main tasks of a pure, as distinguished from a psychological, epistemology.) The concept of reality occurring in these internal questions is an empirical, scientific, non-metaphysical concept. To recognize something as a real thing or event means to succeed in incorporating it into the system of things at a particular space-time position so that it fits together with the other things recognized as real, according to the rules of the framework.

From these questions we must distinguish the external question of the reality of the thing world itself. In contrast to the former questions, this question is raised neither by the man in the street nor by scientists, but only by philosophers. Realists give an affirmative answer, subjective idealists a negative one, and the controversy goes on for centuries without ever being solved. And it cannot be solved because it is framed in a wrong way. To be real in the scientific sense means to be an element of the system; hence this concept cannot be meaningfully applied to the system itself. Those who raise the question of the reality of the thing world itself have perhaps in mind not a theoretical question as their formulation seems to suggest, but rather a practical question, a matter of a practical decision concerning the structure of our language. We have to make the choice whether or not to accept and use the forms of expression in the framework in question.

In the case of this particular example, there is usually no deliberate choice because we all have accepted the thing language early in our lives as a matter of course. Nevertheless, we may regard it as a matter of decision in this sense: we are free to choose to continue using the thing language or not; in the latter case we could restrict ourselves to a language of sense-data and other "phenomenal" entities, or construct an alternative to the customary thing language with another structure, or, finally, we could refrain from speaking. If someone decides to accept the thing language, there is no objection against saying that he has accepted the world of things. But this must not be interpreted as if it meant his acceptance of a *belief* in the reality of the thing world; there is no such belief or assertion or assumption, because it is not a theoretical question. To accept the thing world means nothing more than to accept a certain form of language, in other words, to accept rules for forming statements and for testing, accepting, or rejecting them. The acceptance of the thing language leads, on the basis of observations made, also to the acceptance belief, and assertion of certain statements. But the thesis of the reality of the thing world cannot be among these statements, because it cannot be formulated in the thing language, or it seems, in any other theoretical language.

The decision of accepting the thing language, although itself not of a cognitive nature, will nevertheless usually be influenced by theoretical knowledge, just like any other deliberate decision concerning the acceptance of linguistic or other rules. The purposes for which the language is intended to be used, for instance, the purpose of communicating factual knowledge, will determine which factors are relevant for the decision. The efficiency, fruitfulness, and simplicity of the use of the thing language may be among the decisive factors. And the questions concerning these qualities are indeed of a theoretical nature. But these questions cannot be identified with the question of realism. They are not yes-no questions but questions of degree. The thing language in the customary form works indeed with a high degree of efficiency for most purposes of everyday life. This is a matter of fact, based upon the content of our experiences. However, it would be wrong to describe this situation by saying: "The fact of the efficiency of the thing language is confirming evidence for the reality of the thing world"; we should rather say instead: "This fact makes it advisable to accept the thing language."

The system of numbers. As an example of a system which is of a logical rather than a factual nature let us take the system of natural numbers. The framework for this system is constructed by introducing into the language new expressions with suitable rules: (1) numerals like "five" and sentence forms like "there are five books on the table"; (2) the general term "number" for the new entities, and sentence forms like "five is a number"; (3) expressions for properties of numbers (e.g., "odd," "prime"), relations (e.g., "greater than"), and functions (e.g., "plus"), and sentence forms like "two plus three is five"; (4) numerical variables ("m," "n," etc.) and quantifiers for universal sentences ("for every n, . . ." and existential sentences "there is an n such that . . .") with the customary deductive rules.

Here again there are internal questions, e.g, "Is there a prime number greater than a hundred?" Here, however, the answers are found, not by empirical investigation based on observations, but by logical analysis based on the rules for the new expressions. Therefore the answers are here analytic, i.e., logically true.

What is now the nature of the philosophical question concerning the existence or reality of numbers? To begin with, there is the internal question which, together with the affirmative answer, can be formulated in the new terms, say by "There are numbers" or, more explicitly, "There is an n such that n is a number." This statement follows from the analytic statement "five is a number" and is therefore itself analytic. Moreover, it is rather trivial (in contradistinction to a statement like "There is a prime number greater than a million," which is likewise analytic but far from trivial), because it does not say more than that the new system is not empty; but this is immediately seen from the rule which states that words like "five" are substitutable for the new variables. Therefore nobody who meant the question "Are there numbers?" in the internal sense would either assert or even seriously consider a negative answer. This makes it plausible to assume that those philosophers who treat the question of the existence of numbers as a serious philosophical problem and offer lengthy arguments on either side, do not have in mind the internal question. And, indeed, if we were to ask them: "Do you mean the question as to whether the framework of numbers, *if* we were to accept it, would be found to be empty or not?," they would probably reply: "Not at all; we mean a question *prior* to the acceptance of the new framework." They might try to explain what they mean by saying that it is a question of the ontological status of numbers; the question whether or not numbers have a certain metaphysical characteristic called reality (but a kind of ideal reality, different from the material reality of the thing world) or subsistence or status of "independent entities." Unfortunately, these philosophers have so far not given a formulation of their question in terms of the common scientific language. Therefore our judgment must be that they have not succeeded in giving to the external question and to the possible answers any cognitive content. Unless and until they supply a clear cognitive interpretation, we are justified in our suspicion that their question is a pseudo-question, that is, one disguised in the form of a theoretical question while in fact it is non-theoretical; in the present case it is the practical problem whether or not to incorporate into the language the new linguistic forms which constitute the framework of numbers.

The system of propositions. New variables, "p," "q," etc., are introduced with a rule to the effect that any (declarative) sentence may be substituted for a variable of this kind; this includes, in addition to the sentences of the original thing language, also all general sentences with variables of any kind which may have been introduced into the language. Further, the general term "proposition" is introduced. "p is a proposition" may be defined by "p or not p" (or by any other sentence form yielding only analytic sentences). Therefore, every sentence of the form " . . . is a proposition" (where any sentence may stand in the place of the dots) is analytic. This holds, for example, for the sentence:

(a) "Chicago is large is a proposition."

(We disregard here the fact that the rules of English grammar require not a sentence but a that-clause as the subject of another sentence; accordingly, instead of (a) we should have to say "That Chicago is large is a proposition.") Predicates may be admitted whose argument expressions are sentences; these predicates may be either extensional (e.g., the customary truth-functional connectives) or not (e.g., modal predicates like "possible," "necessary," etc.). With the help of the new variables, general sentences may be formed, e.g.,

(b) "For every p, either p or not-p."
(c) "There is a p such that p is not necessary and not-p is not necessary."
(d) "There is a p such that p is a proposition."

(c) and (d) are internal assertions of existence. The statement "There are propositions" may be meant in the sense of (d); in this case it is analytic [since it follows from (a)] and even trivial. If, however, the statement is meant in an external sense, then it is non-cognitive.

It is important to notice that the system of rules for the linguistic expressions of the propositional framework (of which only a few rules have here been briefly indicated) is sufficient for the introduction of the framework. Any further explanations as to the nature of the propositions (i.e., the elements of the system indicated, the values of the variables "p," "q," etc.) are theoretically unnecessary because, if correct, they follow from the rules. For example, are propositions mental events (as in Russell's theory)? A look at the rules shows us that they are not, because otherwise existential statements would be of the form: "If the mental state of the person in question fulfills such and such conditions, then there is a p such that . . ." The fact that no references to mental conditions occur in existential statements (like (c), (d), etc.) shows that propositions are not mental entities. Further, a statement of the existence of linguistic entities (e.g., expressions, classes of expressions, etc.) must contain a reference to a language. The fact that no such reference occurs in the existential statements here, shows that propositions are not linguistic entities. The fact that in these statements no reference to a subject (an observer or knower) occurs (nothing like: "There is a p which is necessary for Mr. X") , shows that the propositions (and their properties, like necessity, etc.) are not subjective. Although characterizations of these or similar kinds are, strictly speaking, unnecessary, they may nevertheless be practically useful. If they are given, they should be understood, not as ingredient parts of the system, but merely as marginal notes with the purpose of supplying to the reader helpful hints or convenient pictorial associations which may make his learning of the use of the expres-

sions easier than the bare system of the rules would do. Such a characterization is analogous to an extra-systematic explanation which a physicist
sometimes gives to the beginner. He might, for example, tell him to imagine
the atoms of a gas as small balls rushing around with great speed, or the
electro-magnetic field and its oscillations as quasi-elastic tensions and vibra-
tions in an ether. In fact, however, all that can accurately be said about atoms
or the field is implicitly contained in the physical laws of the theories in
question.[3]

The system of thing properties. The thing language contains words like
"red," "hard," "stone," "house," etc., which are used for describing what
things are like. Now we may introduce new variables, say "*f*," "*g*," etc., for
which those words are substitutable and furthermore the general term
"property." New rules are laid down which admit sentences like "Red is a
property," "Red is a color," "These two pieces of paper have at least one
color in common" (i.e., There is an "*f* such that *f* is a color, and . . ."). The
last sentence is an internal assertion. It is of an empirical, factual nature.
However, the external statement, the philosophical statement of the reality
of properties—a special case of the thesis of the reality of universals—is
devoid of cognitive content.

The systems of integers and rational numbers. Into a language containing
the framework of natural numbers we may introduce first the (positive and
negative) integers as relations among natural numbers and then the rational
numbers as relations among integers. This involves introducing new types of
variables, expressions substitutable for them, and the general terms "inte-
ger" and "rational number."

The system of real numbers. On the basis of the rational numbers, the real
numbers may be introduced as classes of a special kind (segments) of rational
numbers (according to the method developed by Dedekind and Frege). Here
again a new type of variables is introduced, expressions substitutable for
them (e.g., "$\sqrt{2}$"), and the general term "real number."

The spatio-temporal coordinate system for physics. The new entities are
the space-time points. Each is an ordered quadruple of four real numbers,
called its coordinates, consisting of three spatial and one temporal coordinate. The physical state of a spatio-temporal point or region is described
either with the help of qualitative predicates (e.g., "hot") or by ascribing
numbers as values of a physical magnitude (e.g., mass, temperature, and the
like). The step from the system of things (which does not contain space-time
points but only extended objects with spatial and temporal relations between
them) to the physical coordinate system is again a matter of decision. Our
choice of certain features, although itself not theoretical, is suggested by
theoretical knowledge, either logical or factual. For example, the choice of
real numbers rather than rational numbers or integers as coordinates is not
much influenced by the facts of experience but mainly due to considerations
of mathematical simplicity. The restriction to rational coordinates would not

be in conflict with any experimental knowledge we have, because the result of any measurement is a rational number. However, it would prevent the use of ordinary geometry (which says, e.g., that the diagonal of a square with the side 1 has the irrational value $\sqrt{2}$) and thus lead to great complications. On the other hand, the decision to use three rather than two or four spatial coordinates is strongly suggested, but still not forced upon us, by the result of common observations. If certain events allegedly observed in spiritualistic séances, e.g., a ball moving out of a sealed box, were confirmed beyond any reasonable doubt, it might seem advisable to use four spatial coordinates. Internal questions are here, in general, empirical questions to be answered by empirical investigations. On the other hand, the external questions of the reality of physical space and physical time are pseudo-questions. A question like "Are there (really space-time points?" is ambiguous. It may be meant as an internal question; then the affirmative answer is, of course, analytic and trivial. Or it may be meant in the external sense: "Shall we introduce such and such forms into our language?"; in this case it is not a theoretical but a practical question, a matter of decision rather than assertion, and hence the proposed formulation would be misleading. Or finally, it may be meant in the following sense: "Are our experiences such that the use of the linguistic forms in question will be expedient and fruitful?" This is a theoretical question of a factual, empirical nature. But it concerns a matter of degree; therefore a formulation in the form "real or not?" would be inadequate.

WHAT DOES ACCEPTANCE OF A KIND OF ENTITIES MEAN?

Let us now summarize the essential characteristics of situations involving the introduction of a new kind of entities, characteristics which are common to the various examples outlined above.

The acceptance of a new kind of entities is represented in the language by the introduction of a framework of new forms of expressions to be used according to a new set of rules. There may be new names for particular entities of the kind in question; but some such names may already occur in the language before the introduction of the new framework. (Thus, for example, the thing language contains certainly words of the type of "blue" and "house" before the framework of properties is introduced; and it may contain words like "ten" in sentences of the form "I have ten fingers" before the framework of numbers is introduced.) The latter fact shows that the occurrence of constants of the type in question—regarded as names of entities of the new kind after the new framework is introduced—is not a sure sign of the acceptance of the new kind of entities. Therefore the introduction of such constants is not to be regarded as an essential step in the introduction of the framework. The two essential steps are rather the following. First, the introduction of a general term, a predicate of higher level, for the new kind of entities, permitting us to say of any particular entity that it belongs to this kind (e.g., "Red is a *property*," "Five is a *number*"). Second, the introduction of variables of the new type. The new entities are values of these variables the constants (and the closed compound expressions, if any) are substitutable for the variables.[4] With the help of the variables, general sentences concerning the new entities can be formulated.

After the new forms are introduced into the language, it is possible to formulate with their help internal questions and possible answers to them. A question of this kind may be either empirical or logical; accordingly a true answer is either factually true or analytic.

From the internal questions we must clearly distinguish external questions, i.e., philosophical questions concerning the existence or reality of the total system of the new entities. Many philosophers regard a question of this kind as an ontological question which must be raised and answered before the introduction of the new language forms. The latter introduction, they believe, is legitimate only if it can be justified by an ontological insight supplying an affirmative answer to the question of reality. In contrast to this view, we take the position that the introduction of the new ways of speaking does not need any theoretical justification because it does not imply any assertion of reality. We may still speak (and have done so) of "the acceptance of the new entities" since this form of speech is customary; but one must keep in mind that this phrase does not mean for us anything more than acceptance of the new framework, i.e., of the new linguistic forms. Above all, it must not be interpreted as referring to an assumption, belief, or assertion of "the reality of the entities." There is no such assertion. An alleged statement of the reality of the system of entities is a pseudo-statement without cognitive content. To be sure, we have to face at this point an important question; but it is a practical, not a theoretical question; it is the question of whether or not to accept the new linguistic forms. The acceptance cannot be judged as being either true or false because it is not an assertion. It can only be judged as being more or less expedient, fruitful, conducive to the aim for which the language is intended. Judgments of this kind supply the motivation for the decision of accepting or rejecting the kind of entities.[5]

Thus it is clear that the acceptance of a linguistic framework must not be regarded as implying a metaphysical doctrine concerning the reality of the entities in question. It seems to me due to a neglect of this important distinction that some contemporary nominalists label the admission of variables of abstract types as "Platonism."[6] This is, to say the least, an extremely misleading terminology. It leads to the absurd consequence, that the position of everybody who accepts the language of physics with its real number variables (as a language of communication, not merely as a calculus) would be called Platonistic, even if he is a strict empiricist who rejects Platonic metaphysics.

A brief historical remark may here be inserted. The non-cognitive character of the questions which we have called here external questions was recognized and emphasized already by the Vienna Circle under the leadership of Moritz Schlick, the group from which the movement of logical empiricism originated. Influenced by ideas of Ludwig Wittgenstein, the Circle rejected both the thesis of the reality of the external world and the thesis of its irreality as pseudo-statements;[7] the same was the case for both the thesis of the reality of universals (abstract entities, in our present terminology) and the nominalistic thesis that they are not real and that their alleged names are not names of anything but merely *flatus vocis*. (It is obvious that the apparent negation of a pseudo-statement must also be a pseudo-statement.) It is therefore not correct to classify the members of the Vienna Circle as nominalists, as is sometimes done. However, if we look at the basic anti-metaphysical and pro-scientific attitude of most nominalists (and the same holds for many materialists and realists in the modern sense), disregarding their occasional pseudo-theoretical formulations, then it is, of course, true to say that the Vienna Circle was much closer to those philosophers than to their opponents.

ABSTRACT ENTITIES IN SEMANTICS

The problem of the legitimacy and the status of abstract entities has recently again led to controversial discussions in connection with semantics. In a semantical meaning analysis certain expressions in a language are often said to designate (or name or denote or signify or refer to) certain extra-linguistic entities.[8] As long as physical things or events (e.g., Chicago or Caesar's death) are taken as designata (entities designated), no serious doubts arise. But strong objections have been raised, especially by some empiricists, against abstract entities as designata, e.g., against semantical statements of the following kind:

(1) "The word 'red' designates a property of things";
(2) "The word 'color' designates a property of properties of things";
(3) "The word 'five' designates a number";
(4) "The word 'odd' designates a property of numbers";
(5) "The sentence 'Chicago is large' designates a proposition."

Those who criticize these statements do not, of course, reject the use of the expressions in question, like "red" or "five"; nor would they deny that these expressions are meaningful. But to be meaningful, they would say, is not the same as having a meaning in the sense of an entity designated. They reject the belief, which they regard as implicitly presupposed by those semantical statements, that to each expression of the types in question (adjectives like "red," numerals like "five," etc.) there is a particular real entity to which the expression stands in the relation of designation. This belief is rejected as incompatible with the basic principles of empiricism or of scientific thinking. Derogatory labels like "Platonic realism," "hypostatization," or "'Fido'-Fido principle" are attached to it. The latter is the name given by Gilbert Ryle to the criticized belief, which, in his view, arises by a naive inference of analogy: just as there is an entity well known to me, viz. my dog Fido, which is designated by the name "Fido," thus there must be for every meaningful expression a particular entity to which it stands in the relation of designation or naming, i.e., the relation exemplified by "Fido"-Fido. The belief criticized is thus a case of hypostatization, i.e., of treating as names expressions which are not names. While "Fido" is a name, expressions like "red," "five," etc., are said not to be names, not to designate anything.

Our previous discussion concerning the acceptance of frameworks enables us now to clarify the situation with respect to abstract entities as designata. Let us take as an example the statement:

(a) "'Five' designates a number."

The formulation of this statement presupposes that our language L contains the forms of expressions which we have called the framework of numbers, in particular, numerical variables and the general term "number." If L contains these forms, the following is an analytic statement in L:

(b) "Five is a number."

Further, to make the statement (a) possible, L must contain an expression like "designates" or "is a name of" for the semantical relation of designation. If suitable rules for this term are laid down, the following is likewise analytic:

(c) "'Five' designates five."

(Generally speaking, any expression of the form "'. . .' designates . . ." is an analytic statement provided the term ". . ." is a constant in an accepted framework. If the latter condition is not fulfilled, the expression is not a statement.) Since (a) follows from (c) and (b), (a) is likewise analytic.

Thus it is clear that *if* someone accepts the framework of numbers, then he must acknowledge (c) and (b) and hence (a) as true statements. Generally speaking, if someone accepts a framework for a certain kind of entities, then he is bound to admit the entities as possible designata. Thus the question of the admissibility of entities of a certain type or of abstract entities in general as designata is reduced to the question of the acceptability of the linguistic framework for those entities. Both the nominalistic critics, who refuse the status of designators or names to expressions like "red," "five," etc., because they deny the existence of abstract entities, and the skeptics, who express doubts concerning the existence and demand evidence for it, treat the question of existence as a theoretical question. They do, of course, not mean the internal question; the affirmative answer to *this* question is analytic and trivial and too obvious for doubt or denial, as we have seen. Their doubts refer rather to the system of entities itself; hence they mean the external question. They believe that only after making sure that there really is a system of entities of the kind in question are we justified in accepting the framework by incorporating the linguistic forms into our language. However, we have seen that the external question is not a theoretical question but rather the practical question whether or not to accept those linguistic forms. This acceptance is not in need of a theoretical justification (except with respect to expediency and fruitfulness), because it does not imply a belief or assertion. Ryle says that the "Fido"-Fido principle is "a grotesque theory." Grotesque or not, Ryle is wrong in calling it a theory. It is rather the practical decision to accept certain frameworks. Maybe Ryle is historically right with respect to those whom he mentions as previous representatives of the principle, viz. John Stuart Mill, Frege, and Russell. If these philosophers regarded the acceptance of a system of entities as a theory, an assertion, they were victims of the same old, metaphysical confusion. But it is certainly wrong to regard *my* semantical method as involving a belief in the reality of abstract entities, since I reject a thesis of this kind as a metaphysical pseudo-statement.

The critics of the use of abstract entities in semantics overlook the fundamental difference between the acceptance of a system of entities and an internal assertion, e.g., an assertion that there are elephants or electrons or prime numbers greater than a million. Whoever makes an internal assertion is certainly obliged to justify it by providing evidence, empirical evidence in the case of electrons, logical proof in the case of the prime numbers. The demand for a theoretical justification, correct in the case of internal assertions, is sometimes wrongly applied to the acceptance of a system of entities. Thus, for example, Ernest Nagel asks for "evidence relevant for affirming with warrant that there are such entities as infinitesimals or propositions." He characterizes the evidence required in these cases—in distinction to the empirical evidence in the case of electrons—as "in the broad sense logical and dialectical." Beyond this no hint is given as to what might be regarded as relevant evidence. Some nominalists regard the acceptance of abstract entities as a kind of superstition or myth, populating the world with fictitious or at least dubious entities, analogous to the belief in centaurs or demons. This shows again the confusion mentioned, because a superstition or myth is a false (or dubious) internal statement.

Let us take as example the natural numbers as cardinal numbers, i.e., in contexts like "Here are three books." The linguistic forms of the framework of numbers, including variables and the general term "number," are generally used in our common language of communication; and it is easy to formulate explicit rules for their use. Thus the logical characteristics of this framework are sufficiently clear (while many internal questions, i.e., arithmetical questions, are, of course, still open). In spite of this, the controversy concerning the external question of the ontological reality of the system of numbers continues. Suppose that one philosopher says: "I believe that there are numbers as real entities. This gives me the right to use the linguistic forms of the numerical framework and to make semantical statements about numbers as designata of numerals." His nominalistic opponent replies:

"You are wrong: there are no numbers. The numeral may still be used as meaningful expressions. But they are not names, there are no entities designated by them. Therefore the word 'number' and numerical variables must not be used (unless a way were found to introduce them as merely abbreviating devices, a way of translating them into the nominalistic thing language)." I cannot think of any possible evidence that would be regarded as relevant by both philosophers, and therefore, if actually found, would decide the controversy or at least make one of the opposite theses more probable than the other. (To construe the numbers as classes or properties of the second level, according to the Frege-Russell method, does, of course, not solve the controversy, because the first philosopher would affirm and the second deny the existence of the system of classes or properties of the second level.) Therefore I feel compelled to regard the external question as a pseudo-question, until both parties to the controversy offer a common interpretation of the question as a cognitive question; this would involve an indication of possible evidence regarded as relevant by both sides.

There is a particular kind of misinterpretation of the acceptance of abstract entities in various fields of science and in semantics, that needs to be cleared up. Certain early British empiricists (e.g., Berkeley and Hume) denied the existence of abstract entities on the ground that immediate experience presents us only with particulars, not with universals, e.g., with this red patch, but not with Redness or Color-in-General: with this scalene triangle, but not with Scalene Triangularity or Triangularity-in-General. Only entities belonging to a type of which examples were to be found within immediate experience could be accepted as ultimate constituents of reality. Thus, according to this way of thinking, the existence of abstract entities could be asserted only if one could show either that some abstract entities fall within the given, or that abstract entities can be defined in terms of the types of entity which are given. Since these empiricists found no abstract entities within the realm of sense-data, they either denied their existence, or else made a futile attempt to define universals in terms of particulars. Some contemporary philosophers, especially English philosophers following Bertrand Russell, think in basically similar terms. They emphasize a distinction between the data (that which is immediately given in consciousness, e.g., sense-data, immediately past experiences, etc.) and the constructs based on the data. Existence or reality is ascribed only to the data; the constructs are not real entities; the corresponding linguistic expressions are merely ways of speech not actually designating anything (reminiscent of the nominalists' *flatus vocis*). We shall not criticize here this general conception. (As far as it is a principle of accepting certain entities and not accepting others, leaving aside any ontological, phenomenalistic and nominalistic pseudo-statements, there cannot be any theoretical objection to it.) But if this conception leads to the view that other philosophers or scientists who accept abstract entities thereby assert or imply their occurrence as immediate data, then such a view must be rejected as a misinterpretation. References to space-time points, the electromagnetic field, or electrons in physics, to real or complex numbers and their functions in mathematics, to the excitatory potential or unconscious complexes in psychology, to an inflationary trend in economics, and the like, do not imply the assertion that entities of these kinds occur as immediate data. And the same holds for references to abstract entities as designata in semantics. Some of the criticisms by English philosophers against such references give the impression that, probably due to the misinterpretation just indicated, they accuse the semanticist not so much of bad metaphysics (as some nominalists would do) but of bad psychology. The fact that they regard a semantical method involving abstract entities not merely as doubtful and perhaps wrong, but as manifestly absurd, preposterous and grotesque, and that they show a deep horror and indignation against this method, is perhaps to be explained by a misinterpretation of the kind described. In fact, of course, the semanticist does not in the least assert or imply that the abstract entities to which he refers can be experienced as immediately given either by sensation or by a kind of rational intuition. An assertion of this kind would indeed be very dubious psychology. The psychological question as to which kinds of entities do and which do not occur as immediate data is entirely irrelevant for semantics, just as it is for physics, mathematics, economics, etc., with respect to the examples mentioned above.[9]

CONCLUSION

For those who want to develop or use semantical methods, the decisive question is not the alleged ontological question of the existence of abstract entities but rather the question whether the use of abstract linguistic forms or, in technical terms, the use of variables beyond those for things (or phenomenal data), is expedient and fruitful for the purposes for which semantical analyses are made, viz. the analysis, interpretation, clarification, or construction of languages of communication, especially languages of science. This question is here neither decided nor even discussed. It is not a question simply of yes or no, but a matter of degree. Among those philosophers who have carried out semantical analyses and thought about suitable tools for this work, beginning with Plato and Aristotle and, in a more technical way on the basis of modern logic, with C. S. Peirce and Frege, a great majority accepted abstract entities. This does, of course, not prove the case. After all, semantics in the technical sense is still in the initial phases of its development, and we must be prepared for possible fundamental changes in methods. Let us therefore admit that the nominalistic critics may possibly be right. But if so, they will have to offer better arguments than they have so far. Appeal to ontological insight will not carry much weight. The critics will have to show that it is possible to construct a semantical method which avoids all references to abstract entities and achieves by simpler means essentially the same results as the other methods.

The acceptance or rejection of abstract linguistic forms, just as the acceptance or rejection of any other linguistic forms in any branch of science, will finally be decided by their efficiency as instruments, the ratio of the results achieved to the amount and complexity of the efforts required. To decree dogmatic prohibitions of certain linguistic forms instead of testing them by their success or failure in practical use, is worse than futile; it is positively harmful because it may obstruct scientific progress. The history of science shows examples of such prohibitions based on prejudices deriving from religious, mythological, metaphysical, or other irrational sources, which slowed up the developments for shorter or longer periods of time. Let us learn from the lessons of history. Let us grant to those who work in any special field of investigation the freedom to use any form of expression which seems useful to them; the work in the field will sooner or later lead to the elimination of those forms which have no useful function. *Let us be cautious in making assertions and critical in examining them, but tolerant in permitting linguistic forms.*

NOTES

From Rudolf Carnap, *Meaning and Necessity* (second edition, suppl. A.), 1956. Reprinted by permission of the University of Chicago Press.

1. I have made here some minor changes in the formulations to the effect that the term "framework" is now used only for the system of linguistic expressions, and not for the system of the entities in question.
2. The terms "sentence" and "statement" are here used synonymously for declarative (indicative, propositional) sentences.
3. In my book *Meaning and Necessity* (Chicago, 1947) I have developed a semantical method which takes propositions as entities designated by sentences (more specifically, as intensions of sentences). In order to facilitate the understanding or the systematic development, I added some informal, extra-systematic explanations concerning the nature of propositions. I said that the term "proposition" "is used neither for a linguistic expression nor for a subjective, mental occurrence, but rather for something objective that may or may not be exemplified in nature ... We apply the term 'proposition' to any entities of a certain logical type, namely, those that may be expressed by (declarative) sentences in a language" (p. 27). After some more detailed discussions concerning the relation between propositions and facts and the nature of false propositions, I added: "It has been the purpose of the preceding remarks to facilitate the understanding of our conception of propositions. If, however, a reader should find these explanations more puzzling than clarifying, or even unacceptable, he may disregard them" (p. 31) (that is, disregard these extra-systematic explanations, not the whole theory of the propositions as intensions of sentences, as one reviewer understood). In spite of this warning, it seems that some of those readers who were puzzled by the explanations, did not disregard them but thought that by

raising objections against them they could refute the theory. This is analogous to the procedure of some laymen who by (correctly) criticizing the ether picture or other visualizations of physical theories, thought they had refuted those theories. Perhaps the discussions in the present paper will help in clarifying the role of the system of linguistic rules for the introduction of a framework for entities on the one hand, and that of extra-systematic explanations concerning the nature of the entities on the other.

4. W. V. Quine was the first to recognize the importance of the introduction of variables as indicating the acceptance of entities. "The ontology to which one's use of language commits him comprises simply the objects that he treats as falling . . . within the range of values of his variables" ("Notes on Existence and Necessity," *Journal of Philosophy*, 40, 1943, p. 118; compare also his "Designation and Existence," *Journal of Philosophy*, 36 [1939], and "On Universals," *Journal of Symbolic Logic*, 12 [1947].)

5. For a closely related point of view on these questions see the detailed discussions in Herbert Feigl, "Existential Hypotheses," *Philosophy of Science*, 17 (1950), 35–62.

6. Paul Bernays, "Sur le Platonisme dans les mathematiques" (*L'Enseignement math.*, 34 (1935), 52–69). W. V. Quine, see previous footnote and a recent paper, "On What There Is" [reprinted in this volume, chapter 16]. Quine does not acknowledge the distinction which I emphasize above, because according to his general conception there are no sharp boundary lines between logical and factual truth, between questions of meaning and questions of fact, between the acceptance of a language structure and the acceptance of an assertion formulated in the language. This conception, which seems to deviate considerably from customary ways of thinking, will be explained in his article ("Semantics and Abstract Objects," *Proceedings of the American Academy of Arts and Sciences*, 80 [1951]). When Quine in the article ("On What There Is") classifies my logicistic conception of mathematics (derived from Frege and Russell) as "platonic realism" (p. 224), this is meant (according to a personal communication from him) not as ascribing to me agreement with Plato's metaphysical doctrine of universals, but merely as referring to the fact that I accept a language of mathematics containing variables of higher levels. With respect to the basic attitude to take in choosing a language form (an "ontology" in Quine's terminology, which seems to me misleading), there appears now to be agreement between us: "the obvious counsel is tolerance and an experimental spirit" ["On What There Is," p. 227.]

7. See Carnap, *Scheinprobleme in der Philosophie; das Fremdpsychische und der Realismusstreit*, Berlin, 1928. Moritz Schlick, *Positivismus und Realismus*, reprinted in *Gesammelta Aufsätze*, Wien 1938.

8. See *Introduction to Semantics* (1943); *Meaning and Necessity* (Chicago, 1947). The distinction I have drawn in the latter book between the method of the name-relation and the method of intension and extension is not essential for our present discussion. The term "designation" is used in the present article in a neutral way; it may be understood as referring to the name-relation or to the intension-relation or to the extension-relation or to any similar relations used in other semantical methods.

9. Wilfried Sellars ("Acquaintance and Description Again," in *Journal of Philosophy*, 46 [1949], 496–504; see pp. 502ff.) analyzes clearly the roots of the mistake "of taking the designation relation of semantic theory to be a reconstruction of *being present to an experience*."

22 KHATCHADOURIAN

The main purpose of Khatchadourian's paper is to demonstrate that there is a class of common nouns that expresses "family resemblances" among objects without at the same time denoting a set of common qualities or characteristics possessed by those objects. The words in the class of common nouns he chooses to analyze refer to man-devised activities and processes and man-made objects such as chairs. Given an assortment of objects denoted by such common nouns, "we find that under certain kinds of conditions they possess a common capacity or set of common capacities (Ca) to serve some purpose (P), to satisfy some need or needs (N), directly or indirectly—in general, that they possess the capacity for being used in a common kind of way (U)."

What man-devised activities and processes and man-made objects have in common, and properly understood in terms of family resemblances, is, fundamentally, the satisfaction of human needs. Such activities, processes, and objects are designed to be used for the purpose of satisfying those needs. In such a way the common noun, e.g. 'chair', never refers to any quality or characteristic inherent in the objects referred to by that term.

In the above quote, Khatchadourian makes reference to "certain kinds of conditions." These are to be understood as standard conditions that are causally necessary for a given activity, process, or object satisfying a need by its use. However, the use of, a chair, for example, typically satisfies the need for which it was designed; but this is not necessarily the case, for a chair can in different circumstances satisfy a need without regard to the purpose for which the chair was designed, for example, propping open a door. Nonstandard conditions are those that causally impede the use of, a chair, for example, in satisfying the need for which it was designed.

Khatchadourian's article bolsters Wittgenstein's notion of family resemblances by exploring their inner workings as applied to a certain class of activities, processes, and objects and in the process strikes a blow to essentialism. Note should be made, however, that his analysis is not all inclusive. It does not include non-man-devised activities and processes or non-man-made objects.

Common Names and "Family Resemblances"

I

In this paper we propose to give, first, a brief analysis of Wittgenstein's notion of "family resemblances." Next we shall try to show that whether or not "family resemblances" constitute a general feature of ordinary language so far as common names are concerned, there are at least some common names such that the things named by them do have one or more features in common, though this feature or these features are not a determinate or relatively determinate *quality* or *characteristic*. Further, we shall argue that this common "feature" or these common "features," in each case, is or are what determine (at least in part) the applicability or uses of the common name concerned, as is shown by an examination of the way in which the latter is used in ordinary discourse. We shall next show how "family resemblances" themselves, where they obtain in the kinds of thing we are concerned with, can be accounted for in terms of our results. Finally, we shall apply our results to the terms 'good' and 'poor' or 'not good' in one sense of these terms, as used in ordinary language.

Briefly, Wittgenstein's notion of "family resemblances" is that the traditional view that in every case where things are called by the same name (when the name is used in the same "sense") there is a quality or a set of qualities which is common to them all, by virtue of which they are all called by that name, is mistaken. Instead of such a common quality or a set of these, examination reveals complex patterns of resemblance different in different cases. Thus, in speaking of "language games," Wittgenstein says:

> Instead of producing something common to all that we call language, I am saying that these phenomena have no one thing in common which makes us use the same word for all,—but that they are *related* to one another in many different ways. And it is because of this relationship, or these relationships, that we call them all "languages."[1]

This is illustrated, for instance, by what we call "games":

> If you look at them you will not see something that is common to *all*, but similarities, relationships, and a whole series of them at that. . . . Look for example at board-games, with their multifarious relationships. Now pass to card-games; here you find many correspondences with the first group, but many common features drop out, and others appear. When we pass next to ball-games, much that is common is retained, but much is lost. . . . (pp. 31e–32e)

Instead of finding characteristics common to all games, "we see a complicated network of similarities overlapping and criss-crossing: sometimes over-all similarities, sometimes similarities of detail" (p. 32e). These similarities

Wittgenstein calls "family resemblances" because "the various resemblances between members of a family: build, features, color of eyes, gait, temperament, etc. etc. overlap and criss-cross in the same way" (p. 32e). The situation involved is like that of a thread in which different fibers overlap but none runs through the whole length of the thread. "And the strength of the thread does not reside in the fact that some one fiber runs through its whole length, but in the overlapping of many fibers" (p. 32e).

It seems clear that the "features" which Wittgenstein has in mind in speaking of "family resemblances" are determinate or relatively determinate characteristics (or relations, or both), and not merely kinds of characteristic or determinables (or kinds of relation, or both). For we can imagine a "family" in which *all* the members have a determinable or a set of determinables but not any determinate or relatively determinate characteristics, in common. All the members of a human family have eyes, ears, a nose, limbs, etc. in common; but we would not (nor would Wittgenstein) say, that these members have certain "family resemblances" by virtue of possessing eyes, ears, a nose, etc. For the determinables these members have in common are shared by most if not all human beings. Rather, what Wittgenstein seems to have in mind is a "family" in which some members have either (1) one or more determinate characteristics in common (say hazel eyes), or (2) relatively determinate characteristics in common (say brown eyes of different shades), and each of these members has one or more *different* determinate, or relatively determinate characteristics in common with some (at least one) or all of the other members. So that some members are directly related by qualitative resemblances to other members, while some or all are also indirectly related to other members through their direct relations to members themselves directly related to the latter.

But how determinate should a characteristic shared by *all* members of a "family" be in order that it may be said to be "something in common" to all the members? For determinateness is a matter of degrees, and is relative: what is a determinate characteristic relatively to a given characteristic may be a determinable relatively to another characteristic. If Wittgenstein is merely repudiating the view that all things called by the same name (in the same "sense") have a qualitatively *identical* "determinate" characteristic (or a set of these), then traditional essentialism will not be completely overthrown; since on the latter view relatively determinate characteristics which are not qualitatively identical *are* counted as the "same." It is obvious that it makes all the difference where we draw the line between qualitative "sameness" and mere qualitative "resemblance." If anything short of qualitative identity is rejected as a common quality, even two copies of the same book, or two dimes, may only have certain "resemblances" but no quality "in common." On the other hand, if the distinction is drawn higher up, so to speak, in the determinate-determinable scale, then the members of the family, all of whom have brown eyes of different shades, will have a common quality and not a "resemblance" in color of eyes. That Wittgenstein himself does not intend to draw the distinction too finely or too stringently is seen by considering his analysis of "games." There he seems to consider games which are amusing as having a common feature; similarly with games which involve competition, or winning and losing; and so on. Yet "amusiveness," for instance, may be different kinds. Nevertheless, the difficulty seems to remain: for on what logical basis or bases (whether the same or different ones in different cases) would Wittgenstein draw the line in a given case, and in different given cases, between qualitative "resemblance" and qualitative "identity"?

There is another point to note before we proceed further. This is that in talking about "family resemblances," Wittgenstein is concerned with things which are called by the same name in one and the same sense, and not in different (literal) senses. Obviously, if what Wittgenstein is maintaining is simply that things which are called by the same name, but in different senses, or with different meanings, have only, "family resemblances" of one sort or another and not any common determinate or relatively determinate characteristics, his view would be of relatively little significance. For hardly anybody would hold the contrary, in the case of at least the majority of common names which have two or more (literal) senses, or meanings. (However, the transition from one sense, or one meaning, of a term to another is subtle and not sharply defined in many cases, and it is no easy matter always to decide where the one sense, or meaning, ends and the other begins assuming that this way of speaking is itself legitimate.)

We shall now analyze the uses or meaning of the name "games," in some detail, as a paradigm for the view we shall argue for; and then apply our results to one class of objects, namely manufactured—in general, man-made—objects.[2]

Wittgenstein seems to me to be quite right in holding that there are no determinate or relatively determinate *characteristics* common to all things called "games." All the games that we have, and all phenomena that we would normally call "games," are played in accordance with certain kinds of rule; so that there is a universal common to them all; but the rules involved differ as we pass from board games to ball games to card games, etc., and from one board game to another, from one ball game to another;[3] and so on. Still, there *is* a more determinate feature common to all kinds of game: namely, the capacity to serve a specific human need or needs, directly or indirectly, under what we shall call "standard" (causal) conditions or in "normal" contexts. The term 'need' is used here in a wide sense, to include emotional, intellectual, aesthetic, "practical," as well as physical and biological needs. Instead of speaking of the "capacity to serve a human need," we might speak of the "capacity to further human ends," or the "capacity to produce certain effects in other things, which, directly or indirectly, serve or can serve human ends." Or we might speak of the phenomena or things whose "capacities" we are talking about as having or as capable of having a specific use or uses for human beings under specified conditions. In the case of "games," this "capacity" is the capacity to evoke or produce pleasure in the player or players and/or the spectators. That this is implicit is some way to be determined later in the meaning or uses of the name 'game' can be seen in a general way by considering some remarks we ordinarily make in connection with "games"; e.g. "What sort of game is this?—it's boring!"; "He always gets angry while playing—and spoils the game"; "This is certainly a queer kind of game: I don't see what pleasure you (or the players, or the spectators) get out of it!"; "You call this a game? Well, you may call it that if you like, but it's certainly a poor game: it's positively irritating!" Also, we do not normally say: "This is a pleasant game" (though we quite frequently say: "This is a *very* pleasant game"), except perhaps to mean that I liked it, or that I find it pleasant. "This is a most unpleasant game" is possible though unusual, and makes one think of games which some would find coarse or vulgar (morally speaking) because it involves, say risqué utterances, or actions ordinarily regarded as indecent. In the last case we tend to think that the term 'game' applies only in a loose or extended or peculiar sense, or that the person making the statement is prudish, that he is judging the game in terms of extrinsic criteria, that he is approaching it in the "wrong spirit." "*I* found this a most unpleasant game" would, however, not be puzzling. But "This is a painful game," seems to be almost a contradiction in terms in "standard" contexts. It raises questions in the hearer's mind, and requires explanation. (It will be explained, however, if the game referred to is bear-baiting, say, and the speaker is thinking of the bear's suffering, or of the pain he feels for the bear's suffering, or of both.) If someone says: "This game made me angry," we think: "He (or his favorite team, or player) lost, that's why"; or that he did not play as well as he knew he could, so he felt frustrated. If a person does not enjoy a game, and we regard the conditions as "standard" conditions so far as the majority of spectators and/or players are concerned, we will think: He's not "in" it; he hasn't caught the "spirit" of the game; he doesn't have the "right" spirit; his mind is wandering; he is preoccupied; he is tired; he has a headache; and so on.

In order to understand these remarks in the light of what we said about "games," we have to consider our crucial qualification that what we call "games" have a common capacity to produce pleasure under *standard conditions* or in *normal contexts*. What we ordinarily call "games" certainly do not actually produce pleasure under just any and all conditions, in all contexts. It is only when certain conditions obtain that a "game" *actually* produces pleasures. This is why we said that "games" have the "capacity" to produce pleasure under "standard" conditions. The word "capacity" is meant to indicate that if certain conditions obtain, pleasure will[4] be produced. To put the matter without using the misleading word 'capacity,' what we are saying is that "games," under certain conditions, produce (either physically or psychologically, or both: in general, causally) by virtue of whatever characteristics they possess, what we call "pleasure" in the player or players, etc. The word 'capacity' is not meant to stand for a mysterious power or property, over and above the ordinary characteristics of a game. If we were not unwilling to complicate matters by using controversial notions, we would say that games have a certain "dispositional property," or a set of these—the property or properties of producing pleasure.

In making the statement "This is a good game, but I don't enjoy it," the speaker tacitly recognizes or implies that although he is not being affected in the way which is normal in those cases in which he would, without hesitation, call a given phenomenon a "good game," the absence of this element in this case is not a sufficient ground for not calling the phenomenon concerned a "good game." In saying that it is a game or a good game, he concedes that it can give, and perhaps is actually giving, others, some, or even a good deal of, pleasure; and also, he implies that his failure to have pleasure is not due to the "game" itself, but to his mood, state of mind, etc. at the time. Thus if somebody asked our friend: "Why do you say so?," on hearing him make the above statement, the answer generally given will be something like: "O, I'm not in the mood today"; or, "I have a toothache"; "I'm worried about my affairs"; and the like. That is, the speaker implies that so far as he is concerned, the conditions are not normal or standard conditions.

But now a doubt arises: is the pleasure produced by different games, or by different kinds of game, of the same kind in every case? Are not the pleasures produced related merely by certain "family resemblances," at least in the case of the pleasure produced by games of different "kinds"? If the answer is in the affirmative—and Wittgenstein would say that it is in the affirmative—then obviously Wittgenstein's analysis of games would be completely true, though here it would be the effects of games that are related by "family resemblances," rather than, or as well as, their characteristics themselves.[5] Now it is certainly true that different kinds of pleasure may be involved in the case of different kinds of game: some kinds, like ball games, involve or may involve both physical and psychological pleasure (a feeling of well-being, enjoyment, etc.), while others, like card games and board games, normally involve only the latter kind of pleasure. But though only some kinds of game produce or can produce physical pleasure, it seems that all games produce or can produce psychological pleasure—though the amount and intensity of pleasure produced may differ with different kinds of game, with different games of the same kind, and with different matches of the same game, depending on the context. But are all these psychological pleasures of the same kind in all cases? No, again. The nature of the specific game determines in good measure the kind of psychological pleasure derived. In chess, the pleasure is said to be "intellectual," while in the case of card games it may be "intellectual" pleasure mixed with "feeling," depending on the context. That is, psychological pleasure may be divided into sub-classes, which are themselves further divisible. Nonetheless, it seems to me (though it is not possible to defend this here), that the classification into "intellectual" and "non-intellectual" (emotional) pleasure more concerns the way in which the pleasure is produced and its general intensity than marks a distinction in the kind of experience involved. Whereas, a difference in kind of experience is involved in the case of the distinction between psychological and physical pleasure, in addition to a difference in the kind of way they are produced in us. Thus a *relatively* determinate kind of effect seems to be produced by all kinds of games.[6] And so far as this relatively determinate kind of effect is produced by all games, it seems to follow that there is some kind of "capacity" in the games themselves, which is (at least) similar in the case of all games; though there need not be (and we are not maintaining that there is) any determinate or relatively determinate characteristic or characteristics common to all games, by virtue of which this kind of effect is produced.

What we have said applies, *mutatis mutandis*, to all other man-devised activities, to man-devised processes, and to man-made objects, like cooking, writing, furniture, instruments, tools, machines. That is, in the case of all activities, processes, or objects of this sort which are called by the same name (in the same literal sense), we find a common capacity or common capacities to serve, directly or indirectly, some human need or some human purpose, the capacity or capacities for being used in the same kind of way. To put the matter abstractly and generally, suppose we take a number of such activities, processes, or objects, $a, b, c, d, e, f \ldots n$, which we ordinarily call "X." If we analyze $a, b, c, d, e, f \ldots n$, we find that under certain kinds of condition they possess a common capacity or a set of common capacities (Ca) to serve some purpose or set of purposes (P), to satisfy some need or needs (N), directly or indirectly—in general, that they possess the capacity for being used in a common kind of way (U). What is more, and this is the central point here, if we examine the way 'X' is used in ordinary discourse—the situations in which we ordinarily apply it and the situations in which we ordinarily refrain from applying it—we find that the conditions under which 'X' is applied are *roughly* those conditions under which $a, b, c, d, e, f \ldots n$, are capable of serving P, of satisfying N, of having U. That is, we find that the notion of a common capacity Ca, or alternatively, of a common use U, is implicit in the meaning or uses of 'X' in ordinary, discourse. It is true that activities, processes, or objects called by *different* names may satisfy the same (kind of) need, may have the capacity of being used in the same (kind of) way; also, that activities, processes, and objects which are called by the same common name can be used in different ways. We can use a table as well as a chair for sitting, and we can use a chair as well as table for eating or writing. But sitting on tables is not ordinarily regarded as the normal or proper way of using tables, nor eating off a chair or writing on it as the normal or proper way of using chairs. (I am not using 'proper' in the sense in which it is used in books on etiquette.) The satisfaction of a certain specific need or a set of needs, the capacity of being used in a specific way, is associated with one "kind" of object, activity, or process (objects, activities, or processes called by, the same name), and another or other specific needs, another or other uses, are associated with another "kind" of object, activity, or process, in the way we speak about these objects, activities, or processes. The reason is simple: it is we, the makers of tables and chairs, who design them in such a way that it becomes possible for them to satisfy the need, or to have the use in view, more efficiently or better than another or other needs or uses. This, as we said, is reflected in ordinary language: the notion of some proper function or use or another (or of the capacity to satisfy a given need) is implicit in the meaning of the common names—of the particular sort we are talking about—which we give to things. It is no accident that the names of manufactured objects (as also the names of man-devised activities, or processes) implicitly involve in their meaning the notion of a capacity to satisfy a specific need or specific needs, to have a given use or uses. "Separate seat for one," a common definition of 'chair,' illustrates this clearly.[7] In many cases, however, dictionaries give a description of the characteristics which the things called by the given name were endowed with by their inventors or original makers (hence, when the particular name was first given to them), and/or those characteristics which they most frequently possess, in addition to mentioning a specific use or specific uses. (Cf. for example the definitions of 'pen' and 'table' in *The Concise Oxford Dictionary*.) Further, as in the case of "games," it is seen that no single determinate or relatively determinate *characteristic*, or set of characteristics, common to all things ordinarily called "chairs," is discoverable. The same is true of things called "tables," "pens," and so on. An object may be made of chromium or of plastic, may be high or low, soft or hard, round or square or polygonal, straight or curved: and yet will not, for that reason, be refused the name 'chair'—so long as it can serve[8] as a "separate seat for one"; i.e., so long as the variation in these and other characteristics does not grossly impede or make impossible the object's possession of the requisite capacity. If an object is made of jelly, it cannot serve as a chair; and we do not apply 'chair' to it in a straightforward sense, even if it has the form of one kind of chair or another. Similarly chair-like objects only a few inches wide and high may be called "toy chairs," but not "chairs" without qualification. They may be called "toy *chairs*" because (1) they have the over-all form of one kind of chair or another, and (2) they can serve to seat tiny "toy men" and "toy women" ('toy man' and 'toy woman' being defined in the same way as 'toy chair'), or little imaginary creatures. How much variation in form and material is compatible with the requisite capacity, depends on the nature and range of the corresponding "standard" (causal) conditions, and on the nature and number of the needs the thing is intended to satisfy. In general, the more specialized and the more complex the need, the smaller the range of variation possible; the less specialized and the less complex the need, the greater the range of variation possible. Similarly, the range of variation is inversely proportional, roughly speaking, to the number of needs meant to be satisfied. The form of chairs designed merely with "utility" in view admits of considerably greater variation than that of chairs designed with an eye to beauty as well as to "utility"; and chairs designed only with an eye to beauty (a mere hypothetical example, however!) admit of greater variation in material than chairs designated with an eye to both beauty and "utility."

From all this we see why no determinate or relatively determinate characteristic or characteristics need run through all things called by the same name for that name to be applicable to them. Hence it is not surprising, if one fixes his attention on the *determinate* or *relatively determinate* characteristics of things, that he tends to conclude that things called by the same name have no determinate "feature" or "features" in common; or that, at most, they have certain "family resemblances." It is especially easy to fall into this line of thought since we become aware or fully aware that a common capacity is or may be involved only by considering the characteristics of a thing from a *very* general standpoint (i.e., by looking at them as general *kinds* of characteristic or as determinables), or by considering a thing in the light of the way we talk about it in actual contexts, under both "standard" and "non-standard" (causal) conditions. For as we have said, things which do satisfy a common need, or have a common use, in certain kinds of situation, may not be capable of satisfying the need or of having that use in other kinds of situation.

II

The preceding—and especially the fact that the possible range of variation in the characteristics of a thing is, roughly speaking, inversely proportional to the complexity and specialization, among other things, of the uses it is ordinarily put to, the ends it serves—gives us one explanation of why we do find "family resemblances" between things called by the same name—the feature on which Wittgenstein fixes his attention. The clearest way to show this is by considering things like chairs, tables, cups, saucers, hammers, nails, and the like. In the majority of cases we unqualifiedly[9] apply the name 'chair' to objects which have a certain kind of over-all structure and shape, and are made of kinds of material falling within some range. This general, over-all pattern imposed by the purpose for which chairs are designed— serving as a separate seat for one—gives things generally called chairs certain over-all similarities in form, and to a lesser degree, in kind of material. A "chair" is expected to have some kind of seat, to rest on some kind of support, to have some kind of support for the sitter's back; and in some cases (where we use the name 'arm-chair') to have supports for the sitter's arms. With regard to material, it has to be made of something relatively hard and firm to support the sitter's weight. But different chairs may serve different, more specialized needs, in addition to serving as a separate seat for one. The kinds of specialized need, or the kinds of specialized use, give us the basis for the ordinary *classification* of chairs into kinds. They impose further restrictions on the form and material of chairs: restrictions over and above those imposed on them by the end-in-view of serving as separate seats for one. These additional restrictions give rise to greater resemblances between chairs of the same "kind" (chairs which satisfy the same kind of specialized need, which have the same kind of specialized use), and to a lesser extent, between chairs of different "kinds" whose specialized uses overlap or are similar in certain respects. Thus a "reclining chair" bears greater resemblances to other "reclining chairs" than to ordinary, plain chairs. But "reclining chairs" may be subdivided into "deck chairs," "Morris chairs," and the like, with still greater resemblances between one "deck chair" and another, one "Morris chair" and another (one kind of still more specialized use being involved in each case). These resemblances in detail between chairs of the same "kind," and more general resemblances between chairs of different "kinds," give us at least some of the overlapping and criss-crossing of resemblances which Wittgenstein speaks about. Also, since the specialized uses of different kinds of chair may have *different* elements in common, the resemblances in form and material may be now with respect to one characteristic, or kind of characteristic, now to another.

The same applies to games, as we see when we consider the general kinds of game: board games, ball games, card games, and the like, and the particular kinds of game falling under one or another of the former: e.g. chess, tennis, bridge. But the general purpose meant to be served by a game, as a game, and the more specialized purposes meant to be served by it as a specific kind of game, determine its characteristics to a lesser degree than the corresponding purposes in the case of a chair, say, because of the former's greater complexity and greater indeterminacy. Pleasure, be it physical or psychological, can be produced in human beings in many different ways. That in the case of games it is actually produced by activities following certain kinds of rule and involving the use of certain kinds of material (such as balls, rackets, boards, cards), must be ascribed to a large extent to the genius of the inventors of games.

III

In talking about games, we gave examples of the kinds of condition which are "standard," and of others which are not "standard," relatively to games in general. It is now time to say something more general and more precise about these. The "standard" conditions, S_1, relative to a thing T, and to a given use U, are:

(1) The kinds of condition—physical, or psychological, or both—which

are causally necessary for T's having U by virtue of its (T's) characteristics. "Non-standard" conditions, S_1, relative to T and U, are the kinds of condition—physical, or psychological, or both—which causally impede, or even make impossible, T's having U; assuming that T itself, as T (i.e., as called "T") is not what we would ordinarily call defective. For even under "standard" or "favorable" conditions relative to T, a thing T, lacking some part it ordinarily possesses, may be incapable of having U. Thus even under "standard" conditions, relative to chairs, a chair with a missing leg, for instance, cannot, as it stands, be used as a chair.

(2) There is no hard and fast dividing line between "standard" and "non-standard" conditions relative to T and U. Also, there does not exist a unique set of conditions which is "standard," and another unique set of conditions which is "non-standard," relatively to T and U. A good deal of flexibility is possible; though mainly in situations where psychological factors are important. A pen cannot be used as a writing instrument without some kind of writing fluid; but a game of baseball may be played and enjoyed even in relatively bad weather, if the players and spectators are in the mood for playing or watching, respectively.

(3) In the case of any given common name 'X' (of the kind we are concerned with in this paper) there are certain conditions, fixed by linguistic usage, which determine whether or not 'X' shall properly apply to a given thing T: conditions under which we would *refrain* from calling a thing an "X" if it did not have a use U the notion of which is implicit in the meaning of 'X.' These conditions may be called the "standard conditions for the use or application of 'X' to a thing T" (symbolized by 'S_2'). In general, S_1 and S_2 coincide. More clearly, conditions S_1 under which a thing T normally has a use U are, generally speaking, the conditions under which T's having or not having use U becomes crucial for determining whether or not a name 'X' (which involved the notion of use U in its meaning) is applicable to it. If T does not have U under standard causal conditions S_1 relative to X's in general, 'X' will not, generally speaking, be applicable to it.

But S_2 and S_1 do not always coincide. For instance, there are cases where we do not refrain from calling a given thing an "X," even though it is incapable, as it stands, of having a use U under the standard causal conditions S_1 relative to X's in general, and though the notion of U is implicit in the meaning of 'X.'[10] For example, a "broken chair," or a "chair with a leg missing," is called a chair even though it cannot be sat on under causal conditions which are standard for intact chairs. The existence of such cases may seem to contradict our general position in sections I and II. But actually it does not materially affect it. As a matter of fact, such apparent exceptions merely constitute borderline cases and are themselves explainable in terms of our general position.

A. Let us take a simple and clear example, that of chairs. Chairs seem unmistakably to have been invented for a specific kind of use, for use in a certain way. That is, the intended use seems to have determined the general characteristics of the original chairs. It is possible, therefore, that originally the name 'chair' did involve, in ordinary discourse, the notion of the capacity to have that use under certain physical conditions such that a thing could *not* be properly called a chair *unless* it possessed that capacity. But since a chair's *characteristics* are causally responsible for the chair's possessing the capacity to be used in a given way, under certain conditions, the term 'chair' would subsequently come to apply to objects which have these kinds of characteristic, *in their own right*, making the possession of these kinds of characteristic a "necessary" condition for the applicability of 'chair,' rather than the capacity to have the use which these characteristics are designed to make possible. Once this shift in "meaning" has been effected, a further complication seems to arise. The term 'chair' now comes to be applied also to objects which merely "resemble"[11] objects hitherto called chairs, provided the "resemblance" is considerable and not tenuous (there being no sharp line of demarcation between "considerable" and "tenuous" resemblance), even though these objects, as they stand, cannot serve as chairs. By an "object which 'resembles' a chair" I have here in mind a so-called broken, battered, or incomplete chair, such as a chair with one leg missing.

B. But the shift in "meaning" described above is not sharp and complete in actual cases. The notion of certain sets of characteristics Ca, or Cb, or Cd, and so on, does not seem to usurp completely, in actual practice, the place of the notion of a given use U which Ca, or Cb, or Cd, and so on, make possible in a given thing T. In deciding whether or not to call a given thing by a certain name, or in justifying the giving of a certain name to a given thing, appeal is made now to the one, now to the other, now to both, notions. When we say: "What sort of chair is this?—it's broken; one of its legs is missing!" our tendency to think of the object referred to as a *broken* chair may be due either to the fact that (a) it lacks certain kinds of characteristics which are generally found in objects called "chairs" without qualification (so-called intact chairs), and/or to the fact that (b) it cannot, as it stands, serve as a chair. But we *do* speak of it as a *"chair"* because we think of it (i) as an object which used to have the kinds of characteristic a chair generally has, or was capable of serving as a chair, or both; and/or (ii) as an object capable of serving as a chair if it were to have certain characteristics it now lacks (i.e., if it were to be "repaired"). Thus if (say) just before a party a servant discovers a chair with a cracked seat, and he remarks: "We can't use this (as a chair): the seat is cracked," he may get the following reply from the hostess: "Yes we can! Get me some glue," or "Yes we can, if you get me some glue."[12] In using qualifying adjectives like 'broken,' 'defective,' 'incomplete,' 'battered,' we reflect in ordinary language the distinction between the kind of case in which a given object called "X" can, *as it stands*, serve as an "X," and the borderline kind of case in which it cannot, as it stands, serve as an "X."

Let us note that there is no hard and fast line dividing the borderline cases themselves, where the name 'chair,' say, is still applied (though with qualification), and cases where the name 'chair' is no longer applied. Thus we uniformly speak of a "*chair* with a leg missing," a "*chair* with two legs missing," a "*chair* with three legs missing"; but we can *either* speak of a "*chair* with all of its legs missing," (or a "legless chair") or of the "*seat* and *back* of a chair"; while we do *not* seriously speak of a "chair with the legs and back missing" but rather of the "seat of a chair," or even of a "wooden board" (or a "wooden board having the shape of a chair's seat"), and the like. In other words, and stated generally, there is no hard and fast line in ordinary discourse between an "X with a part missing," a "part *a* of X," and a "not-X and not-*a*."

IV

Our discussion would be grossly incomplete if we do not consider, at least briefly, one use of 'good' and of 'poor' or 'not good'; namely, their use in such statements as "This is a good knife," "That wasn't a good game of tennis," "He played a poor game of chess." Such an analysis shows that there is a very intimate relationship between the uses of common names of the kind we have concerned ourselves with in this paper, and the above uses of 'good' (also 'very good,' 'excellent') and 'poor' or 'not good' (also 'very poor,' 'extremely poor,' 'not very good,' 'not good at all,' etc.).

A. If we examine cases in which we ordinarily call a man-made object, or a man-devised activity or process, a "good X" and not merely "X," we find, first, that we do so both (a) when the prevalent causal conditions (viz., in general, the conditions for the application of the name 'X') are standard, and (b) when the causal conditions are non-standard, for "X's" in general. In the case of (a) we further discover that in calling the given thing a good "X," we indicate one or both of two things: (i) that this thing "X" is capable of having, or actually has, *in an eminent or outstanding degree* (these terms being used in a relative sense) a given use U; (ii) that "X" possesses one or more *characteristics* by virtue of which it is capable of having, or actually has, a use U, in an eminent or outstanding degree. In both (i) and (ii), the use U involved is found to be the use associated with "X" *qua* "X" or the notion of which is implicit in "X's" meaning. For instance, if we point to a knife and say: "This is a *good* knife," we ordinarily indicate that it is capable of cutting, or is actually cutting, certain kinds of thing (meat, butter, bread, and so on) well, efficiently, without effort, and/or it is either sharp or very sharp, *or* has a firm and comfortable grip, *or* has a long and wide blade, *or* its blade has a saw-like edge, or some or all of these characteristics together—that is, one or more characteristics which make it capable of cutting certain kinds of thing well, efficiently, with ease. We may also speak of a knife as a good knife if it has one or more characteristics that make it capable of being used to cut (of serving as a knife), or to cut well, *for a relatively long time*: in general, characteristics which enable it to preserve its peculiar use. Thus a knife may be said to be a good knife because it has a rust-proof blade and/or has a sturdy handle.

Examples illustrating these points can be easily multiplied. Also, these points can be readily applied *mutatis mutandis*, to the use of 'very good,' 'excellent,' and the like, corresponding to the use of 'good' we are talking about.

In the case of (b), i.e., when we apply the term 'good' to a thing "X" under causal conditions which are non-standard for "X's" in general, we indicate that "X" is capable of having, or actually has, use U *even though the prevalent conditions are non-standard for it qua "X,"* and therefore even though it is not expected to have U. If "X" has U, or seems capable of having it (or if it has characteristics which seem to show that it has this capacity) in an outstanding degree, even though the prevalent causal conditions are non-standard, we tend to call it a "very good X," or an "excellent X," and not merely a "good X." We will call a knife a good (or a very good) knife if it cuts (and better still, if it cuts well) things which it is not designed—and therefore not expected—to cut. Similarly, we would ordinarily apply the term 'good' (or 'very good,' etc.) to an all-purpose knife just invented, tacitly comparing its performance with the performance of ordinary knives. But once we get used to this kind of knife and ordinary knives go out of use or become rare, we tend to bestow these terms only on a specific all-purpose knife (or a whole brand of it) which cuts better the things all-purpose knives are expected to cut, or cuts more kinds of things than other all-purpose knives, under conditions which now come to be regarded as standard for *them*, but which include conditions which are non-standard for ordinary knives. (Cf. the case of quill pens and fountain pens. This example also illustrates the converse of what we have just said: we tend at present to speak of a quill pen as a *poor* pen, judging its performance in terms of the performance of fountain pens, when originally it must have been the opposite.) It may be noted that in case (b) in general, (i) the degree in which a thing "X" has or seems to have use U associated with it *qua* "X," and (ii) the degree in which the prevalent causal conditions are non-standard (or unfavorable), wherever such variation in degree in these conditions is possible, ordinarily determines the judge's assessment of *how* eminently "X" has or is capable of having U. Consequently, they determine whether 'good,' or 'very good,' or 'excellent,' shall be applied. These points may be illustrated by the following statements: "It was a very good game of tennis! The players rarely missed the ball, despite the strong wind"; "It was an excellent game of tennis! The players rarely (or better still: "hardly ever," or "never") missed the ball, and did some fast footwork, despite the strong wind and the soggy ground."

Our remarks in (a) and (b) above apply equally, *mutatis mutandis*, to objects, activities, and processes with relatively, or highly, specialized uses, such as carving knives, chess games, sledge hammers, writing desks, arm chairs, ice cream, and so on.

B. Coming now to uses of 'poor' or 'not good' in the sense in which we are here concerned with these terms, a man-made object or a man-devised activity, or process, is ordinarily said to be a "poor X" or "not a good X" in the following situations:

(1) If it is regarded as completely incapable of having a given use U associated with it *qua* "X," provided that (a) it is regarded as intact *qua* "X," and that (b) the prevalent causal conditions are regarded as standard, that is, when "X" is expected by the person calling it a "poor X" or "not a good X" to have use U. (In this type of case, however, we generally tend to use a stronger expression than 'poor' or 'not good' alone: we say: "This is a very poor X.") A knife with a completely blunt blade is intact as a knife—it has the general structural characteristics of one kind of knife or another, though not all the characteristics which are necessary for cutting. Hence it *is* called a knife, and not, say, "junk" (except as a hyperbole). But since it is incapable of cutting things which knives are ordinarily expected to cut, it is called a poor knife or is said to be not a good knife. (On the other hand, we will probably call it "junk," or something equivalent in meaning to 'junk,' instead of a "poor knife," if it has no blade; though we might still call it a handle-less knife" and not "junk" if it has a blade but no handle. For the possession of a blade is regarded as—and is—causally more *necessary* for cutting, for an object's serving as a knife, than the possession of a handle.)

(2) If, as it stands, it is capable of having the associated use U—or is regarded as capable of having use U—but in a lower degree than the person calling it a "poor X" expects a thing called "X" to have, it being again assumed that the prevalent causal conditions are standard conditions and that "X" is intact *qua* "X." Taking knives again as our illustration, a knife may be said to be a poor knife if its blade, say, is rusty or is somewhat blunt, if it has a very short handle, or a very short blade, or has several or all of these defects together. In other words, if it lacks certain characteristics which would have enabled it to have the peculiar use—cutting—associated with it *qua* knife, with the ease and efficiency expected of a knife; or has certain characteristics which prevent it from serving as expected.

The above analysis, as well as further analysis, tends to indicate that in such statements as "*a* is a good X," "*b* is a poor X," where 'X' and 'Y' are common names of the kind we are dealing with in this paper, (a) 'good' does not refer to any specific determinate or relatively determinate characteristic or characteristics common to all things ordinarily called "good X's," by virtue of which these things function better than is generally expected of things called "X's," or by virtue of which they are called good "X's"; (b) that, similarly, 'poor' or 'not good' do not refer to any specific determinate or relatively determinate characteristic or characteristics *present* in all things called "poor Y's," which prevent them from functioning well or even functioning at all; nor do these terms refer to any specific determinate or relatively determinate characteristic or characteristics *absent* from all things called "poor Y's" or "not good Y's," as a result of which they are incapable of functioning well or even functioning at all. The determinate or relatively determinate characteristics of a knife may vary qualitatively and in degree, and yet we may still properly call it a good knife—so long as it serves well (and/or for a relatively long time) as a knife. Similarly a knife may be capable of cutting things it is not ordinarily expected to cut, by possessing one or more of a variety of determinate or relatively determinate characteristics of certain kinds. The same applies to "poor knives" or "not good knives." Of course many knives said to be good knives may and do have one or more determinate or relatively determinate characteristics in common, in the same way as many knives in general (say those of the same brand) whether good or not, may and do have such characteristics in common. But our point is that we do not restrict the ordinary application of the term 'good' to knives which have one or more specific characteristics in common. What determines in ordinary usage the application—and the range of application—of 'good' is something other than the possession of certain characteristics in common: as we have been trying to show, it is the *degree*, and the *nature of the conditions* under which, a given kind of use is possessed. On this basis, there is no necessity, no need for all things called "good X's" to have one or more determinate or relatively determinate characteristics in common, in order that they may properly be called "good X's." Similarly, *mutatis mutandis*, with 'poor' or 'not good.'[13]

One final word. There is no hard and fast dividing line between cases where an object or phenomenon would be called a "poor X" and cases where it would not be called "X" at all. Consider an object having the general structure of an armchair, but with one of its legs considerably shorter than the rest. This object we call a poor armchair or not a good armchair (as well as, say, a "lame" armchair), rather than something else— say "junk." The situation here is relatively straightforward, since the object in hand does serve as a separate seat for one, etc., though less satisfactorily than anything generally called a "chair" or "armchair" without qualification. A chair is required to afford the sitter some degree of rest or comfort; whereas this particular chair is uncomfortable. But one can still sit upon it. Now suppose we have a similar object, but with one of its "legs" missing. This object cannot, as it stands, serve as a separate seat for one. Despite that, we would still call it a chair—qualified with (say) 'broken.' In this case, however, we would *not* speak of it as a "poor chair." We call it a chair though we know that it cannot, as it stands, serve as one; but at the same time we do not expect it to serve as a chair. That is why we do not call it a "poor chair." Finally, if we rip a chair apart, leaving the "seat" intact, we do not call the latter *either* a "poor chair," *or* a "broken chair," but rather, the "seat of a chair." All this goes to show that the transition from (i) "chair" (without qualification) to (ii) "poor chair" (or "not a good chair"), and, say, "chair with cracked seat" to (iii) "broken chair" (say in the case of a chair with a leg missing), but *not* "poor chair" to (iv) "junk," is not clear-cut and fixed, but gradual and continuous and blurred. This also goes to show that there is no sharp demarcation line between "standard" conditions for the use of a name 'X' (say 'chair') and "non-standard" conditions.[14]

NOTES

From *Philosophy and Phenomenological Research* 18 (1957–58). Reprinted by permission of the author and the editor of *Philosophy and Phenomenological Research*.

1. [L. Wittgenstein,] *Philosophical Investigations*, translated by G. E. M. Anscombe, (Oxford, 1953), p. 31e.
2. Whether our results apply to natural objects and to psychological phenomena in general we shall not inquire in this paper.
3. Cf. what Wittgenstein says about skill and luck in games. "Look at the parts played by skill and luck; and at the *difference* between skill in chess and skill in tennis." (P. 32e.) (Italics mine.)
4. The statement: "If standard conditions obtain, pleasure will be produced by a game" is meant to be, and is, an analytic statement; and not either an *a priori* synthetic judgment, or an empirical generalization. For our contention is that the notion of "standard" conditions here is built into the meaning of the word 'game' in such a way as to make the above statement analytic. The essential point here is that we are not arbitrarily introducing the notion of "standard" conditions in order to guarantee the truth of the statement. Our contention is that if we analyze the uses of the term 'game,' we *discover* this notion of "standard" conditions implicit in it. That this is so is, however, an empirical assertion about the uses or meaning of 'game.' Similarly with the other common names which we shall discuss later on. (But see above for the distinction and difference between two kinds of "standard" condition which are used indiscriminately here.)
5. Wittgenstein himself sometimes thinks of the characteristics, sometimes of the effects produced, in speaking of "family resemblances." For instance, he asks whether all games are amusing (effects), whether they always involve winning and losing, or competition between the players, or skill, or luck (the characteristics of the games themselves). (Cf. p. 32e.)
6. It is noteworthy that many of the phenomena Wittgenstein analyzes are complex "psychological" processes, such as thinking, doubting, learning; and it may well be that there *only* "family resemblances" can be discovered. But supposing that to be true, and even if in the case of games themselves, only "family resemblances" are discoverable in their effects, our position seems to remain secure as far as the names of manufactured objects are concerned—and also of activities which do not appreciably include psychological elements in their effects.
7. Cf. Max Black, *Language and Philosophy*, (Ithaca, New York, 1949), pp. 30–31.
8. For the precise meaning of 'can' here, and for a discussion of an important qualification of the above, see above and note 12.
9. This qualification is necessary in the light of our later discussion below. But the borderline cases we shall discuss there can themselves be explained in terms of the principles underlying the above discussion.

10. There are also cases where a thing T does have a use U under (at least some of the) standard causal conditions S₁ relative to things called "X's," and yet we refrain from calling it an "X" ('X' being a name which implicitly involves the notion of U in its meaning). A log can be sat on, and yet we do not call it a chair—not without some qualification at least. About these cases we have already said something in connection with the notion of a thing's "proper" or "normal" use. Further discussion must be left to a future paper.

11. I am not here referring to the kind of resemblance which obtains, say, between so-called "irrational numbers" and so-called "cardinal numbers," on the basis of which (taking this merely as a hypothetical possibility) the former may have come to be called "numbers." This kind of extension of a name's meaning does not consist in the creation of borderline cases, as in the case of a so-called "broken chair's" being called a chair despite its being "broken." Incidentally, the former is one way in which the existence of "family resemblances" between things called by the same name may be accounted for.

12. It is important to note that in the above interchange 'can' is used in two different senses by the servant and the hostess respectively. The former is using the word in a narrower and stricter sense. He is saying, in effect, that *as it stands*, and under the *prevailing circumstances*, the "chair" cannot serve as a chair. The hostess, on the other hand, is using 'can' in a less stringent sense. What she says, in effect, is that the broken chair can serve as a chair, even in that particular situation, since it can be (easily) repaired, and therefore *made to serve* as a chair. In this sense of 'can,' our statement that an object (activity, process, of the kind we are concerned with) may be called "X" even if it cannot serve as an "X," etc., will be false. In this sense of 'can,' "can serve as an X" can be taken as a (conventionally determined) "necessary" condition for properly calling a man-made or a man-devised thing an "X." However, let us add that the ordinary uses of 'can,' in our second sense, are relative to the particular situation involved. A chair with a slightly cracked seat "can (be made to) serve" as a chair, even in the urgency of preparations for a party; but a chair with a leg missing cannot (even in the second sense of 'can'). So the hostess would not say: "Yes we can, get me some glue!" if the chair referred to had a leg missing. (But she would still refer to the object as a "chair.") Still, a chair with a leg missing "can (be made to) serve" as a chair if there is plenty of time, say, to send it to a carpenter and have it repaired. Thus the distinction between 'can' and 'cannot' in this sense is not clear cut and sharp: whether or not a given object is thought of as capable of having a given use depends on the state of the object in a particular situation.

13. It is interesting to note that in English there is no meaning or sense of 'bad' (with the exception, perhaps, of 'bad' in 'bad food') which corresponds to the above meaning or sense of 'good.' The antonym of 'good' in this meaning or sense is 'not good' or 'poor,' and not 'bad.' We cannot properly say "a bad knife," "a bad game," "a bad pen," in the same way in which we speak of a "good knife," a "good game," a "good pen," and so on. In other words, there does not seem to be a meaning or sense of 'bad' in English which is synonymous with 'not good' (or 'poor') in the above sense or meaning. But there may be some languages in which we can properly say "This is a bad knife," "This is a bad game," and the like, in the sense of "This is a poor knife," "This is not a good game." As a matter of fact, this is admissible in one Asiatic language I know, namely in *colloquial* or *conversational* (though not in literary) Armenian.

14. I wish to thank Professor Bernard Peach of Duke University for his criticisms of an earlier draft of this essay.

23 BAMBROUGH

Bambrough offers a succinct explanation of Wittgenstein's view of universals. The uneasiness one feels with respect to universals is understandable and straightforward. On the one hand, the realist quite correctly understands that, for example, all chairs must have something in common; otherwise they simply would not be chairs. From this he mistakenly concludes that there must be some subsistent entity or other that is the universal all chairs have in common. However, no one has been able to isolate this or any other universal, and this is a source of uneasiness. On the other hand, the nominalist concludes that there is no such subsistent entity over and above individual chairs, and consequently all that such particulars have in common is that they are referred to as chairs. The uneasiness we are left with here is the feeling that the correct use of common nouns is something more than an arbitrary naming game. There simply must be something more than the name 'chair' that all chairs have in common.

Wittgenstein's solution to the problem of universals appreciates both the realist's and the nominalist's respective points of view and the uneasiness we feel with respect to both of those positions. His solution is to agree with the realist that all chairs have something nonarbitrary in common, that is, something more than a name. He also agrees with the nominalist that the "something" that all chairs have in common is not some elusive subsistent entity called a universal. Wittgenstein's solution to the problem of universals is that what all chairs have in common is that they simply are chairs, nothing more and nothing less. Assigning a common noun, e.g., 'chair', to a class of particulars is not arbitrary because all those particulars *are* chairs. That is the end of the matter. To hunt for something beyond the fact that all chairs are chairs, a something that we call a universal, is to go on an ontological wild goose chase. There simply are no such "things" as universals.

Universals and Family Resemblances

I believe that Wittgenstein solved what is known as "the problem of universals", and I would say of his solution, as Hume said of Berkeley's treatment of the same topic, that it is "one of the greatest and most valuable discoveries that has been made of late years in the republic of letters."

I do not expect these claims to be accepted by many philosophers.

Since I claim that Wittgenstein solved the problem I naturally do not claim to be making an original contribution to the study of it. Since I recognize that few philosophers will accept my claim that Wittgenstein solved it, I naturally regard it as worth while to continue to discuss the problem. My purpose is to try to make clear what Wittgenstein's solution is and to try to make clear that it is a solution.

Philosophers ought to be wary of claiming that philosophical problems have been finally solved. Aristotle and Descartes and Spinoza and Berkeley and Hume and the author of the *Tractatus Logico-Philosophicus* lie at the bottom of the sea not far from this rock, with the skeletons of many lesser men to keep them company. But nobody suggests that their journeys were vain, or that nothing can be saved from the wrecks.

In seeking for Wittgenstein's solution we must look mainly to his remarks about "family resemblances" and to his use of the example of games. In the *Blue Book* he speaks of "our craving for generality" and tries to trace this craving to its sources:

> This craving for generality is the resultant of a number of tendencies connected with particular philosophical confusions. There is—
>
> (a) The tendency to look for something in common to all the entities which we commonly subsume under a general term.—We are inclined to think that there must be something in common to all games, say, and that this common property is the justification for applying the general term "game" to the various games; whereas games form a *family* the members of which have family likenesses. Some of them have the same nose, others the same eyebrows and others again the same way of walking; and these likenesses overlap. The idea of a general concept being a common property of its particular instances connects up with other primitive, too simple, ideas of the structure of language. It is comparable to the idea that *properties* are *ingredients* of the things which have the properties; e.g., that beauty is an ingredient of all beautiful things as alcohol is of beer and wine, and that we therefore could have pure beauty, unadulterated by anything that is beautiful.
>
> (b) There is a tendency rooted in our usual forms of expression, to think that the man who has learnt to understand a general term, say, the term "leaf", has thereby come to possess a kind of general picture of a leaf, as opposed to pictures of particular leaves. He was shown different leaves when he learnt the meaning of the word "leaf"; and showing him the particular leaves was only a means to the end of producing "in him" an idea which we imagine to be some kind of general image. We say that he sees what is in common to all these leaves; and this is true if we mean that he can on being asked tell us certain features or properties which they have in common. But we are inclined to think that the general idea of a leaf is something like a visual image, but one which only contains what is common to all leaves. (Galtonian composite photograph.) This again is connected with the idea that the meaning of a word is an image, or a thing correlated to the word. (This roughly means, we are looking at words as though they all were proper names, and we then confuse the bearer of a name with the meaning of the name.) (Pp. 17–18).

In the *Philosophical Investigations* Wittgenstein again speaks of family resemblances, and gives a more elaborate account of the similarities and differences between various games:

66. Consider for example the proceedings that we call "games". I mean board-games, card-games, ball-games, Olympic games, and so on. What is common to them all?—Don't say: "there *must* be something common, or they would not be called 'games'"—but *look and see* whether there is anything common to all.—For if you look at them you will not see something that is common to *all*, but similarities, relationships, and a whole series of them at that. To repeat: don't think, but look!—Look for example at board-games, with their multifarious relationships. Now pass to card-games; here you find many correspondences with the first group, but many common features drop out, and others appear. When we pass next to ball-games, much that is common is retained, but much is lost.—Are they all "amusing"? Compare chess with noughts and crosses. Or is there always winning and losing, or competition between players? Think of patience. In ball games there is winning and losing; but when a child throws his ball at the wall and catches it again, this feature has disappeared. Look at the parts played by skill and luck; and at the difference between skill in chess and skill in tennis. Think now of games like ring-a-ring-a-roses; here is the element of amusement, but how many other characteristic features have disappeared! And we can go through the many, many other groups of games in the same way; can see how similarities crop up and disappear.

And the result of this examination is: we see a complicated network of similarities overlapping and criss-crossing: sometimes overall similarities, sometimes similarities of detail.

67. I can think of no better expression to characterize these similarities than "family resemblances"; for the various resemblances between the members of a family: build, features, color of eyes, gait, temperament, etc. etc. overlap and criss-cross in the same way.—And I shall say: "games" form a family.

Wittgenstein expounds his analogy informally, and with great economy. Its power can be displayed in an equally simple but more formal way by considering a situation that is familiar to botanical taxonomists.[1] We may classify a set of objects by reference to the presence or absence of features ABCDE. It may well happen that five objects *edcba* are such that each of them has four of these properties and lacks the fifth, and that the missing feature is different in each of the five cases. A simple diagram will illustrate this situation:

e	d	c	b	a
A B C D	A B C E	A B D E	A C D E	B C D E

Here we can already see how natural and how proper it might be to apply the same word to a number of objects between which there is no common feature. And if we confine our attention to any arbitrarily selected four of these objects, say *edca*, then although they all *happen* to have B in common, it is clear that it is not in virtue of the presence of B that they are all rightly called by the same name. Even if the actual instances were indefinitely numerous, and they all happened to have one or more of the features in common, it would not be in virtue of the presence of the common feature or features that they would all be rightly called by the same name, since the name also applies to *possible* instances that lack the feature or features.

The richness of the possibilities of the family resemblances model becomes more striking still if we set it out more fully and formally in terms of a particular family than Wittgenstein himself ever did. Let us suppose that "the Churchill face" is strikingly and obviously present in each of ten members of the Churchill family, and that when a family group photograph is set before us it is unmistakable that these ten people all belong to the same family. It may be that there are ten features in terms of which we can describe "the family face" (high forehead, bushy eye-brows, blue eyes, Roman nose, high cheekbones, cleft chin, dark hair, dimpled cheeks, pointed ears and ruddy complexion). It is obvious that the unmistakable presence of the family face in every single one of the ten members of the family is compatible with the absence from each of the ten members of the family of one of the ten constituent features of the family face. It is also obvious that it does not matter if it happens that the feature which is absent from the face of each individual member of the family is present in every one of the others. The members of the family will then have no *feature* in common, and yet they will all unmistakably have *the Churchill face* in common.

This example is very artificial, and it may seem at first sight that its artificiality plays into my hands. But on the contrary, the more natural the example is made the more it suits my purpose. If we remember that a family face does not divide neatly into ten separate features, we widen rather than reduce the scope for large numbers of instances of the family face to lack a single common feature. And if we remember that what goes for faces goes for features too; that all cleft chins have nothing in common except that they are cleft chins, that the possible gradations from Roman nose to snub nose or from high to low cheekbones are continuous and infinite, we see that there could in principle be an infinite number of unmistakable Churchill faces which had no feature in common. In fact it now becomes clear that there is a good sense in which *no two* members of the Churchill family need have *any* feature in common in order for all the members of the Churchill family to have the Churchill face.

The passages that I have quoted contain the essence of Wittgenstein's solution of the problem of universals, but they are far from exhausting his account of the topic. Not only are there other places where he speaks of games and of family resemblances: what is more important is that most of his philosophical remarks in *The Blue and Brown Books* and in the *Philo-*

sophical Investigations are concerned with such questions as "What is the meaning of a word?" "What is language?" "What is thinking?" "What is understanding?" And these questions are various forms of the question to which theories of universals, including Wittgenstein's theory of universals, are meant to be answers. There is a clear parallel between what Wittgenstein says about games and what he says about reading, expecting, languages, numbers, propositions; in all these cases we have the idea that there is a common element or ingredient, and Wittgenstein shows us that there is no such ingredient or element. The instances that fall under each of these concepts *form a family*.

It is already clear that the point Wittgenstein made with the example of games has a much wider range of application than that example itself. But exactly how wide is its application meant to be? Wittgenstein's own method of exposition makes it difficult to answer this question. In his striving to find a cure for "our craving for generality," in his polemic against "the contemptuous attitude towards the particular case," he was understandably wary of expressing his own conclusions in general terms. Readers and expositors of Wittgenstein are consequently impelled to make use of glosses and paraphrases and interpretations if they wish to relate his work to philosophical writings and doctrines that are expressed in another idiom; that is to say, to most other philosophical writings and doctrines.

I believe that this is why Wittgenstein's solution of the problem of universals has not been widely understood, and why, in consequence, it has not been widely seen to be a solution.[2] In avoiding the generalities that are characteristic of most philosophical discussion he also avoided reference to the standard "problems of philosophy" and to the "philosophical theories" which have repeatedly been offered as answers to them. He talks about games and families and colors, about reading, expecting and understanding, but not about "the problem of universals." He practiced an activity which is "one of the heirs of the subject which used to be called 'philosophy'", but he did not relate the results of his activity to the results of the enquiries to which it was an heir. He did not, for example, plot the relation between his remarks on games and family resemblances and the doctrines of those philosophers who had been called Nominalists and Realists.

When I claim that Wittgenstein solved the problem of universals I am claiming that his remarks can be paraphrased into a doctrine which can be set out in general terms and can be related to the traditional theories, and which can then be shown to deserve to supersede the traditional theories. My purpose in this paper is to expound such a doctrine and to defend it.

But first I must return to my question about the range of application of the point that is made by the example of games, since it is at this crucial first stage that most readers of Wittgenstein go wrong. When we read what he says about games and family resemblances, we are naturally inclined to ask ourselves, "With what kinds of concepts is Wittgenstein *contrasting* the concepts of game, language, proposition, understanding?" I shall consider three possible answers to this question.

The first answer is suggested by Professor Ayer's remarks about games and family resemblances on pp. 10–12 of *The Problem of Knowledge*. Ayer contrasts the word "game" with the word "red", on the ground that the former does not, while the latter does, mark "a simple and straightforward resemblance" between the things to which the word is applied. He claims that, "The point which Wittgenstein's argument brings out is that the resemblance between the things to which the same word applies may be of different degrees. It is looser and less straightforward in some cases than in others." Now this contrast between simple and complicated concepts is important, and the games example is a convenient means of drawing attention to it, but I am sure that this is not the point that Wittgenstein was making with his example. In the *Brown Book* (p. 131) he asks, "Could you tell me what is in common between a light red and a dark red?" and in the *Philosophical Investigations* (Section 73) he asks, "Which shade is the 'sample in my mind' of the color green—the sample of what is common to all shades of green?" Wittgenstein could as easily have used the example of red things as the example of games to illustrate "the tendency to look for something in common to all the entities which we commonly subsume under a general term." Just as cricket and chess and patience and ring-a-ring-a-roses have nothing in common *except that they are games*, so poppies and blood and pillar-boxes and hunting-coats have nothing in common *except that they are red*.

A second possible answer is implied by a sentence in Mr. P. F. Strawson's *Individuals*: "It is often admitted, in the analytical treatment of some fairly specific concept, that the wish to understand is less likely to be served by the search for a single strict statement of the necessary and sufficient conditions of its application than by seeing its applications—in Wittgenstein's simile—as forming a family, the members of which may, perhaps, be grouped around a central paradigm case and linked with the latter by various direct or indirect links of logical connexion and analogy." (p. 11). The contrast is not now between simple and complex concepts, but between two kinds of complex concepts: those which are definable by the statement of necessary and sufficient conditions and those which are not. But once again the contrast, although it is important, and is one which the family resemblances simile and the example of games are well able to draw, is not the point that Wittgenstein is concerned with. In the sense in which, according to Wittgenstein, games have nothing in common except that they are games, and red things have nothing in common except that they are red, *brothers have nothing in common except that they are brothers*. It is true that brothers have in common that they are male siblings, but their having in common that they are male siblings is their having in common that they are *brothers*, and not their having in common something in addition to their being brothers. Even a concept which can be explained in terms of necessary and sufficient conditions cannot be *ultimately* explained in such terms. To satisfy the craving for an ultimate explanation of "brother" in such terms it would be necessary to define "male" and "sibling", and the words in which "male" and "sibling" were defined, and so on *ad infinitum* and *ad impossibile*.

What then *is* the contrast that Wittgenstein meant to draw? I suggest that he did not mean to draw a *contrast* at all. Professor Wisdom has remarked that the peculiar difficulty of giving a philosophical account of universals lies in this: that philosophers are usually engaged in implicitly or explicitly comparing and contrasting one type of proposition with another type of proposition (propositions about minds with propositions about bodies, propositions of logic with propositions about matters of fact, propositions about the present and the past with propositions about the future, etc.) whereas propositions involving universals cannot be compared or contrasted with propositions that do not involve universals, since *all* propositions involve universals.[3] If we look at Wittgenstein's doctrine in the light of this remark we can understand it aright and can also see why it has been misunderstood in just those ways that I have mentioned. It is because of the very power of the ways of thought against which Wittgenstein was protesting that philosophers are led to offer accounts of his doctrine which restrict the range of its application. They recognize the importance of Wittgenstein's demonstration that *at least some* general terms can justifiably be applied to their instances although those instances have nothing in common. But they are so deeply attached to the idea that there must be something in common to the instances that fall under a general term that they treat Wittgenstein's examples as special cases, as rogues and vagabonds in the realm of concepts, to be contrasted with the general run of law-abiding concepts which *do* mark the presence of common elements in their instances.

Here we come across an ambiguity which is another obstacle to our getting a clear view of the problem of universals and of Wittgenstein's solution of it. Ayer remarks, in the passage to which I have already referred, that, "It is correct, though not at all enlightening, to say that what games have in common is their being games." It is certainly correct, but I strongly deny that it is unenlightening. It is of course trivially and platitudinously true, but trivialities and platitudes deserve emphatic affirmation when, as often in philosophy, they are explicitly or implicitly denied, or forgotten, or overlooked. Now the platitude that all games have in common that they *are* games is denied by the nominalist, who says that all games have nothing in common except that they are *called* games. And it is not only the nominalist, but also his opponent, who misunderstands the central importance of the platitude that all games have in common that they are games. When he is provoked by the nominalist's claim that all games have nothing in common except that they are called games, and rightly wishes to insist that games have something more in common than simply that they are called games, he feels that he must look for something that games have in common apart from *being* games. This feeling is entirely misplaced. The very terms of the nominalist's challenge require only that the realist should point out something that games have in common apart from *being called* games, and this onus is fully discharged by saying that they *are* games.

Although the feeling is misplaced, it is a very natural feeling, as we can see by considering the kinds of case in which we most typically and ordinarily ask what is in common to a set of objects. If I ask you what these three books have in common, or what those four chairs have in common, you will look to see if the books are all on the same subject or by the same author or published by the same firm; to see if the chairs are all Chippendale or all three-legged or all marked "Not to be removed from this room." It will never occur to you to say that the books have in common that they are books or the chairs that they are chairs. And if you find after close inspection that the chairs or the books do not have in common any of the features I have mentioned, and if you cannot see any other specific feature that they have in common, you will say that as far as you can see they have nothing in common. You will perhaps add that you suppose from the form of my question that I must know of something that they have in common. I may then tell you that all the books once belonged to John Locke or that all the chairs came from Ten Rillington Place. But it would be a poor sort of joke for me to say that the chairs were all chairs or that the books were all books.

If I ask you what *all* chairs have in common, or what *all* books have in common, you may again try to find a feature like those you would look for in the case of *these three* books or *those four* chairs; and you may again think that it is a poor sort of joke for me to say that what all books have in common is that they are books and that what all chairs have in common is that they are chairs. And yet this time it is not a joke but an important philosophical truth.

Because the normal case where we ask "What have all *these* chairs, books or games in common?" is one in which we are not concerned with their all being chairs, books or games, we are liable to overlook the extreme peculiarity of the *philosophical* question that is asked with the words "What do *all* chairs, *all* books, *all* games have in common?" For of course games *do* have something in common. They *must* have something in common, and yet when we look for what they have in common we cannot find it. When we try to say what they have in common we always fail. And this is not because what we are looking for lies deeply hidden, but because it is too obvious to be seen; not because what we are trying to say is too subtle and complicated to be said, but because it is too easy and too simple to be worth saying: and so we say something more dramatic, but something false, instead. The simple truth is that what games have in common is that they are games. The nominalist is obscurely aware of this, and by rejecting the realist's talk of transcendent, immanent or subsistent forms or universals he shows his awareness. But by his own insistence that games have nothing in common except that they are called games he shows the obscurity of his awareness. The realist too is obscurely aware of it. By his talk of transcendent, immanent or subsistent forms or universals he shows the obscurity of his awareness. But by his hostility to the nominalist's insistence that games have nothing in common except that they are called games he shows his awareness.

All this can be more fully explained by the application of what I will call "Ramsey's Maxim." F. P. Ramsey, after mapping the course of an inconclusive dispute between Russell and W. E. Johnson, writes as follows:

"Evidently, however, none of these arguments are really decisive, and the position is extremely unsatisfactory to any one with real curiosity about such a fundamental question. In such cases it is a heuristic maxim that the truth lies not in one of the two disputed views but in some third possibility which has not yet been thought of, which we can only discover by rejecting something assumed as obvious by both the disputants." (*The Foundations of Mathematics*, pp. 115–116.)

It is assumed as obvious by both the nominalist and the realist that there can be no objective justification for the application of a general term to its instances unless its instances have something in common over and above their having in common that they *are* its instances. The nominalist rightly holds that there is no such additional common element, and he therefore wrongly concludes that there is no objective justification for the application of any general term. The realist rightly holds that there is an objective justification for the application of general terms, and he therefore wrongly concludes that there *must* be some additional common element.

Wittgenstein denied the assumption that is common to nominalism and realism, and that is why I say that he solved the problem of universals. For if we deny the mistaken premiss that is common to the realist's argument and the nominalist's argument then we can deny the realist's mistaken conclusion and deny the nominalist's mistaken conclusion; and that is another way of saying that we can affirm the true premiss of the nominalist's argument and can also affirm the true premiss of the realist's argument.

The nominalist says that games have nothing in common except that they are called games.

The realist says that games must have something in common, and he means by this that they must have something in common other than that they are games.

Wittgenstein says that games have nothing in common except that they are games.

Wittgenstein thus denies at one and the same time the nominalist's claim that games have nothing in common except that they are called games and the realist's claim that games have something in common other than that they are games. He asserts at one and the same time the realist's claim that there is an objective justification for the application of the word "game" to games and the nominalist's claim that there is no element that is common to all games. And he is able to do all this because he denies the joint claim of the nominalist and the realist that there cannot be an objective justification for the application of the word "game" to games unless there is an element that is common to all games (*universalia in rebus*) or a common relation that all games bear to something that is not a game (*universalia ante res*).

Wittgenstein is easily confused with the nominalist because he denies what the realist asserts: that games have something in common other than that they are games.

When we see that Wittgenstein is not a nominalist we may easily confuse him with the realist because he denies what the nominalist asserts: that games have nothing in common except that they are called games.

But we can now see that Wittgenstein is neither a realist nor a nominalist: he asserts the simple truth that they both deny and he also asserts the two simple truths of which each of them asserts one and denies the other.

I will now try to put some flesh on to these bare bones.

The value and the limitations of the nominalist's claim that things which are called by the same name have nothing in common except that they are called by the same name can be seen if we look at a case where a set of objects literally and undeniably have nothing in common except that they are called by the same name. If I choose to give the name "alpha" to each of a number of miscellaneous objects (the star Sirius, my fountain-pen, the Parthenon, the color red, the number five, and the letter Z) then I may well succeed in choosing the objects so *arbitrarily* that I shall succeed in preventing them from having any feature in common, other than that I call them by the name "alpha." But this imaginary case, to which the nominalist likens the use of all general words, has only to be described to be sharply contrasted with the typical case in which I apply a general word, say "chair", to a number of the instances to which it applies. In the first place, the *arbitrariness* of my selection of alphas is not paralleled in the case in which I apply the word "chair" successively to the chair in which I am now sitting, the Speaker's Chair in the House of Commons, the chair used at Bisley for carrying the winner of the Queen's Prize, and one of the deck chairs on the beach at Brighton. In giving a list of chairs I cannot just mention anything that happens to come into my head, while this is exactly what I do in giving my list of alphas. The second point is that the class of alphas is a *closed* class. Once I have given my list I have referred to every single alpha in the universe, actual and possible. Although I *might* have included or excluded any actual or possible object whatsoever when I was drawing up my list, once I have in fact made my arbitrary choice, no further application can be given to the word "alpha" according to the use that I have prescribed. For if I later add an object that I excluded from my list, or remove an object that I included in it, then I am making a different use of the word "alpha." With the word "chair" the position is quite different. There are an infinite number of actual and possible chairs. I cannot aspire to complete the enumeration of all chairs, as I can arbitrarily and at any point complete the enumeration of all alphas, and the word "chair", unlike the word "alpha", can be applied to an infinite number of instances without suffering any change of use.

These two points lead to a third and decisive point. I cannot teach the use of the word "alpha" except by specifically attaching it to each of the objects in my arbitrarily chosen list. No observer can conclude anything from watching me attach the label to this, that, or the other object, or to any number of objects however large, about the nature of the object or objects, if any, to which I shall later attach it. The use of the word "alpha" cannot be learned or taught as the use of a general word can be learned or taught. In teaching the use of a general word we may and must refer to characteristics of the objects to which it applies, and of the objects to which it does not apply, and indicate which of these characteristics count for the application of the word and which count against it. A pupil does not have to consult us on every separate occasion on which he encounters a new object, and if he did consult us every time we should have to say that he was not *learning* the use of the word. The reference that we make to a finite number of objects to which the word applies, and to a finite number of objects to which the word does not apply, is capable of equipping the pupil with a capacity for correctly applying or withholding the word to or from an infinite number of objects to which we have made no reference.

All this remains true in the case where it is not I alone, but a large number of people, or all of us, who use the word "alpha" in the way that I suggest. Even if everybody always called a particular set of objects by the same name, that would be insufficient to ensure that the name was a general name, and the claim of the name to be a general name would be defeated by just that necessity for reference to the arbitrary choices of the users of the name that the nominalist mistakenly claims to find in the case of a genuinely general name. For the nominalist is right in thinking that if we always had to make such a reference then there would be no general names as they are understood by the realist.

The nominalist is also right in the stress that he puts on the role of human interests and human purposes in determining our choice of principles of classification. How this insistence on the role of human purposes may be reconciled with the realist's proper insistence on the objectivity of the similarities and dissimilarities on which any genuine classification is based can be seen by considering an imaginary tribe of South Sea Islanders.

Let us suppose that trees are of great importance in the life and work of the South Sea Islanders, and that they have a rich and highly developed language in which they speak of the trees with which their island is thickly clad. But they do not have names for the species and genera of trees as they are recognized by our botanists. As we walk round the island with some of its inhabitants we can easily pick out orange-trees, date-palms and cedars. Our hosts are puzzled that we should call by the same name trees which appear to them to have nothing in common. They in turn surprise us by giving the same name to each of the trees in what is from our point of view a very mixed plantation. They point out to us what they called a mixed plantation, and we see that it is in our terms a clump of trees of the same species. Each party comes to recognize that its own classifications are as puzzling to the other as the other's are puzzling to itself.

This looks like the sort of situation that gives aid and comfort to the nominalist in his battle against the realist. But if we look at it more closely we see that it cannot help him. We know already that our own classification is based on similarities and differences between the trees, similarities and differences which we can point out to the islanders in an attempt to teach them our language. Of course we may fail, but if we do it will not be because we *must* fail.

Now *either* (a) The islanders have means of teaching us their classifications, by pointing out similarities and differences which we had not noticed, or in which we had not been interested, in which case *both* classifications are genuine, and no rivalry between them, of a kind that can help the nominalist, could ever arise;

or (b) Their classification is arbitrary in the sense in which my use of the word "alpha" was arbitrary, in which case it is not a genuine classification.

It may be that the islanders classify trees as "boat-building trees", "house-building trees", etc., and that they are more concerned with the height, thickness and maturity of the trees than they are with the distinctions of species that interest us.

In a particular case of *prima facie* conflict of classifications, we may not in fact be able to discover whether what appears to be a rival classification really *is* a classification. But we can be sure that *if* it is a classification *then* it is backed by objective similarities and differences, and that if it is *not* backed by objective similarities and differences then it is merely an arbitrary system of names. In no case will it appear that we must choose between rival systems of genuine classification of a set of objects in such a sense that one of them is to be recognized as *the* classification for all purposes.

There is no limit to the number of possible classifications of objects. (The nominalist is right about this.)[4]

There is no classification of any set of objects which is not objectively based on genuine similarities and differences. (The realist is right about this.)

The nominalist is so impressed by the infinite diversity of possible classifications that he is blinded to their objectivity.

The realist is so impressed by the objectivity of all genuine classifications that he underestimates their diversity.

Of course we may if we like say that there is one complete system of classification which marks all the similarities and all the differences. (This is the realist's summing up of what we can learn by giving critical attention to the realist and the nominalist in turn.)

Or we may say that there are only similarities and differences, from which we may choose according to our purposes and interests. (This is the nominalist's summing up.)

In talking of genuine or objective similarities and differences we must not forget that we are concerned with similarities and differences between *possible* cases as well as between actual cases, and indeed that we are concerned with the actual cases only because they are themselves a selection of the possible cases.

Because the nominalist and the realist are both right and both wrong, each is driven into the other's arms when he tries to be both consistent and faithful to our language, knowledge and experience. The nominalist talks of resemblances until he is pressed into a corner where he must acknowledge that resemblance is unintelligible except as resemblance *in a respect*, and to specify the respect in which objects resemble one another is to indicate a *quality* or *property*. The realist talks of properties and qualities until, when properties and qualities have been explained in terms of other properties and other qualities, he can at last do nothing but point to the *resemblances* between the objects that are said to be characterized by such and such a property or quality.

The question "Are resemblances ultimate or are properties ultimate?" is a perverse question if it is meant as one to which there must be a simple, *single* answer. They are both ultimate, or neither is ultimate. The craving for a single answer is the logically unsatisfiable craving for something that will be the ultimate terminus of explanation and will yet itself be explained.

NOTES

From the *Proceedings of the Aristotelian Society* 61 (1960–61). Reprinted by courtesy of the editor of the *Proceedings of the Aristotelian Society*.

1. I have profited from several discussions with Dr. S. M. Walters on taxonomy and the problem of universals. On the more general topics treated in this paper I have had several helpful discussions with Mr. R. A. Becher. Miss G. E. M. Anscombe kindly lent me the proofs of her essay on Aristotle, which is to appear in *Three Philosophers* by Miss Anscombe and Mr. P. T. Geach.
2. Of recent writings on this topic I believe that only Professor Wisdom's *Metaphysics and Verification* (reprinted in *Philosophy and Psycho-analysis*) and Mr. D. F. Pears' *Universals* (reprinted in Flew, *Logic and Language*, Second Series) show a complete understanding of the nature and importance of Wittgenstein's contribution.
3. Professor Wisdom has pointed out to me that further discussion would be necessary to show that claims of the form "This is Jack" are not exceptions to this rule.

4. Here one may think of Wittgenstein's remark that "Every application of every word is arbitrary," which emphasizes that we can always find *some* distinction between any pair of objects, however closely similar they may be. What might be called the principle of the diversity of discernibles guarantees that we can never be *forced* to apply the same word to two different things.

24 WOLTERSTORFF

Realists maintain that qualities refer to universals. Nominalists maintain that qualities refer to aspects of particulars. Wolterstorff argues that both offer equally plausible accounts of qualities. Central to Wolterstorff's argument is the notion of identity criteria, which are the circumstances under which one identifies X as the same "thing" as Y. In one set of circumstances one may be interested in the similarity of two or more particulars. Take, for example, the class of three things: one is red and soft, another is soft and round, and the third is round and red. Each member of the class is similar to the other without there being any one quality that they all have in common. Such similarity lends itself quite favorably to a nominalistic analysis.

However, there may be circumstances in which one is interested in the qualities themselves possessed by particulars, such as in matching paint samples on the basis of similarity. Here the identity criteria lend themselves particularly well to a realistic analysis of qualities where the particulars in possession of a common quality are most easily understood to be mere proxies for the instantiation of a universal.

The contrast between nominalism and realism is often drawn by saying that the former makes use of the relation of similarity holding between particulars, whereas the latter makes use of the notion of universals shared by particulars. And it is because both theories use the relation of resemblance that any vagueness which appears in the one theory as a result of vagueness in the notion of resemblance will make a parallel appearance in the other.

That the criteria for identity of particulars are no more clear than those for universals and neither theory is simpler than the other indicates to Wolterstorff that one is just as good as the other.

Qualities

1. Pointing is a kind of drawing attention to. Suppose, then, I point at the tail of a dog. How does this differ from pointing at a dog? That it does differ is clear. For if someone asks me, "Are you pointing at a dog?" I can say "No I am pointing at the tail of a dog." And if, pointing, I say, "This would not be so short, but it became gangrenous and we had to cut it off," I cannot be viewed as pointing at a dog. But then, how do these pointings differ? Someone might venture that, since pointing usually involves an aiming of the finger, perhaps one aims one's finger differently in the two cases. This will

not do at all, however, for it takes only a moment's reflection to see that the same aiming may be used either to point at a dog or to point at the tail of a dog. So knowing what someone is pointing at involves knowing more than the rule: when someone points, follow the aim of his finger in order to know what he is pointing at.

But what else does it involve? Well, suppose you point at a dog, and as the direct result of your pointing my attention is drawn to the dog's tail and not to the dog. In this case something has gone wrong; I failed to know what you were pointing at. And, it would seem, the cause of the failure was that my attention was not drawn to what you intended it to be drawn to. You intended to draw my attention to the dog, and instead it was drawn to the dog's tail. So pointing seems to be an intentional action, an intentional drawing attention to something; and knowing what you are pointing at involves knowing your intention. Hydras can and do aim their limbs in certain directions, and their aiming of limbs may well draw our attention to things, but they cannot point.

Yet this seems clearly wrong, for we do say that the weather vane is pointing to the west, and that the spinner is pointing to the 7. But how does the weather vane's pointing to the west differ from its pointing to the large oak? And how does the spinner's pointing to the 7 differ from its pointing to the red background? It seems to me it does not. We can say, indifferently, that the spinner points to the 7 or to the background, though gamblers seem by and large to be interested in the numbers and not in the colored backgrounds. But when a man points at a number he is not pointing at a colored background. So what we should have said above is that *one kind* of pointing involves a reference to intention, and that this is the kind which is relevant when we say that a man is pointing at the tail of the dog and not at the dog.

But how can *you* know what I intend to call your attention to? The simplest method is, of course, for me to accompany my pointing with the words "this dog" or "the tail of this dog." But such verbalization is not essential; indeed, it is clearly subsidiary. For we call attention to things not only *by means* of words, but *in order to teach* words; the words "dog" and "tail," for example, are customarily taught children by pointing. So imagine that these words are not available; how then can I let you know that I am pointing at the dog and not at his tail? The most straightforward way is probably to point again, this time aiming my finger at the dog's head and not at his tail. But just this is certainly not enough. For how are you to know that I am pointing twice at the same dog and not once at his tail and once at his head? The answer to this is simple enough: I accompany my second pointing with the words "This is the same as that," or words to this effect. Of course, I do not first point at the dog's tail and then at his head, and say "This is the same as that"; for a dog's tail is not the same as a dog's head. Rather I aim my finger first at the dog's tail, then at his head, and, by then affirming the identity of the object pointed at, I show it to be something bigger than and different from either the dog's tail or his head.[1] It is, in short, a dog. And to make my intention more and more unambiguous, I point more and more times at the dog, each time affirming the identity of the object pointed at.

So for you to know what I am pointing at, you must know the circumstances under which I would be willing to say that I am pointing at the same thing as that at which I pointed previously. I shall call this *knowing the identity criteria* for the thing pointed at. The utility of using terms like "dog" and "tail of a dog" to accompany our pointings may then be viewed as due to the fact that singular terms like these are, in a sense, ossified identity criteria. Telling you that I am pointing at a dog is a way of informing you of the circumstances under which I would be willing to say that I am pointing at the same thing as that at which I pointed previously.

Now I wish to suggest, as preliminary to what I shall argue in this paper, that the difference between qualities and particulars is to be explicated in essentially the same way in which I have explicated the difference between a dog and a tail of a dog. Suppose, for instance, that I point and say, "This is green." What then am I pointing at; that is, does "this" refer to a particular or to a quality? I suggest that it may be either, and that the way to find out is to determine the identity criteria of the entity referred to. Suppose I say, "This is green and that is green, only this is a tree and that is a carpet, so this is not identical with that"; here it is clear that I am pointing at two distinct particulars and not at one identical quality. But if I say "This is green" while pointing in the direction of a tree, and then, pointing in the direction of my carpet, say "And this is green, and this is identical with that," then I would be pointing at a quality. And so would a father who in teaching his child says, "Here's green, and here's green, and here's green again." (And incidentally, if we *do* say these things, it disposes of the traditional prejudice that qualities and universals cannot be pointed at.) But what I have shown does not quite prove what I have concluded; for how do I know that, when you are apparently pointing at a quality, you are not rather pointing at a larger and scattered particular? The difference lies, I suggest, in the *reason* that you give for asserting the identity. Though every case of pointing at a certain quality *might* also be viewed as pointing at a scattered particular, the difference lies in the *criteria* used for asserting identity.

Now what I wish to discuss in this paper are the identity criteria for qualities. And my fundamental thesis will be that there are two distinct interpretations of these criteria, each being perfectly intelligible and consistent in itself, but that our ordinary language about qualities gives us no ground for saying that either is the correct, or even preferable, interpretation. In the tradition one of these interpretations has been preferred by nominalists and the other by realists—meaning by "nominalist" one who holds that qualities are to be interpreted in terms of particulars and classes of particulars, or *quality-classes* as I shall call them; and meaning by "realist" one who holds that qualities are *universals*. Hence I can also put my thesis thus: the dispute between nominalists and realists is a pointless dispute, incapable of solution except by arbitrary fiat. But in spite of this it is not a meaningless dispute, for the position of each disputant can be given an intelligible and consistent, yet distinct, formulation.

2. For the issue which I wish to discuss a consideration of predicates is irrelevant. Indeed, if the case for the existence of qualities or universals rested on an analysis of such terms, I should regard it as a very shaky case. For to hold that, in "Socrates is wise," "Socrates" refers to a particular and "wise" to a universal, is certainly to confuse names with predicates.[2] And to hold that the repeated applicability of predicates like "red" can be explained only by saying that each of the entities to which it is applicable possesses redness, is to utter something uninformative at best and tautologous at worst.[3] But then I do *not* think that the case for the existence of qualities and universals rests on an analysis of such terms.

Rather the issue first joins, I think, when we consider expressions like "the color of his hat," "the wisdom of Socrates," and "the pitch of St. Mary's bell." Each of these is a description in which the word preceding the "of" ordinarily names or refers to a quality, and the word succeeding the "of" ordinarily names or refers to a particular. I shall henceforth call these *quality-descriptions*, without implying anything as to their analysis. Now the offhand inclination of the nominalist is to take these expressions as referring to aspects of particulars, to "abstract particulars" if you will, whereas the offhand inclination of the realist is to take them as referring to qualities. I shall eventually show that neither the realist nor the nominalist need stake his case on his ability or inability to follow out this original inclination; but it will be important first to consider who is right on this issue.

The realist would hold that, if the color of my coat is in fact green, then "the color of my coat" refers to the same entity as does "greenness." Is there anything in our use of quality-descriptions to show that this view is mistaken? One fact which seems to show its incorrectness is that we say such things as, "What *was* the color of your coat?" (when the coat is destroyed) and "What *was* the pitch of St. Mary's bell?" (when the bell is broken). The use of the past tense here would seem to indicate that we are referring to something which was destroyed when the coat or the bell was destroyed; and what could this be but a certain aspect of the coat or the bell? For colors are not destroyed by burning coats, nor pitches by breaking bells. But this argument is inconclusive. For one might also say, while pointing in the direction of a color sample, "This *is* the color that my coat *was*," and while playing a note on the piano, "This *is* the pitch that St. Mary's bell *had*." And this seems to indicate that tenses here are determined by the fact that the coat which formerly possessed the indicated color no longer exists, rather than by the fact that the color of the coat is an aspect of the coat which is destroyed along with the destruction of the coat. And second, we some-times even tense the verb in statements which refer unambiguously to qualities. We would not say, of course, that "green *was* a color"; but we might say, "What *was* the pitch you just gave?" and "The cloying sweetness you smelled *was* insect repellant."

But there is another class of cases which conclusively shows that the realist cannot be wholly right. For suppose a painter friend of mine comes to me one day and says, "I want you to see the wonderful green on my latest canvas." So I pull a color chart from my pocket and ask him to point to the color he has in mind. He may then point to one and say, "This is it." But he may also summarily wave the chart aside and say, "No, that won't do, you'll have to see my canvas in order to see what I'm referring to." In this latter case "the green on my canvas" is used to refer not to a certain color but to a particular qualitative aspect of my friend's canvas; for the friend might admit that the color of my sample was just like that on his canvas, but still deny that they are identical, since after all his canvas is not in the same place as my sample. Thus it is clear that quality-descriptions are not always used to refer to qualities.

So is the nominalist then right, or are there also cases in which quality-descriptions *must* be viewed as referring to qualities and not to aspects? The sort of case one naturally thinks of here is "The color of this hat is the same as the color of this blotter"; and "The pitch of this chorale is the same as the pitch of St. Mary's bell." In these cases it seems that we are asserting the existence of a quality shared by two different particulars. But these examples raise a new issue which is central to the whole debate over universals. For "the same" is an ambiguous expression, meaning either "identical" or "similar." Thus if two children have the same father, they have the identical father and not two similar ones, and if two college boys wear the same tuxedo so that they cannot go to dances together they wear the identical tuxedo.[4] But on the other hand, though every soldier wears the same uniform, all soldiers can appear on parade clothed. The difference between these two senses of "the same" is also clear from our use of qualifying adverbs. One speaks of two things as being almost the same, or nearly the same, or not at all the same. And here we clearly mean "similar," for identity does not hold in degrees.

Now with this distinction in hand the nominalist can easily show that statements like "The color of his coat is the same as the color of this blotter" do not refute his position. For "is the same as" can here be construed to mean "is exactly or closely similar to"; hence the statement does not say that this quality is identical with that but that this aspect is similar to that. The realist obviously has a way of blocking this answer, however; for one might also say, "The color of this blotter is *identical* with the color of his coat." And though this is a rather stiff way of speaking, and though the nominalist may wish to hold that, in some sense, no information is conveyed by this sentence which is not conveyed by "The color of this blotter is exactly similar to the color or his coat," yet the two sentences are not synonymous.

There is also another class of statements which gives the nominalist trouble. Examples are, "This is the color of his coat," said while pointing in the direction of a blotter; "This is the pitch of *Nun ist das Heil*," said while playing a note on the piano; and "You too can have the wisdom of Socrates," proclaimed by an encyclopedia advertisement. Here we seem unambiguously to be asserting that one quality is shared by two distinct particulars; and the nominalist cannot now escape by distinguishing senses of "the same." Of course, on the analogy of "He has his father's hands," he might attempt to reformulate these and say that "This is the color of his coat" *really* means "This is exactly similar to the color of his coat." But I see no defense that could be given for such a reformulation.

In summary, then, quality-descriptions may be used to refer either to aspects or to qualities; and in ordinary speech we usually do not make it clear how we are using them. The reference can, however, be made clear by asking for the circumstances under which the speaker would be willing to say that he was referring or pointing again to the same entity, with "the same" understood now as meaning "identical" and not "similar." Having done this, it turns out that neither the realist's inclination to regard these expressions as referring to qualities, nor the nominalist's inclination to regard them as referring to aspects, can be wholly correct. This, however, need give the realist no anxiety, since all he has to show is that, whatever else there be, there are universals. The nominalist, however, contends that there are *only* particulars and classes of particulars; so unless he can find a nominalistic interpretation of these references to qualities, an analysis of quality-descriptions will show already that nominalism is not a possible view.

But before considering the two alternative analyses of qualities, I think it worth remarking that a good many confusions in the history of philosophy have been caused by a failure to see that quality-descriptions may refer either to particulars or universals. For example, I think this failure is responsible for the extreme ambivalence in all classical modern philosophy on whether we really perceive only particulars or only universals. And it is clearly responsible for the views of G. F. Stout[5] and D. C. Williams,[6] and for G. E. Moore's total failure to understand Stout.[7] Stout says, for instance, that "of two billiard balls, each has its own particular roundness separate and distinct from that of the other, just as the billiard balls themselves are distinct and separate. As Jones is separate and distinct from Robinson, so the particular happiness of Jones is separate and distinct from that of Robinson." Of course, Stout is wrong in holding that "the roundness of this ball" can refer *only* to a particular; but Moore is equally wrong in holding that it can refer *only* to a universal.

3. In addition to quality-descriptions referring to qualities, the terms we must now consider are ones like "greenness," "circularity," and "stickiness." I shall give these the traditional name of *abstract singular terms*. And what I wish to see is whether, at this stage, either realism or nominalism can be shown to be mistaken.

In analyzing abstract singular terms, the nominalist seems in general to have two courses open: he can say that all statements using such terms can be translated into synonymous statements whose singular terms refer only to concrete particulars; or, failing this, he can say that abstract singular terms refer not to universals but to certain classes of particulars, quality-classes.

According to the first suggestion, a statement like "Greenness is a color" is to be paraphrased as "For every entity, if it is green, then it is colored." Now is this paraphrase really synonymous with the original? It is not, I think. For the analysis assumes that "is a color" is synonymous with "is colored." But this is surely false, if for no other reason than that the ranges of meaningful application of these two terms are different. Green is a color but is not colored; and a blotter is colored but is not a color. There are also other flaws in the paraphrase; for certainly the connection between being green and being a color is in some sense a necessary connection, as well as being in some sense a relation of subsumption. But neither of these features is brought out by the proposed analysis. Thus the only plausible interpretation of nominalism seems to be that which regards hues, pitches, virtues, and so forth as classes of particulars.

Now the strongest objections to the class theory are based on the belief that the classes which nominalism proposes to identify with qualities cannot actually be defined. I think, however, that they can be; and so I shall take it as my main task to show that this objection is invalid.

Classes, according to the usual conception, are identical if and only if they have the same members. Hence the first thing we must do is decide when quality-classes do and when they do not have the same members; and for this we shall first have to know what criterion is used in determining the membership of such classes. Well, what criterion *do* we use? Suppose I come into a paint store with a sample of the color of my living room wall, and ask for some paint of the same (identical) color. How do I go about deciding whether the color of the paint handed to me is or is not identical with that on my wall? The answer seems clear: I bring a sample of the paint and a sample of the wall-color close together, and if they resemble each other I say they have the same (identical) color. Similarly, to find out whether St. Mary's bell has a pitch identical with that of St. Thomas' bell, I listen carefully to a peal from each and compare. In short, similarity is the criterion for membership in quality-classes; and our chief task is therefore this: given particulars and the relation of similarity holding among pairs of particulars, how can qualities be defined as certain kinds of classes?

But before describing what sort of class a quality actually is, we must deal with several complexities in the ordinary concept of similarity. In ordinary language things are not merely similar but are more or less similar, and, to make the situation worse, they are more or less similar in two quite different ways. For by saying that x is more similar to y than to z I may mean either that x is similar to y in more respects than it is to z, or that, whatever the respect in which they are similar, x is more closely similar to y in that respect than to z. For example, a nickel resembles a dime in both color and shape, while resembling a penny only in shape; and the color of a dime is more like that of a quarter than like that of a nickel. Now both the fact that things are similar in different respects, and the fact that things are similar in varying intensities, give trouble to the nominalist.

Consider first the difficulties arising from the varying intensities of similarity. The problem is just this: what degree of similarity is necessary for identity of qualities? That it is less than exact similarity seems to be implied by the fact that green things are by no means all exactly similar in color. Sage, lakes, blotters, grass, lamps, flower pots, bruises—all are green, but all are not exactly similar in color. On the other hand, if I ask for paint of the same color as that already on my wall, I would not be satisfied with just a green, or even an olive-green. And if a psychologist tells me to adjust a second light until it has the same brightness as the first, he clearly means *exactly* the same. Indeed, it always makes sense to say of qualities that they are almost the same but still not identical. So it is not clear what degree of similarity is necessary for identity of qualities. I am inclined to think, however, that it is exact similarity, and that the difference in shades of green can be given another explanation. But whether I am right or wrong on this point will make no difference. For I shall show later that precisely the same difficulties arise for the realist; and hence the difficulties arising from varying intensities of similarity cannot be used as a ground for preferring realism. I shall, in what I say further, mean by "similarity" always exact similarity; but this will in no way prejudge my central thesis.

The difficulties arising from the fact that things are similar in various respects are more troublesome. A quality-class would seem, quite clearly, to be a class of all and only those things which are similar in a certain respect. Or, to put it more precisely, a quality-class is a class which fulfills these two requirements: (i) of the members of the class, each is similar to every other; (ii) no thing outside the class is similar to every member of the class. But it would seem that, unless we introduce more conditions, this definition by no means yields only those classes which can plausibly be identified with qualities.

One of the difficulties which arises is called by Goodman the difficulty of imperfect community.[8] Suppose the universe included a class of things of the following description: one is green and hard, another is hard and square, and a third is square and green—symbolized as *gh*, *hs*, and *sg*. Now this class fulfills our requirements for a quality-class, since each member is similar to every other, and we are to suppose that there is nothing outside the class which is similar to every member of the class. Yet there is no quality common to the three members, and consequently the class cannot be identified with a quality. A second difficulty Goodman calls the companionship difficulty. Suppose that everything green is sticky, and everything sticky is green. In this case the class of green entities would be identical with the class of sticky entities. But then the qualities greenness and stickiness cannot be identified with this class; for greenness is not identical with stickiness.

Now it would seem that, to prevent these difficulties, we must somehow get at the inside of particulars and distinguish the different respects in which they resemble each other. Thus we might try taking similarity as a triadic relation, saying always that x is similar to y in respect to z, and then defining a quality-class as a class of particulars similar to each other in only one respect, and that the same respect throughout. But this would be to give up the game immediately. For suppose we do regard similarity as a triadic relation, always saying, for instance, that the blotter is similar to the coat in respect to its color. What then does "color" refer to? A class of particulars? If so, we have precisely the same difficulty that we were trying to escape. So apparently it refers to a universal, with the usage of "the same respect" determined according to the criteria recommended by the realist. But this was just what the nominalist wanted to avoid. Thus, since respects in this context are universals, the nominalist can make no use of them.

But there *is* a way of avoiding the difficulties of companionship and imperfect community, and this is just to keep in mind that the class of particulars includes not only concrete physical objects and events but also what I have called the aspects of these. The color of the Taj Mahal (on one interpretation of this phrase), as well as the Taj Mahal, is a particular; and a color patch as well as a tree is an instance of greenness. Furthermore, there are aspects of aspects, for instance, the hue of the color of the Taj Mahal. We are, then, to remember that the relation of similarity holds among aspects as well as among concrete particulars.

Now no doubt an apprehension will arise over using qualitative aspects of things in order to define qualities. I do not think, however, that such a procedure is circular. For I may very well recognize the shape of Eisenhower's face without having an independent recognition of that shape itself—without knowing what kind of shape it is, without being able to say in what way this shape differs from other shapes, without being able to sketch it, and so forth.

The inclusion of aspects in our quality-classes immediately eliminates the companionship difficulty. This arose, it will be remembered, whenever we had a class of things of this schematic form: gs, gs, gs. But now we also have the two particulars g and s. According to our rules then, gs, gs, gs, g will form one quality-class; and gs, gs, gs, s will form another. The two classes have different memberships, and are therefore not identical, because s and g do not resemble each other. The difficulty of imperfect community is likewise solved. Our example illustrating this was, schematically, gh, hs, sg. We are now directed to allow also the three aspects g, h, and s. This gives us the three classes gh, sg, g; gh, hs, h; and hs, sg, s; and the difficulty is resolved.

In summary then, a quality, according to a nominalist, is a class of all and only those particulars which bear a certain resemblance to each other. Hence qualities A and B are identical if and only if they have the same instances (members); and we determine whether they do or do not have the same instances by observing the relations of similarity and dissimilarity among the instances.

4. Now the realist regards all this as wrong, and insists that qualities are not classes of particulars but are instead universals. Such classes may, in some way, be associated with qualities, but they are not to be identified with them.

What then does the realist propose as the identity criterion for qualities? Consider again the example of my coming into the paint store and asking for some paint of the same color as that on my wall. How *do* I decide whether the color of the paint is identical with the color of my wall? Obviously what I do is compare the colors. And if I find that they resemble each other exactly, I say that this color is identical with that. Similarly, to find out whether the pitch of St. Mary's bell is identical with the pitch of St. Paul's, I listen carefully to see whether I can discern any difference in pitch. And to find out whether the flavor of this cheap Scotch is really identical with the flavor of this expensive Scotch, I taste each carefully and compare the flavors. Thus the relation of similarity constitutes the identity criterion for universals.

The contrast between nominalism and realism is often drawn by saying that the former makes use of the relation of similarity holding between particulars, whereas the latter makes use of the notion of universals shared by particulars.[9] But it can now be seen that this contrast between resemblance-theorists and universals-theorists is improperly drawn. Both theories make use of the relation of resemblance, the only difference being that they use it in different ways. The nominalist uses resemblance as the criterion for membership in quality-classes, whereas the realist uses resemblance as the criterion for identity of universals. And it is because both theories use the relation of resemblance that any vagueness which appears in the one theory as a result of vagueness in the notion of resemblance will make a parallel appearance in the other.

Now the usual objections to the realistic interpretation of qualities are made, not on the ground that it involves a program impossible of being carried out, but rather on the ground that it involves a commitment to queer and weird entities, things best shunned. This seems to me a baseless prejudice, and I shall concentrate my attention on showing why the objection is not applicable.

There is, for instance, a long and by no means dead tradition to the effect
that only particulars can be perceived, that universals may be objects of
reason but not of perception. But this is certainly mistaken. For we can play
a pitch on a violin, relish a sweetness on our tongues, feel annoyed by an
acridity, and watch admiringly an old man's tenacity. The usual doctrine is
that we can play sounds but not pitches, taste stuffs but not sweetness, be
annoyed by smells but not by acridity, and observe an old man but not
tenacity. But once we see that the reference of terms and of pointings is fixed
by the identity criteria of the entity referred to, and once we see that there
are identity criteria for universals as well as for particulars, there seems no
reason at all to defend the dictum that only instances of universals can be
perceived but not universals themselves. Psychologists, in speaking of
brightness and loudness scales, have had the correct intuition.

Immediately associated with the view just considered is the belief, present
in Western philosophy almost since its inception, that universals are indifferent to the buzz of space and time, composing a still and immutable world of
their own. But this is equally mistaken; for if we can point to and perceive
universals, then universals *must* be locatable. The basis of the traditional
doctrine is, I suppose, a vague intuition of the fact that places and times play
no role in determining the identity of universals. But of course it does not
follow from this that universals are outside of space and time. Greenness
does appear at certain times and places; the father in teaching his child says,
"Here's green, and here's green, and here's green again." And though we
would probably never ask, "Where is green?" men have asked "Where is
virtue to be found?" and conductors have no doubt inquired "Where is that
F-sharp coming from?"

So the usual dread of admitting the existence of universals is quite
unfounded. They are quite as humdrum and quite as circumambient as
particulars, differing just in the fact that the criteria for saying "This is the
same universal as that" are different from those for saying "This is the same
physical object as that."

5. We have seen, then, that both realism and nominalism can be given
consistent and plausible interpretations. According to the nominalist, similarity is a relation holding among particulars, and we use it as the criterion
for membership in quality-classes. According to the realist, similarity is a
relation holding among qualities as well, and we use it as the criterion for the
identity of universals. Which theory, then, is correct? What statements do
we make about qualities which show that the one interpretation is right and
the other wrong?

(i) We might consider, first, the statements which gave the nominalist
trouble previously—for example, "The color of this table is identical with
the color of that table." Now the realist interprets this to mean that there is
here one entity, a universal, shared by two particulars; and he holds that we
establish the identity of this entity by comparing the color of this table with

the color of that. And this is certainly a plausible interpretation. Unfortunately, however, the nominalist's interpretation is equally plausible. For he interprets the sentence to mean that there is here one entity, a class, of which these two particulars are members; and he holds that we establish the fact that they are members of the same class by comparing the two tables. So this sort of statement—statements asserting an identity of qualities—can be handled easily by both theories.

(ii) But there is another kind of statement which, prima facie at least, offers more promise. According to the nominalist, similarity holds only among particulars. Apparently all we need do then to refute nominalism is find statements asserting similarity among qualities. And such are immediately at hand; for instance, "Yellow is more like orange than like purple." But will this really turn the trick; is it impossible to give a nominalistic interpretation of this sentence? One paraphrase which the nominalist might suggest is this: take anything yellow, anything orange, and anything purple; then the yellow thing is more like the orange thing than like the purple thing. But there is no assurance that this statement is even true; for though, *in respect to color*, yellow things are more like orange things than like purple things, this may well not be true in general. The way around this objection, however, is just to make the paraphrase refer to aspects and not to concrete things, thus: for anything yellow and anything orange and anything purple, the color of the yellow thing is more similar to the color of the orange thing than to the color of the purple thing. And though this is by no means as straightforward an interpretation of our original statement as that which the realist can give, there seems to be no consideration which would show it to be actually mistaken.

So apparently there is no way of showing either theory to be incorrect. But it might still be felt that there are grounds for *preferring* one theory to the other. So let us consider various suggestions to this effect.

(i) Is there any way, for instance, of showing the one theory to be simpler than the other? I think not. For the realist assumes the existence of universals, whereas the nominalist assumes the existence of quality-classes. Consequently on this level they are precisely comparable. Furthermore, the definition of quality-classes does not seem to me significantly more or less complicated than that of universals. So the test of simplicity yields inconclusive results.

(ii) It has sometimes been argued that the criteria for the identity of classes are clearer than those for universals; and if this were true, it would certainly be a reason for preferring nominalism. But whether or not universals are in *general* vaguer entities than classes (and I suppose they are), they are certainly no more vague than quality-classes. For as we have already seen, both the realist and the nominalist make use of the notion of similarity; consequently any vagueness in the one theory will find its parallel in the other. So the criterion of clarity also gives no ground for preference.

6. My conclusion to this whole discussion, therefore, is that there is no ground whatever for preferring either realism or nominalism. Now in such a situation, the intuitive response of the contemporary philosopher is to suspect that the dispute is meaningless. But it is clear that this is not the case. For if the color of two tables is indistinguishable, the realist says the color of the one is *therefore* identical with the color of the other, whereas the nominalist says they are exactly similar and *therefore* belong to the same quality-class. But "is similar to" is not synonymous with "is identical with"; and regarding entities as identical if and only if they have the same members is not the same as regarding entities as identical if and only if they are exactly similar. Hence we find that we have here the anomalous situation of a meaningful but pointless dispute.

To see more clearly the source of this anomaly, consider a hypothetical case in which the distinction between similarity and identity cannot, as a matter of fact, be drawn. Suppose, for instance, that identity of persons were determined by identity of memories; and imagine that I find a person with memories the same as mine in all respects. Are his memories then identical with mine, or are they merely exactly similar? I think it is easily seen that such a question cannot be answered. The distinction between the two senses of "the same" is here inoperative; for there is no defense which one could give of the contention that they are similar but not identical, but there is also no defense which one could give of the contention that they are not only similar but identical. The distinction between qualitative and numerical sameness is vacuous.

But the situation with respect to qualities is not quite like this, for the nominalist *can* point to something which will distinguish similarity from identity, namely, difference of place; and his contention is that, though x and y may be qualitatively similar, this does not prove that they are identical. So the issue here is not whether similarity *can* be distinguished from identity, but whether difference of place shall establish nonidentity. Now in the case of physical objects it does; all 1959 Fords may be qualitatively alike, but they are not identical. And if this were the only permissible criterion for the identity of entities, realism would be an impossible view; indeed, one could not even distinguish between the meaning and the criteria of identity. But suppose on the other hand that all our singular terms referred to universals. In this case nominalism would be an impossible view, and again there would be no way of distinguishing between the meaning and the criteria of identity. As a matter of fact, however, identity *can* be determined according to different criteria; and so the issue is joined. But it cannot be settled. For though the nominalist may insist on diversity of places as implying nonidentity, he can give no justification for his insistence; and though the realist may insist that nonidentity of places does not always determine nonidentity of entities, he too can give no reason for his insistence.

The debate is thus clear enough, and it may seem surprising that our language fails to reflect it. Still, it may *not* be so surprising. For in the first place, both theories regard similarity as, directly or indirectly, determining the identity of qualities. And secondly, in our existing language the reference of quality-descriptions is ambiguous, and it is this ambiguity which is fundamental to the whole issue. For though there are indeed some cases in which quality-descriptions cannot be interpreted as referring to particulars, we saw that the nominalist can, by using the notion of classes, still interpret them as referring *in a roundabout way* to particulars. Hence we end where we began.

Whatever be the reasons, though, it is clear that, given our actual language, there is no point in distinguishing senses of "this is the same as that" when dealing with qualities. For whatever our theory, we would all agree that a person knew what colors were if, upon being asked to bring something of the same color as the green thing I have, he always brought something green.[10]

NOTES

From *Philosophical Review* 69 (1960). Reprinted by permission of the author and the editor of *Philosophical Review*.

1. Cf. W. V. Quine, "Identity, Ostension, and Hypostasis," in *From a Logical Point of View* (Cambridge, Mass., 1953), pp. 65–79.
2. Cf. M. Lazerowitz, "The Existence of Universals," *Mind*, LV (1946), 1–24.
3. Cf. D. F. Pears, "Universals" in *Logic and Language*, II, ed. by A. Flew (Oxford, 1955), pp. 51–64.
4. This example is from D. C. Williams, "On the Elements of Being," *The Review of Metaphysics*, VII (1953), 6.
5. "The Nature of Universals and Propositions," Hertz Lecture, *Proceedings of the British Academy*, X (1921–1923), 157–172.
6. [D. C. Williams, "On the Elements of Being."]
7. "Are the Characteristics of Particular Things Universal or Particular?" symposium in *Proceedings of the Aristotelian Society*, Supp. vol. III (1923), 95–113.
8. N. Goodman, *The Structure of Appearance* (Cambridge, Mass., 1951), pp. 124 ff.
9. Cf. H. H. Price, *Thinking and Experience* (London, 1953), ch. I.
10. I have profited a great deal in writing this paper from conversations with Mr. Noel Fleming.

25 ALLAIRE

Allaire's goal is to demonstrate that the nominalist position is mistaken. Quite simply, the nominalist maintains that while red things exist, red does not exist. This view results from a prior commitment to the ontological proposition "What exists is independent." With this view, in conjunction with the claim that "Characters (i.e., qualities) are dependent," the nominalist is able to conclude that "Characters do not exist." However, the term "independent" is ambiguous. Both the realist and nominalist admit that there are independent entities, for whether or not characters are dependent, the subjects that exemplify the characters are understood by both parties to be independent of one another.

The Platonist denies the claim that (1) "Neither individuals nor characters are *independent* of each other," thereby committing himself to the independent existence of characters. Allaire views the nominalist as primarily motivated by a fear of Platonic realism. Nevertheless, one can remain a realist, although not of the Platonic variety, and consistently maintain the mutual dependence of individuals and characters in which universals are presented to us "through" or "by means of" individuals. Consequently, two individuals can, and most reasonably do, exemplify the *same* character, which therefore must give characters a different ontological status than individuals.

However, the nominalist, as a result of his Platonic paranoia and his confusion over the different senses of "independent," bypasses (1) in favor of (2), namely, "An individual is *independent* whereas a character is *dependent*." In this claim he tries to have it both ways. On the one hand, he wants a character to be identified with the individual that possesses the character and that exists independently of any other individual possessing the same character. The consequence of this is that two individuals cannot possess the same character. On the other hand, the nominalist is aware that in some sense the same character is revealed by the presence of, for example, two red individuals. The nominalist could overcome this difficulty by realizing that the acceptance of (1) does not commit him to Platonic realism, and that the more moderate approach to universals implied by (1) actually and more accurately reflects his views of universals.

Existence, Independence, and Universals

Consider a visual field which contains two red spots (of the same shade). At least two sentences are true of it: (a) "This is red" and (b) "That is red."

294

One question which ontologists frequently ask themselves, when considering such sentences and what they refer to, is: What is the meaning of "is" in
(a) and (b)? How one answers this question determines in large measure
whether one is a nominalist or a realist.

The realist claims that the "is" in both sentences is the predicative is.
Accordingly, his analysis runs as follows. Each spot is a fact which consists
of an individual and a character standing in the exemplification relation. The
individuals are referred to by "this" and "that," respectively; the charac-
ter(s) by "red." Thus, the individuals are different; the character(s) the same.
Upon the realist's analysis, therefore, there are in this situation three
existents. Or, to say the same thing differently, diversity and non-diversity
are primary. This, in fact, is one of the basic considerations which guide his
analysis. For to him it is obvious that the spots are, as one says, numerically
different—that is, two—and are yet in one respect the same.

The nominalist is less explicit regarding the meaning of "is." Implicitly,
though, he assimilates it to the "is" of identity. Upon the nominalist's
analysis there are but two existents, the two red spots. Thus he maintains
that "this" and "that" name the two existents *properly*, whereas "red"
names them *commonly* or indifferently. However, even though "this" and
"red" both name the same existent, the meaning of "is" in this case cannot
be that of non-diversity, that is, literal sameness. For, if it were, there would
be only one spot and not, as there are in fact, two—a fact which no
ontologist can afford to lose sight of. It follows that if the nominalist wishes
to maintain that there are only two existents, he must also maintain that they
are both complex. Or, to say the same thing as it was said above, the
nominalist like the realist must maintain that diversity and non-diversity are
primary. That the nominalist does maintain this is implicit in his admission
that the application of "red" to the *two* spots is not arbitrary but somehow
grounded in the fact that they are both red and not, say, one red, one green.
This means that the sameness (qualitative) as well as the difference (numerical) of the two spots is grounded in the spots. Now four comments.

1. In both analyses the existents are named. Nominalist and realist both
implicitly accept the following proposition. (N) *What is named exists.*
According to the realist, however, "this" and "red" name different things,
namely, an individual and a character, respectively. According to the nominalist, "this" and "red" both name the same thing, namely, a red spot. (So
do "that" and "red.") This is as it should be. For the realist accepts the
existence of characters (universals); the nominalist does not. According to
the latter, red does not exist; only red things do.

2. The realist accepts another ontological proposition which the nominalist does not. (S) *What exists is simple.* The full dialectics of this notion is
extremely subtle.[1] It is, in fact, at the core of much current criticism of
logical atomism. However that may be and however many strands the
notion of simplicity may contain, in one clear and significant sense the

nominalist is willing to accept a complex entity—namely, our red spot—as one existent. Thus he must at least implicitly reject (S).

3. (S) and (N) jointly yield another proposition. (SN) *What is named is simple*. The realist accepts (SN). The nominalist must reject it; for, though he takes "red" to be a name, what it refers to is in at least two senses not simple. Like "this" and "that," "red" refers to something complex. This is the first sense. Unlike "this" and "that," "red" refers to two existents. This is the second sense. In contrast, the realist asserts that "red" refers to one and only one existent, the character red, which, like all characters, can be exemplified by several individuals. So, too, with "this" and "that." Each refers to one and only one individual.

4. According to the realist the "is" in both (a) and (b) is the predicative is. The meaning the nominalist assigns to it has not yet been clarified, except negatively. We saw that it could be neither the predicative is nor that of identity. Positively, the meaning that may plausibly be assigned to it is "part-whole." That is, (a) may be rephrased as "Red is a part of this." In other words, (a) may be analyzed by saying that "this" refers to a whole of which red is a part, "red" referring to the part. A nominalist who accepts (N) cannot, however, propound this analysis. For it would be tantamount to saying that universals exist. Our nominalist may, therefore, try to discard (N), replacing it by (N'). (N') *What exists is what is properly named* (named, that is, by a proper and not a common name). Then he could accept the suggested analysis (part-whole). This analysis has indeed the merit of at least rendering intelligible the meaning of "is" in (a) and (b), a merit which the more traditional common-name doctrine lacks. It also fits more closely the over-all nominalistic pattern. For the nominalist wishes to maintain that only individuals exist. (N') is a convenient explication of this claim. It must not be overlooked, however, that upon this gambit, as upon the other, the nominalist's individuals are radically different from the realist's. The realist's are simple, the nominalist's complex, consisting of both the realist's individuals and characters.

These four comments show what the basic difference between nominalist and realist implies. More importantly, they are meant to show that the nominalist's attitude toward (S), (N), and (SN) is not determined by a claim concerning the constitution of the spot that differs significantly from the realist's. For in both analyses diversity and non-diversity are primary and there obtains in both a (logical) relation between the two constituents of each spot. The nominalist's reluctance to admit the existence of universals must, therefore, not be ascribed to his attitude toward (S), (N), and (SN). Rather, it is the other way around. His nominalism determines his attitude toward (S), (N), and (SN). If this is so, as I believe I have shown, then one must ask oneself: What is the cause of the nominalist's reluctance to acknowledge that universals exist? That is, why does he insist that only the complex entity (the spot) exists while its constituents do not? Historically speaking, his insistence or, if you please, his position echoes the classical doctrine of hylomorphism. If made explicit, this position is unobjectionable as a choice of terminology. We continue our probe, however: What are the (terminological) consequences the nominalist tries to avoid by insisting that universals do not exist?

One of the deepest roots of nominalism, the one which I hope to unearth, emerges in the nominalist's claim that, while red things exist, red does not. Few would deny what underlies this claim. One is never acquainted with red alone but always with something that exemplifies red. This is the common-sense core of nominalism. The question is: Is this core incompatible with the claim that universals exist? The nominalist apparently believes that it is. I now hope to show that his belief is mistaken.

The heart of the matter is the notion of independence. The nominalist is implicitly guided by still another ontological proposition. (I) *What exists is independent.* Unhappily, the nominalist fails to distinguish the several meanings of "independent." That is why he is misled by spurious arguments of the following sort. "What exists is independent. Characters are dependent. Hence, characters do not exist." This is a crude paradigm of his confusion. I call him confused because "independent" does not mean the same thing in the two premises of the spurious argument.

Four uses of "independent" are relevant. They occur in the following sentences. (I1) There are *independent* entities. (I2) An individual is *independent* whereas a character is *dependent*. (I3) Neither individuals nor characters are *independent* of each other. (I4) Atomic facts are *independent* of each other. Each sentence is the crux of a philosophical controversy. The atomist-holist controversy centers on (I1).[2] (I4) is the focal point of the synthetic-a priori issue.[3] Both (I2) and (I3) are central to the arguments concerning the ontological status of characters and individuals.[4]

Every atomist (pluralist) accepts (I1), asserting it in the teeth of the holist's (monist's) claim that only the Absolute is real. The issue is whether or not there is more than one "independent entity." To recover this meaning of "independent" it will be profitable to consider the following proposition. (P) *A thing is what it is independently of all the characters it exemplifies and of all the relations in which it stands.* Not surprisingly, (P) is at the heart of the "internal relations" struggle. That struggle, however, does not concern us directly. The point is that either explicitly or implicitly (P) is frequently embraced by philosophers who wish to maintain, say, that a physical object is "more than" the "class" of its properties (and relations). That is, one holds (P) in order to be able to deny that a physical object can be "defined" in terms of its properties (and relations). There must be something in which those properties (and relations) inhere. Furthermore, that in which they inhere "is what it is" regardless of what in fact inheres in it. Consider the sentences "Socrates is white" and "Socrates is red." Assuming that "Socrates" refers to what properties inhere in, it follows from (P) that both sentences are about the same thing and that no matter which of the two is true Socrates is not altered, that is, not different. Only the facts would differ. Or, to say the same thing differently, to accept (P) is to maintain that the "meaning" of "Socrates" remains the same regardless of what true (or false) sentences "Socrates" occurs in.

(P), however, does not assert that Socrates, in order "to be what he is independently," must not have any properties (or relations). Nor does it even suggest that Socrates may ever be without properties. That is not the point. The point is, rather, that no matter what properties a thing may have, its "essence" is not changed, though, to be sure, the fact may be. Another way of expressing this meaning of "independent" is to say that there is no logical connection whatsoever between knowing what the word "Socrates" refers to and knowing in which sentences (true or false) it occurs.[5]

In its broadest sense (P) does not apply only to what are usually called individuals or substances. An extreme Hegelian, for example, who like all Hegelians must reject (P), is yet willing to allow "thing" to refer not only to individuals but also to characters and whatever else there may be. For one who denies (P) thus broadly interpreted, "individuation involves negation." Again, this is individuation in the broad sense, which includes distinguishing an individual from its characters as well as two characters from each other. To know green, according to the extreme Hegelian, one must therefore know everything that green is not. Or, to put it a bit captiously, to really know anything one must know everything. That something is wrong here, that indeed "language has gone on holiday," many will allow. What exactly is wrong is another story, one which need not detain us. The following suggestion, however, is relevant to the meaning "independent" has in (I1). One mistake which, according to some atomists,[6] the Hegelians make is their failure to distinguish between knowing what a word refers to (in one sense of "meaning") and knowing true sentences in which it occurs (another sense of "meaning"). If these senses of "meaning" are not distinguished, then the claim of the Hegelians that to know (the meaning of) anything one must know (the meaning of) everything can easily lead to the absurdity that to know, say, the difference between red and green one must know everything. In this connection the following passage from the Tractatus is worth examining.

> 2.0122   The thing is independent, in so far as it can occur in all *possible* circumstances, but this form of independence is a form of connexion. (It is impossible for words to occur in two different ways, alone and in the proposition.)

Here we encounter an explicit use of "independent" in the sense of (I1).[7] Wittgenstein's point, I submit, is that what is meant by the "independence of the thing" can be clarified by saying that its name can occur in any sentence provided only that the "type rule" is observed. This rule, however, is held to be purely syntactical. That is, the formation rules of the language depend on the shapes of the sign and not on what they refer to.[8]

Let me restate the main features of the first meaning of "independent." First, to say that an individual or a character is *independent* is to say that the word referring to it can occur in any sentence provided only that the syntactical rules are observed. Second, a thing is *independent* in the sense that there is no logical connection between what the thing is and in what facts it occurs. Or, to put the matter linguistically, there is no logical connection between the referent or meaning of a word, in one sense of "meaning," and true or false sentences in which it occurs. Third, the *independence* of a thing is expressed by saying that the word which refers to it is a "mere label" (a name) and that the formation rules on which its place in sentences depends are syntactical, not semantical. Fourth, the thing's *independence* can also be expressed by saying that what a word refers to (its meaning in one sense of "meaning") is not altered by its occurrence in sentences which were not previously known to be true.

(I1) is, of course, intimately connected with (S). The logical atomists all embraced (S). Naturally, they all believed that there were "independent entities" in sense (I1). Often (S) itself carried this weight for them. However, the connection extends further. If there were no (ontological) simples which could merely be labeled by linguistic simples such as "this" and "red," there would plausibly be at least a quasi-logical connection between the referent of a word and the facts expressed by true (or false) sentences in which it occurs. To grasp this, consider that, if the linguistic simple "this" is to refer to a complex entity, knowledge of what it refers to would in some sense depend "logically" on knowing the constitution of the entity, which distinguishes it from others, that is, on knowing facts expressed by sentences. Since the nominalist maintains, at least implicitly as we saw, that "this" does refer to a complex entity, he is in danger of asserting such a "logical" connection. For, as we also saw, upon his analysis the referent of "this" contains the referent of "red." This may explain why some nominalists prefer the fuzzy common-name doctrine to the part-whole analysis.[9]

Whether the logical atomists' program can be realized is controversial. The language they undertake to construct would of course contain no primitive descriptive terms which are not mere labels. The point I wish to make, however, does not depend on whether the program is realizable, that is, whether such a language can be constructed. My point is rather that, whether or not it is, both the realist and nominalist must consistently believe it to be realizable. For if they do not, then, as I have shown, they implicitly deny (I1). And, as I have also shown, the denial of (I1) leads to monism, that is, to the obliteration of distinctions on which both nominalist and realist insist.

That concludes the discussion of (I1), the first use of "independent." I turn next to the third, (I3).

The "form of connection" of which Wittgenstein speaks in the quoted passage (2.0122) and which he himself so poignantly explicates is closely related to (I3). Wittgenstein's point is that a language cannot even be a candidate for the role of ideal language (L)[10] unless there is a sharp distinction among its words and its sentences. Words are not sentences, they only occur in them. That is why words "cannot stand alone." The formation rules of L are such that only strings of words count as sentences. This restriction on L, however, is weaker than (I3), which maintains that no character word can occur in a sentence without having first occurred in an atomic sentence of the form "fx." Let me sharpen this. There are two points which, though they are closely related, must be clearly distinguished. First, there is the interpretation of L. In this context (I3) merely means that, say, no color word can be introduced into L as a primitive term unless its referent is first exemplified by an individual. That we never do know what a color word refers to unless we have once seen the color exemplified is undeniable indeed. Second, one may know, in some sense of knowing, without actually being acquainted with the color red, that "red" refers to a color. But then this kind of knowledge can be accounted for without disrupting the import of (I3). That is why the two points must be distinguished.

(I3) is the heart of the realism issue. One who denies both (I3) and Wittgenstein's thesis in 2.0122 I would call an extreme Platonist. One who merely denies (I3) I call a Platonist.[11] Aristotle certainly accused Plato of denying (I3) with respect to the "Forms." Whether he also accused him of denying the weaker requirement is difficult to say.[12]

(I2) takes for granted that the exemplification relation is asymmetrical and that individuals are the lowest-level items, that is, that individuals are referred to by terms which occur only in the subject place. (I2) thus rests on the type distinction. Many metaphors are associated with this meaning of "independent." Some deserve mention, for they contribute to the nominalist's perplexity. First, an individual (or substance) is often said to "need no support" while a character does. Second, it is said that characters "cannot stand alone" while individuals can. The latter metaphor may tempt one to claim, as Russell once did,[13] that the world could consist of only one individual and nothing else. Clearly such an individual could not be of the realist's sort. Russell, therefore, made it an individual of the nominalist's sort, that is, one which "contains" characters. Third, since words referring to individuals occur only in the subject place, they are often called "proper names."[14] This may tempt one to believe that a predicate term, say, "red," is a different *kind of name*, and not just a name of a different *kind of thing*. This, I submit, is one reason why the nominalist calls "red" a common name. Fourth, in the hylomorphic scheme a substance is a composite of form and matter, neither of which exists. Some medieval philosophers who held this doctrine believed that a substance could exist without accidents, that is, they denied (I3). One reason was their concern with immortality. A contemporary nominalist who takes his cue from these philosophers obviously is misled. Furthermore, the composite substance of the hylomorphic scheme is, of course, not really a thing but a fact, namely, a "form informing matter." The nature of the informing relation remains obscure in the hylomorphic scheme, just as the meaning of "is" in (a) and (b) remains obscure upon the common-name analysis. Nor is this an accident. The doctrine of common names has its historical root in the hylomorphic scheme.

The explication of (I4) is standard and familiar. In L no (atomic) sentence of the form "fx" (or "rxy," and so forth) logically entails any other. This and only this is the meaning of the *Tractatus* thesis that (atomic) facts are independent of each other. Accordingly, one may say that it is logically possible (in the sense explicated by the truth tables) for the world to consist of only one atomic fact. This suggests that, carelessly construing "independent" as "capable of standing alone," one may be tempted to propound a fact ontology: that is, an ontology according to which only atomic facts *exist*. (I) and (I4) create a similar temptation; for taken together, they yield the same doctrine. Moreover, there is a significant connection between (I1) and (I4). One possible way of securing the privileged status of "a priori truth" for certain sentences is to claim that, in some (to me) obscure sense of "follow," their truth follows from the "meaning" of the words which occur in them.[15] This claim I have shown to be incompatible with (I1).

One is never acquainted with red alone but always with something exemplifying red. This is the common-sense core of nominalism. Is it compatible with the existence of universals? The nominalist answers that it is not. I have in this paper set myself the task of showing that his answer is mistaken. To accomplish the task I maintained that one must distinguish among four uses of "independent" and the philosophical issues which they control. Having made the distinctions, I now return to the task.

The realist holds that individuals as well as (some) characters exist because both are independent in sense (I1), because they are simple (S), and because they can be named (N). But the realist must also know how to distinguish between these kinds of existents. The distinction he secures by accepting (I2). Nor need he maintain that this is the only difference between individuals and characters.

What does the realist claim with respect to (I3) and (I4)? If he wishes to avoid the pitfalls of either Platonism or extreme Platonism, he will be wise to adopt (I3). One who adopts (I3) in this spirit may be called an "empiricist." At least, that is one reasonable specification of that overworked word. With respect to (I4) the realist is free to choose. His choice, if he knows what he is about, will depend on the position he takes in the analytic-synthetic controversy.

If I am right, then I have already solved the task I set myself. One need not reject the common-sense core of nominalism in order to hold that universals exist. The nominalist thinks that one must. It remains to exhibit the anatomy of his belief. To do that one must keep two things in mind. One is that the nominalist is mesmerized by his desire to prevent universals from flying off into Plato's heaven. The other is that the nominalist, as I portray him, fails to distinguish the four meanings of "independent."

There is indeed a sense in which only individuals are independent, namely (I2). This gives the nominalist his start. Yet a clever nominalist is fully aware that universals are in some sense presented to us. Thus he puts them in his individuals, which become, therefore, qualitied things. In this fateful move he receives aid and comfort from (I4). To see that, one merely has to consider that to speak of a qualitied thing is to speak of a fact, namely, of a thing having a quality. At this point, therefore, the nominalist takes advantage of all the verbal suggestions contained in such phrases as "standing alone" and "needing no support." If one wonders whether in thus attributing to the nominalist an implicit fact ontology I am not going too far, I would say this. On the one hand, a consistent nominalist must deny that the "is" in (a) and (b) is the *is* of non-diversity. On the other hand, he must maintain that (a) and (b) refer to two things rather than to two facts. If one now wonders that so awkward a predicament was not noticed for so long, I reply that the spurious doctrine of common names may well have kept one from noticing it. After all, nominalism has a distinguished history.

I should like to close by answering a general objection that may be raised against this paper. The objector, I imagine, calls my explications arbitrary. Why, for instance, select (I1), rather than (I4), for the explication of the philosophical proposition that what exists is independent (I)? My answer is two-fold. First, if one says that what exists is independent, he uses "exist" as well as "independent" philosophically. Such uses, just as those which some call ordinary, have their context. I believe I have shown that the context which most closely relates "existence" and "independence" is (I1). Second, if a philosopher wishes to use his words so that facts and only facts exist because they and they alone are independent in the sense of (I4), he may surely do so. All we may expect from him is that he tells us exactly how he uses "independent." Once such explications are given and the distinctions made, what is there left to argue about?

NOTES

From *Philosophical Review* 69 (1960). Reprinted by permission of the author and the editor of *Philosophical Review*.

1. Some realists construe "simple" as Moore did (in *Principia Ethica*). Briefly, a *simple* is the referent of an undefinable term, e.g., "yellow"; a *complex* the referent of a definable term, e.g., "horse." The referents of the former are said to *exist*. The explications would appear to uncover the core of the ontological

enterprise. Again briefly, that enterprise is to show what is made of what and tends to claim that what is *composed* does not, in this special sense, *exist*.

2. This controversy in its contemporary dress is discussed by Gustav Bergmann, "The Revolt Against Logical Atomism," *The Philosophical Quarterly*, VII (1957), 323–339 and VIII (1958), 1–14.

3. For an analysis of this issue see Edwin B. Allaire, "*Tractatus* 6.3751," *Analysis*, XIX (1959), 100–105.

4. Cf. Gustav Bergmann, "Frege's Hidden Nominalism," *The Philosophical Review*, LXVII (1958), 437–459.

5. There is, however, an intimate connection between knowing the referent of a word and knowing the synactical rules which govern its use. Cf. Gustav Bergmann, "Ineffability, Ontology, and Method" in *The Philosophical Review*, LXIX (1960), 18–40.

6. Cf. Bertrand Russell, "The Philosophy of Logical Atomism," reprinted in *Logic and Knowledge* (London, 1956), pp. 203–204. Lectures II and III of this essay are worth reading in connection with the several meanings of "independent." For Russell's confusions are transparent and instructive.

7. Whether the early Wittgenstein was a nominalist or realist is controversial. What he means in 2.0122 does not, however depend on his being either. For no matter what the primitives of his improved language are, they certainly are mere labels.

8. See note 5.

9. It is to be noted that upon both nominalistic analyses the referent of "this" cannot be "defined." For "this" in both cases refers to a whole, only one part of which is or can be named. The individuating constituent, if I may so express myself, is not named. Again, one hears the echo of the hylomorphic doctrine.

10. As was shown above, the thesis of this paper does not depend on whether or not such a language can be constructed. It merely depends on both nominalist and realist admitting that it can. For in so doing they both embrace (I1).

11. It is interesting to note that both types of Platonism in their relation to the doctrine of simples are a major concern of the later Wittgenstein. Cf. *The Blue and the Brown Books* (Oxford, 1958), p. 17, and *Philosophical Investigations* (New York, 1953), Secs. 37–59. Secs. 57 and 58 are especially interesting in this regard.

12. Wittgenstein's thesis is sometimes expressed by saying that "thought is propositional." This means that the object of awareness (in the generic sense) is always referred to by a sentence. Cf. *Tractatus* 2.0121 and 3–3.144.

13. Russell, *op. cit.*, p. 202. For a discussion of Russell's individuals see J. O. Urmson, *Philosophical Analysis* (London, 1956), pp. 54–57.

14. "Proper name," in so far as it is used philosophically, I call a metaphor. For I do not know what it means to be a name without naming one and only one thing.

15. See note 3.

26   DONAGAN

Donagan observes that in *The Problems of Philosophy*, Russell adheres to what the former calls the Realist Principle; "namely, that primitive predicates occurring non-redundantly in true propositions denote real things." When pushed to the extreme, the Realist Principle forces one to accept unknown negative facts into one's ontology, which some obviously find uncomfortable. However, the only way to avoid this conclusion is to demonstrate the impossibility of unexemplified universals or to show "that all negative propositions are reducible to affirmative ones." That neither has been accomplished so far is demonstrated by an examination of four objections. They are "(1) the classical difficulty, with which Plato struggled, that the very concept of a unitary universal which is 'shared by' many particulars appears to be self-contradictory; (2) that although some realist principle may be true, the Realist Principle which Russell held is false; (3) that Russell's argument depends on features peculiar to certain languages, which may be dispensed with in an artificial language, and perhaps in some natural languages; (4) that Russell's theory of universals, as a whole, is 'circular and uninformative'."

None of these objections succeeds in undermining Russell's position. Furthermore, an examination of these criticisms exposes the perils of a nominalist or idealist interpretation of universals. These are far greater than the pitfalls of Russell's realism. It is in this sense that Donagan sees Russell's brand of realism winning by default.

Universals and Metaphysical Realism

The late Friedrich Waismann once remarked that, while you may confute and kill a scientific theory, a philosophy dies only of old age. The realist theory of universals, which G. E. Moore and Bertrand Russell revived in the brilliant fifteen years which preceded the first World War,[1] seems to have aged more rapidly than its authors, and to have died, or fallen into oblivion, during the 'forties. In the United States, the very different conception of realism propounded by Professor Quine and Goodman,[2] and nicknamed by Quine "Plato's Beard," has displaced it, leaving Professor Bergmann almost alone to defend it.[3] In Britain, a polished essay by Mr. Pears seems to have been received as its epitaph.[4] In this paper I propose to re-examine Moore's and Russell's principal argument for the reality of universals, in order to determine whether any spark of life remains in it. Is it truly dead, or only neglected?

I

Russell's *The Problems of Philosophy* is a convenient and familiar point of departure. Lucidly and simply, it states the position which Moore and Russell held, and their reason for holding it. In its eighth chapter, Russell wrote this:

> Suppose, for instance, that I am in my room. I exist, and my room exists; but does "in" exist? Yet obviously the word "in" has a meaning; it denotes a relation which holds between me and my room. This relation is something, although we cannot say that it exists *in the same* sense in which I and my room exist. The relation "in" is something which we can think about and understand, for, if we could not understand it, we could not understand the sentence "I am in my room."[5]

The conclusion that we are to investigate is that the relation denoted by "in" *is*, or is real. Russell's distinction between being and existence, according to which the relation denoted by "in" has being (*is* or is real) but does not exist, is notoriously difficult, and we shall defer investigating it. Yet, even apart from that distinction, Russell's argument and conclusion are puzzling.

His reasoning seems to have been as follows:

(i) Some propositions of the form "*x* is in *y*," where "*x*" and "*y*" deputize for names or descriptions of things which in a familiar sense exist, can be thought about and understood.

(ii) They could not be thought about or understood unless the word "in" were thought about and understood; *i.e.* "in" is not redundant.

(iii) Some propositions in the form "*x* is in *y*" are true. (I take this to be presupposed in Russell's opening injunction: "Suppose, for instance, that . . .")

(iv) The non-redundant elements of true propositions denote things that are real or have being, if not things that exist.

(v) Therefore, "in" denotes something which *is* or is real, if not something which exists; and since if "in" denotes anything at all it is a relation, it follows that at least one relation *is* or is real.

If relations are real, then universals are real: for "a *universal* will be anything which may be shared by many particulars";[6] and at least two pairs of particulars, namely, Russell and his room, and Moore and his room, may share the relation denoted by "in."

Neither Russell nor Moore believed that all universals were relational. In *The Problems of Philosophy* Russell had much to say of justice and whiteness, which he considered to be non-relational qualities; and in *Some Main Problems of Philosophy* Moore strove to demonstrate that in some sense *whiteness* is a universal which is neither a relation (like *in*) nor a relational property (like *in Russell's room*). Yet both Moore and Russell considered the being of relations and relational properties to be far more evident than that of non-relational (qualitative) universals; and both ascribed the nominalist tendencies in the work of Berkeley and Hume to their error that, unlike qualities, relations are evidently the work of the mind.[7] Russell plainly agreed with Moore that "it is . . . comparatively easy to distinguish universals of both these two sorts [relations and relational properties]; and if it were quite clear that they were the only sorts, the whole question about universals would be . . . comparatively simple."[8]

Simple or not, it is the question we are to investigate. In doing so, I shall assume that Moore and Russell were in the right when they declared that whether or not there are qualities which are irreducible to relational properties has not the slightest bearing on whether or not there are universals.

Despite Russell's lucidity, there are obscurities in his argument as I have analysed it. It only applies to expressions which are non-redundant, i.e. which must be thought about and understood if the meaning of the sentences in which they occur is to be thought about and understood. Clearly if, instead of saying "I am in my room," Russell had added some expletive to "room," e.g. "God-forsaken," that expletive would have been redundant, and his argument would not have shown that there is something which "God-forsaken" denotes. To show that, it would be necessary to produce a true statement in which "God-forsaken" was not redundant. But is it enough to exclude redundant expressions? Some expressions, for example in mathematics, are rigorously defined. If the definition of "triangle" were substituted for the word "triangle" in a theorem of Euclid, the meaning of that theorem would remain unchanged. Are we to interpret Russell's argument as showing that there is a universal denoted by "triangle," *as well* as those denoted by "figure," "plane," and "three-sided?" In his later work Russell construed his argument as applying only to expressions which are primitive. Hence, the fact that you can think about and understand the expression "in" shows *either* that "in" denotes something that is real or has being, *or* that "in" is definable, and that the primitive expressions by which it is ultimately to be defined denote things that are real or have being.

Even after this clarification, the scope of Russell's argument remains obscure. Suppose that the sentences with which Russell began were, "You are *or* I am in my room" or "I am an *individual* (or a *particular*)." The expressions "or" and "individual" (or "particular") are, in Russell's own view, not redundant. Once more, we must turn to his later works for guidance. If all logical connectives such as "and," "or," "if . . . then" be interpreted truth-functionally, then they must be excluded from the fundamental propositions from which compound propositions are constructed. It must be conceded that a difficulty remains about the sentence, "'I am in my room' is true." To understand that sentence, it is necessary to understand the expression "true"; and if truth-functional analyses of the logical connectives are to be admitted, such sentences must be indispensable. However, Russell might plead that the expressions "true" and "false," which signify, not properties of objects, but properties of propositions about objects, call for separate elucidation and interpretation. I shall therefore assume that his argument applies neither to them nor to their derivatives.

Expressions like "individual," "particular," and "universal" must also be treated separately. Frege's technique of quantification enables us to dispense with them as they most commonly occur in such sentences as, "Some individual both took office under Caesar and conspired to murder him," by replacing them with variables, e.g. "For some value of 'x,' 'x took office under Caesar and x conspired to murder Caesar' is true." As for sentences which cannot be so analysed, e.g. "Brutus is an individual," what they say is *shown* by allowing certain expressions, e.g. "Brutus," to be substituted for certain variables, e.g. "x" in the above function; and it may be expressed in the formal mode by such sentences as, "The expression 'Brutus' is a legitimate value of the variable 'x'." Russell was to accept Wittgenstein's view that expressions like "individual," "particular," and "universal," which can be eliminated by such devices, signify formal concepts,[9] and should not be mistaken for predicates signifying properties which a thing may or may not possess.

These elucidations affect only the scope of Russell's argument. What of its nature? If our analyses and clarifications are sound, it asserts that the reality of the universal *in* follows from three facts: (i) that the sentence "I am in my room" can be thought about and understood; (ii) that on the occasion when Russell wrote it he expressed a true proposition; and (iii) that the word "in" neither is definable nor is a logical connective nor signifies a formal concept, and is predicable of many particulars (henceforth I shall call such expressions "primitive predicates"). That universals are real is held to follow from these facts by the general principle that the non-redundant elements of true propositions denote things that are real or have being. That principle, however, applies to proper names as well as to predicates. Russell's argument requires only a narrower principle, which I shall henceforth call "the Realist Principle"; namely, that primitive predicates occurring non-redundantly in true propositions denote real things, or, as Moore liked to say, "real constituents of the world." It is plain why Russell and Moore adhered to this Principle. They could not conceive how otherwise propositions containing primitive predicates could state facts about the world.[10] And certainly this consideration is weighty. If the ultimate non-logical and non-formal constituents of true propositions refer to nothing in the world, in what can the truth of such propositions consist?

Before proceeding to consider objections to Russell's argument one more elucidation is called for. While it presupposes that there are true propositions containing expressions which stand for universals, it does not stipulate that those propositions must assert that those universals are exemplified. In his example Russell laid it down that the relation *in* was supposed to be exemplified; for he invited his readers to suppose that he was in his room.

But, since "in" is as much a constituent of the negative proposition "Russell is not in his room," as of the affirmative one, "Russell is in his room," the reality of the relation *in* would seem to follow from the truth of either one.

This point can be generalized. Let "... *R* ..." signify a relational expression, and let the only true propositions containing "... *R* ..." be of the form -*R (x,y)* or -*xRy*. In other words, let it be true that -(∃*x,y*) *xRy*. Six years after writing *The Problems of Philosophy*, Russell stoutly maintained the possibility that there are negative facts, i.e. that there are facts expressible by propositions of the form -*fa*, which cannot be reduced to facts express- ible by propositions that contain no sign of negation.[11] If that is possible, then it is logically possible that the only true propositions containing a given predicative expression, whether "*F* ... ," or "*R*(... , ...)" or some other, should be negative. By Russell's argument, such an unexemplified universal would have exactly the same claim to being or reality as exemplified ones.

Both in *The Problems of Philosophy* and "The Philosophy of Logical Atomism" Russell avoided admitting this by adopting the Principle of Acquaintance, namely, that "in every proposition that we can apprehend (i.e., not only in those whose truth and falsity we can judge of, but in all that we can think about) all the constituents are really entities with which we have immediate acquaintance."[12] It follows that we cannot think about any proposition the primitive expressions in which do not stand for constituents with which we are acquainted; and we can be acquainted with the constit- uent denoted by a qualitative or relational expression only if that constituent is exemplified and we are acquainted with an instance of it. In short, we cannot even think about a negative proposition containing "... *R* ... ," e.g. "-*aRb*," unless we have been acquainted with a state of affairs asserted by a proposition of the form "*xRy*."

The metaphysical problem, however, cannot be dodged in that way. First, the question whether universals have being or are real is quite distinct from the question whether every universal of which we have formed a concept has been exemplified somewhere at some time. Nothing in Russell's argument confines its application either to affirmative propositions, or to propositions we know. Of course, he might stipulate that its application be so confined; but such an arbitrary stipulation would carry no weight. Secondly, the problem of unexemplified universals can be propounded even if the Princi- ple of Acquaintance be accepted. That Principle entails neither that any given language, English say, contains expressions for all exemplified qualities and relations, nor that speakers of English are acquainted with instances of all of them. It cannot, therefore, forbid a speaker of English to opine that two objects, say the Atlantic and the Pacific Oceans, stand to each other in some relation with which he is not acquainted. It follows that somebody who said, in English, "(∃*R*) the Atlantic Ocean *R* the Pacific Ocean, and I am not acquainted with *R*," would make an intelligible statement.

Now if you can opine that a pair of objects exemplifies a relation with which you are not acquainted, you can equally opine that it does not. For example, you might intelligibly say:

(1) "($\exists R$) -R (the Atlantic Ocean, the Pacific Ocean) and I am not acquainted with R."

Having said that, you might generalize it:

(2) "($\exists R(x,y)$) -$R(x,y)$ and I am not acquainted with R."

If (2) were true, an infinite number of statements of the form -$R(x,y)$ would be true, in each of which the value of the variable "R" would signify an unexemplified relation. The Principle of Acquaintance entails, not that there is no such relation, but that no language contains a predicate denoting it. Although the limits of my language may be the limits of *my* world, they are not the limits of *the* world.

Since I am not tempted to endorse any metaphysical Principle of Plenitude, I am inclined to think the proposition (2) above to be true. If it is, then there are innumerable negative facts which, if the Principle of Acquaintance be true, nobody will ever know. From that, if Russell's argument is sound, it follows that an unexemplified relation is a real constituent of the world. Those who countenance Russell's argument can escape this conclusion in only two ways: either by demonstrating that unexemplified universals are impossible (not merely that they cannot be directly known), or by demonstrating that all negative propositions are reducible to affirmative ones. Up to now, neither has been established.

II

Realist arguments like Russell's have been rejected for such a variety of reasons that I cannot here examine them all. I shall, therefore, select those few which I judge to be cardinal. I cannot even justify my selection; for to do so it would be necessary to show that none of the objections I do not discuss has more weight than any of those I do.

The four objections I have selected are: (1) the classical difficulty, with which Plato struggled, that the very concept of a unitary universal which is "shared by" many particulars appears to be self-contradictory; (2) that although some realist principle may be true, the Realist Principle which Russell held is false; (3) that Russell's argument depends on features peculiar to certain languages, which may be dispensed with in an artificial language, and perhaps is in some natural languages; (4) that Russell's theory of universals, as a whole, is "circular and uninformative."

(1) *The Classical Difficulty.* In the *Philebus* Plato drew attention to two difficulties in his theory of forms: if there are many things in which a form may be said to be present, it would seem that "we must think [either] that [the form] is dispersed and has become many," or "that it is still entire and divided from itself, which latter would seem to be the greatest impossibility of all" (*ibid.* 15B). Russell's theory appears to avoid the first difficulty, but

not the second. He recognized a universal denoted by "in" which may be "shared" or, to avoid metaphor, "exemplified" by, many pairs of particulars, e.g. by Russell and his room, and by Moore and his. However, he did not think that only part of the universal *in* would be exemplified by each pair that exemplifies it: that is, he did not think that it could be "dispersed" among those pairs, and so "become many." A universal remains unitary. Yet, since Russell did think that Moore could be in his room at the very same time as he was in his, the two rooms being necessarily at different places, he could not avoid concluding that at the same time the unitary universal *in* could be exemplified at different places. Does that not imply what to Plato seemed "the greatest impossibility of all," that it is "still entire and yet divided from itself?"

A tempting way out of this difficulty is to deny that because the *in* is exemplified by Russell and his room, both of which are at a certain place, the universal itself must be at that place, or at any place. Yet that way lies destruction. It is true that the question form, "Where is the universal?" has no established use in non-philosophical discourse. But then, neither has the term "universal" such a use; and questions of the impugned form naturally arise out of Russell's theory. Moreover, there is a strong reason for thinking that if universals are exemplified in space and time, they are where they are exemplified. You can verify the statement that Russell is in his room by looking into it and seeing him there. When you look, you see not only him and his room, but also that he is in it. It is true that it is not good English to say that you see *in*, along with Russell and his room; but, as the late J. L. Austin once pointed out, neither is it good English to say that you do not see it, or that you intuit it. "I [see] what in English is described by means of two demonstrative pronouns and an adverbial phrase. To look for an isolable entity corresponding to the latter is a bad habit. . . ."[13] Now, if what you see includes what is described by the adverbial phrase ". . . is in . . . ," *i.e.* a universal, must it not be where you are looking? And if one man was to see that Russell was in his room at the same time as another was to see Moore in his, would it not follow that the universal *in* was in the two different places where the two were looking? If so, would not the universal *in* be both "entire and yet divided from itself"?

At this juncture, realists should act on the principle that the best defense is attack, and protest that *by its very nature* a universal is the sort of thing that can be exemplified by particulars in different places at the same time. To say that it is "entire and yet divided from itself" is objectionable, because it presupposes that to be exemplified in two different places at once implies being divided. It is true that a *particular* can only be in two places at once if one part of it is at one place, and another part at the other; but, by their very nature, universals are not divisible into parts. Exasperated, the Platonic Mephistopheles may retort that what is seen to be exemplified at two different places is seen at those places; and that, since what is seen at one place is not what is seen at the other, the *in* which is seen to be exemplified in Russell's room cannot be the same as the *in* which is seen to be exemplified in Moore's room. In his turn, a realist may reply that the second premise of this argument, namely that what is seen at one place is not what is simultaneously seen at the other, holds for particulars but not for universals. If he is asked how that can be, he need not hesitate to reply that you cannot explain what is fundamental. At a certain time Russell is in his room and Moore is in his; and one and the same relation, namely that denoted by "in," is a constituent of both facts. If that is impossible, then all discourse is impossible.

Even this resounding affirmation may not exorcise the Platonic imp. We have supposed that realists may avoid metaphorical expressions like "share" and "participate in" when speaking of the connection between particulars and universals, and have employed instead the non-metaphorical "exemplify." But what does "exemplify" denote? In his 1911 essay "On the Relations of Universals and Particulars," Russell wrote that,

> . . . according to the theory which assumes particulars, there is a specific relation of subject to predicate . . . [O]rdinary sensible qualities will be predicates of the particulars which are instances of them. . . . Predication is a relation involving a fundamental logical difference between its two terms . . . [T]he question whether predication is an ultimate simple relation may be taken as distinguishing the two theories [i.e. that there are particulars and that there are not]; it is ultimate if there are particulars. (*Logic and Knowledge*, p. 123)

Plainly Russell's "predication" has the same sense as our "exemplification" ("exemplification" is better because it is convenient to reserve "predication" for the relation between a linguistic expression and what it is predicated of); and Russell is saying that predication (or exemplification) itself is an "ultimate simple relation."

In the first of his articles on Plato's *Parmenides*, Professor Ryle showed that there cannot be such a relation.[14] By Russell's own exposition, it would be anomalous. Whereas ordinary relations relate particulars (John is *to the left of* James) or universals (Yellow *is a lighter color than* red), exemplification is supposed to relate particulars *to* universals. Suppose, nevertheless, that there is such a relation. Applying this supposition to Russell's example, exemplification will relate the two particulars, Russell and his room, to the relation *in*, and the two particulars, Moore and his room, to the same relation. It follows that exemplification is a universal. For, although Russell defined a universal as "anything which may be shared by many particulars," by explicitly acknowledging that "predicates themselves may have predicates,"[15] i.e. that there may be universals which are exemplified only by universals, he showed that he considered it a sufficient condition of universality that a thing be predicable of or exemplifiable by many other things whether particulars or not.

The ultimate simple relation of exemplification is then a constituent of each of the two facts:

(i) The relation *in* is exemplified by Russell and his room;
(ii) The relation *in* is exemplified by Moore and his room.

It follows that,

(ia) The relation of exemplification is exemplified by Russell, his room, and the relation *in*,

and that,

(iia) The relation of exemplification is exemplified by Russell, his room, and the relation *in*.

But the facts (ia) and (iia) are stated in sentences which contain the expression "is exemplified by." What does that expression denote? It cannot denote the relation of exemplification which is said to be exemplified, because a relation cannot relate anything to itself. It must therefore denote either nothing at all or a second-order relation of exemplification. It cannot denote nothing at all, if the first-order relation of exemplification is genuine, as it must be if universals are related to what they exemplify by an ultimate simple relation. Hence it must denote a second-order relation of exemplification. Manifestly, this regress is interminable and vicious. For, since second-order exemplification must in turn be a genuine universal, exemplified by Russell, his room, the relation *in*, and first-order exemplification, there must be a third-order relation of exemplification, and so *ad infinitum*.[16]

Since vicious infinite regresses cannot be stopped, they must not be allowed to start. Once you concede to the Platonic imp that particulars and universals need a further universal, and an anomalous one at that, to relate them, you cannot deny that that further universal requires yet a further one and so *ad infinitum*. Nor will it help to plead that the relation of exemplification is unique. It is *not* unique in the only respect that matters: namely, that many sets of universals and particulars share it or exemplify it.

Why did Russell postulate a relation of exemplification at all? Presumably because he perceived that even if he and his room are real particulars, and the relation *in* a real universal, it does not follow that he is in his room, any more than it follows that he is not in his room. The relation *in* is a constituent of both the positive and the negative fact. What is the difference between those facts? It is natural to suggest that in the positive fact the relation *in* is tied to Russell and his room by an ultimate simple relation, and that in the negative fact it is not. But by accepting that suggestion, you generate Ryle's regress.

The only possible escape is to deny that the statement "Russell is in his room" asserts any relation, whether ultimate or not, between the relation *in* and the particulars it is said to relate. The relation *in* may relate Russell and his room, or it may not; but, supposing it does relate them, it does not follow that some further relation relates it to them. In the same way, a certain rose may be red or not; but, supposing it is red, it does not follow that *being red* is related to it.

Ryle's regress can only be forestalled by conceiving the exemplification of a universal by a particular or set of particulars as non-relational. Language inevitably misleads us here. Having recognized that expressions like ". . . is red" and ". . . is in . . ." denote constituents of facts, it is tempting to think that the difference between the facts asserted by the pairs of sentences:

"*a* is red" and "*a* is not red,"
"*a* is in *b*" and "*a* is not in *b*,"

must be found in the presence or absence of some further constituent, the relation of exemplification. That would be a mistake. The fact, if it be a fact that *a* is red, has exactly the same constituents as the fact, if it be a fact, that *a* is not red. There is an ultimate difference between the two facts, but it is not a difference in their constituents.

I have argued: (1) that Plato's objection to the realist theory of universals does not arise if it is presupposed that a universal may be simultaneously exemplified by many particulars without being divided from itself; and (2) that Ryle's regress cannot begin if it is presupposed that the difference between the facts asserted by propositions of the forms $f(x)$ and $\bar{f}(x)$ is not a difference in their constituents, i.e. is not a relational difference. Neither presupposition seems to me to be inconsistent. Whether or not Russell's Realist Principle is true, Plato's objection does not refute it.

(2) *Even if some realist principle is true, must it be Russell's?* It is well known that, ever since the Nominalist controversy vexed the medieval Schools, most of those who have claimed to be realists have adopted a position less extreme than Russell's.

The most familiar form of "moderate" realism is the commonly ascribed to Aristotle. According to it, while something in the world must correspond to a true proposition, that correspondence need not be point for point. As Aquinas urged, "*Alius est enim modus intellectus in intelligendo quam rei in essendo.*" If "Russell is in his room" is true, then something in the world must correspond to that proposition; but there need not be a constituent in the world for each constituent of the proposition. If we take the true propositions "Socrates is a man," and "Plato is a man," there must once have been something in the world corresponding to each of them. But it was not that the particulars Socrates and Plato each exemplified the universals denoted by the primitive predicates into which "is a man" is supposedly analysable. (Nor was it that the particulars of which the complex particulars Socrates and Plato are supposedly composed exemplified the universals denoted by certain primitive predicates.) Rather, it was that the essence *man*, which in itself is neither universal nor particular, was *in rerum natura* individuated in Socrates and Plato, as well as in other men. *In rerum natura* the same essence may therefore be multiplied. However, when somebody forms the proposition that Socrates is a man, or that Plato is a man, he does so by abstracting the individuated essence both from the different parcels of matter which it informed and from the accidents with which it was associated. Since the abstracted essence of Socrates is the same as that of Plato or of any other man, it is universal. It follows that an essence exists in two distinct ways: *in rerum natura* as a many, and in the mind as a one. The universal term "man" stands for the essence *man* as it exists in the mind abstractly. The essence itself, being neutral with respect to universality and particularity, can exist *in rerum natura* as individuated in Socrates, Plato, and other men.[17]

Against this theory, Russell would presumably argue that it is unintelligible to suppose that a neutral essence should be capable of existing both as many individuals, and as an abstract unitary universal. In what sense can the same neutral thing exist as both a many and a one? An Aristotelian would retort that this seems absurd only because of the dogma that everything is either universal or particular. If Russell may protest that universals are unitary and yet exemplified by many things, why may not an Aristotelian protest that essences, while neither universal nor particular, may exist in the world as many particulars and in the mind as unitary universals?

Set against Russell's, the Aristotelian theory has two drawbacks. First, it postulates not merely one problematic entity, as Russell's does, but one problematic entity and two problematic forms of existence for it. By Ockham's Razor, Russell's theory, if tenable at all, is preferable. Secondly, the question cannot be suppressed: If the essence *man* is individuated in Socrates and Plato, are Socrates and Plato nothing but two individuals? Are they not both men? And if they are both men, can you stop short with saying that the essence *man* is individuated? Must you not add that the individuals, Socrates and Plato, exemplify the same thing, namely man?

A very different criticism of Russell's Realist Principle has been made by Goodman and Quine.[18] Like Russell, they hold that in some way true statements correspond in their structure to the structure of the world, but they altogether reject Russell's doctrine that there must be real universals which correspond to the primitive predicates of true propositions. In their view, only one part of any statement carries ontological commitment: its quantified variables. To find out what a man's ontological commitments are, you must find over what variables the statements he believes to be true compel him to quantify. "Entities of a given sort," Quine wrote, are ontologically assumed by a theory "if and only if some of them must be counted among the values of the variables in order that the statements affirmed in the theory be true."[19]

On this view, if in the proposition, "Russell is in his room," you permit "Russell" and "his room" to be replaced by the non-predicative name variables "x" and "y," and those variables to be quantified, i.e. if you assert that $(\exists x,y)$ x is in y, you commit yourself to a world containing individuals, but not to the reality of the relation *in*. It is true that in "*(∃x,y) x* is in *y*," you use the word "in," and presuppose that it has meaning. But Quine has insisted that "there is a gulf between *meaning* and *naming*."[20] In the same spirit Goodman has defined nominalism as "the refusal to countenance any entities other than individuals," while at the same time allowing "the nominalist's language" to contain "one-place and many-place predicates of individuals."[21] He can consistently do so, because, like Quine, he does not consider predicates to stand for any entity.[22] In the opinion of both Goodman and Quine then, a philosopher would commit himself to rejecting nominalism only if he were to allow ". . . is in . . ." to be replaced by a variable, and that variable to be quantified, as in "*(∃R)* Russell *R* his room," for only by doing so would he expressly assert that there is some relation (and relations are universals) in which Russell stands to his room.

This position can be assailed from several directions. Professor Sellars, for example, has forcibly argued that to quantify over a variable does not commit you to accepting the values of that variable denoting anything real.[23] Russell would approach the matter from another quarter. Holding, as he does, that what you quantify over has no special ontological significance, he might nevertheless urge that the alleged gulf between admitting predicates of individuals and quantifying over predicate variables is imaginary. Of course a logician may for his own convenience eschew such quantification. Russell himself discovered that unrestricted quantification over predicate variables generates the paradox which bears his name, nor could he deny force to Quine's charge that "our precautions against [such] contradictions [e.g. Russell's Theory of Types] are *ad hoc* devices, justified only in that, or in so far as, they seem to work."[24]

Yet he might rejoin that to prohibit *all* quantification over predicate variables because unrestricted quantification gives rise to contradiction would be a remedy worse than the disease. Quine himself admits such facts as that more than one dog is white, and that roses and sunsets are red. Well, if it is true both that Fido is white and that Rover is white, must it not also be true that there is some color which Fido and Rover both have? More generally, if *Fa* and *Fb* are both true, must it not be true that *(∃f) fa* and *fb*? It will not do for a logician to say: in my system, quantification over predicate variables is forbidden. The device of quantification is not private property; and any logician may be called upon to answer whether the result of a particular quantification is or is not true. Prima facie, that Fido and Rover are both white is a sufficient condition of the truth of the proposition *(∃f) f* (Fido) and *f* (Rover); and if any proposition expressed by means of quantification over predicates is true, then *some* quantification over predicates is legitimate, and no considerations of elegance or convenience can justify prohibiting it.

By arguing against Quine in this way, Russell would not surrender to Quine's criterion of ontological commitment. He might continue to hold the

Realist Principle that the primitive predicates of true propositions must each denote something real. He would overcome Quine's criterion by showing that, rightly employed, it yields exactly the same results as his own. If by asserting the truth of a proposition containing a primitive predicate you oblige yourself to assert the truth of a proposition containing a quantified predicate variable, then quantified variables are not unique in disclosing ontological commitments.

Yet Quine has another argument. "We may say," he wrote, "that some dogs are white and not thereby commit ourselves to recognizing either doghood or whiteness as entities. 'Some dogs are white' says that some things that are dogs are white; and in order that this statement be true, the things over which the bound variable 'something' ranges must include some white dogs, but need not include doghood or whiteness."[25] Russell of course knew that in the proposition "Something is white," the bound variable "something" does not range over a class of things which includes whiteness; and wisely, he did not couch his argument in terms of abstract nouns like whiteness or doghood. His rejoinder to Quine would be: If some things that are dogs are white, is there not some quality which things that are dogs have? Otherwise how do white dogs differ from those which are not white? How can it be a fact that this dog and that are white, if the predicate ". . . is white" does not stand for something which dogs can either be or not be?

(3) *Does Russell's argument depend on features peculiar to certain languages?* Russell began by defining a universal as "anything which may be shared by many particulars." Now it is manifest that in English, as in all modern European languages, innumerable true propositions can be expressed by joining predicative expressions like verbs, adjectives, and common nouns to proper names or demonstrative pronouns; and that in many of the sentences so constructed the same predicative expression, used in the same sense is joined to a variety of proper names and demonstrative pronouns. Inasmuch as those propositions are faithfully reflected in English (or French, or German, or Italian) sentences which express them, there must by the Realist Principle be universals corresponding to those predicative expressions. Russell evidently recognized this; for he wrote that, "broadly speaking, proper names stand for particulars, while other substantives, adjectives, prepositions and verbs stand for universals."[26]

But what if the very same propositions which are expressed in English by predicative expressions can be expressed in some other language, whether artificial or not, without them? A suggestion with which Russell toyed in *An Inquiry into Meaning and Truth* is to the point here. Imagine a language in which what is expressed in English by "That wall is white" is expressed, not by a predicative expression corresponding to ". . . is white," but by a proper name, say "White," which is taken to be the name of a spatially and temporally discontinuous particular. This particular can be said to be wherever any part of it is, much as a salesman can be said to be in a house if he has his foot in the door. Instead of saying, as in English, "That wall is white," speakers of our imaginary language would say "White is there," pointing to that wall (or possibly, "White and Wall are there").

In *An Inquiry into Meaning and Truth* (London, 1940), Russell proposed a similar interpretation of many statements in modern European languages. "I wish to suggest," he wrote, "that 'this is red' is not a subject-predicate proposition, but is of the form 'redness is here'; [and] that 'red' is a name, not a predicate . . ." (p. 97). In *Three Philosophers*, Miss G. E. M. Anscombe attributed an apparently similar view to Aristotle. "It would be closer to [Aristotle's] view," she wrote, "if we ascribed to him an alternative that Plato proposes: namely, that a single form is divided up and becomes many. . . . Thus if there were only one large lump of [gold] in the world, the division of it would make gold, which had been only one thing, become many" (pp. 31–32).

Prima facie, an expression like "White" in this imaginary language would not denote anything which may be shared by many particulars. It is not shared by many places; for while White is in many places, a different part of it is at each of them. And although it would seem very strange to us to speak of In, say, as being where Russell and his room are, it is not obviously impossible that a language could be constructed in which even relational predicates like ". . . is in . . ." would be replaced by proper names of discontinuous particulars. If this could be done, there would be no reason to suppose that there are any constituents of reality which may be exemplified by many particulars. That supposition would be dismissed as an illusion created by the structure of certain languages. It could not survive the discovery that non-predicative structures are possible.

Unfortunately, not even in imaginary languages can predicative expressions be completely replaced by names of particulars. Suppose there to be a language in which everything said in English about what is white or not white is said by means of a proper name "White" of the kind I have described, i.e. the name of a spatially and temporally discontinuous particular. We may then inquire how saying that this particular is in two places is synonymous with saying that two different regions are white. Obviously, if the discontinuous particular "White" were many-colored, the two could not by synonymous. "The particular White is both here and there" could express the same proposition as "This region and that region are white," only if the particular White were of one color, and that color were white. But that condition cannot even be stated in our imaginary language. Manifestly, to introduce a further discontinuous particular, Albus say, and to lay it down that Albus is wherever White is, would only put off the evil day; for the regions where Albus is need not be white unless Albus itself is white all over.

Neither the belief that predicative expressions could be replaced by names of discontinuous particulars, nor Russell's notion that logically "This is white" is "not a subject-predicate proposition, but is of the form '[White-ness] is here,'"[27] would be tempting were not the predicative expression itself, or one of its derivatives, used as the name of the discontinuous particular. Suppose that particular to be named "Jack." The proposition "Jack is here" can only express the same proposition as "This is white" if Jack fulfills certain conditions. Those conditions can be stated in English, by means of the predicative expression, ". . . is white"; but I cannot conceive how they could be stated except by predicative expressions or their equiva-lents, i.e. by combining the same linguistic element used in the same sense with a number of other linguistic elements, in order to say the same thing about the things for which those other linguistic elements stand. The nature of the elements and the modes of combining them fall within the province of grammar, and Russell placed no limitation on their variety. He presupposed only that any language in which what can be said in modern European languages can be said, must contain predicative expressions or their equiva-lents. That presupposition has not been shown to be false by any argument known to me.

(4) *The objection that Realism is "circular and uninformative."* Having survived, bloody but unbowed, the objections of candid friends like Plato, and nominalist foes like Goodman and Quine, it would be an anti-climax if realism should succumb to the objection, not that it is inconsistent, but that it is trivial. Yet Mr. D. F. Pears has put that objection vigorously:

> [R]ealism is necessarily a circular explanation of naming . . . [U]ltimately there must be some exit from the maze of words, and, whenever this exit is made, it will be impossible to give an informative reason except by pointing . . . [It is true that] at the place where the exit is made it is always possible to give a detailed reason like "we are able to call things red because they are red," . . . [but that] is too obviously circular to look informative. . . . What philosophers who propose the existence of univer-sals do is to propose a general reason which looks informative because it shifts to another level, but unfortunately it is not. It merely marks time. . . .[28]

The form of realism which Pears chose to attack is not precisely Russell's. Russell's premise was not that we are able to call things red, but that some propositions containing the primitive predicate ". . . is red" are true; and his argument did not purport to explain such truths, but only to exhibit a necessary condition of their existence. However, it is beyond doubt that Pears would be willing to adapt his objection to Russell's theory.

In one respect, Pears is less than clear. He accuses realists like Russell of proposing a "reason which looks informative because it shifts to another level, but unfortunately it is not." Literally, this means that, because it shifts to a new level, Russell's reason *looks* informative, although in fact it is not. In other words, Russell argued that a necessary condition of the truth of propositions of the form "*x* is red" is that the universal *red* be real: this "shifts to another level," i.e. shifts from the level of words like ". . . is red" to the level of real beings, and so looks informative. Pears, however, contends that it is not. But if Russell's argument does shift to a new level, is it not informative? To be told that real beings correspond to the primitive predicates of true propositions—is not that information?

A second interpretation of Pears' objection is possible. If the clause "because it shifts to another level" falls within the scope of the verb "looks," then what Pears meant is that Russell's "reason" only *seems* to shift to another level, and so is not informative, although it seems so. Pears' example of a detailed realist "reason" supports this interpretation: "it is always possible to give a detailed reason like 'We are able to call things red because they are red.'" Observe that he does not write, "we are able to call things 'red' because they are red"; for, if he had, he could not have added that this "is too obviously circular even to look informative." By placing quotation marks around the word "red," he would have shown that his realist is looking to a fact about the world to explain a fact about language, i.e. that he does "shift to another level."

Pears did not leave the matter there. He went on to dismiss as vain all realist efforts to escape from the maze of words by postulating real entities corresponding to primitive predicates, on the ground that entities so postulated would be no more than "shadows" of their corresponding predicates.[29] Realism is "like a dream"—a dream the "manifest content [of which] is little more than a harmless caprice, but . . . [the] latent content [of which] is a serious error."[30] I doubt whether I understand what Pears meant by this simile; but I interpret him as meaning that a universal is like a dream-object, an unreal image constructed in the realist's mind, which, since it merely reproduces a fact about the objects from which it has been derived, i.e. that they are called by the same name, "taken literally . . . seems to be of little importance."[31] Its manifest content is therefore harmless. But, since it easily passes over into full-blown Platonism, thus becoming both important and false, its latent content is dangerous.

This criticism is odd, not because it affirms anything paradoxical, but because it affirms nothing (so far as its "manifest content" goes) which Russell need deny. Russell himself would reject full-blown Platonism,[32] i.e. the doctrine that only universals are real, and that objects in the world of sights and sounds are "between unbeing and being." Nor would he deny that universals are "shadows" of primitive predicates in the sense that the reality of universals is inferred from the fact that primitive predicates are irreducible components of true propositions. Of course he would deny that universals are shadows of primitive predicates in the sense that if the predicates had never been conceived, then the universals would not be real. That universals are in that sense shadows is the harmful latent content of Pears' simile.

Let it be conceded that the latent content of realism is false: to Russell, that was never in question. Is its manifest content, Russell's theory as I have elucidated it, also false? Pears' only objection to that manifest content, namely, that it is circular, that it only seems to escape from the maze of words, I think I have shown to be false. Realism asserts that something in the world corresponds to, and in that sense is a shadow of, every primitive predicate; but that assertion is neither circular nor uninformative.

III

Wise philosophers defer to plain men; but a plain man who has accompanied us so far will hardly contain his derision. To swallow the doctrine that universals are constituents of the world, just as a certain morsel of flour is a constituent of a pudding mixture, is painful, even when it is stipulated that the universals in question be exemplified. But that unexemplified universals are as much constituents of the world as exemplified ones! Is not that as though you were to say that flour is a real constituent of ice-cream because it is true that ice-cream is *not* made of it?

Should our plain man turn for aid and comfort to Moore's *Some Main Problems of Philosophy*, he would be confirmed in his outrage. Moore there invited his readers to distinguish two kinds of objects we can think about: "those which do have *being*, and those which simply have not got it, are purely imaginary, and don't belong to the Universe at all." To the second class he assigned "pure fiction[s]" like griffins and chimaeras. He then proceeded:

> If you fix clearly in your mind the sense in which there certainly are no such things as griffins and chimaeras, . . . it seems to me quite plain . . . that universals are not in any way to be classed with griffins and chimaeras; that, on the contrary, there is *the* most fundamental difference in the world between the two, a difference ever so much more important than that which separates universals from particulars (p. 373).

At this, any plain man who has learned a little Russellian logic will protest: "The fictitiousness, the non-being, of griffins and chimaeras consists in the fact that nothing is a griffin or a chimaera; but in your argument that universals are real you don't even attempt to show that they are all exemplified; in fact, it has been urged that your argument proves that unexemplified universals are as much constituents of the world as exemplified ones."

Such a protest is certainly justified. Moore himself, in his essay "The Conception of Reality," later accepted Russell's and Frege's view that the question whether or not griffins and chimaeras are real is the same as the question whether or not the predicates ". . . is a griffin" and ". . . is a chimaera" are each truly predicable of something.[33] And it is quite clear that the Realist Principle on which Russell's argument for the reality of universals depends, namely, that primitive predicates occurring non-redundantly in true propositions denote real constituents of the world, does not mean that such predicates are truly predicable of something. To show this, it is not necessary, although it is sufficient, to demonstrate that nothing in Russell's argument precluded its application to negative facts involving unexemplified universals. One need only point out that Russell began by supposing that he was in his room, *i.e.* that the relational predicate "... is in ..." was truly predicable of something, namely, himself and his room. It follows that if by his conclusion that the relation *in* is a real constituent of the world he had meant no more than that it is exemplified, then his argument would have been a gross *petitio principii*. To attribute such a blunder to Russell would be ridiculous.

Moore, then, was simply wrong when he implied that the sense in which realists claim to prove that universals are real constituents of the world is the sense in which griffins and chimaeras are not. Whether universals are real or have being in the sense of Russell's (and Moore's) proof is a question altogether distinct from the question whether they are or are not exemplified.

We may go further. Expressions like "real constituent of the world," and descriptions of the task of Philosophy or Ontology as being "to give a general description of the *whole* of the Universe, mentioning all the most important kinds of things which we *know* to be in it,"[34] inevitably suggest that philosophers are looking for the ingredients of which the world is composed, much as a chemist looks for the ingredients of a chemical mixture, or perhaps a zoologist for the species of fauna inhabiting a given region. Plain men are led to expect that philosophers will place before them a list of distinct ingredients or species, like flour and sugar, or lions and antelopes, although of course it is not required that they be material or even observable. And indeed some philosophers, for example the neo-Platonists and Aristotle and his medieval followers, with their hierarchies of beings, have done something like that. For example, Aquinas's catalogue—God or *Esse subsistens*, the Separate Substances or pure subsisting forms, and material substances or beings whose forms actualize matter—together with his account of their ordering with respect to one another, is in the ordinary sense a general description of the whole Universe, mentioning all the important kinds of things which Aquinas believed he knew to be in it.

Since the sense in which Aquinas believed God and the Separate Substances to be "in the Universe" (he would not, of course, have used that phrase) is the same as that in which Moore believed griffins and chimaeras *not* to be in it, namely that the predicates "... is God" and "... is a Separate Substance" are each truly predicable of something, we have already shown that Russell did not even profess to prove that universals are real in that sense. In what sense, then, did he profess to prove it? According to his Realist Principle, the non-redundant primitive predicates of true propositions denote things that are real or have being: but how are the expressions "things that are real," "things that have being" to be understood? If Moore, who in 1910 was as close to Russell as any man was, nevertheless misunderstood, have we any hope of doing better?

Wittgenstein once alleged that "Nothing is more likely than that the verbal expression of the result of a mathematical proof is calculated to delude us with a myth";[35] and whether he was right or wrong about mathematics, his remark holds good of Russell's proof of the reality of universals. Wittgenstein's prescription for getting rid of such delusions was to look at the proof "[T]he *sense* of the result is not to be read off from [the result] by itself but from the *proof*."[36]

Why did Russell accept his Realist Principle? What proof did he give of it? He seems to have thought that a proof of it would fall into two parts. First, it would be necessary to show that predicative expressions could not all be analysed into non-predicative ones. Both Russell and Moore held that traditional nominalism, e.g. that of Berkeley and Hume, had attempted such analyses, and had failed, because it had not been able to dispense with the relational predicate ". . . is similar to. . . ."[37] Secondly, it would be necessary to show that whether or not a proposition is true depends on how the world is, and not on how anybody, plain or scientific, chooses to think about it. If "F" and "G" are primitive predicates, then what "Fa" says about the world is different from what "Ga" says about it. The difference in what they say can only arise from the difference of their predicates. Suppose both to be true: then the world is as they say it is, and what they say it is depends in part on their predicates. Suppose either or both to be false, then the world will be as the negatives of either or both say it is, and that too depends in part on their predicates. This argument does not show that any bit of the world is named by "F" or "G"; for it is not about the elements or ingredients of the world in the way in which a chemical analysis is about the elements or ingredients of a chemical compound or mixture. But it does show that "F" and "G" refer to the world in the sense that they are descriptive and not merely formal parts of statements about it, the truth of those statements being determined by how the world is. And since, for any predicate "f" and any individual name "x," it is true either that fx or that $\neg fx$, every primitive predicate must be a descriptive and not merely a formal part of a true full description of the world, the truth of that description being determined by how the world is. That, if anything, is what Russell's proof proves; and that is what I think he meant when he asserted that a universal like *in* "is something, although we cannot say that it exists *in the same sense* in which I and my room exist."[38]

Russell confirmed this interpretation of his theory of universals in an almost mocking remark in his "Reply to Criticisms" in P. A. Schilpp's *The Philosophy of Bertrand Russell*.

If it is true [he wrote], as it seems to be, that the world cannot be described without the use of the word "similar" or some equivalent [i.e. without the use of predicates], that seems to imply something about the world, though I do not know exactly what. This is the sense in which I still believe in universals. (p. 688)

In this passage, Russell took the realist theory of universals to consist in repudiating two errors: the nominalist error that predicates can be dispensed with in a true description of the world; and what we may call the "idealist" error that the repudiation of the nominalist error implies nothing about the world, because the truth of a description depends, not on how the world is, but on how thinkers think.

Even if I have interpreted Russell's theory correctly, I have not shown that it is true; for I have proved neither that predicates cannot be dispensed with in a true description of the world, nor that whether a description of the world is true depends on how the world is. However, Moore's and Russell's criticism of Berkeley and Hume, and the difficulties I have pointed out in the proposal to replace qualitative predicates by the names of discontinuous particulars, show how difficult it is to carry out the nominalist programme. As for what I have called "the idealist error," like Moore and Russell I consider it to merit exposure rather than refutation.

A plain man might accept all my explanations, and yet object that the realist theory of universals, although true, is of little importance. In one respect, he would be right. The major questions of metaphysics are either about the substance of the world (e.g., What sorts of individuals does it contain? What are the space and time in which some, if not all, of them exist? Do they persist through time? Are they substances or processes? Are any or all of them phenomenal?) or about mind and knowledge (e.g., What is a mind? How are minds related to bodies? Is thinking a physical process? How can we think of individuals, their kinds, and their properties? How is thinking related to perceiving?). The realist theory of universals does not lead to a solution of any of these problems. Its importance, like its character, is negative. If you reject it, that is, if you accept the nominalist or the idealist theories that conflict with it, you cannot avoid serious errors when you try to answer the major questions. Although negative, it is fundamental.[39]

NOTES

From *The Monist* 47, no. 2 (1963). Reprinted by permission of the editor of *The Monist*.

1. G. E. Moore, "The Nature of Judgment," *Mind*, 8 (1899), esp. pp. 178–83; "Identity," *Proc. Aris. Soc.*, 1 (1900–1), esp. pp. 105–15; *Some Main Problems of Philosophy* (London, 1953), hereafter cited as *Main Problems*, pp. 301–5, 312–77 (composed in 1910–1); and Bertrand Russell, "On the Relations of Universals to Particulars" (composed 1911) in *Logic and Knowledge*, ed. Robert C. Marsh (London, 1956); *The Problems of Philosophy* (London, 1912), chs. 8–10.
2. W. V. Quine, *From a Logical Point of View* (Cambridge, Mass., 1951), chs. 1, 6; Nelson Goodman, *The Structure of Appearance* (Cambridge, Mass., 1951), ch. 2.
3. Gustav Bergmann, *Meaning and Existence* (Madison, Wis., 1959), esp. chs. 4, 13. My debts in this essay to Professor Bergmann, particularly in what I say about the attempts of Professors Quine and Goodman to shave Plato's Beard, are

heavy and obvious, though no doubt he would reject most of my conclusions.

4. D. F. Pears, "Universals," in *Logic and Language*, 2nd series, ed. Antony Flew (Oxford, 1953).
5. Bertrand Russell, *The Problems of Philosophy* (London, reset edn. 1946), hereafter cited as *Problems*, p. 90.
6. Russell, *Problems*, p. 93; cf. Moore, *Main Problems*, p. 304.
7. Russell, *Problems*, pp. 95–7; Moore, *Main Problems*, pp. 305, 313–4.
8. Moore, *Main Problems*, p. 353; cf. Russell, *Problems*, pp. 93–4, 97.
9. Ludwig Wittgenstein, *Tractatus Logico-Philosophicus* (London, 1922), 4.126–4.12721.
10. Russell, *Problems*, pp. 90 (cf. 80–8), 97–8; Moore, *Main Problems*, pp. 303–5.
11. Russell, *Logic and Knowledge*, pp. 211–6, esp. 213.
12. Russell, *Problems*, p. 58; *Logic and Knowledge*, pp. 195, 270–80. For a criticism of the Principle of Acquaintance see Max Black, *Language and Philosophy* (Ithaca, 1949), pp. 130–4.
13. J. L. Austin, *Philosophical Papers* (Oxford, 1961), p. 18.
14. Gilbert Ryle, "Plato's *Parmenides*," *Mind*, 48 (1939), pp. 137–8.
15. *Logic and Knowledge*, p. 123; cf. *Problems*, pp. 102–3.
16. Ryle truly observed that his regress is not the same as F. H. Bradley's celebrated regress of relations, "though reminiscent of it" (*loc. cit.* p. 138). The question which generated Bradley's regress, namely, How can "a more or less independent" relation relate its terms? arises from Bradley's doctrine that a relation between A and B "implies really a substantial foundation within them" (*Appearance and Reality* [Oxford, 1946], pp. 17–18). Neither Russell nor Ryle saw any difficulty in the "independence" or externality of relations.
17. The traditional Aristotelian doctrine is clearly explained by Henry B. Veatch in *Intentional Logic* (New Haven, 1952), pp. 105–13, esp. 111–3. Fr. Joseph Owens, C.Ss.R., has argued that the "Aristotelian" doctrine really was Aristotle's: see *The Doctrine of Being in the Aristotelian Metaphysics* (Toronto, 1957) pp. 242–3.
18. W. V. Quine, *From a Logical Point of View*, pp. 9–14, 102–29, esp. 122–4; Nelson Goodman, *The Structure of Appearance*, pp. 33–41.
19. Quine, *op. cit.* p. 103.
20. *Ibid.* p. 9.
21. Goodman, *op. cit.*, pp. 33–4.
22. *Ibid.* pp. 34–5.
23. W. S. Sellars, "Grammar and Existence: A Preface to Ontology," *Mind*, 69 (1960), esp. pp. 499–503, 507–17. Although my position in this paper is reactionary while his is revolutionary, my debt to Sellars' writings and conversation is too great to be indicated in detail: in particular, his criticism over many years at Minnesota showed me that realism is still an issue, and that Russell's and Moore's views deserve serious consideration.
24. Russell did not, however, plead guilty. "The theory of logical types," he wrote, ". . . has also a certain consonance with common sense which makes it inherently credible." (*Principia Mathematica* [2nd ed., Cambridge, 1927], p. 37).
25. Quine, *op. cit.* p. 13.
26. Russell, *Problems*, p. 93.
27. Russell, *An Inquiry into Meaning and Truth* [London: Allen and Unwin, 1940], p. 97.
28. D. F. Pears, "Universals" in *Logic and Language*, 2nd series, ed. Antony Flew (Oxford 1953), pp. 53–4.

29. *Ibid.* p. 54.
30. *Ibid.* p. 58.
31. *Ibid.* p. 58.
32. "These mystical developments [i.e. Platonism] are very natural, but the basis of the theory is in logic, and it is based in logic that we have to consider it" (Russell, *Problems*, p. 92).
33. G. E. Moore, *Philosophical Studies* (London, 1911), p. 212.
34. Moore, *Main Problems*, p. 1.
35. Ludwig Wittgenstein, *Remarks on the Foundations of Mathematics* (Oxford, 1956), II, 26 (p. 77).
36. *Ibid.* II, 25 (p. 76).
37. Russell, *Problems*, pp. 95–7; Moore, *Main Problems*, pp. 313–7.
38. Russell, *Problems*, p. 90.
39. Although I doubt whether any of them will agree with most of my conclusions, this essay originated in conversations with my colleagues Herbert Hochberg, Reinhardt Grossmann, Henry B. Veatch and Roger C. Buck, and both in design and in particular points is heavily indebted to them.

27 AARON

Aaron argues that (1) universals are natural recurrences, and (2) universals are principles of grouping or classifying. Both (1) and (2) go beyond Aristotelian realism in different ways, but neither in the direction of extreme or Platonic realism.

It is undeniable that recurrences are found in the natural world. These recurrences are of two kinds, identities and resemblances. Two or more things can and do possess an identical quality that often serves as their sole distinguishing feature. Relations, such as "to the north of," as well as qualities, are recurring identities. However, universals are not just identities, but resemblances as well. As Aaron observes, "Certain qualities are similar without being identical and the similarities recur. For instance, shades of blue which are not identical but similar constantly recur and we learn to speak of the color 'blue', covering by this token all shades of blue, as a class of colors." However, it is necessary to include things along with qualities and relations when resemblances are understood to be real recurrences. For example, horses are similar but not identical.

Our use of general words in thinking may indeed be initiated by natural recurrences, but it certainly does not end there. Imaginative universals, be they things (e.g., a dragon) or situations (e.g., the slaying of the dragon), serve as principles of classification, and human thinking is to a great extent dependent upon them. Aaron does not deny that this aspect of his analysis smacks of conceptualism.

Finally, some universals are principles of grouping that are neither an image nor a concept, but are verbal in nature. These are the universals of abstract thinking and take the form of general words. We can, for example, carry on a meaningful conversation about the nature of a proposition, characterized by a series of words to elucidate what constitutes a proposition, itself a linguistic "entity." Consequently, the universals of intellect and abstract thinking appear to have some of the trappings of nominalism. Aaron is not upset with this eclectic view of universals, for his primary concern is the development of a theory of thinking.

The Theory of Universals

A THEORY OF UNIVERSALS

85. After the examination of common quality, disposition, and concept we now find ourselves in a position to offer a theory of universals. It will be

one resting on the discussions of the previous chapters, discussions which have ranged over a wide field. We may thus hope to be saved from basing the theory on too narrow a foundation. Often when some one fact or a few facts seem to point in the direction of one of the traditional theories, this is at once assumed to be the true theory. And this procedure is particularly dangerous if, as is usually the case, one's theory of knowledge and one's philosophy in general rest on this assumption from that point forward. Thus the conviction that the common quality is concrete may cause a philosopher to jump at realism; a feeling that we are guided in thinking by elements not given in perception may lead to conceptualism. Recently the drift has been towards nominalism. But it does not appear to be a nominalism conscious of itself in any positive sense, indeed, it is most difficult to find any positive statement of contemporary nominalism. What is attractive in it is its denials, its criticisms of other theories of universals. Yet it is dangerous to assume that nominalism is true because realism and conceptualism are false. If we are to accept it we must accept it in itself as a positive theory which we have considered and understood.

After taking as broad a view as possible of all the issues involved I find at the end of this study that I cannot accept any one of the traditional theories and I must explain first why I think it necessary to reject them. In speaking of the traditional theories I mean Aristotelian realism, conceptualism, and nominalism, omitting realism of the *ante rem* kind. The latter has been discussed already and, except possibly in the moral field where it may be contended that it alone does justice to the facts, the theory is hardly relevant to present discussions and need not be re-examined here.

86. The case against Aristotelian realism is a strong one. On this theory a universal is something we discover; it is part of the objective world of nature. Not that it is an object in nature, one amongst other objects, as is the chair or table; it is rather a common quality *in rebus*, a quality of this table, for instance, which is also a quality of that table and of other tables, and is as real as the tables themselves. Common relations, too, may be said to be universals in this sense. Many of these universals may be discovered to go together; for instance, the qualities a, b, and c go together in the object O, and we may discover this combination of universal qualities. Knowledge of universals in this sense gives us a basis for classification. Things which have certain qualities or relations in common are perceived to form a class which we may know, and we may further discover wider classes of which this class is a member, as when we find many species in one genus.

Such is the position of the Aristotelian realist; but it is at once disturbing to find that though the realist ought on this account to limit his universals to qualities and relations, he never does so. Man, it appears, is a universal, as well as white or triangular; and yet man is neither a common quality nor a common relation. This apparent inconsistency arouses suspicion; it suggests that the realists' original position is not one that can be sustained, and this is indeed the case.

Two major criticisms of realism can be made, and I shall limit myself to these. In the first place, the realist holds, and holds rightly if our previous argument is correct, that there are discoverable common qualities and relations; but he then concludes that all universals are either such common qualities or common relations. Yet, for instance, the quality human is not discovered as ultramarine is discovered. It is simply not true that all men have this quality, human, in common, so that we can observe it and discover it in observing them. Nor is it the case that we discover qualities *a*, *b*, and *c*, combined together to make up the complex quality human, in all men. Most men are two-legged, but some have lost a leg. Most men are rational, but some are idiots. If we say that to be human is to be two-legged and rational we are stating a standard or an ideal, what ought to be the case; we certainly do not discover two-leggedness and rationality as a common quality or combination of common qualities in all men. The realist account of these matters is misleading.

Logically it is not impossible for all men to share a quality by virtue of which they could be classified as men, an *x* which would belong to them all as the color ultramarine is shared by these objects now before me. But it is clear that we do not discover this quality in experience. Yet we do speak of human as a quality, and the sentence '*A* is human' is quite significant. It is also a universal, at least in this sense that we can say '*B, C, D* . . . are human'. It would thus appear that some universals are not discovered. The quality human or being human is apparently a quality for which we ourselves are partly responsible. We frame it out of material derived from experience and on the suggestion of experience; nevertheless it is *post rem* and, to a certain degree, 'the workmanship of the mind'. Consequently, we must deny the realist position that all universals are discovered, for if human is a universal then it certainly is not discovered. This will hold too of the universal man. There can be no objection to this universal on a *post rem* theory, but it is palpably neither a discovered common quality nor a common relation. The universal man is certainly suggested by experience but yet it is determined finally in respect both to its content and to its limits by the thinker himself who uses the universal.

The second main objection to the realist thesis is the following. Realism assumes that classification is only possible on the basis of discoverable, identical qualities or relations *in rebus*. In fact, this is not the case. If we were confined to identical qualities and relations as bases for classification, classification even of natural objects into species and genera would have been impossible. For instance, it is this characteristic of being human, which is not a discoverable common quality or relation, which determines the class man. The classification is suggested by experience and is in this sense founded on the real, but it is not based on the discovery of identical qualities. Our primitive classifications and much adult classification, as we have seen, rest not on the conscious observation of identical qualities, but on a familiarity with the recurring elements of experience which leaves us disposed to group in certain ways. On the other hand, a Linnacus will take greater care in classifying than the ordinary man and he will state explicitly the characteristics which he uses as bases for his classification, but these characteristics again are frequently not the common, identical qualities of the realist. For resemblances guide us in classifying as much as identities, and they bring in a more extensive field of objects. Obviously, in the practical affairs of life a loose classification of objects that resemble one another without, possibly, resembling one another closely, is frequently very useful. The demand for close resemblance, not to say identity, may prove a hindrance.

If the realist replies that all observation of resemblance presupposes awareness of identical qualities, since things resemble only in so far as they have qualities in common, this reply, as we have seen, is of doubtful validity. In some cases we do discover identical qualities which provide a foundation for the resemblance; in others we entirely fail to do so, and we have no right to assume that they must be there. Moreover, it is not things only which resemble one another but qualities themselves resemble, and resemble in circumstances which make it absurd to speak of an identity as the basis of the resemblances. We certainly cannot admit that we observe resemblances, and so frame our universals, only in so far as we discover identical qualities.

Thus the realist is at fault both in holding that all universals are discovered identical qualities and in supposing that classification is only possible when the characteristics determining the class are such identical qualities. This criticism, in my opinion, finally refutes Aristotelian realism and makes any rehabilitation of this theory impossible. Certainly no rehabilitation will be attempted here. Nevertheless, two points should be made. First, the criticism, while it refutes the traditional Aristotelian realism, in no way establishes either conceptualism or nominalism. Secondly, granted that the arguments prove that certain universals are not identical qualities nor complexes of such qualities, it yet does not follow that there are no universals of this kind. On the contrary, the evidence is plain, as we have seen in discussing common qualities, that identical qualities can be discovered by us, and it may well be the case that these are sometimes what we mean when we speak of universals.

87. In turning to conceptualism we recall the argument of the previous chapter. There we sought to feel our way towards a more satisfactory theory of concepts than the one provided by the traditional or classical conceptualists. The latter, the conceptualism for instance of Locke, is hardly a living theory and there are few philosophers who would subscribe to it. As we have seen, it leads to skepticism about human knowledge. It also leads to a deep suspicion of abstraction and a growing emphasis on the value of 'the bare, naked particular'. We begin, however, with this traditional theory and

ask what these conceptualists meant to convey by their doctrine that the universal was the concept.

The answer they gave is clear—up to a point. The concept (or idea) was what was 'before the mind', that of which the mind was aware, at the same time it was not an object independent of the mind. In saying, therefore, that the universal was the concept they were saying, in the first place, that the universal was not part of the concrete, real world. Concrete particular things alone existed and there was no universal amongst them. But, in the second place, though the concept was dependent on the mind, it was none the less an entity, that is to say, an abstract entity. It was a cognized object. Thus the theory that the universal was the concept was for them definite and precise, since the concept itself was precisely conceived.

But it was precise so long as one did not probe too deeply. As has been seen, the empiricists themselves were uneasy about one or two points in the theory. First, if all things are particulars, are not ideas particular too? For consistency's sake, should not one say that what one was aware of was a particular idea? Could one then think of this particular idea as in some way representative of many and so give it a sort of universality? But this suggestion considerably clouds the previously clear theory. Secondly, the conceptual entity has not quite the same objectivity as a particular, concrete object. It is mind's creation. It is abstracted, possibly compounded, a complex construction of the mind. This makes it very different from the concrete object independent of mind. Is it then proper that we should speak of it as an entity? Yet if the concept is not an entity the traditional theory ceases to be clear and precise and becomes something vague instead.

But, if difficulties of this sort arose, the traditional conceptualists were still in a better position to make sense of the theory that universals were concepts than later conceptualists have been. At least, a case could be made that it makes sense to speak of ideal objects of awareness as *universalia post rem*. But suppose we adopt the view that concepts are mental capacities, can we then sensibly talk of these capacities as *universalia post rem*? To defend the view that a universal is a mental faculty would be a formidable task. If, on the other hand, we think of conceiving in terms of the use of general words, we might be tempted to say that the universal was the general word, but in that case conceptualism would be no different from nominalism, whereas the conceptualist has always insisted that it is different.

The conceptualist of course does not say that the concept is the general word. I have suggested that the safest way to state the theory of verbal concepts today is the following: the concept is the general word plus all the accretions necessary for its successful use. Now where, on such a theory, are we to find the universal? If the accretions are thought of as mental dispositions or mental capacities they scarcely provide us with the universals we are searching for, if as internal accusatives we are back with the traditional theory. Perhaps we should conclude that contemporary conceptualism, critical of the traditional doctrine, cannot provide us with a theory of universals and that it is misguided to seek for any such theory in it. And if we are speaking of a precise, clear theory this seems to me to be the case. On the other hand, it is true that we do use the general word successfully and that through its use we know how to apply a predicate which can characterize more than one object. Our successful use of general words too presupposes—as does our use of imagery in thinking—that we possess principles or rules of grouping and are applying them. Reflection on these phenomena may help to provide us with a theory of universals, but the one definite theory that conceptualism has put forward, namely, that the universal is the internal accusative, is to be rejected.

88. Now traditionally the only theory which remains is nominalism. But we should not be justified in assuming that since realism and conceptualism have both been shown to be false, nominalism must be true. We must examine the nominalist case in itself.

Yet as has been seen, it is not easy to find a positive statement of nominalism; it is easy enough to trace 'nominalist' tendencies in contemporary thought, and it is not difficult to find out what is denied. Yet the doctrine is rarely set forward positively. One of the earliest attempts to do so in modern philosophy, that of Hobbes, is also one of the neatest: 'there being nothing in the world universal but names'. This means presumably that, for instance, each cat is an individual creature; it has individual, particular qualities. The universal is neither a common quality in cats, not a natural class, nor a concept. It is the 'name' or general word 'cat', and we should not seek beyond the verbal for any other universal.

Such nominalism has sometimes been interpreted to mean that the one thing cats have in common is the name 'cat', but this account of it makes it at once absurd. To begin with, it is not the case that all cats share this name. Only those cats which are spoken of in English are called 'cats'. If we followed this interpretation strictly the universal 'cat' and the universal 'chat', being different words, would be different universals. In the second place, if it be granted that cats really have one quality in common, namely, having the name 'cat', there seems to be no inherent objection to their having other qualities in common, for instance, a liking for fish. The door is open for the realist.

The nominalist, however, would no doubt object to this interpretation. If we do deny the theory of common qualities, he would say, we do deny it, and two cats must not be supposed to have a common quality in being both called 'cat'. What Hobbes really meant was that universals only come into being with classifying, and that classifying is a verbal technique. In the physical world each object is individual and different from every other. Yet in using a general word we know how to speak of many of them at one and the same time. We have learnt the use of language and part of that learning consists in knowing how to use general words. Now it is here and here only that the universal comes into being, when we classify, using general words for the purpose. It thus belongs essentially to the verbal.

In examining this theory it must first be admitted that the nominalist has the right to use the term 'universal' as he chooses and may use it as a synonym for the general word, and only in this way. This is a matter of convention, and though it is true that normally the word has been used in other ways, yet it may be thus used if the nominalist chooses. But when he goes on to imply that classifying is merely using general words and is solely a verbal matter he is surely on less firm ground. One would have thought it obvious that a classifying is a grouping and grouping is not the same thing as using a general word. Grouping may well proceed without the use of a general word. Very young children group things together manipulatively before they begin to speak. Ribot's deaf-mutes grouped things together though they had no words. Normally we group things together because we discover recurrences. In any case, grouping is not just using a general word. Yet this appears to be the nominalist position as now interpreted, and it is obviously false.

But the nominalist might argue that he is prepared to admit a grouping other than the using of the general word, as long as it is understood that the grouping is wholly arbitrary and that it is not the consequence of the observation of recurrences in nature. He could not admit the latter without giving the case away to the realists. But we may group things together arbitrarily, he might say. Take any four objects; there is nothing to prevent our grouping them together into a class and now giving them a name. The universal would come into being only in the classifying; no recurrence, no common quality and no resemblance between the objects, would be presupposed.

Now it is a question whether we can ever find four objects of which we can say, 'These have nothing whatsoever in common'; but even if we could it would be agreed that any grouping on this basis would be most unusual. And yet the nominalist, to maintain his position, has to hold that *all* grouping is of this kind. He denies that there is any non-verbal universal element, acquaintance with which guides us in our grouping. But this is an impossible position. In normal grouping we are guided by observing recurrences in our experience and by the empirical suggestion of natural sorts. We did not entirely arbitrarily decide on the constituent members of the cat-group. We might conceivably have done so. A linguistic dictator could enact that henceforth the word 'cat' was to be the name for all the objects that he had put together at a certain place, and perhaps along with creatures which we now call 'cats' he had also included objects that we now call 'bicycles' and 'tomatoes'. We should then have to call them all 'cats'. But this would prove nothing about the way we have in fact come to use the word 'cat' and nothing about universals. The nominalist has to disprove that there are *universalia in rebus* and our ordinary usage of the term 'cat' suggests that there are. For ordinarily the entities covered by the term 'cat' have not been determined by any such arbitrary fiat, but by experience. We have become accustomed to the recurrence of a creature that is domesticated, purrs, likes fish, has fur, and so on. Our classifying is guided by the recurrences. It will not help us to ignore these recurrences or to refuse to call them universals. Yet if we recognize them, nominalism as a positive theory is no longer possible.

The nominalist might seek to defend himself in still another way. Do we not, he might ask, use words significantly in conceptual thinking without having in mind any of the realist's recurrences, and does not this fact support the nominalist case? All we make use of in these circumstances is the word itself, and if there is a universal present in our thought it must be verbal. But this again, we must reply, gives no real support to a thorough-going nominalism. We may use such a word as 'cat' in imageless thinking but obviously not all its uses are of this kind, and even when it is so used we use the word significantly in speaking and thinking because we have learnt from experience how the word should be used, though we do not now explicitly recall these experiences. Thus it would be erroneous in the extreme to suppose that such occasional uses of words in imageless thinking justify the nominalist thesis.

Finally, it must be admitted that there are words in use which operate, as it were, solely within the verbal, and which do not presuppose recurrences or common qualities, for instance, the words 'but' and 'or'. Yet the presence of such words in speech is hardly a justification of nominalism, for the nominalist would certainly not be prepared to admit that his theory applies to such words only, if it applies to them at all. Sometimes, it is true, nominalism is presented as if it were simply the theory that words can be used without reference to a world other than the verbal. But a moment's reflection will show that this doctrine, which I in no way dispute, is not a theory of universals.

To sum up, if nominalism is the doctrine that the members of a class share one thing in common and one thing only, the name, then its absurdity soon becomes apparent. If, on the other hand, it is the assertion that classifying is a purely verbal process and involves no prior knowledge of common features or relations which are nonverbal, then it is false. On either interpretation strict nominalism seems wholly unacceptable.

89. But, if nominalism on either of these interpretations is rejected, it must not be assumed that every doctrine which has been described as 'nominalist' must thereby be rejected. On the contrary these doctrines may well be accepted even when nominalism is denied.

For instance, the 'elimination' or 'abolition' of the class by the authors of *Principia Mathematica* is sometimes supposed to establish nominalism. But this is not so. The claim is made that classes can be eliminated in favor of quantification and propositional functions, and there is a sense in which this is true. But this reduction in no way establishes nominalism. For, as I ventured to point out in my British Academy Lecture,[1] in 'For all x's, if x is human then x is mortal' we are still left with the universals human and mortal and there is no suggestion that these universals are 'abolished'. That is to say, if *Principia Mathematica* 'abolishes' the class it leaves the problem of universals very much where it finds it. It certainly offers no nominalist theory of, for instance, the universal human.

There are other doctrines described as nominalist which a realist could accept without giving up his realism. Indeed, the present tendency to describe all philosophers who are not 'platonist' as 'nominalist' paradoxically puts many who are realists, but not platonists, into the 'nominalist' camp.[2] Even the renunciation of abstract entities' which was the mark of nominalism according to the celebrated article 'Steps towards a Constructive Nominalism' by Quine and Goodman in 1947[3] is something of which a realist might well approve. This article opened, 'We do not believe in abstract entities. No one supposes that abstract entities—classes, relations, properties, etc.—exist in space-time; but we mean more than this. We renounce them altogether.' Unfortunately, no analysis is provided of the key phrase 'abstract entities', though classes, relations, and properties are said to be instances. No one, it is said, supposes that they exist in space-time but, unlike the authors, most people apparently suppose that they do exist—not in space-time but, presumably, as objects for the mind, as Lockean internal accusatives. But if 'renouncing abstract entities' is renouncing internal accusatives, and if all who do renounce them are nominalists, then many realists are nominalists; for a realist may certainly reject the doctrine of internal accusatives and yet remain a realist.

Both writers have moved away from this position since 1947; Quine does not consider himself a nominalist,[4] and Goodman, though still a nominalist, has varied his emphasis. He now holds 'that the nominalist insists on the world being described as composed of individuals, that to describe the world as composed of individuals is to describe it as made up of entities no two of which have the same content, and that this in turn is to describe it by means of a system for which no two distinct entities have exactly the same atoms'.[5] Yet nominalism in this sense too might be accepted by a realist. Certainly it is good Aristotelian realist doctrine that what exist are individuals; further the realist accepts the identity of indiscernibles, if this is Goodman's point, from which it follows that no two distinct individuals can be identical in all respects. If the point is, however, that individuals can never have anything in common then Aristotelian realists would reject this theory. But it is not clear whether Goodman is saying this. If he is, what account would he give of the quality of *ultramarine*? The empirical evidence is that we have in the ultramarine of these two pieces of silk an instance of an identical quality in the Aristotelian realist sense.

Unlike Goodman, Quine is prepared to recognize classes. He admits the difficulties, particularly the paradoxes that follow if we do recognize them. 'Yet the admission of classes as values of variables of quantification brings power that is not lightly to be surrendered.'[6] What he is not prepared to recognize is the attribute, and he refuses to recognize it because of its 'referential opacity' and even more because of our inability to identify 'attributes attributed by two open sentences'. The 'referential opacity' of most attributes must be granted, though in defence of Aristotelian realism the case of *ultramarine* should again be studied. It must also be granted that anyone who looks at human thinking from the standpoint of modern logical theory finds difficulty with intentional entities. Yet in my view classes presuppose attributes; to admit classes is to presuppose rules or principles for classifying, and these principles I take to be the attributes and the universals which we speak of in terms of general locutions or open sentences.

90. We must now consider the theory which emerges from our discussions up to the present, but before doing so a word should be said about certain problems which I take to be, in this connection, secondary, but which are sometimes held to be central. It is occasionally argued or implied that the problem of universals consists (*a*) in distinguishing between token words and type words, (*b*) in distinguishing between determinables and determinates, or (*c*) in making clear the nature of quantification. These three problems are important, particularly the third, and require attention; but in my view the problem of universals is different from all three and is not to be identified with any one of them.

Thus while it is necessary to recognize the difference between token and type words it is surely obvious that the key to the understanding of universals is not to be found in the recognition of this difference. The distinction may be illustrated in the following way. If we confine ourselves for the moment to written, rather than spoken, words then the word 'problem', let us say, occurs more than once on this page. Each appearance is a token word and is numerically different from every other appearance of this word. None the less the printed shape of the various token words is the same and this enables us to use it as a type word. It need not be identically the same, similarity is enough. If we now proceed to say that though there are many appearances of the word 'problem' on this page yet it is one and the same word that appears, we are then thinking of the type word. This distinction, it should be noted, applies to proper names as much as to general words; we can distinguish between the token word 'Peter' and the type word. And this fact at once suggests that we should not expect to find here any special insight into our use of general words. It is important for any language theory that the same shape can recur, and that we know how to make use of this recurrence. The recurrence of shapes is itself an instance of a universal, in one sense of that term. But the simple distinction between token word and type word throws no light on the nature of the universal.

No doubt if we began to inquire into the use of the type word we should find universals involved in some cases of its use, but that inquiry would take us farther than the distinction itself.

In the same way the distinction between determinables and determinates is relevant to the problem of universals, though again I cannot agree that making this distinction solves the problem. With occasional straining, it is possible no doubt to speak of each and every quality as a determinable and a determinate; for instance, color is a determinable and red and blue are determinates, or, again, red is a determinable and the various shades of red are determinates. Relations do not lend themselves so easily to this treatment, though we may say, for instance, that being to the left of is a determinate of the determinable, spatial relation. And we can always say that such and such a relation is a determinate of the determinable, relation. In the case of things, men, tables, dragons, the division would presumably follow the lines of the traditional genus-species division. In this way it might be possible to speak of all universals as either determinables or determinates. But I should still hold that the distinction presupposes universals and does not itself provide a solution of the problem of universals. For if we consider a determinate, say ultramarine, the realization that it is a determinate is subsequent to the realization that ultramarine is a common quality, yet our awareness of the universal in this case is one with the latter realization. I am here speaking of the distinction in empiricist terms. Admittedly, if it was meant that we know the final nature of things, knowing that the real consists of so many determinables which are the ultimate metaphysical forms or principles explanatory of all being, this doctrine would certainly be of the first importance and could not be said to be secondary. But, presumably, those who draw our attention to this distinction do not do so because they have metaphysical knowledge of this kind, but because experience has taught them that some qualities lend themselves to the determinable-determinate distinction. Clearly in their case the solution of the problem of universals cannot be identified with the making of this distinction. The same holds true of the distinction between species and genus.

Thirdly, I believe it a mistake to identify the theory of universals with quantification theory, that is to say, with the logic of the use of such quantifiers as 'all', 'some', and 'any'. It is true that the language of traditional logic itself sometimes suggests this identification. In particular, when the quantifier 'all' is used in a sentence, as in 'All men are mortal', the proposition is traditionally called a 'universal proposition'. Such language makes it easy to suppose that the problem of universals is one about our use of 'all' and is related to the problem of numbers, so that mathematical logicians alone can solve it. *In my opinion quantification presupposes the universal.* Not that it is necessary for the logician to set down a theory of universals before explaining quantification, although perhaps it would be best if he did proceed in that order. Most often, however, he assumes universals without presenting a theory of universals. To resolve 'All men are mortal' into 'For all x's, if x is human then x is mortal' is to explain the quantification with the help of the variable x, but also with the presupposition of universals, namely, those involved in the use of the general words 'human' and 'mortal'. The fact that resolution is possible in this way makes it clear that the theory of universals cannot be identified with quantification theory, though the two are related. No doubt a thorough and complete quantification theory would include a solution of the problem of universals, but it would also contain over and above this solution, the explanation of our use of such words as 'all' and 'some'. This is a problem pre-eminently for the mathematical logician and is bound up with theory of number.

91. I turn then to the final question: what sort of theory of universals is suggested by the argument of this book? The approach has been from the study of thinking and it has become increasingly clear that our adult human thinking is possible only because of our ability to speak in general terms. It is also clear that part of the explanation of how we are able to use general words successfully lies in a natural fact, and it is with this fact that I begin.

The world around us, as revealed in experience, is populated by beings and things which, while being individual and distinct, have yet much in common. Not only in our thinking but in our general behavior our conduct rests upon the assumption that individual being, for instance, individual human beings, have many features in common. The tailor, cutting out ready-made suits, knows the general run of men's sizes; the teacher has a rough idea of the capacities of next year's freshmen; and the mother who believes her baby to be unique, as he certainly is, reads with avidity the nursing-book which is written on the assumption that all babies are more or less alike. So, too, with animals, plants, and all living things; we see the individuals but find in them common features; and it is these common features which concern us in our zoological, veterinary, and botanical sciences. This then is the fact with which we start, our thinking rests in part on the observation of recurrences. Here is part explanation of our successful use of general words. The same features recur in different individual beings and individual things and we are aware of this fact.

By universals, then, I mean, in the first place, recurrences found in the natural world. To that extent the theory here put forward is realist. In dealing with universals we are not confined to a world of imaginative or logical constructions and are certainly not concerned with words only. On the contrary, our thinking rests upon foundations empirically given; it is because our experience is what it is that we think as we do and use general words in the way we do. We are able to say that an object we saw yesterday was ultramarine, and that this present object is ultramarine, and that possibly the next object we shall see will be ultramarine, because ultramarine is a shade which recurs in the natural world observed by us. Accordingly when we speak and think, using such general words as 'ultramarine', we are not turning away from the real, that is to say, from the experienced real, but are speaking and thinking about it.

As we examine these recurrences more closely, however, we see that they are of two sorts, identities and resemblances. We may first consider identities. In a previous chapter I have shown that we can quite safely speak of identities in this context, and that we fail to do justice to the facts if we speak of resemblance or similarity only, even of close similarity. The color of this postage stamp does not resemble the color of the second stamp but is identical with it; to speak of resemblance here would be to speak falsely. We do observe identical qualities and there are *universalia in rebus*. These qualitative identities are one and the same not only through a passage of time, as a thing may be said to be identical with itself, but also as contemporaneously present at different places. This is their distinguishing feature: one and the same shade of red is here *and* there, in two places at one and the same time.[7]

On considering this matter, however, as has been seen, a very important and very necessary qualification must be borne in mind. The identity is an *observed* identity and nothing more is being claimed for it. Admittedly, what I now take to be identical might turn out to be distinguishable, given more acute sensory powers. There is the disturbing fact that occasionally we find ourselves unable to distinguish the shade *a* from the shade *b* and the shade *b* from the shade *c* and yet we can distinguish between the shades *a* and *c*. What is experienced as indistinguishable is clearly not necessarily identical in the metaphysical sense ('really' identical). None the less, some queer results follow if real identity of quality be denied; for instance, there would be, apparently, as many shades of color as there are colored things and this certainly appears absurd. However, fortunately, it is not necessary for us to come to any final decision on this metaphysical point. The question whether there are or are not metaphysically identical qualities does not affect our theory of universals. The latter begins with the observing of qualities which, so far as we can see, are identical. When we say that these are *universalia in rebus* it is understood that the *res* in question are things experienced by us.

Qualities are not the only discoverable identities, there are also relations. The relation of being to the left of, for instance, is one and the same relation in contexts A and B, and no language except that of identity fits the case. To take another example, this line stands perpendicularly upon the other line, so forming a right angle. That relation is precisely the same wherever I find it. The importance of such identical relations as these in our thinking need not be emphasized. Unlike identical qualities they are not universals *in*, but universals *between*, things, not *in rebus* but *inter res*. Yet they are in the world experienced by us, quite as concretely as are the qualities. They too are discovered. It is true that just as in the case of qualities I may see two qualities to be identically the same but later by looking more closely am able to distinguish between them, so I may see one line to fall perpendicularly on another, thus forming a right angle, but later discover, for example, on measuring the angle with a protractor, that though it looks a right angle yet the protractor shows it to fall short of 90 degrees. But the fact remains that I began by seeing one line fall perpendicularly on another. Here is a relation which is constantly recurring in my experience; I look around me at this moment and see many lines falling perpendicularly on other lines in this room. Here is the recurrence and, in that sense of the term, the universal, though not a recurring, identical quality but a recurring, identical relation. So universals are identical relations as well as identical qualities.

92. Now in so far as universals are identities of this kind there can be no objection to speaking of them as objects of which we are aware; that is to say, they are recurrences which we observe. Having observed them we know how to use our observations as principles in accordance with which we group and classify. On the basis of this classification we know what to expect if something is said to be so and so and we learn how to use the relevant general words significantly. The tokens, the sounds used in spoken language and the shapes in written, are a convention of the language used, but our successful use of them rests on our acquaintance with natural recurrences.

But this is only a beginning. The next step in the theory comes with the realization that the recurrences examined thus far, namely, identical qualities and relations, are not the only recurrences in our experience. Certain qualities are similar without being identical and the similarities recur. For instance, shades of blue which are not identical but similar constantly recur and we learn to speak of the color 'blue', covering by this token all shades of blue, as a class of colors. Behind the use of 'ultramarine' lies the observation of the identical shade, but behind that of 'blue' lies the observation of identical shades together with the observation of likenesses between them. In the same way certain relations are similar to one another and the recurrence of these similarities suggests new classifications. But once similarities are introduced we cannot stop with qualities and relations. For *things* are similar, and we classify on the basis of the similarity of things. Men are roughly alike, so are the different cats we meet, and the different spades we see. And not only things but processes and situations are similar. Once again parliamentary candidates seek to win our favor, once again the postman walks up the path or the sun sinks over the horizon. The recurrence of these similarities is as useful a basis for classification as is the recurrence of identical qualities and relations. Here too are universals. Perhaps it is not so easy to pinpoint them in this case as in the case of ultramarine. They are recurring likenesses. Sometimes, as in the case of the family face, we are aware of 'overall' likenesses between objects though we cannot single out any identical (or even resembling) quality which they all possess. But they are amongst the likenesses we observe and use, along with other likenesses, as empirically based principles of grouping. So recurring similarities as well as identities are universals, and we consciously use them to classify and order our experience, and are thus able to use a further set of general words successfully.

To hold that the recurring similarity is a universal, along with the recurring identical quality or identical relation, is to go beyond Aristotelian realism. Nor can the latter be maintained by the argument that all similarities must rest in the end on identities, for this, as we have seen, is not the case. Sometimes, it is true, two objects are similar because they have identical qualities; at other times we find no identical qualities and yet the objects are similar. Moreover, simple qualities can be similar where there is no possibility of an underlying identical quality. It follows that a recurring similarity that does not, so far as we can see, rest upon an identity, can none the less be a basis for grouping. Thus while our theory begins with the Aristotelian realist position it soon leaves it behind. Yet, it should also be added, if we begin in this way, if we say that the universal on which grouping rests may be the recurring identity, we already rule out nominalism. Indeed, we rule out nominalism when we say that we group on the basis of an observed similarity. It is curious that nominalists, whilst recognizing that their theory is incompatible with realism, appear to think that it is compatible with the doctrine that we group on the observation of similarities. Yet if we group objects as they are found to resemble one another, then we begin not with so many individuals, as the nominalists wish to say, but with so many *resembling* individuals. The resemblance or similarity is as much objective or natural fact as is the identity of common qualities and common relations. In other words, the Resemblance theory is as unsatisfactory a foundation for nominalism as is the Identity theory. In both cases a universal in nature is presupposed. Thus in asserting that universals are recurring similarities as well as recurring identities our theory is shown to be different from both Aristotelian realism and nominalism.

93. Thus far we have been speaking of the universal mainly as the natural recurrence, the recurring identity or similarity. But the other sense of the word has already emerged according to which a universal is a principle of grouping enabling us to determine the limits of the group and providing a standard whereby to recognize a member of the group when we come across one. Ultramarine is a shade of color that recurs in our experience, but we use it consciously as a principle for grouping, as when we divide things into those which are ultramarine and those which are not. From this point forward in our statement of the theory it is this second sense of the term 'universal' which more and more engages our attention.

Not all principles of grouping have been gained in the way that ultramarine has been gained and not all of them are used in the way in which it is used. Some of the principles which guide us are far more ambiguous and in using them we are less conscious of what we are doing. Our thinking is carried on at different levels. Thinking on a high level, which is throughout logical and precise, where the justification of every step taken is wholly clear, where nothing is taken for granted and nothing implied of which the mind is not fully conscious—such thinking is very different from normal thinking. Normally our thinking is loose, much is assumed and much vaguely implied and the mind is more passive than active, more controlled than controlling. Now part of the explanation of such loose thinking is to be found in the character of the principles which then guide us in classifying. Our familiarity with certain recurrences in experience has brought into being various habits, we group without being fully conscious of the principle on which we group, indeed, without being fully conscious that we are grouping, and when we do later come to reflect upon this grouping we realize that the principles used were vague and lacked precision.

Traditional conceptualism was at fault in its failure to recognize the occurrence of such primitive classifying. It was justified in its view that not all the universals guiding our thought were universals of the same kind as ultramarine, that such a universal as human, for instance, could not be adequately accounted for in strictly realist terms. But its doctrine that all non-observable universals were of necessity conscious fabrications, conscious compoundings of the observable universals, was false. The classificatory principles essential to our thinking and our use of general words are, as Hume hinted, frequently of a more primitive kind. Experience of houses, tables, and men has given us principles of classification before we become conscious of these principles. Before we ever consciously frame an imaginative concept of, and before we are able to give the precise meaning of, 'house', 'table', and 'man', we know how to use these words. But when we reflect upon these primitive principles and when we seek to clarify them, it is then we realize the extent to which our thought is dominated by them. For we are here concerned not merely with house, man, table, but also with such important categorical notions as substance, cause, space, time, and the rest, whose further analysis proves so difficult. They too are originally gained in this way and must be included amongst these primitive principles. Moreover, it is here that we find the explanation of our primitive inductions, namely, in our acquiring principles of grouping or class-determinants, not as the product of conscious and purposive fabrication, but as the consequence of the working of hidden mental processes.

These primitive principles of grouping are the universals which lie at the base of so much of our normal thinking. They cannot be neglected. Yet it is also necessary to admit as universals the consciously formulated principles with which the conceptualists concerned themselves. They are framed out of observed identical qualities or relations or similarities. They also include elements found to be present in the more primitive principles, though the conceptualists had not understood this point. In framing these principles we define the boundaries of our group more precisely, if arbitrarily, and set down the limits, so that henceforth we have no difficulty in recognizing any member and are able to exclude from the class any object lacking in any of the requisite and essential characters. These are imaginative constructions and the primary purpose of the constructing is to make clear to ourselves the vague principles which, we find, guide us in grouping and classifying. But such construction does not consist entirely in clarificatory analysis. In addition there is what may be termed free fabrication. We construct in imagination such objects as dragons, mermaids, chimaeras, and so on. We combine elements isolated by abstraction in an order we freely choose, and bring into being new imaginative creations. Now these too are used as principles of classification, though the classes in this case have no members (unless we regard drawings and paintings of, for instance, mermaids as members of the class). Nevertheless, the principle in this case is as genuinely a universal as any other, in the sense that it would, for instance, enable us to recognize a mermaid if we saw one. In addition to the creation of imaginative objects we create imaginative situations involving various relations. It is as easy to imagine the situation in which the dragon is slain as it is to imagine the dragon itself. Slaying the dragon, running the hundred yards in nine seconds, conquering cancer, linking the planets by air communication—all such imagery may serve as principles of classification. And it is obvious that universals such as these, imaginative and hypothetical though they may be, play a highly important part in human thinking.

94. Lastly, we must consider the thinking which is predominantly verbal rather than imaginative. In imaginative thinking the universal is exemplified in the use of an image or of images as a principle of grouping together with all the accretions necessary to the use. Since imaginative thinking is rarely wholly nonverbal, one of these accretions is likely to be language. We have now to consider the situation in which the major part of the thinking is verbal and in which images, if they are present at all, are few and faint.

The more intellective and abstract thinking is usually supposed to be predominantly verbal, relying less and less on imagery as it develops. We are agreed that it is mistaken to speak of such thinking in terms of apprehending abstract entities, or as the conceiving of a concept which is an internal entity and of which the general word is the name. We reject too the view that the universal is a concept in this sense. We are not to look for the universal amongst the internal accusatives of the traditional conceptualist.

In the case of predominantly verbal thinking, therefore, we cannot look to the image or to the concept (as defined traditionally) for our theory. In what direction then should we look? Clearly, in the direction of general words. Just as consideration of the use of imagery in the more imaginative thinking gives us understanding of the universal in that thinking, so too does consideration of the use of general words give us understanding in the case of verbal thinking. Suppose, for instance, we examine our use of the general word 'proposition'. Our use of it, we say, is determined by what we think is and is not a proposition, by what we suppose can or cannot complete the open sentence '. . . is a proposition'. If we proceed to explain what we take the word 'proposition' to mean, by saying, for instance, that it is a form of words in which something is affirmed or denied about something, what we are doing then is explaining in other words the principle which rules our thinking in our use of the word. Our thought is in terms of a class that is determined by a principle. Of x, y, and z we can say that each is a series of words in which something is affirmed or denied about something, that is, on this definition, each is a proposition; whereas the series of words a is not determined in this way and is accordingly not a proposition. Now this principle is the universal we seek.

The universal is not an image and it is not a concept, that is, an abstract, internal entity. Nor is there any suggestion that it is a word, or even a general word. It is a principle of classification. Such principles rule our thought as we use imagery and general words to think about our world, to classify the objects within it, and to relate the classes with one another. Without the principles we should be tied to immediate experience, but with them significant general statements, science and what Quine has called 'eternal sentences', become possible.

95. Our conclusion then is that a universal is a principle of grouping or classifying. But a little earlier (§ 91) it was said that a universal is a natural recurrence. How are we to relate these two statements? I argue that both of them are necessary for an adequate theory of universals.

Philosophers are free to define the word 'universal' as they choose, and some are content to say that the universal is a common quality *in rebus* and to leave it at that. The term 'common quality' is interpreted either in a narrow sense to cover identical qualities and relations only or in a wider sense to cover resemblances as well. In either case the universal is a natural recurrence. As far as it goes I accept this account of the universal, and find in it the foundation upon which to build a theory of thinking. But it is inadequate; for to say that ultramarine, for example, is a universal, in the sense of being a common quality, leaves something important unsaid, namely, that since it is a common quality it can be used as a principle of grouping. Now this too is part of what is meant when we say that ultramarine is a universal. It is a universal as being a natural recurrence, but also as being a principle of grouping.

But not every principle of grouping is also an observed natural recurrence. On the other hand, familiarity with the features of our world, as opposed to the fully conscious apprehension of a common quality, has disposed us to classify in certain ways. On the other we use imagery which we ourselves have fabricated, for instance, the image of the unicorn, to provide us with a basis for grouping. Again verbal description, which may be vague or precise, provides us with principles. Thus there are many ways in which we acquire principles of grouping in addition to the use of common qualities directly observed.

We cannot then simply say that a universal is a natural recurrence. Any principle of grouping is a universal and we cannot identify principle of grouping with natural recurrence. This is an avowal that the question 'What is a universal?' cannot be answered in one sentence, but needs two. *Universals are natural recurrences; universals are principles of grouping or classifying.*

At the same time it would seem to be the case that the fundamental basis of all generalizing and grouping is this observation of natural recurrences. The use of general words would seem to rest finally on this observation, even though the full explanation of our principles of grouping involves more than reference to this observation alone. In this way our thinking is always linked to the experienced world. There is admittedly a metaphysical problem in the existence of these natural occurrences which this book does not attempt to solve. What is the final explanation of the recurrences in nature? It might be said that this is the real problem of universals and that the one attempt to tackle it thus far is the attempt made by the advocates of the theory of Forms. Certainly, this is not the question which has concerned us in this book. Here we have been concerned with a less ultimate problem, that of analyzing in phenomenological terms the universal element in thinking, and that of making clear the factors which lie behind our use of general words in thinking. This problem is one that can be solved at the phenomenological level, even if certain ultimate questions are left unanswered.

Our purpose is to prepare the way for a satisfactory theory of thinking. An adequate theory of universals, as I conceive it, is necessary for the further theory of thinking. I do not suggest that the theory of universals contains the whole analysis of thinking; at most it is part of that theory. Thinking involves the successful use of general words and the theory of thinking explains how general words are used. In this part of its task the latter theory is one with that of universals, as here conceived. But clearly there are other problems in the theory of thinking. An obvious problem is that of presenting an adequate account of classes. We have here considered merely a preliminary problem, that of principles presupposed in classifying, and we regard these as universals. I have referred also to the important element of steering and purposeful control which is present in the thinking of intelligent man, and this element needs examination. There is further the question of the nature of insight and of the inferences which rest upon it, together with the whole question of the relation between thinking and knowing. These, and many other matters, need to be discussed in the full theory of thinking. But their discussion lies outside the scope of this book.

NOTES

From R. I. Aaron, *The Theory of Universals* (second edition, 1967). Originally published by Clarendon Press, London, 1952. Reprinted by permission of Oxford University Press.

1. [Aaron,] *Our Knowledge of Universals*, [British Academy Lecture], 1945, § 4.
2. This regrettable tendency in modern logic and philosophy leads to considerable confusion. In his Geneva lecture (1934) entitled 'On Platonism in Mathematics', Paul Bernays describes Hilbert's axioms system (as contrasted with Euclid's) as 'platonist'. This may possibly be the source of the modern dichotomy. It would be good if logicians reconsidered their use of 'platonist' and 'nominalist'. For Bernays's lecture cf. *L'enseignement mathematique*, vol. 34 (1935), pp. 52–69, translated for Benacerraf and Putnam, *Philosophy of Mathematics*, 1964, pp. 274–86.
3. *Journal of Symbolic Logic*, vol. 12, pp. 105–22.
4. Cf. [W. V. Quine,] *Word and Object* [Cambridge, Mass.: The MIT Press, 1960], p. 243, n. 5.
5. Benacerraf and Putnam, *Philosophy of Mathematics* [Englewood Cliffs, N.J.: Prentice Hall] 1964, p. 203. Reprinted from Goodman's *The Problem of Universals*, 1956.
6. *Word and Object*, p. 266.
7. Blanshard, *Reason and Analysis* [La Salle, Ill.: Open Court Publishing Co., 1962], p. 393, refers to such universals as 'specific universals'.

28 NAMMOUR

The problem of universals is based on the assumption that there is the world as it is, which is metaphysically distinct from any language used to represent it. Both the Common Property thesis (e.g., that two red things *really* possess a common property) and the Resemblance thesis (e.g., that two red things are *really* similar) arise from this view. The former thesis emphasizes the dominance of the world, with language reflecting the common properties found in it. The latter thesis comes down on the side of language and stresses that the notion of sameness depends upon the context in which language users find themselves. Consequently, sameness is a reflection of our interests and needs.

Nammour demonstrates that both the Common Property thesis and the Resemblance thesis are fraught with difficulty primarily because of the aforementioned metaphysical assumption. Upon examination of, for example, color words, we cannot, as J. L. Austin suggested we can, separate the world from the words we use to represent it for the purpose of establishing an unbiased view of the world, because there is no such unbiased view of the world (nor can there ever be). Any and every view of the world is necessarily linked to the language and therefore to the language user doing the viewing. That viewer, no matter how earnest, cannot separate himself from his interests and needs, and his language reflects that fact. Once this fact is recognized, the debate over universals versus resemblances and the problem of universals in general can be properly understood to be a pseudo-problem.

Resemblances and Universals

It is fairly obvious that there is no agreement among philosophers about the range to which Wittgenstein's notion of Family Resemblances can be applied. There are those who hold that Wittgenstein's notion applies only to complex words like 'chair' and 'game' and not to simple words like 'red' and 'yellow'. To this it is often added that the Common Property solution to the problem of Universals is basically sound. Originally all general words in our language referred to things which shared a common and peculiar characteristic. But as new objects 'continually presented themselves to men', the application of a general word was extended on the basis of their similarities to the original cases.[1] The virtue of color words lies not only in that it is taken as evident that the Common Property thesis holds for them, but also in that they serve as paradigms or reminders of how Family Resemblance words used to be before they were extended and their connotation became, in Mill's words, 'vague' and 'unsettled'. Against this view, however, some philosophers hold that the Resemblance view applies to all general words. Thus Mr. Renford Bambrough, in his famous article 'Universals and Family Resemblances', insists that 'there is no classification of any set of objects which is not based on genuine similarities and differences'. And that 'we can be sure that if it is to be a classification then it is backed by objective similarities and differences, and if it is not backed by objective similarities and differences, then it is an arbitrary system of names'.[2] Bambrough makes it clear that color words are not exceptions to this rule. In what follows I wish to look closely at this controversy. I hope to show that both the Common Property thesis and the Resemblances thesis are fraught with difficulties. At the end of the paper I shall make very brief suggestions as to what Wittgenstein's estimate of the problem of Universals is.

II

In order to get clear about the precise nature of the controversy it would be worthwhile to consider a few examples in which color words are used.

(1) Suppose that an art student has spent some time in frustration trying to come up with a blue color he had in mind. Suppose further that in an act of sympathy you tried to help him by showing him a sample of blue. 'Here is one which Degas used for the asters, there is one which Matisse used for this vase', and so on. In each case he says, 'No, that is not it'. After coming up with the color he wants, he says (and you can see) that it is *altogether different* from the samples you showed him—that it is not the same. Altogether different? Yes. An art teacher will understand him well when he says this. Indeed, he would be surprised if the student were to say otherwise. With his sensitivity to colors, shades, fineness of the grind, etc., he knows that the two colors are not the same. In this context two blue things are not the same. They are altogether different.

(2) Two casual visitors to an art gallery may say of the same two colors I considered in the above example that they are the same. The circumstances, the interests, and the background are different here. Two blue objects are said to be the same in this context.

(3) A housewife who is looking for red curtains to match her couch might comment on a suggested color by the store clerk by saying, 'It does not match well, although it is similar to what I want'. Here two red things are said to be similar although they are not the same.

These examples, which can be easily multiplied, show that what counts as the same, different, and similar with regard to color will depend on the contexts, on our interests, who we are, and where we are. They also seem to threaten both the simplicity claimed for color words by the Common Property thesis and the insistence on similarities by the Resemblance thesis.

It may be said, however, that the objections raised by these cases can be met. It will be conceded by the proponents of both views that what we count the same, different, and similar depends on the many circumstances and interests we have. It will be further conceded that we say that two red objects are similar, the same, or that they are totally different. But it will be objected that what we say in these circumstances is not a reliable index of how things really are. For red things are *really* the same (Common Property) or *really* similar (Resemblance thesis) regardless of what we say of them in these circumstances. Our interests, the complicated weaves and patterns of our lives impose a twisted order on things and this is reflected in the way we speak. We have to be on guard with what we say. And we should look at the world without the veils and blinkers that what we say can put on our eyes. J. L. Austin in "A Plea for Excuses" expresses this point:

> Words are not 'except in their own little corner' facts or things: we need therefore to prise them off the world, to hold them apart from and against it, so that we can realize their inadequacies and arbitrarinesses, and can relook at the world without blinkers.[3]

Now several things must be noted before looking closely into this new move. First, what is being claimed by both the Common Property and the Resemblance theorists is that there are certain features which the world exhibits independently, as it were, of our interests and language. On the Common Property view this feature is the property of 'being red'. On the Resemblance view it is 'objective similarities and differences'. Second, the Resemblance theorist does not altogether deny the role which our interests and language play in determining the range of application of a general word. For he allows that the 'sameness' or 'being red' come from the side of language. He insists, however, that what the world exhibits can be seen independently of language and hence serves as an external check for it. This is, if I understand him at all, the force of Bambrough's remark that 'there is no classification of any set of objects which is not *objectively* based on genuine similarities and differences'. And that 'we can be sure that if it is a classification then it is backed by objective similarities and differences. And if it is not backed by objective similarities and differences then it is an arbitrary system of names'. His further remark that 'all red things have nothing in common except that they are red' indicates to me that the 'sameness' or 'being red' is language dependent. Third, Bambrough is not alone in holding to this view. J. L. Austin seems to have held a similar one. In his article on 'Truth' he insisted:

> That things are similar or even 'exactly' similar, I may literally see, but that they are the same I cannot literally see—in calling them the same color a convention is involved additional to the conventional choice of the name to be given to the color which they are said to be.

And:

'The same' . . . is a device for establishing and distinguishing the meaning of ordinary words. . . . It is part of our apparatus in words for fixing and adjusting the semantics of words.[4]

III

Now that the issue between the Common Property and the Resemblances theorists is more clearly defined, the question arises as to how one should go about finding out whether the world exhibits similarities or samenesses. How does one decide which comes from the side of language and which comes from the side of the world? It is obvious that one cannot decide this matter by considering cases in which color words are ordinarily used. For such cases show that what counts the same, different, and similar will depend on our circumstances and interests. And this has already been discredited by the new move. Perhaps the way to do it is by following Austin's instruction to 'prise words off the world' and 'hold them apart from and against it'. But how should I or anyone carry out these instructions? Should I take two red flowers and gaze at them very hard and pretend that I do not know the conventions governing the use of the language of colors? This obviously will not do. But this need not render our attempt hopeless. We should think of cases in which one is confronted by colored objects without any previous knowledge of what we call that color. It is perhaps here that one gets to decide on the sameness and similarities of color without the color word. Thus consider the following.

I stop at a toy shop to buy some colored blocks for children. While looking at the assortment of blocks they have, I notice a color I have never seen before. I ask the clerk about it and he says it is fuchsia. Now, in looking at the fuchsia blocks, I have certainly noticed that they are all the same color. In recalling the incident I could have said this before finding out what the color was. But this case and other similar cases will not do for what the philosophical thesis I am investigating requires. For although I did not know what the color I have seen was, i.e. I did not know that it was fuchsia, I certainly knew that it was a color. I knew what the word 'color' means and what 'the same color' means. I also knew a host of color words. In recounting the incident to someone I could have described what I saw in the toy shop in terms of other color words I know. I could have said that the blocks were of the same reddish-purple color, which is what fuchsia is. In short, I knew the conventions (Austin's phrase) that govern the language of colors. What I need is a case in which one not only does not know the word 'fuchsia' but also the word 'color' and the rest of the color words. An ideal case would be one in which one does not have a language of colors. But what could such a case be?

Perhaps imagining an adult visitor from a distant planet where everything is color-free will do. I can imagine him speaking English as we do. I can then introduce him to colors and color words. He should be in a position to answer my question. The trouble with this case, however, is not only that I do not really know how my visitor will react or what he will say, but also that it is extremely difficult to understand. For what would a color-free world be like and what kind of an English language have I endowed my visitor with? Does my imaginary visitor ever close his eyes? Does he not know what darkness and what black and white are? Are there no shades and shapes on his planet? What kind of a creature am I imagining here? The case of the imaginary visitor will not do. Nor will it do to imagine someone who belongs to a totally different culture, with a totally different system of colors from our own. For here, too, it is not clear how such a person might react to our use of color words. Nor do I see any *a priori* reason to think that he would be able to learn our language or that we would be able to learn or understand his.[5] But perhaps we can still decide our philosophical issue by observing children at the time they learn color words. This suggestion, however, will not do either. Suppose I present a child with a number of color blocks. The child already knows what a block is. He does not know, however, the difference between a blue block and a red one. He does not yet know the language of colors. In pointing to a red one, I say 'these are red', and to the blue ones, I say 'these are blue'. I repeat this procedure several times while we are playing. Then I ask him to bring me a red block and he brings me a blue one. Later on, however, he catches on to the distinction. But how does he catch on? Does he find out that the red blocks are the same or similar? Does he then 'associate' or 'label' what he already saw with the color words he hears from me or others? And before he caught on, i.e. when I said 'bring me a red block' and he brought a blue one, did he see the sameness (or similarities) in color but think that I was pointing to the shape of the blocks or their glossy texture?

I want the child to answer all these questions. The trouble is, however, that he cannot. He will not understand what I am talking about. And by the time he does, he is in no better position to know how he caught on than I am now in trying to find out what happened in my own case.

I cannot 'prise [color] words off the world' as Austin suggests. There does not seem to be a way to follow his instructions or to get a feel for what they involve. In Austin's view as well as in the essentialists' view we should be able, as Austin says, to 'hold the words apart from and against the world . . . [and] relook at the world without blinkers'. What is demanded from us is to achieve the impossible. It is for this reason that it is an impossible demand. We do not understand what it involves.

I said in connection with my wanting to ask the child whether he sees the 'sameness (or similarities) of color in the world' i.e. prior to or separately from the language of colors, that the child would not understand what I am talking about and therefore he could not answer me. I want to say now that I do not know what I thought I could ask the child. My own questions are, I think, unintelligible. This is not only because the child cannot answer them, but more radically, because I do not understand what I am asking for. In wanting to ask the child whether he sees that the colored blocks are the same (or similar) prior to his learning color words or independently of them, I have imagined that I can speak of the 'same' and 'similar' without the word 'color' and color words. Indeed, I must have imagined myself without the use of the words 'same' and 'similar'. Thus, not only do I not know how the child catches on, on further reflection I do not know what I imagined myself to be wanting to ask the child. I cannot understand my own questions.

The fact that I cannot understand my own questions here is of paramount importance. It must be kept in mind when, in philosophizing, we avail ourselves of examples of bulls that can charge at red flags and birds like chickens and crows of which we say that they make color distinctions. These cases may be invoked to substantiate the thesis I am considering. Since the crow can make color distinctions, and since the crow does not have language then, the argument might go, it must be meaningful to speak of the 'world' without language. And it must be the case that there are similarities and differences in the 'world'. But what is involved in saying that the crow makes color distinctions? How does one understand his saying: 'The crow makes color distinctions?' Notice, I am not questioning here the fact that the crow makes color distinctions. Nor am I questioning that we say of the crow that it makes color distinctions. Indeed what else would we say of the crow? What I am questioning, however, is the contention that the case of the crow can ever substantiate the thesis I am considering. For the only way that it can do so would be *for us who say that the crow* makes color distinctions to be able to understand *color distinctions* without color words. We must be able to understand a sense of 'distinction' without qualification, indeed without the word 'distinction' and without language. It is after all *we who say* of the crow that it makes color distinctions. And since we cannot understand in *our own case* a sense of 'distinction' and 'similar' without language, indeed without the words 'similar' and 'distinction', then in saying that the crow makes color distinctions we could not be saying anything that would substantiate the separation of language and the world. If we were, we should not understand what we are talking about. We should not understand the sentence, 'The crow makes color distinctions'. Of course, it would be nice to look at the world through the crow's eyes. And it would be nice to look at the world through the baby's eyes. But then this would require that we become crows or babies, and in that case no philosophical problem would arise.

I am not saying here that there are no similarities or sameness in the world. Nor am I saying that the similarities and sameness come from the language. Nor am I saying that the thesis I am considering is wrong (if only because I do not know what it would be like for it to be right). All that I am saying is that we cannot understand the things that such a thesis leads us to say.

Three final remarks:

(1) I did not address myself in this discussion to the possible claim that the child has a non-verbal language—a kind of mental picture or primitive awareness of the similarities or sameness in the world prior to language. The reason for this omission is as follows. Even if we allow (How?) this claim to pass the objections to the impossible question of how the child catches on and what the child knows before language, we should theoretically still have the same trouble in understanding the language-world division. For we still have the non-verbal language *and* the world. We would also have the non-verbal language and the verbal one. In fact, introducing a private non-verbal language makes the whole thing most mysterious and incomprehensible.

(2) The Problem of Universals trades, it seems to me, on the metaphysical assumption that there is language on one side and the 'world' on the other side. Given this assumption, the question arises as to how general words in our language 'refer' to or 'designate' things in the 'world'. Do they do so *because* of common properties or *because* of similarities and resemblances? The word 'because' in this context indicates the metaphysical division between 'language' and the 'world'. But if my investigation has been correct thus far, it should be clear that this division will not do. It is impossible to divest ourselves from language and look at the 'world' or 'reality' independently of it and our variegated interests which are internally connected with it. It should be clear furthermore that the question of Universals which arises out of this division is also an impossible question. It demands the impossible for an answer—namely that we arrive at something nonlinguistic or extra-linguistic. It is like someone attempting to saw a tree branch while the branch is necessary if he is to be up on it at all or even to begin sawing.

(3) It was not my intention in this paper to deal directly with Wittgenstein's own remarks about Family Resemblances. If I am allowed to be dogmatic, however, I would say that these remarks are an unfortunate hangover from his *Tractatus* period. His admonition to 'look and see' in *Philosophical Investigations* No. 66 and his contention that we shall find similarities and resemblances after looking and seeing, give the impression that there are, in Bambrough's words, 'objective similarities' to be seen independently of our interests and language. All this, however, is not in line with his overall view on this and related issues. For not only does he reject an earlier complex-simple view of things on the grounds that what counts as simple and complex will depend on our variegated interests and language (forms of life), but he also rejects any sense of reality or objectivity independent of these forms of life. In *Zettel* No. 331 he attacks the justification of the rules of grammar 'which is construed on the model of justifying a sentence by pointing to what verifies it'.[6] I believe that Wittgenstein's ultimate answer to the question: 'How do we apply a general word consis-

tently to a multitude of individuals?' would not be different from his answer to the question: 'How do I know that this color is red?' In *Philosophical Investigations* No. 381 he answers: 'I have learnt English'.[7]

NOTES

From *Mind* 82 (1973). Reprinted by permission of Oxford University Press.

1. This view was originally advanced by J. S. Mill and was recently echoed by P. F. Strawson. *Cf.* J. S. Mill, *A System of Logic* in Nagel, ed., *John Stuart Mill's Philosophy of Logic and Scientific Method* (New York, 1950), pp. 32 ff. *Cf.* P. F. Strawson, *Individuals*, p. XV, Anchor Books (New York, 1963).
2. Renford Bambrough, 'Universals and Family Resemblances', *Proceedings of the Aristotelian Society*, LXI (1960–61), 207–222.
3. J. L. Austin, *Philosophical Papers* (Oxford, 1961), p. 130.
4. J. L. Austin, *Philosophical Papers* (Oxford, 1961), pp. 88, 90.
5. It is perhaps this point which Bambrough fails to see and which leads him to the view that there must be 'objective similarities' in the world independent of our interests and language. How else is he to explain the possible existence of two different color systems and at the same time reject the nominalist's charge of linguistic arbitrariness. My point against Bambrough here is similar to Barry Stroud's point about our concepts of measurement. Stroud argues on behalf of Wittgenstein that although it may be conceivable that a community with a totally different system of measurement might exist, there is no logical guarantee that we can understand their system or their way of life. *Cf.* Barry Stroud, 'Wittgenstein and Logical Necessity', *Philosophical Review*, Vol. LXXIV, 1965.
6. When Wittgenstein speaks of the 'rules of grammar' he does not have in mind rules that can be extracted and written out like the rules of chess. He has in mind our linguistic practices—what he calls 'agreement in language' (*Philosophical Investigations*, nos. 221–230, 241–242). This agreement cannot be justified by nor is it in itself something extralinguistic. It is an agreement *in* language and the notion of the consistency of our application of a general word goes with that.
7. Although he has not read this paper nor would necessarily agree with it my deep indebtedness to Professor Frank B. Ebersole should be obvious to those who either have read his writings or have had the good fortune to work with him.

BIBLIOGRAPHY

BOOKS AND COLLECTIONS

Allan, D. J. *The Philosophy of Aristotle*. Oxford and New York, 1952.

Anscombe, G. E. M., and P. T. Geach. *Three Philosophers*. Oxford and New York, 1961.

Aristotle. *De Interpretatione*. Translated by J. L. Ackrill. Oxford and New York, 1963.

Bambrough, R., ed. *New Essays on Plato and Aristotle*. London and New York, 1965.

Bochenski, I. M., A. Church, and N. Goodman. *The Problem of Universals*. Notre Dame, Ind., 1956.

Butchkarov, P. K., *Resemblance and Identity*. Bloomington, Ind., 1966.

Cohen, L. J. *The Diversity of Meaning*. London, 1962.

Crombie, I. M. *An Examination of Plato's Doctrines*. Vol. 2. London and New York, 1963.

Frege, G. *Philosophical Writings*. Translated and edited by P. T. Geach and M. Black, Oxford, 1952.

Geach, P. T. *Mental Acts*. London and New York, 1957.

———. *Reference and Generality*. Cornell, N.Y., 1962.

Goodman, N. *The Structure of Appearance*. Cambridge, Mass. 1951.

Holloway, J. *Language and Intelligence*. London, 1955.

Hume, D. *Introduction Treatise of Human Nature*. Edited by A. D. Lindsay. London and New York, 1960.

Joske, W. D. *Material Objects*. London and New York, 1967.

Kovesi, J. *Moral Notions*. London and New York, 1967.

Kung, G. *Ontology and the Logistic Analysis of Language*. Dordrecht, Holland, and New York, 1967.

Loux, M. J. ed., *Universals and Particulars*. New York, 1970.

Luschei, E. C. *The Logical Systems of Lesniewski*. Amsterdam and New York, 1962.

Passmore, J. *Philosophical Reasoning*. London and New York, 1961.

Plato. *Parmenides*. In *Plato and Parmenides*, translated with commentary by F. M. Cornford. London, 1939.

———. *Phaedo*. In *The Last Days of Socrates*, translated by H. Tredennick. Baltimore, 1954.

Quine, W. V. *Word and Object*. Cambridge, Mass., 1960.

———. *Ontological Relativity and Other Essays*. New York, 1969.

Robinson, R. *Plato's Earlier Dialectic*. Oxford and New York, 1950.

Russell, B. *The Analysis of Matter*. London and New York, 1927.

———. *Introduction to Mathematical Philosophy*. London and New York, 1930.

———. *Inquiry into Meaning and Truth*. London and Baltimore, 1956.

Searle, J. R. *Speech Acts*. Cambridge and New York, 1969.

Shwayder, D. S. *The Modes of Referring and the Problem of Universals*. Berkeley, Calif., 1961.

Stout, G. F. *The Nature of Universals and Propositions*. London, 1921.

Strawson, P. F. *Individuals*. London and New York, 1959.

Wittgenstein, L. *The Blue and Brown Books*. Oxford and New York, 1958.

————. *Philosophical Investigations*. Translated by G. E. M. Anscombe. 2nd ed. Oxford and New York, 1963.

Woolhouse, R. S. *Locke's Philosophy of Science and Knowledge*. Oxford and New York, 1971.

Woozley, A. D. *Theory of Knowledge*. London and New York, 1949.

Zabech, F. *Universals*. The Hague, 1966.

ARTICLES

Aaron, R. I. "Locke's Theory of Universals." *Proceedings of the Aristotelian Society* 33 (1932–33).

————. "Two Senses of 'Universal.'" *Mind* 48 (1939).

————. "Hume's Theory of Universals." *Proceedings of the Aristotelian Society* 42 (1941–42).

Acton, H. B. "The Theory of Concrete Universals." Parts 1, 2. *Mind* 45 (1936); 46 (1937).

Aldrich, V. C. "Colors as Universals." *Philosophical Review*, 41 (1952).

Alston, W. P. "Ontological Commitments." *Philosophical Studies* 9 (1958).

Ayer, A. J. "Universals and Particulars." *Proceedings of the Aristotelian Society* 34 (1933–34).

————. "On What There Is." *Aristotelian Society Supplementary* 25 (1951).

Bacon, J. "Ontological Commitment and Free Logic." *Monist* 53 (1970).

Baylis, C. A. "Meanings and Their Exemplifications." *Journal of Philosophy* 47 (1930).

————. "Logical Subjects and Physical Objects." *Philosophy and Phenomenological Research* 17 (1957).

Bemays, P. "On Platonism in Mathematics." In *Philosophy of Mathematics*, edited by P. Benacerraf and H. Putnam. Englewood Cliffs, N.J., 1964.

Bennett, J. "Substance, Reality and Primary Qualities." *American Philosophical Quarterly* 2 (1965).

Bergmann, G. "Particularity and the New Nominalism." *Methodos* 6 (1954).

————. "Strawson's Ontology." *Journal of Philosophy* 58 (1961).

Black, M. "The Elusiveness of Sets." *Review of Metaphysics*, 24 (1971).

Bochenski, I. M. "The Problem of Universals." In *The Problem of Universals*, edited by I. M. Bochenski, A. Church, and N. Goodman, Notre Dame, Ind., 1956.

Braithwaite, R. B. "Universals and the 'Method of Analysis.'" *Aristotelian Society Supplementary Volume* 6 (1926).

Brandt, R. B. "The Languages of Realism and Nominalism." *Philosophy and Phenomenological Research* 17 (1957).

Brody, B. A. "Natural Kinds and Essences." *Journal of Philosophy* 64 (1967).

Butchkarov, P. K. "Concrete Entities and Concrete Relations." *Review of Metaphysics* 10 (1957).

Campbell, K. "Family Resemblance Predicates." *American Philosophical Quarterly* 2 (1965).

Carmichael, P. "Derivation of Universals." *Philosophy and Phenomenological Research* 8 (1948).

Carnap, R. "The Methodological Character of Theoretical Concepts." *Minnesota Studies in the Philosophy of Science* 1 (1956).

Chomsky, N., and I. Scheffer. "What Is Said to Be." *Proceedings of the Aristotelian Society* 59 (1958–59).

Church, A. "Propositions and Sentences." In *The Problem of Universals*, edited by

I. M. Bochenski, A. Church, and N. Goodman. Notre Dame, Ind., 1956.
————. "Ontological Committment." *Journal of Philosophy* 55 (1963).
Cooper, N. "Ontological Committment." *Monist* 50 (1966).
Cornman, J. W. "Language and Ontology." *Australasian Journal of Psychology and Philosophy* 41 (1963).
Darrant, M. "Feature Universals and Sortal Universals." *Analysis* 139 (1970).
Dawes-Hicks, G. "Are the Characteristics of Particular Things Universal or Particular?" *Aristotelian Society Supplementary Volume* 3 (1923).
Durcasse, C. J. "Some Critical Comments on a Nominalistic Analysis of Resemblance." *Philosophical Review* 49 (1940).
Dummett, M. "Nominalism." *Philosophical Review.* 49 (1940).
————. "Truth." *Proceedings of the Aristotelian Society* 59 (1950).
Duncan-Jones, A. E. "Universals and Particulars." *Proceedings of the Aristotelian Society* 34 (1933–34).
Emmett, E. R. "Philosophy of Resemblances." *Philosophy* 39 (1954).
Ewing, A. C. "The Problem of Universals." *Philosophical Quarterly* 21, no. 84 (1971).
Frege, G. "Concept and Object." Translated in *Philosophical Writings*, edited by P. T. Geach and M. Black. Oxford, 1952.
Furlong, E. J., C. A. Mace, and D. J. O'Connor. "Abstract Ideas and Images." *Aristotelian Society Supplementary Volume* 27 (1953).
Gasking, D. "Clusters." *Australasian Journal of Psychology and Philosophy* 38 (1960).
Geach, P. T. "On What There Is." *Aristotelian Society Supplementary Volume* 25 (1951).
————. "What Actually Exists." *Aristotelian Society Supplementary Volume* 42 (1968).
Ginascol, F. H. "The Question of Universals and Problem of Faith and Reason." *Philosophical Quarterly* 9 (1959).
Goddard, L. "Predicates, Relations and Categories." *Australasian Journal of Psychology and Philosophy* 44 (1966).
Goodman, N. "A World of Individuals." In *The Problem of Universals*, edited by I. M. Bochenski, A. Church, and N. Goodman. Notre Dame, Ind. 1956.
————. "On Relations That Generate," *Philosophical Studies* 9, (1958). Also in *Philosophy of Mathematics*, edited by P. Benacerraf and H. Putnam. Englewood Cliffs, N.J., 1964.
Goodman, N., and W. V. Quine. "Steps Towards a Constructive Nominalism." *Journal of Symbolic Logic* 12 (1947).
Haack, R. J. "Natural and Arbitrary Classes." *Australasian Journal of Philosophy* 47 (1969).
Hacking, L. "A Language Without Particulars." *Mind*, 77 (1968).
Hartshorne, C. "Are There Absolutely Specific Universals?" *Journal of Philosophy* 68, no. 3 (1971).
Hintikka, J. "Existential Presuppositions and Existential Commitments." *Journal of Philosophy* 56 (1959).
Jones, J. R. "Are the Qualities of Particular Things Universal or Particular?" *Philosophical Review* 58 (1949).
————. "What Do We Mean by an 'Instance?'" *Analysis* 11 (1950).
————. "Characters and Resemblance." *Philosophical Review* 60 (1951).
Joseph, H. W. "Universals and the 'Method of Analysis.'" *Aristotelian Society Supplementary Volume* 6 (1926).
Kearns, J. T. "*Sameness and Similarity*." Discussion with B. Blanshard, *Philosophy and Phenomenological Research* 29 (1969).

Khatchadourian, H. "Natural Objects and Common Names." *Methodos* 13 (1961).

Klemke, E. A. "Universals and Particulars in a Phenomenalist Ontology." *Philosophy of Science* 27 (1960).

Knight, H. "A Note on the 'Problem of Universals.'" *Analysis* 1 (1933).

Knight, T. A. "Questions and Universals." *Philosophy and Phenomenological Research* 27 (1966).

Korner, S. "On Determinables and Resemblances." *Aristotelian Society Supplementary Volume* 33 (1959).

Kultgen, J. H. "Universals, Particulars, and Change." *Review of Metaphysics* 9 (1956).

Leonard, H. S. "Essences, Attributes and Predicates." *Proceedings and Addresses of the American Philosophical Association* 37 (1964).

Lloyd, A. C. "On Arguments for Real Universals." *Analysis* 11 (1951).

Lomansky, L. "Nominalism, Replication and Nelson Goodman." *Analysis* 29 (1968–69).

Long, P. "Are Predicates and Relational Expressions Incomplete?" *Philosophical Review* 78 (1969).

Loux, M. J. "'The Problem of Universals.'" In *Universals and Particulars*, edited by M. J. Loux. New York, 1970.

Manser, A. R. "Games and Family Resemblances." *Philosophy* 42 (1967).

Margolis, J. "Some Ontological Policies." *Monist* 53 (1970).

McCloskey, H. J. "The Philosophy of Linguistic Analysis and the Problem of Universals." *Philosophy and Phenomenological Research* 24 (1964).

Mei, T. L. "Chinese Grammar and the Linguistic Movement in Philosophy." *Review of Metaphysics* 14, no. 3 (1961).

———. "Subject and Predicate: A Grammatical Preliminary." *Philosophical Review* 70 (1961).

Moore, G. E. "Are the Characteristics of Particular Things Universal or Particular?" *Aristotelian Society Supplementary Volume* 3 (1923).

Moravscik, J. "Strawson on Ontological Priority." In *Analytical Philosophy*, edited by R. J. Butler. Oxford and New York, 1965.

O'Connor, D. J. "On Resemblance." *Proceedings of the Aristotelian Society* 46 (1945–46).

———. "Stout's Theory of Universals." *Australasian Journal of Psychology and Philosophy* 27 (1949).

———. "Names and Universals." *Proceedings of the Aristotelian Society* 53 (1952–53).

O'Shaughnessy, R. J. "On Having Something in Common." *Mind* 79, no. 315 (1970).

Pap, A. "Nominalism, Empiricism, and Universals." *Philosophical Quarterly* 9 (1959); 10 (1960).

Parsons, C. "Ontology and Mathematics." *Philosophical Review* 80 (1971).

Parsons, T. "Ontological Commitment." *Journal of Philosophy* 64 (1967).

———. "Criticism of 'Are Predicates and Relational Expressions Incomplete?'" *Philosophical Review* 79 (1970).

Pears, D. F. "A Critical Study of P. F. Strawson's *Individuals*." *Philosophical Quarterly* 11 (1961).

Phillips, E. D. "On Instances." *Analysis* 1 (1934).

Pompa, L. "Family Resemblances." *Philosophical Quarterly* 17 (1967).

Prior, A. N. "Determinables, Determinates, and Determinates." *Mind* 58 (1949).

Quine, W. V. "On Universals." *Journal of Symbolic Logic* 12 (1947).

———. "On Carnap's Views on Ontology." *Philosophical Studies* 2 (1951).

———. "Ontology and Ideology." *Philosophical Studies* 2 (1951).

————. "A Logistical Approach to the Ontological Problem." In *The Ways of Paradox*, by W. V. Quine. New York, 1966.

————. "Russell's Ontological Development." *Journal of Philosophy* 63 (1966).

Quinton, A. "Properties and Classes." *Proceedings of the Aristotelian Society* 58 (1957–58).

Ramsey, F. P. "Universals and the 'Method of Analyses.'" *Aristotelian Society Supplementary Volume* 6 (1926).

Rankin, K. W. "The Duplicity of Plato's Third Man." *Mind* 77 (1969).

————. "Is the Third Man Argument an Inconsistent Trial?" *Philosophical Quarterly* 20, no. 81 (1970).

Raphael, D. D. "Universals, Resemblance, and Identity." *Proceedings of the Aristotelian Society* 55 (1954–55).

Roma, E., and S. B. Thomas. "Nominalism and the Distinguishable Is Separable Principle." *Philosophy and Phenomenological Research* 28 (1968).

Russell, B. "On the Relations of Universals and Particulars." *Proceedings of the Aristotelian Society* 12 (1911–12).

Ryle, G. "Systematically Misleading Expressions." *Proceedings of the Aristotelian Society* 32 (1931–32).

Sachs, D. "Does Aristotle Have a Doctrine of Secondary Substances?" *Mind* 58 (1948).

Scheffler, I. and N. Chomsky. "What Is Said to Be." *Proceedings of the Aristotelian Society* 59 (1958–59).

Searle, J. R. "On Determinables and Resemblance." *Aristotelian Society Supplementary Volume* 33 (1959).

Sellars, W. "Logical Subjects and Physical Objects." *Philosophy and Phenomenological Research* 17 (1957).

————. "Grammar and Existence: A Preface to Ontology." *Mind* 69 (1960).

————. "Abstract Entities." *Review of Metaphysics* 16 (1963).

Simon, M. A. "When Is a Resemblance a Family Resemblance." *Mind* 78 (1969).

Sinisi, V. F. "Nominalism and Common Names." *Philosophical Review* 71 (1962).

Smith, N. K. "The Nature of Universals." *Mind* 36 (1927).

Sommers, F. "Types and Ontology." *Philosophical Review* 72 (1963). (Also in *Philosophical Logic*, edited by P. F. Strawson. Oxford and New York, 1967.)

Stoothoff, R. H. "What Actually Exists." *Aristotelian Society Supplementary Volume* 42 (1968).

Stout, G. F. "Things, Predicates, and Relations." *Australasian Journal of Psychology and Philosophy* 18 (1940).

————. "Are the Characteristics of Particular Things Universal or Particular?" *Aristotelian Society Supplementary Volume* 42 (1968).

Strawson, P. F. "Singular Terms and Predication." *Journal of Philosophy* 58 (1961).

————. "The Asymmetry of Subjects and Predicates." In *Language, Belief and Metaphysics*, Vol. I of *Contemporary Philosophic Thought*, edited by H. E. Kiefer and M. K. Munitz. New York, 1970. (Also in Strawson, P. F. *Logico-Linguistic Papers*. London, 1971.)

Stroll, A. "Meaning, Referring and the Problem of Universals." *Inquiry* 4 (1961).

Taylor, C. C. W. "Forms as Causes in the Phaedo." *Mind* 78 (1969).

Teichmann, J. "Universals and Common Properties." *Analysis* 29 (1968–69).

Thomas, W. J. "Platonism and the Skolem Paradox." *Analysis* 28 (1967–68).

Thompson, M. H. "Abstract Entities." *Philosophical Review* 69 (1960).

————. "Abstract Entities and Universals." *Mind* 74 (1965).

Toms, E. "Non-Existence and Universals." *Philosophical Quarterly* 6 (1956).

Urmson, J. O. "Recognition." *Proceedings of the Aristotelian Society* 56 (1955–56).

Vision, G. "Searle on the Nature of Universals." *Analysis*. New Series no. 137 (1970).

Wallace, J. R. "Sortal Predicates and Quantification." *Journal of Philosophy* 62 (1965).

Welker, D. D. "Linguistic Nominalism." *Mind* 79, no. 316 (1970).

Wolterstorff, N. "Are Properties Meanings?" *Journal of Philosophy* 57 (1960).

———. "On the Nature of Universals." In *Universals and Particulars*, edited by M. J. Loux. New York, 1970.

Woodger, J. H. "Science Without Properties." *British Journal for the Philosophy of Science* 2 (1952).

Woozley, A. D. "Universals." In *Encyclopaedia of Philosophy*, 8, pp. 194–206, edited by P. Edwards. New York, 1967.

INDEX

111.2 P94

The Problem of universals

DATE DUE		

111.2 P94

The Problem of universals

DATE DUE	BORROWER'S NAME